PEREGRINE BOOKS

ERASMUS:
ECSTASY AND THE PRAISE OF FOLLY

Desiderius Erasmus, born about 1469, led the humanist reformation of the Northern Renaissance in theology, education, classical studies and above all in the rediscovery of the power of early
Christian authors, both Greek and Latin. He was a brilliant satirist
whose evangelical humanism brought him into conflict both with
the more reactionary theologians of Paris and Louvain and with
Luther, for whose theology he nevertheless had a respect. Erasmus
studied in Paris and Italy and came to England, where he spent
some of the happiest years of his life and became a close friend of
Thomas More, to whom he dedicated the *Praise of Folly*. Italy,
where Pope Julius II led his armies in battle, disappointed him,
and he ended his life, saddened by the sharpening of the religious
conflict, in Basle, where he died in 1536.

His extensive correspondence shows that he was in touch with
many of Europe's leading princes and thinkers, and his prolific
writings make him a figure not only of scholarly interest but also
of outstanding literary, theological and political importance.

Dr M. A. Screech is a Senior Research Fellow of All Souls College,
Oxford, a Fellow of the British Academy and a Fellow of University College, London. He long served on the committee of the
Warburg Institute as the Fielden Professor of French Language and
Literature in London, until his election to All Souls in 1984. He is
a Renaissance scholar of international renown. He is editing a
French edition of selected *Essais* of Montaigne and an English
edition of complete *Essais* of Montaigne for Penguin Classics, the
first volume of which, *An Apology for Raymond Sebond*, was
published in 1987. He is also writing a book on the 'folly' of
the Cross. His other books include French editions of works by
Rabelais and Du Bellay; in English, *Montaigne and Melancholy* and
Rabelais; and in Latin, with Anne Screech, *Erasmus' Annotations on
the New Testament: The Gospels*.

Phillips

Erasmus:
Ecstasy and the
Praise of Folly

M. A. SCREECH

PENGUIN BOOKS

PENGUIN BOOKS

Published by the Penguin Group
27 Wrights Lane, London w8 5TZ, England
Viking Penguin Inc., 40 West 23rd Street, New York, New York 10010, USA
Penguin Books Australia Ltd, Ringwood, Victoria, Australia
Penguin Books Canada Ltd, 2801 John Street, Markham, Ontario, Canada L3R 1B4
Penguin Books (NZ) Ltd, 182–190 Wairau Road, Auckland 10, New Zealand

Penguin Books Ltd, Registered Offices: Harmondsworth, Middlesex, England

First published by Duckworth 1980
Published in Peregrine Books 1988

Copyright © M. A. Screech, 1980
All rights reserved

Reproduced, printed and bound in Great Britain by
Hazell Watson & Viney Limited
Member of BPCC plc
Aylesbury Bucks
Filmset in Bembo

*For my father, Richard John Screech, MM,
in time for his eighty-fourth birthday*

Except in the United States of America,
this book is sold subject to the condition
that it shall not, by way of trade or otherwise,
be lent, re-sold, hired out, or otherwise circulated
without the publisher's prior consent in any form of
binding or cover other than that in which it is
published and without a similar condition
including this condition being imposed
on the subsequent purchaser

Contents

Abbreviations

AV	:	Authorised version
CCSL	:	*Corpus Christianorum: Series Latina*
CR	:	*Corpus Reformatorum*
EE	:	*Erasmi Epistolae*, ed. P. S. and H. M. Allen, Oxford, 1906–1947
LB	:	'Lugduni Batavorum' : the Leyden edition of Erasmus' *Opera Omnia* edited by Johannes Clericus, 1703–06
PG	:	*Patrologia Graeca*, ed. Migne
PL	:	*Patrologia Latina*, ed. Migne
RV	:	Revised version
Kan	:	*Morias Encomion. Stultitiae Laus Des. Erasmi Rot. Declamatio*, ed. I. B. Kan, The Hague, 1898
Scheurer	:	*Moriae Encomium Erasmi Roterodami Declamatio*, 'Argentorati in aedibus Matthiae Schurerij, M.D.XI' (This text where faulty has been corrected against the edition, with the same title, published 'Argentorat. Ex aedibus Schureriansis Mense Octobri. Anno M.D.XII' and other editions.)
Undated [1515] *Moria*	:	the edition listed as E 846 in F. van der Haeghen's *Bibliotheca Belgica* (second series, XIII), Ghent – The Hague, 1891–1923.
1515 *Moria*	:	the edition listed by van der Haeghen as E 847.
1516 *Moria*	:	the edition listed by van der Haeghen as E 848.

Preface

Erasmus can be made to seem all things to all men. He was born in the late 1460s, about the time that Philip II of Burgundy succeeded Charles the Bold, extending his domains into Liège, Alsace, Breisgau and Ghent. When Erasmus was a child, Lorenzo the Magnificent was ruling in Florence where the platonising Academy flourished. But when he died on 12 July 1536, the face of Europe had changed. So had the face of Christendom. The fall of Athens to the Turks in 1456 had been followed by further relentless conquests in Christian Europe; throughout his life-time the Turkish threat dominated political and religious thinking, not least in Germany. But while armies fought in eastern Europe, Francis I of France was more inclined to make an ally of the Turk against his own enemies, the papacy not excluded. When Erasmus died, Henry VIII had broken with Rome, and Charles V, the Holy Roman Emperor, ruled the greatest empire that the world had ever seen.

During his full and industrious life (he died aged 67 or so) he poured out book after book, letter after letter. At various times he has been above all thought of as the author of part only of what he wrote, as some of his works achieved prominence and others fell into comparative neglect.

At times he may seem to be primarily the editor of the first Greek New Testament, which was accompanied by a more elegant Latin translation as well as by copious annotations. From there, to classify him with other Biblical scholars and translators—Lefèvre d'Etaples, Coverdale, Luther, Calvin or even Cranmer, is but a short step. Erasmus can be made to seem a proto-Protestant, especially when much of what he stood for was rejected by the Council of Trent, his own works being placed on the Index of 1564. Not infrequently copies of his books in ecclesiastical libraries were heavily censored in black ink, his portrait defaced, the volumes confined to certain trusted readers.

Then there is the other Erasmus, the friend of Thomas More, the champion of free-will against Luther on behalf of Pope Leo X. If these complex matters are simplified, Erasmus can readily be made to seem more traditionally orthodox than he was—especially if orthodoxy is judged by later standards.

The wider public of the Renaissance probably knew his *Adages* best of all—Montaigne said, with a smile, that if he had called on Erasmus he would have expected him to talk in proverbs and adages. That little book published in 1500, recast in 1508 and much expanded throughout thirty-six years of his life, became one of the great formative source-books of Europe, read by schoolboys at one extreme and yet pillaged by intellectuals such as Rabelais at the other.

Then there are the *Praise of Folly* (1511?) or the *Colloquies* (1519). (Both these books were also considerably expanded.) When Erasmus is judged primarily against these, he can be made to seem, above all, an irreverent mocker of religion and superstition, such as that ancient Greek satirist Lucian whom he took as his model. When it is known that Rabelais wrote to Erasmus in 1532, calling him his intellectual father and his intellectual mother, it is easy to read into him not only all that Rabelais stands for, but all that he is wrongly said to stand for as well.

Erasmus' life can also be thought of in many different ways. Those who come to him through the pages of Froude or through the romanticised fibs which he himself encouraged and which form the basis of Charles Reade's *The Cloister and the Hearth,* see him as the wronged love-child, bundled into a monastery by grasping provincial Dutchmen yet ending his days as the man most courted by Pope and Princes.

The more scholarly views, based upon the voluminous correspondence of Erasmus which P. S. and H. M. Allen so magnificently edited, can also mislead. There are gaps in it; and Erasmus is an adept at putting his own case well. Judged primarily from the letters, Erasmus seems a man more inclined to temporise and to avoid committing himself than his works themselves justify. For, judged from his works, Erasmus, while retiring as a man, was bold, outspoken, even rash and imprudent in an age of rival orthodoxies, of torture and of burning at the stake.

Since this present study has as its starting-point the end only of one of his books, it could clearly run analogous risks. I am at least aware of them. And while it starts where it does, it ranges through the whole of Erasmus' writings, from his earliest to his latest. What is perhaps most striking is what was (for me at least) a discovery: there is not one man who was More's friend, another who wrote the *Praise of Folly,* another who quietly edited the New Testament in Greek, and yet another who paraphrased the same work in elegant Latin and who poured out his interpretation of the Christian religion—what he called the 'philosophy of Christ'—in books of paedagogical theory, in commentaries on the psalms, in treatises of practical piety. They are one and the same man. And one of the many aspects of his religion which helped to integrate the character of this subtle, complex, attractive man, was a particular concept of ecstasy.

At times ecstasy dominated the Renaissance mind. The Renaissance scholar found it—and rightly found it—in Greek and Latin pagan writers, in his Old Testament, in his New Testament, in the early fathers, in the mediaeval—and what was then the modern—Church. Many of those who wrote about it knew, or believed they knew, what ecstasy was at first hand.

This ecstasy and what it implies has little or no connexion with what often passes as 'charismatic' Christianity today. It was marked by discretion, by prudence, by a kind of shyness. It was not based on anti-intellectualism; on the contrary, those who believed that they knew what it was at first hand included many of the greatest intellects, who found themselves, in this, following Plato and St Paul as well as St Bernard, say, and St Bonaventura.

And what Erasmus meant by ecstasy was something which helped to win him the unwavering support of Thomas More, a man not inclined to emotional and anti-intellectual self-indulgence.

The Renaissance was an international affair. Scholars reared in Holland might study in Paris, go on to Florence, pass time in Rome, call in at Oxford, teach in Cambridge, and then thrive in a London which already over-shadowed its provincial cousins.

It is only natural that, in dealing with an author reared in such an age, this book should start with another book perhaps first conceived on the way from Rome to London; probably written in London itself; published in Paris; re-published fundamentally changed in Strasbourg; again republished with several vitally important changes in Basle; read avidly throughout learned Europe, but eventually banned in 1564 at Trent—a banning which, as such follies often do, did not stay its triumphant course, but added to it the piquant salt of official disapproval.

'If it had been anyone else we might conjecture he was in prison.' P. S. Allen (*The Age of Erasmus*, 1914, p. 143) states the problem with humour but without exaggeration. There is a gap in our knowledge of Erasmus and his doings, stretching from the autumn of 1509, when he was tempted back to England from Italy, until April 1511, when he was at Dover, about to leave again for Paris. The *Praise of Folly*, written during this period, forms the basis of this book. It is our main clue to what happened to Erasmus during those important months. And in itself it is a work of great fascination.

This silence is staggering. In 1509 Erasmus was no minor figure. He had been drawn back to England by Andrew Ammonius—or rather by Mountjoy, in whose name Erasmus' English-based Italian friend had written the famous letter of 29 May 1509 (*EE* I. 215). Henry VIII had just succeeded to the throne of England (21 May 1509). Erasmus was told how the young king's accession rejoiced the hearts of the good and the learned: he was a monarch who sought not gold, jewels or precious metals but glory, virtue, immortality. 'Accept wealth,' the letter said, skilfully applying a line of Martial (8. 56. 11), 'and be our greatest seer' (*vates*). Erasmus somewhat sadly recalled this period in 1535, towards the end of his life: he would have been happy to grow old in Italy, he wrote, if he had not been enticed to England by promises of golden mountains (*LB* 9. 1750E; *A Reply to the Defence of Peter Cursius*). In 1509 he had every right to expect direct royal patronage. The gentle William Warham, Archbishop of Canterbury, added his own promises of financial help (*EE* I. 214). Thomas More and other staunch friends awaited him.

Erasmus hastened back to London. Then, for eighteen months, the rest is silence . . .

He stayed most of the time in Thomas More's house in London—at Bucklersbury (More had yet to move to Chelsea). He apparently frequented Ammonius and William Grocyn, a scholar who had much in common with him despite an almost superstitious attachment to traditional piety. But what he did, whom he met, what his plans were, what became of the great promises that had been made to him—such things are known, if known at all, by inference and conjecture. The lion came to London and did not roar. He did not even purr. And we do not know why.

What we do know is that Erasmus left England, with his friendship for More deepened. That was on or about 11 April 1511, when he wrote to Ammonius from Dover. The *Praise of Folly* was soon to be published in Paris. We may infer that he took the manuscript with him. But that is not what he would have us believe.

Today, the *Praise of Folly* is by far Erasmus' most famous work, though other ages gave greater importance to his *Adages* and at one time it was rivalled in literary popularity by the *Colloquies*. Nowadays the book of Erasmus which is most often printed in translation and most widely read by both scholar and general reader alike is, without a shadow of doubt, the successor to the little volume which first saw the light in Paris, almost certainly in 1511.

Because the *Praise of Folly* is so well-known in translation, it comes as a surprise to realise that the Latin text is not. Most scholars know it either from the great *Opera Omnia* published by Leclerc in Leyden in 1703–6 or from I. B. Kan's handier edition published by Nijhof at The Hague in 1898. Both give a late version of the text. This has resulted in the total eclipse of the original version; so much so, that few realise that what Erasmus wrote during those silent months is not the work that modern editions and translations place before them. A series of misunderstandings, misdatings of ideas, and misconceptions about the significance of the book itself, results from this fact. In this book an attempt is made to put the record right, at least in one respect.

The general drift of Erasmus' satire in the greater part of the *Praise of Folly* presents no great problems to most who are likely to read it. Modern readers are attuned to irony—much more than many of Erasmus' contemporaries were. Moreover, the objects of his mockery no longer stir up that mixture of incomprehension, frustration and aggression which was more typical of the time when he published and republished his important little book. The laughter at the expense of rhetoricians, grammarians, poets, lawyers, philosophers, monks, cardinals, popes and kings has been softened by the passage of time. These figures from the past appear clothed in fancy dress. We do not identify with them. We can laugh and let it go.

The contemporary reader was differently placed. As edition after edition was thumped off the presses, the face of political and religious Europe changed. Luther came and broke from Rome; Calvin was about to set his seal on a fundamental reform of life and doctrine; Henry VIII broke from Rome; More lost his life, and so did many others on many sides of the great new divides which cut across the unity of western Christendom. Monks left their cloisters and married: many despaired of ever reforming the monasteries. All too many were inclined to make Erasmus responsible for what was happening. Those who were in favour of radical measures often believed that he was really on their side: how could he have written such scathing satire of the weaknesses of the Old Religion without actually siding with them! The enemies of the Reformers were often inclined to agree.

Erasmus had many friends. Many of these were made by the *Praise of Folly*. But he had many enemies, both within his own church and within the new churches being born outside the fold of Rome. Princes courted him. At least one prince of the Church hated him. The satirical implications of the *Praise of Folly* are not the main subject of this book. The pages that follow are devoted to what is probably an even more important aspect of it—its truly astonishing end.

The *Praise of Folly* concludes in a way which would have been hard to foresee: a witty, erudite, sustained and moving praise of a form of religious ecstasy which is indistinguishable from a bout of temporary madness. I have tried to bring out what this praise of ecstasy means, both in itself and within the wider context of Erasmus' conception of the philosophy of Christ. The principal method I adopt is to give the original text of this part of the *Moria* (as the book has been very usefully called from at least 1511), dividing it up into sections convenient for study. Each of these sections is also given in translation. The meaning of the original work is gauged, partly by comparing it with the later modifications which Erasmus felt obliged to make to it, partly by finding out what Erasmus wrote on such matters in other works; partly, again, by reading what he is known or believed to have read.

A very different Erasmus emerges out of my book from the one often met in both scholarly and popular works. I believe it to be an authentic sketch of a crucial aspect of the man and his thought. Erasmus worshipped a God who saved the world by an act of divine madness: the mission of his Son as the incarnate Christ. God incarnate also acted like a madman. So did his chief disciples. And so too—according to Erasmus—do his true followers in all ages. One of the forms in which this madness is found is the bewildered, ecstatic amazement of those who, some time in their lives, either by special revelation or by the word of God transmitted in speech or writing, catch a glimpse of the face of their transfigured Lord. It is then that they see for a moment the glorious majesty hiding behind the cloak of that lunatic Man of Sorrows who was the manifestation of a God who had, as it were, given up hope of saving the world by wisdom, deciding to save it by an act of infinitely costly madness.

Erasmus' concern with the folly of God reaches far beyond the pages of the *Moria*. It influenced the very choice of words for his Latin translation of the New Testament. It informs many of the annotations which accompanied that revolutionary work. It conditioned the way he read his Old Testament and the way he wrote about it. The implications of this divine folly penetrate through to the very kernel of what he believed the Christian religion to be.

One of the reasons why his contemporaries found his ideas hard to grasp, and so deeply offensive to their traditional piety, is that the theme of the madness of God is more at home in Greek Christianity than in western Catholicism. The *Moria* may well be written in elegant Latin, but its conception of divine folly, in God, in Christ, in his ecstatic followers, is one which emerges more readily from the Greek New Testament than from the Latin Vulgate. It was also given its most authentic slant by Greek fathers. A favourite among these, for Erasmus, was Origen. From the Latins he preferred those who were open to the influence of these Greeks. His favourites include Ambrose, Jerome and Augustine . . . and Bernard of Clairvaux.

The Greek fathers knew their Plato at first hand in their own language. In the eyes of Erasmus and of some other Renaissance humanists this placed them immeasurably above the scholastic theologians of mediaeval Catholicism. For most of the scholastics Plato was a closed book. So too was the Greek New Testament.

Renaissance humanists of Erasmus' mould sought to syncretise what they admired in Graeco-Latin thought with the religion they found in their Greek Bibles and in their Greek fathers. Inevitably this led to an increase in the influence of Plato and of his master Socrates. For Erasmus, Socrates was in some ways a prefiguration of Christ, analogous in this to David. Yet even a major mediaeval scholastic such as Thomas Aquinas knew no Greek. What reliance could a humanist like Erasmus place in a school of theology whose very professors could not read the words of Matthew, Mark, Luke or John, not to mention Paul, Peter, James or Jude?

Little is certain about the circumstances in which the *Moria* was written. Erasmus' own statements do not bear the stamp of literal truth and have to be taken with a grain of salt, not crudely swallowed whole. One can be sure of little else than that it was composed at least partly in More's house, and that its writing was associated with a period of illness. More was not only a close friend; he was a gentleman. Such a man was to be trusted with his friends' most private thoughts and their most private hopes and fears. If ever a man knew what the *Moria* meant, he did. And he championed it throughout his life. But of the circumstances in which it was written he says nothing

The *Moria* is sometimes said to date from 1509, since Erasmus states, in a doubtless conventional literary disclaimer, that it was composed on the way back from Italy. Others date it more cautiously from the presumed year of its printing, 1511. Both these statements are misleading. Much of the *Moria* as read and translated today had not even been conceived in 1512, let alone in 1509 or 1511. The text which was entrusted to the careless compositors of the Parisian printer Gilles de Gourmont—in 1511 no doubt—is most decidedly not the one which forms the basis of modern studies.

The 1511 *Moria* has, to date, never been re-edited, never given in any variants. (The Amsterdam edition of Erasmus' works will put that right; the *Moria* is in the hands of Professor Clarence Miller. So is a new English translation for Yale.)

The first version—the only one until 1514—is a much shorter work. It was reprinted in 1511 and 1512—more than once. Page after page of the book known today first saw the light in 1514, when Scheurer of Strasbourg was entrusted with a fundamentally revised and expanded text. Most of the 1514 additions arose out of later preoccupations. They cannot be explained in terms of 1509 or 1511. To talk of the 1511 *Moria* as though it contained, in germ or in bloom, all that was added in 1514 is to distort historical perspective.

In some ways the first version can, with due caution, be connected with the *Enchiridion Militis Christiani*, which Martens of Antwerp published in 1503/4. The links between the *Enchiridion* and the 1511 *Moria* are very real. But so too are the differences. There is ecstasy, if you know where to look for it, but no sign of Lucianesque laughter in the *Enchiridion*. From the first version of the *Moria* onwards, the kind of humour which Erasmus, More, Melanchthon and Rabelais learned to appreciate in Lucian's works occurs in Erasmus where one might least expect it—in the expanded *Moria* and the *Colloquies*, of course, but also in the *Annotations on the New Testament*. So, too, does ecstatic folly.

The 1514 *Moria* belongs to another world from that of the *Enchiridion*. In between 1511 and 1514 the warlike pope Julius II had died, being succeeded by Leo X, a welcome protector of Erasmus as well as an understanding reader. And attempts had been made to lure Erasmus back to his cloister!

The 1514 *Moria* echoes these changes with unmistakable clarity. It belongs to an age whose controversies had been sharpened and exacerbated by the 1511 *Moria* itself. Erasmus was a man of peace, capable of arousing deep affection and loyal friendship. He never seems to have realised how wounding his laughter could be to those who lacked his sense of humour.

In the history of Erasmus' thought, both the 1511 and the 1514 versions occupy pivotal positions.

The edition of 1511 is not a light-weight work of 'literature', to be set apart from his scholarship or his scriptural erudition. It is intimately connected with the major concerns of his humanist Christianity. Under a suitable veil it alludes to a key moment in his religious development. As for the later versions—for there are more than one—they are intimately bound up with his principal scholarly preoccupations. The closing pages are shot through and through with Erasmus' interpretation of the philosophy of Christ, which they expound with a fervour which is enhanced, not hindered, by the subtle humour and Lucianesque laughter. English Christians at least do not need reminding that humour and piety can make very good bedfellows. Neither did the readers of Brant, Boccaccio and Rabelais.

The flavour of the last pages of the *Moria* owes much to a happy alliance of St Paul and those platonising (rather then neo-platonising) fathers of the Church whose influence on Erasmus' Christianity it is almost impossible to overstate—Origen, Basil, Ambrose, Augustine . . . This platonising evangelism is very different in emphasis from the magical mysticism of Ficino, or of Pico della Mirandola or even of John Colet. Only in comparatively superficial ways can it remind one of the mysticism of Plotinus or the daemon-ridden world of Proclus. Erasmus has no time at all for Ficino's magic rings, his respect for the legendary and antedated Hermes Trismegistus or for quasi-magical practices generally. He was influenced by the Platonism he came across in Italy: it was probably there that he first saw how powerful a contribution Plato had made to the doctrines of ecstasy with his teachings in the *Phaedrus* about the divine forms of madness which produce prophets, poets or lovers. But Renaissance Platonism in Italy was given a special twist from the start. If we are to believe Ficino in his commentary on Plotinus, it was the Byzantine scholar Gemistus Pletho who, visiting Italy for the Council of Florence (1438–9), inspired Cosimo de' Medici to conceive the project of resuscitating Plato. Some twenty years later Cosimo provided Ficino with Greek texts of Plato and Plotinus. He encouraged him to translate them both, as well as the writings of Hermes Trismegistus. Pico further encouraged him to translate and comment on Plotinus after Cosimo's death.

This genealogy of interest and scholarship meant that Florentine Platonism was, from the outset, intimately connected with neo-Platonism and with that 'ancient theology', that *prisca theologia*, of Hermes Trismegistus, Moses, Orpheus and Pythagoras, which D. P. Walker has made so well-known.[1]

Spiritual and demonic magic, as well as the entire *prisca theologia*, are totally foreign to Erasmus. He may owe something to the school of Ficino, but much of what they stood for he jettisoned, ignored or opposed. Much which passed for neo-Platonism in the fifteenth and sixteenth centuries he heartily disliked.

The same applies to some of the authors whom the Florentines held in high esteem: Plotinus, Proclus, Pseudo-Dionysius among them. With the exception of the last they play next to no part in Erasmus' thought. Even Pseudo-Dionysius was partially eclipsed between the *Enchiridion* and the *Moria*.

From the *Moria* onwards, Erasmus' philosophy of Christ has much more in common with Origen than with the intense neo-Platonic mysticism of Pseudo-Dionysius, whose authenticity he doubted—without however dismissing him entirely, as Luther and Calvin later did. (Origen flourished at the beginning of the third century. The publishing of his works in the sixteenth century was an important event.)

A major influence on Erasmus' theology was not an ancient one

[1] On these points, see his *Spiritual and Demonic Magic from Ficino to Campanella*, Warburg Institute, London, 1958, esp. chapter 3.

at all. The Greek Orthodox theologian Theophylact, a mediaeval archbishop of Ochrida (Bulgaria) was once thought by Erasmus to be a certain Vulgarius. Others of his contemporaries believed him to be no less than St Athanasius, to whom was attributed the most firmly orthodox of the creeds. Erasmus only untangled these knots after the *Moria* was written. Together with Chrysostom, whom he largely followed, Theophylact exerted a major influence over Erasmus' thought, not least in the *Annotations on the New Testament* and the *Paraphrases*. But that was later. It is likely that he encouraged Erasmus to link Pauline and Socratic ecstasy together in the *Moria* when he read him earlier, in Latin translation, under the name of Athanasius. If this were so, Erasmus believed that he had behind him not only the heterodox Origen but the impeccably orthodox Athanasius, his near contemporary. (The real Athanasius flourished at the end of the third century.)

Themes such as these are developed in this book. The idea first came to me in the late 1940s. In 1949, when completing my degree after the war at University College London, I had already stumbled on the fact that the first version of the *Moria* was significantly different from later ones. But only gradually did it transpire that this was not common knowledge, even among scholars. I am most grateful to Professor Walker who, over the years, tempted me to give several series of classes on Erasmus in the Warburg Institute. There, this study could mature, stimulated by his presence and that of his colleagues, as well as by those keen young scholars who miraculously appear, year after year, in both my College and his Institute. He read this study, spotted several errors and made helpful suggestions. A further debt of gratitude is owed to Dr Margaret Mann Phillips, for several years now an honorary lecturer of University College London; her love for Erasmus is infectious. Yet another debt was incurred to Sir Ernst Gombrich; in 1975, he arranged an informal lecture at the Warburg Institute, during which the themes of this book were outlined. As a result a marked copy of Kan was placed in the Warburg Library. Scholars who asked for their own copy were given one.

Also in 1975 the late Jean Boisset insisted that something about all this should be said in French at his *Centre National* for Reformation Studies at Montpellier.[1]

---

[1] See J. Boisset, ed., *Réforme et Humanisme; Actes du IVe Colloque*, Montpellier, 1977: '*L'Eloge de la Folie' et les études bibliques d'Erasme*, pp. 149–165. Scholars who asked to see the typescript were given a copy of that too, as Jean Boisset's long illness and untimely death naturally held up publication.

This book will, I hope, be useful to those with no Latin or Greek. Erasmus' Latin is always given in, or with, a translation. When Greek is absolutely necessary, it is transliterated and translated. No Latin or Greek is used when an English translation alone suffices to bring out the points at issue. (References to the original texts are always given, of course.) All languages other than English are accompanied by translations, on those occasions where the original text must be given to bring out particular points. With the exception of the quotations from the Loeb *Philo*, all the translations are my own. They claim no literary merit whatsoever: they are designed purely and simply to help to clarify the problems and to make the solutions proposed easier to grasp. An awkward literal translation can often do this better than a polished literary one.

'Literary' versions of Erasmus risk betraying his meaning—not least in the closing pages of the *Moria*. With the help of more literal translations, Erasmus can often be left to speak for himself; but such translations constitute a challenge which I have not always managed to rise to. I have done my best.

Erasmus expresses himself by means of copious allusions to Biblical and classical texts. A consistent effort has been made to identify them and to bring out their force. It is not enough to note where an allusion comes from; the fuller force of its use may echo passages in a father such as Origen or in a theologian such as Theophylact. This has been constantly borne in mind.

The *Moria* is infused with subtle humour. Not all the jokes have been pointed out. Readers have their own sense of humour, which can gain nothing from being constantly nudged. But religious and philosophical jesting demands a knowledge of the intellectual system within which it arouses its humour: it is that system of thought and reference which is emphasised in this book. Up to a point Erasmus' humour works within the same terms of reference as that of Rabelais. Occasional allusions are made to my book *Rabelais* published just before this one. I was working on both books at the same time; what was said in one can occasionally be useful to the other. Certainly the comedy of both Rabelais and Erasmus becomes much more deep and satisfying when one knows what they are getting at. They were often getting at similar things. But not always.

This book owes much to those many people who have patiently listened to me talking or lecturing about Erasmus and ecstasy. Both questions and challenges helped to clarify what I have to say. Mrs Sally North and Miss Anne Reeve, both research assistants in the Department of French Language and Literature in College, did indeed assist with research. Mrs Sonia Wakely proved as always an intelligent, patient and ingenious typist. So did Mrs Pam King, who moved in during Mrs Wakely's absence.

This book was a pleasure to think about and a pleasure to write. If the readers get a tithe of that pleasure, then they will have had their money's worth.

Part of the time I spent at the Institute for Research in the Humanities (University of Wisconsin—Madison) as the 1978–9 Johnson Visiting Professor was devoted to lecturing on Erasmus and ecstasy, as well as correcting the proofs and improving the original version of this study. I am grateful to Professor Robert Kingdon and the other members of the Institute for their encouragement and friendly interest.

Students of Erasmus will naturally compare what I say in this volume with the important and original English translation of the *Praise of Folly* made by Professor Clarence H. Miller, published by Yale University Press while this book was printing.

Geneva, 1979   M.A.S.

CHAPTER ONE

The *Moriae Encomium* of 1511 and 1512

The first edition of the *Praise of Folly* was published in Paris by Gilles de Gourmont. It bears no date.

At this time Erasmus was in his forties. The work is not a youthful extravaganza. Even if this first version were actually written in 1509, Erasmus was then forty years of age, assuming that his birth is correctly dated from 1469. His years at Deventer and 'sHertogenbosch were far behind him (1478–87). Such influences as the gentle and practical piety of the Brethren of the Common Life had had upon him were by now overlaid, complemented and enriched by wisdom and knowledge he had acquired as a widely travelled humanist scholar. At this time his years as an Augustinian at Steyn (1487–93) must also have seemed far away—though he was soon to find, in 1514, that old virtues have long shadows no less than old sins, when his prior Servatius wrote to him suggesting that he return to the cloister. He had been a student in Paris; he had visited England and Italy, learning much, frequenting the circles of great men as well as acquiring valued friends. His international reputation stood high. Many pious scholars had influenced him, including, I think, Grocyn, as well as John Colet. Besides such men of lasting renown must be placed the all-but-unknown Jean Vitrier, whom Erasmus praises with fervour as being a man of great goodness and integrity—it was Vitrier who first introduced him to Origen (see Festugière, *Enchiridion*, Paris, 1971, p. 12f.). And he had also met the great, good, warm-hearted, formidable and incorruptible Thomas More.

As a scholar Erasmus was now at his best, his subtle understanding coupled with wide reading and an industry which never ceases to amaze. He was at home with classical learning and classical literature generally; encouraged by Vitrier, he had discovered for himself the force of the theology of Origen. The Greek fathers were becoming as well-known to him as Augustine and Jerome. In these authors he found powerful allies in his fight against the dominant scholastic

orthodoxies of the universities of western Europe. He had been be-
friended by Aldus, the scholarly printer of Venice. He had lived in his
household and discovered the realities of printing and publishing. He
had seen Julius II's Rome with his own eyes and found it wanting. He
had discovered a special bent in his ever-expanding editions of the
Adages. The main elements of his theology had been settled. This once
poor, orphaned, second son of a concubinary Low German priest was
now a man whom kings could write to and who could write to kings.
The *Praise of Folly* is no mere *jeu d'esprit*. It is the work of a mature man
at a turning-point in his life. It represents some of his most dearly
treasured thoughts. To the end of his career he was destined to feel the
need to defend such thoughts in several ways, both openly and indirectly. And perhaps, in the end, he drew back slightly from some of his
bolder enthusiasms: but not from many—and then never entirely.

Gilles de Gourmont was a printer of some importance—a humanist
who could manage Greek. Among the works he published was Guillaume du Bellay's *Peregrinatio* (1509) and Thomas More's *Utopia* (after
1 November 1516).

Erasmus tells us that the *Moria* was seen through the press by
Richard Croke. This statement can hardly be the whole truth: for one
thing, Erasmus was in Paris at the time. P. S. Allen was almost
certainly right to date this first edition from 1511 and to assume that
Erasmus himself was responsible for its being published (*EE* I. 222).

Moriae Encomium: Stulticiae Laus is dedicated to Thomas More, the
title being, of course, a play on his name. This encouraged the reader
who knew More, or who knew of More, to associate the kind of folly,
the *mōria*, both praised and praising in this book, with the learned,
unpretentious, unfussy humanist Christianity that More espoused
through practical piety in public and private life. Our knowledge of
the later years of More's life should be laid firmly aside. Even *Utopia*
(1516) had yet to cross the Channel and seek its first buyers on the
bookstalls of Paris.

The dedicatory letter to Thomas More is simply dated 'From
the country, 9 June' (*Ex rure*, *Quinto Idus Junias*). The words 'from the
country' are probably part of the literary convention to which the
Moria belonged (W. Kaiser, *Praisers of Folly*, 1964, p. 31f.) But the
Quintus Idus Junias probably refers to 9 June 1511, when Erasmus was
indeed in Paris.

The Gilles de Gourmont edition is not well printed. It contains over
two pages of *errata*, presumably attributable to Erasmus' last-minute
vigilance. In a letter to John Botzheim (from Basle, 30 January 1523)
Erasmus appears to be blaming Croke for the shabby way the text was

first set up in type. That would be a very ungenerous thing to do if it were quite untrue. It would fit the facts if Croke had been entrusted with seeing the book through the press, Erasmus intervening when it was too late to correct the proofs but still in time to insist that the principal errors be listed in the blank pages at the end of the last gathering. What makes it hard to be sure is that Erasmus in this letter was striving to play down the importance of the *Moria* as well as his own involvement in its publication (*EE* I. p. 19, 6f.).

To appreciate the original text of the *Moria* it is vital to get rid of several preconceptions. The book of 1511 and its re-editions bear little resemblance to the elegant volumes produced by Froben in 1515 and 1516 with annotations which certainly owed much to Erasmus himself (*EE* II. no. 495, Introduction). Hans Holbein's illustrations which have given so much pleasure to so many readers were yet to be conceived, let alone sketched in the margins of the Basle copy and eventually made known to a wider public.

The Gourmont edition of the *Moriae Encomium Erasmi Roterdami declamatio* is a little book of a mere 48 leaves alternately signed in eights and fours (a^8, b^4, c^8, d^4, e^8, f^4, g^8, h^4). Except for some very elementary illumination of initial capitals, there is no division into paragraphs or chapters—a headlong typographical presentation which lends a breathless quality to the book: one feels one has to read it all at one go. The text ends (without the final *telos*) on the first page of the penultimate leaf. The rest of this page and two of the three which follow are filled with the corrigenda. The last page is blank.

This book (and the other editions based on it in 1511 and again in 1512) can only be read in such libraries as possess it. The major changes made in 1514 and later fall into several categories. A very few simply find a more elegant way of saying something which Erasmus found to be inadequately phrased in 1511. Some of the more important changes quickly correct or justify theological points made slackly or too baldly in 1511. The majority are scathingly satirical. In 1515–16 prudence is to the fore, though only in the part concerned with ecstasy.

The additions made in the dedicatory letter to Thomas More strengthen the classical antecedents of the *Moria* by citing additional examples of ancient authors who wrote a jesting encomium, a *lusus*, in an allegedly similar vein. (Curiously these variations are ignored even by Allen and the Toronto translators of the *Letters*.) Such additions are not of minor interest, but even they pale into insignificance when compared to the many phrases, paragraphs and whole pages at a time added to the body of the *Moria* in 1514.

Scheurer's edition of 1514 was the basis on which Froben produced his texts of the *Moria* in 1515–16.

These three editions which Froben produced in 1515–16 need to be distinguished from each other, especially the third one.

The first of these is undated, but is assumed to have been on sale early in 1515. (In this book I refer to it as the undated [1515] *Moria*. There is a copy in the Bodleian Library at *Vet. D. 1. d.6*.)

In essentials it follows the Scheurer 1514 text, with the addition of some of the marginal notes attributed to Listrius. This text was the basis for a second edition, often found joined to Seneca's *Apocolocyntosis* and Synesius' praise of baldness. The colophon of the Synesius is dated March 1515. There is a copy in the Bodleian at *Mar. 865 (2)*. Hans Holbein drew his famous illustrations for the *Moria* in the margins of the copy now in the public art collection of the Basle City Museum. (There is a reproduction of this *Moria*, edited by H. A. Schmid and published by Henning Oppermann of Basle in 1931.) This text is referred to as the dated 1515 *Moria*.

This text was followed by the much more interesting Froben edition which appears to bear the date 1515. It must have actually been published in 1516. There is a copy in the Bodleian at *Mar. 860 (1)*.

The text of this edition has been carefully expurgated, as far as the closing pages devoted to ecstasy are concerned. It is presented as being *pro castigatissimo castigatius*—the more absolutely correct text, better even than previous editions. In significant ways it differs from all others; as far as ecstasy is concerned, these differences are very important. In addition, the text is accompanied by even more marginal notes attributed to Listrius. They are some of the most interesting ones.

This must be the edition that Froben refers to in his letter to Erasmus, which P. S. Allen dates as 17 June [1516]. He stresses what personal attention he gave to its printing (*EE* II, no. 419. lines 15f.).

It is referred to here as the Froben 1516 *Moria*. It is one of the most revealing of Erasmus' writings.

Between these last two editions Erasmus had been brought to see the importance of the criticisms made against him. The best-known of these were those of Martin Dorpius; these he answered in a letter which was regularly prefixed to the *Moria* from 1516 onwards, but first published by Froben in August 1515 in a volume of J. Damian's *In Turcas Elegeia* (*EE* II, p. 599, 'A'. It figures in P. S. Allen's editions of the *Erasmi Epistolae*, in volume, II, no. 337). Erasmus wrote it from Antwerp, on his way to Basle after his third and last long stay in England.

But Dorpius was not his only critic. That can be inferred by what Erasmus had to defend.

Erasmus claimed to have dashed off the original *Moria* in a week. He also claimed that his books had not caught up with him after his journey from Italy. But he said that in his explanations of the adage *Ollas ostentare* ('To make a show of kitchen pots'), which has close affinities to the additions he made to the 1514 version of the dedicatory letter to More. (*Ollas ostentare* was added to the *Adages* in 1515. It is, therefore, contemporary in composition with the 1514 *Moria*, not the 1511; *Adagia* II. 2. 40; M. M. Phillips, p. 96; p. 355.) The 1514 *Moria* was certainly not the product of seven or eight days feverish writing. Nor were those of 1515–16. Whether or not we accept that the first version was written so quickly is a matter of judgment.

Less easy to dismiss as pure convention or light-hearted appeals to the rules of *lusus* are the excuses and explanations to be found in the letter to Dorpius. We nevertheless find much the same unconvincing assertions put forward: Erasmus had written the book in More's home, soon after his return from Italy; he was suffering from a kidney complaint; he did not have his books about him; even if he had done so, he could not have devoted himself to serious writing. The *Moria*, we are told, was sketched out as a pastime, with no idea of publication; it was simply a way of taking his mind off his illness. When his friends saw what he had written, they enjoyed the joke and prevailed upon him to continue with it. He spent a week or so on it—*septem plus minus dies*—too much for so light a thing. But then, the same friends who urged him to write it whisked it off to Paris, having it printed from a poor incorrect manuscript . . . That is all very well! It could apply at a pinch, I suppose, to the first edition: we know hardly anything for certain about the circumstances in which it was written. But this letter to Dorpius dates from 1515 (*EE* II. no. 337). By that year Erasmus had added many a satirical page to his book and could in no way shuffle off his full responsibility for what, from then on; became known as the *Praise of Folly*—the 1514 *Moria* completely eclipsing its shorter pre-decessor. Several of the 1514 additions are among the most bookish things Erasmus ever wrote. In so far as he is to be taken seriously, Erasmus is deliberately misleading a colleague—and, by publishing the letter, misleading a wider public. He defends his book by emphasising its light-heartedness, the short time he took to write it, the fact that it is, after all, a jest, a *lusus*, with a sound classical pedigree. We, at least, must not allow ourselves to be misled by this. Erasmus revised his work while preparing his *Annotations on the New Testament*. Both his revision and the original text belong to the mainstream of his thought. It is a bold work, expounding ideas which remain fresh and attractive still. He was moved to speak lightly of his *lusus* not merely out of convention, not simply because some of his readers did perhaps sometimes find it rather light, but as an act of self-protection. Some of his critics by no means liked the theology he expounded through the mouth of Folly. Some, of course, did not understand it: others understood it only too well.

The first edition of 1511 was swiftly followed by others, giving what is essentially the same text, incorporating the corrections. Whether Erasmus authorized any of these re-editions is not known. Matthew Scheurer of Strasbourg brought out an edition in August 1511. Theodoric Martens of Antwerp followed suit in 1512 and Conrad Badius of Paris in July of the same year. Finally, Scheurer brought out yet another edition in October 1512. The text of these early editions remained the standard one until November 1514, when Erasmus entrusted to Scheurer an expanded version closely resembling the standard one of today.

The 1511 Scheurer edition is the most interesting of the early ones. At the end it contains a letter to Erasmus, dated *xiiii Kal. Septembres. Anni Salutis Nostrae. M.D. XI.* This date—in modern terms 19 August 1511—is the first definite one we have where the *Moria* is concerned. The letter (for which no other source is known) was written by Jacob Wimfeling of Schlettstadt, a mature scholar of considerable importance. He was afraid that his own book against Jacob Locher ('Philomusus') and his defence of certain aspects of scholastic theology could be taken as an attack on the *Moria* and its author, whereas he admired Erasmus and delighted in his new book. He believed that Erasmus and he were fighting the same battles. Having enjoyed the *Moria*, he persuaded Scheurer to reprint it so that his countrymen could share the pleasure (*EE* 1, no. 224). Erasmus, far from being annoyed by this pirating of his book, moved closer in sympathy with Scheurer and his circle. One might even wonder whether the 1511 reprinting was in fact unauthorised, especially when one considers that it was to Scheurer that he entrusted the full-blooded *Moria* of 1514. In one way, certainly, Erasmus' future scholarship was closely bound up with Scheurer and his circle. In 1512 Scheurer printed Johannes Kono's Latin version, *De Natura Hominis*, of a work of Pseudo-Gregory of Nyssa, basing himself on the same volume that contains the manuscript of 'Vulgarius' (Theophylact) which, when Erasmus read it in Basle, radically influenced his scriptural exegesis.

An exciting opuscule awaiting anyone who reads the Scheurer edition of 1511 is the little poem at the end. It is addressed to Erasmus by Sebastian Brant, no less. Critics have often compared and contrasted Brant's *Ship of Fools* (1495) and the *Praise of Folly*. This poem is proof that such comparisons are justified in contemporary terms. Brant, whom Jacob Wimfeling deeply admired, was an ally of note in those early days when the *Moria* was stirring up a hornet's nest (*EE* II, no. 305, no. 302, iif.). In his poem Brant draws a comparison between his *Narrenschiff* and Erasmus' *Moria*. His support for Erasmus was all the more noble in that he foresaw real trouble ahead:

> Vulgares nostra stultos vexisse carina
>   Contenti, intactam liquimus ire togam;
> Moria nunc prodit, que byrrhum, syrmata, fasces
>   Taxans, philosophos convehit et druidas.
> Heu mihi quas turbas, quas sanguinis illa lituras
>   Eliciet, biles cum stomachisque ciens.

Content to have carried vulgar fools in our *Narrenschiff,* we allowed the toga to go untouched. *Moria* now comes forth who, censuring the *burrha* [the red cloak of Cardinals], the *syrmata* [academic gowns] and the *fasces* [the insignia of State], conveys as well philosophers and druids [the clergy]. Alas, what commotions, what smears of blood she will call forth, arousing anger with wrath.

After the prefatory letter to Thomas More, the 1511 *Moria* starts off with a bang: *STULTICIA LOQUITUR*, 'Folly Speaks'. The reader is warned, from the title-page onward, that the *Moriae Encomium* is a declamation—one of those rhetorical *declamationes* which humanists delighted in and which allowed, within one short work, an ever-shifting change of emphasis from pure banter, deliberately weak arguments on matters of no importance, to ideas cogently expressed and deeply held. (Henry Cornelius Agrippa gives a good description of this subtle literary genre in his *Apology* against those who calumniated his own declamation *On the Vanity of all Sciences and on the Excellence of the Word of God*.)

The conventions attached to the *declamatio* provided Erasmus with a permanent way of escape from aggressive censure. When, for example, a group of Spanish monks condemned—among other things—his theology of marriage expounded in the *Encomium Matrimonii,* Erasmus could blandly reply that the work was a declamation, and as such subject to certain rules: first of all, in a *declamation* it is not the truth we have in view but the ability to speak with ingenuity *(ingenii dicendique facultas)* (*LB* 9. 1089E).

The humanist reader would have recognised that Erasmus' elegant *lusus* conformed in the main to the advice of the two classical rhetorical theorists most admired in their circles, Quintilian and Aphthonius. This is as one would expect, for the *Moria* is not a eulogy of folly by an author called Erasmus speaking in his own name: it is a eulogy of folly, an encomium made by a character called Folly in the form of a

declamation. Both Quintilian and Aphthonius had established para-
digms for such encomiums. Attempts to analyse the relationships of
the *Moria* to the theories of the classical rhetoricians have partly
broken down, but only because later versions have been taken as the
basis for modern studies. The 1511 version fits into them far more
snugly. But such questions need not delay us here.[1]

This declamatory mask of Folly is maintained until the last word of
the book. Except for the dedicatory letter, nothing is presented in
Erasmus' own name. Folly's declamation proceeds uninterruptedly to
its conclusion, with a pace which is lacking in the expanded edition of
1514.

My main aim in this book is to throw more light on the climax of
this headlong *declamation*, as well as on the pages which prepare us for
it. We are not only concerned with the actual *epilogus* (which Kan calls
chapter 68) but with the profound eulogy of Christian folly which
begins with what is now called chapter 68, occupying the whole of
that 'chapter' as well as 'chapter 69'.

In the Gourmont edition there is no break of any kind at this point
(or indeed anywhere else). Folly embarks upon her climax half-way
through the third line of a page and goes on right to the end, through
six and a half pages of dense print. Much the same applies to the
Scheurer edition of 1511: there the climax starts in the third from the
last line on G6v°, running straight on through six pages of equally
dense print. It is not an arbitrary act to concentrate on these
pages—provided that full weight is also given to the evangelical
preparation which precedes them. Folly herself invites us to see this
part of the *Moria* as a peroration, bringing her declamation to its close:

> Ac ne quae sunt infinita persequar utque summatim dicam . . .
> Scheurer, 1511, G6v°

> But lest I should chase after the infinite, I shall briefly say that . . .

The pages which follow hard upon this call to our attention are
concerned to elaborate a powerful exposition of Christian ecstasy—not a specifically and exclusively Platonic or neo-Platonic
ecstasy, but a fully Christian form of ecstasy. Basic texts of the New
Testament are called into play. The ecstatic experiences of St Paul and
St Peter are drawn upon directly. These important authorities are
interpreted in ways redolent of Christian mysticism, interpreted in the
light of Erasmus' constant concern with the spiritual as against the
carnal, the invisible as against the visible. This theology is inspired by

---

[1] Cf. with the reservations just expressed, W. Kaiser, *Praisers of Folly*, 1964, p. 3ff.

the New Testament, interpreted with the help of the early, often platonising, Church fathers whom Erasmus so much admired—and by Theophylact who is treated as a kind of honorary ancient.

For Erasmus, ecstasy—which he normally, but not always, identifies with rapture—is the highest manifestation of Christian folly. The praise of ecstasy in the *Moria* is a most fitting climax to those pages where Lucianesque irony gives way to Evangelical fervour, as the full 'folly of the Gospel' is expounded by Folly with subtlety and learned wit.

Folly, as a characteristic of the Christian life, plays a significant part in the theology of St Paul. Erasmus was a Christian scholar for whom the New Testament, spiritually understood in the original Greek, was the focal point of his scholarship and of his piety. It is not really surprising, therefore, that Christian folly should occupy so large a place in his developed thought. (Any reader of this book whose knowledge of the New Testament is rusty would be well advised to re-read the key folly epistles of St Paul, I and II Corinthians.) But Erasmus also found folly and ecstasy in many other parts of the Bible.

Although Erasmus turned for inspired guidance to the Greek New Testament, western Christendom had for centuries been inclined to take as normative the Latin of the Vulgate—the Latin translation of St Jerome. Erasmus was one who doubted whether the Vulgate—at least as it stood, with all its errors, inaccuracies and infelicities—could in fact be the work of St Jerome. This doubt in itself made him enemies. Erasmus could never ignore the Vulgate text: he corrected it at his peril: any departure at all was bound to arouse the wrath of some powerful theological conservatives. Béda, the theological 'monster' of Paris, the syndic of his faculty, a man whose spite and censuring power spread far beyond his college of Montaigu until he was finally squashed by the combined might of the kings of England and France and the du Bellay family—openly opposed the teaching of Greek and Hebrew because it encouraged students who knew these tongues to correct their professors who did not. He was for a time one of Erasmus' most influential enemies, smearing both him and Lefèvre d'Etaples with the name of 'clandestine Lutherans'. Béda and his kind not only feared that a Greek New Testament they could not read would overthrow their venerated Vulgate. Equally seriously, those who gave primacy to the Greek original over the Latin translation devalued at a stroke much of the writings of some of the pillars of scholastic theology, who were nearly all Greekless. On many an occasion Aquinas, say, or Duns Scotus, Nicolas of Lyra or Hugo Carrensis, can be shown to be hopelessly wrong in their theology, reading into their Latin New Testament meanings which had no warrant whatsoever in the original Greek. Erasmus delighted in rubbing this lesson home.

Erasmus' passionate concern for the exact nuance of the divinely revealed truth of the New Testament was accompanied by a parallel concern to extract the truths figuratively foreshadowed by the *Veritas Hebraica,* the true text of the Old Testament. He never managed to learn Hebrew. As often as not he turned for guidance to the standard Greek translation of the Hebrew Scriptures, the Septuagint. This practice could be partly justified by the fact that the New Testament writers themselves normally quote from the Septuagint, sometimes finding doctrines in the Greek for which the Hebrew gives little or no justification. Moreover, the early Greek fathers piously allegorised the Old Testament, acknowledging the inerrancy of the literal meaning in theory, but often treating it as far less important than the spiritual allegories they found beneath the surface. Erasmus does refer to the distinguished Jewish scholar Rabbi Solomon, but with caution and a certain distaste. When writing on the 2nd Psalm (*Quare fremuerunt:* 'Why do the Nations so furiously rage together') he declares that he does not consider what Jewish scholars have to say—especially the ancient ones—to be a total loss, but their works are full of fog and silly fables, not to mention falsification of Christian matters and a hatred for Christ (*LB* 5. 202C).

Erasmus' neglect of Hebrew was not without its dangers. But it also had advantages: it shielded him from that widespread humanist concern with the Kabbala and Jewish mysticism generally which, while being of keen interest to modern Renaissance scholars, could easily have deflected him from the main direction of his intellectual Christian life: to extract from the New Testament a spiritual theology and a guide to practical piety. This he did by opening his mind to the riches of the Greek Bible and of the early Greek fathers of the Church, as well as to the Christian insights of the great early Latins, especially Jerome, Ambrose, Augustine. These sources enabled him to lay aside the complexities of mediaeval western theology, which he saw, often unjustly, as barren, arrogant and ignorant logomachias. He plunged himself into another world of scholarship, elegant and more serene, finding in it a depth of Christian experience far more attractive than what he had learned in the universities of his youth.

There was a danger, too, in going back so enthusiastically to these early fathers. Some, like Origen, were at least partly heretical, even in those of their works which had survived centuries of neglect or of perhaps systematic attempts to destroy them. Others were writing at a time when later orthodoxies had yet to be imposed on to a more or less willing western Church. For some of his contemporaries Erasmus seemed to be saying that all mediaeval scholastic theology could be swept aside: that orthodoxy did not have to be sought in the definitions and anathemas of later times; that the early fathers already held the essentials of the faith.

Inevitably he aroused hostility, hatred and exasperated suspicion. Personally, I do not believe that Erasmus, in anything he wrote, ever put in doubt the credal orthodoxies or the essentials of the Catholic faith. But even men of good will can be understood if they thought he had. He was so often appealing to authorities which lesser scholars did not know and which they often did not even have access to. He did not attract only suspicion and enmity of course: he also attracted support from all over Europe. And his gift for friendship won him the honour of a lasting place in history as the darling of Thomas More.

The last pages of the *Moria*, written probably in More's own house, call upon the developed resources of Erasmus' scholarship. Naturally, such an important climax is carefully prepared for.

CHAPTER TWO

The Preparation for the Praise of Ecstasy: Christian Folly

1. *The theology of the* Enchiridion *as narrated by Lucian?*

The climax of the *Moria* is indeed carefully prepared for. It starts with the words:

Atqui fortassis apud Christianos, horum levis est auctoritas: (1511 Scheurer, G5r°, line 14; Kan, p. 159).

However, among Christians the authority of these [arguments] is no doubt light.

On page 159, Kan (in accordance with standard practice) begins a new chapter at this point. Then follow some twenty pages of largely scriptural argument and polemic, ending a few lines up on page 180. In no part of the *Moria* are the traditional texts and translations so misleading. For these pages of Kan's contain some fifteen interpolations. Some are small but not unimportant. Others are large (15 lines on page 161, 41 lines on pages 163–48), or very large (all the end of 'chapter 65' from line 5 of page 179); in one case the interpolation is massive (everything from line 3 of page 165 to the last line of page 173).

To read the text as it first appeared is a refreshing experience. The absence of bitter polemics is heartening. The light, but single-minded, presentation of the paradoxical Scriptural case for Christian folly is effective and arresting. Since the Scheurer text is free of the misprints of the Gourmont *editio princeps* I use it here. It follows the original edition, with which, of course, I have checked it.

In his defence of the *Moria*, written from Antwerp towards the end of May 1515, Erasmus declared that he was only doing in jest what he had already done straightforwardly in the *Enchiridion Militis Christiani*—'The Manual of the Christian Soldier'—which he first published in 1503.[1] Erasmus maintained that he had kept his works free from aggressiveness. His writings were harmless (*innoxiae*); they shed no blood (*incruentae*). He named no names. In this the *Moria* was no different from his other books; only it took a different route (*tametsi via diversa*):

In the *Enchiridion* we propounded the pattern of the Christian life. In our little treatise *On the Education of the Christian Prince* we openly gave advice about the matters a Christian prince should be taught. And in the *Praise* [*of Folly*], under the guise of an encomium, we did the very same thing obliquely as we had done there straightforwardly.

Plato and Horace approved of such bantering (*EE* II, no. 337, 84f.).

This is the truth. But it is not the whole truth. Erasmus remains loyal in the *Moria* to the *Enchiridion*'s concern with the spiritual rather than the carnal, the invisible rather than the visible, the moral rather than the formal. He remains textually loyal to an interpretation of man as a creature compounded of body, mind and spirit which, under Origen's guidance, he found expounded in St Paul, especially in I Thessalonians 5:23 (see below, p. 96). But the new element—which put even Martin Dorpius on the wrong track—was the Lucianesque humour. One has to wait a long time, when reading even the 1511 *Moria*, before the paradoxes, jests, ironies and obliquities of Folly are finally and clearly resolved in the very last section of the work. Even the few pages which lead up to the final resolution are not without their jests and their arresting paradoxes. Moreover, since the writing of his earlier works Erasmus had deepened his theological commitment, embracing now—still largely under the guidance of Origen and of Greek theology generally—a religious conviction which gave the last serious word in the *Moria* to a passionate exposition of the joys of a mad ecstatic union of a man with his God and his neighbour.

The pages about to be studied prepare for the serious conclusion and partly share in its seriousness. They begin on sig. G5r° of the 1511 Scheurer edition (p. 159 of Kan). I give both Scheurer and Kan references. When quoting Scheurer I remain as close as practicable to the text, simply changing the punctuation where it would be unhelpful to stick over-scrupulously to the original practice. Italics are introduced in order to draw attention to the Scriptural or other quotations. Throughout this book all the italics are my own. (A few minor misprints are tacitly corrected against the 1512 Scheurer edition.)

The text of the praise of ecstasy is given in Appendix B.

[1] There is a useful introduction to the *Enchiridion* in A. J. Festugière's French translation, Paris, 1971.

2. *Lucian gives way to the manhood of Christ*

This section of the *Moria* starts off still in the vein of Lucian to which the previous pages have accustomed the reader. Only with hindsight do we realise that we are being presented with a skilful transition from bantering satire to lightly-borne, yet earnestly preaching, erudition. We have a brief mockery of the Sorbonne and of Duns Scotus—the theologians of Paris were fair game for evangelical humanists, as was Scotus, whom it was normal to caricature as the archetypal scholastic booby (a *dunce* in fact).

Then follows a series of allusions to folly texts taken from the Old Testament. They are loosely cited at times. The carelessness with which some of the texts of both the Old and New Testaments are cited towards the end of the 1511 *Moria* is striking. Such carelessness cannot be used to lend support in the contention that the first version of the *Moria* was written when Erasmus' books had not arrived from Italy. It would be hard to believe that Erasmus could not lay his hands on a Vulgate in More's house. The distortions include textually incorrect citings of some vital words of St Paul. What seems to have happened—where St Paul is concerned at any rate—is that Erasmus did not check his quotations because he was sure he was right. Who among us has not done the same thing, especially under the pressure of emotion or commitment? In the case of the Old Testament quotations a certain apparent slackness of allusion is found in other writers on folly too—in Viguerius, for example, who is quoted below (p. 28). At all events, none of the Old Testament texts which Erasmus cites is so august or so grave as to raise an eyebrow when used in jest: 'The number of fools is infinite' (Ecclesiastes 1:15), 'Vanity of vanities, all is vanity' (Ecclesiastes 1:2, etc.); 'Folly is a joy to a fool' (Proverbs 15:21), and, again from Proverbs (30:2), 'I am the most foolish of men'. (This text can have deeper overtones. Erasmus does not develop them.) Ecclesiastes also supplies: 'He that increases wisdom increases sorrow, and in much wisdom is much indignation' (1:18).

Of the texts marshalled at this point, only one gives cause for reflection. We are misled into thinking that Folly is simply being ingenious, twisting words to fit her case:

Rursum sapiens ille qui dixit, *stultus mutatur ut Luna, sapiens permanet ut sol,* quid aliud innuit nisi mortale genus omne stultum esse? . . . (Scheurer G5v°; Kan 162).

Again that wise man [Solomon] who said: 'The fool changeth like the moon, the wise man remaineth like the sun'—what else does he imply but that the mortal race is all foolish? . . .

The text alluded to, Ecclesiasticus 27:12, does not in fact contrast the fool (*stultus*) and the wise man (*sapiens*); it contrasts the fool and 'the man holy in wisdom' (*homo sanctus in sapientia*). Folly twists this to her purposes by introducing the word *sapiens* twice, once with the reference to *sapiens ille*, once in the loose quotation itself. The Septuagint could not encourage the fool/wise-man jest, since, like the Vulgate, it also opposes the fool (*aphrōn*) to the pious man (*eusebēs*). Moreover it does not compare the pious man's permanence to the sun (LXX Ecclesiasticus 27:11). What gave rise to Folly's development here is that part of the ancient Latin translation of Origen's *Commentary on St Matthew* which has survived. There, explaining the episode of the lunatic in Matthew 17, Origen (in the Latin, not the Greek version) does cite Ecclesiasticus 27:12 just as Folly does. *Sapiens sicut sol permanet* is applied to the just, who is the 'wise man' who 'remaineth like the sun'. Similarly, to the changeableness of the sinner is applied the words 'the fool changeth like the moon': *Insipiens sicut luna immutatur* (PG 13. 1103–4, *Vetus Interpretatio*). Few of the *Moria's* readers would have recognised this debt to Origen. Most of them probably thought it was simply an ingenious piece of jesting, as, up to a point, it may well be. But for the scholarly reader of today the clue is a valuable one, reminding him from the outset that one of the major sources of Erasmus' theology is Origen, especially in the *Commentary on Matthew*, the Old Testament *Homilies* and his exegesis of *The Song of Songs which is Solomon's*.

Just when we have congratulated ourselves on seeing the joke, a new element is introduced. The sentence quoted above continues in an unexpected way:

> *soli deo* sapientis nomen competere.
>
> . . . and that the name of wise belongs to God alone.

With these words a major theme of the climax is introduced: the wisdom of God which is to be compared and contrasted with both the wisdom and the foolishness of men. The words *soli deo*, 'to God alone', are in context an appeal to Luke 17:19. Erasmus also hints at a more profound theme: that Christ in his manhood, emptied of his divine wisdom, was a kind of fool. (There is also a play on words: the wise man who remains like the *Sol*—the Sun—resembles *soli deo*—God alone.)

Folly continues by asserting that many interpret the moon as human nature and the sun as God, the fount of all light. And then we are abruptly confronted with the authority of Christ:

Huic astipulatur quod ipse *Christus* in evangelio *negat quemquam appellandum bonum, nisi deum unum* (Scheurer G5vº; Kan 162).

With this agrees the fact that Christ himself in the Gospel denies that anyone is to be called good, except God alone.

The phrase *negat quemquam appellandum bonum, nisi deum unum* is an allusion to Mark 10:18: *Nemo bonus nisi unus Deus* ('No one is good, except one God'). It is interesting that Erasmus has altered the order of the words, *nisi unus deus* becoming *nisi deu[s] unu[s]*. Why he does this is clear from his annotation on the cognate verse of St Matthew's gospel (19:17; *LB* 6. 101D), where he prefers the Greek reading to the Vulgate's. The Greek he renders there as *nullus est bonus, nisi unus, nempe Deus* ('No one is good, except one, namely God'). He annotates Mark 10:18 the same way (*LB* 6. 191E); and, to the corresponding verse of Luke 17:19, he adds a note pointing out the parallels and stressing that Christ is speaking here in his humanity not in his deity (*LB* 6. 304F). The text serves then as the highest conceivable authority for Christians who wish to humble the pretensions of men to virtue in the sight of God. Even Christ in his manhood denied the epithet good; that epithet is reserved not to 'one God' (*unus Deus*) but to God alone (*Deus unus*). In the *Moria* this point is emphasised a few lines earlier with the contention that the name of good belongs to 'God alone' (*soli deo*). For that is what St Luke reports Christ as saying.

3. Paul: the more foolish apostle

This introduction of a serious theological element into Folly's oration is managed with considerable art; it is so imbedded in the light-hearted allusions to the verses from Ecclesiastes, Proverbs and Ecclesiasticus that the point is made—and apparently done with—almost before we have noticed it. Even the more sombre note provided by Ecclesiastes 1:18 does not break the spell: 'Who increases knowledge (*scientia*) increases pain, and in much understanding (*sensus*) is much displeasure (*indignatio*).' Here again, the borrowing is not closely literal and it could still all be taken as an impish joke on the part of Folly (Scheurer G5vº; Kan 163). But then we are suddenly plunged into the folly of the Gospel, associated directly with the name of St Paul.

Neque Paulus ille magnus gentium doctor, stulti cognomen illibenter agnoscit: *Insipiens quis est*, inquiens, *plus ego*, perinde quasi turpe sit vinci stulticia Et *libenter fertis insipientes*, ad se refert.

And neither did Paul, that great teacher of the Gentiles, ungladly accept the surname of fool, saying, 'Who is unwise? I am more', as though it were disgraceful to be surpassed in folly. And he applies to himself the words, 'Ye bear fools gladly'.

The texts alluded to are Romans 15:16 (St Paul acknowledged as the apostle to the Gentiles) and two folly commonplaces from II Corinthians 11. The first is badly mangled; *Insipiens quis est? plus ego* (Who is unwise? I am more), corresponds to verse 23, *minus sapiens dico, plus ego* ('Less wise, I say, I am more'). Erasmus has conflated it with II Corinthians 11:29, *Quis infirmatur, et non infirmor* ('Who is weak, and I am not weak?'). This text is subject to correction and to such a massive explanatory and polemical addition in 1514 that it can be left over to Appendix A. One may simply note that, with this calling upon the authority of St Paul, the move towards the praise of ecstasy is well under way. The Vulgate reading *minus sapiens* is a very weak rendering of the Greek original. So too is the Authorised Version's 'I speak as a fool'. The word St Paul uses is *paraphroneō*— (*paraphronōn lalō*); Paul is speaking as one who is 'out of his wits', who is 'insanely beside himself'; (cf. Erasmus' *Annotations, LB* 6. 790F). The text in its original form is an excellent preparation for what is to follow. But Erasmus blunted its point—his verbally slack allusion weakens Folly's case more than somewhat. St Paul did not write 'Who is a fool? I am more', but 'Are they servants of Christ?—I am speaking like a madman—I am more'. That makes a great deal of difference within the context of the *Moria*. This erroneous citing of a text central to the theme of Christian folly helps to explain, at least in part, why this phrase of the 1511 *Moria* was so fundamentally expanded in 1514. Erasmus was wrong, and knew it.

The second of the allusions to II Corinthians is from verse 19, 'For ye bear fools gladly' (*Et libenter fertis insipientes*). It poses no great problems. It closely renders the Vulgate text, simply changing *suffertis* to *fertis*, a change which Erasmus does not maintain in his own *Novum Instrumentum*. There is of course a play on words here, *libenter* (gladly) corresponding to the hardly classical *illibenter* used just before: Paul did not *illibenter*, 'ungladly', accept the name of fool.

But the tone is becoming more serious and passages of Scripture are being used to make points which, however paradoxical, form part of the serious eulogy of Christian folly. The next words are

Quid quod palam stulticiam praecipit: *Qui videtur esse sapiens inter vos, stultus fiat, ut sit sapiens.*

That clearly teaches folly: 'If any man among you seemeth to be wise, let him become a fool, that he may be wise' [I Corinthians 3:18] (Scheurer G5v°; Kan 165).

The paradox of this is more carefully explained in the paraphrase of I Corinthians 3:18. What is condemned is seeking happiness in philosophy [like the Greeks] or in the law of Moses [like the Jews]. If a man wishes to be truly wise, 'let him become wisely foolish' (*sapienter stultescat*). Once he ceases to profess foolish wisdom he becomes suitable to be a disciple of wisest folly (*LB* 7. 868F–869A).

Both the quotation from I Corinthians 3: 18 in the *Moria* of 1511 and its subsequent development in Erasmus' other writings show that banter has been thrust aside. This foolish wisdom, this wise folly, is the philosophy of Christ.

4. *God's folly, according to Origen*

The urgent change of tone proceeds apace in 1511:

Illud haud scio an mirum videatur, cum deo quoque nonnihil stulticiae tribuit: *Quod stultum est*, inquit *dei, sapientius est hominibus*. Porro Origenes interpres obsistit, quo minus hanc stulticiam ad hominum opinionem possis referre, quod genus est illud, *gentibus quidem stulticiam* (Scheurer G5v°–G6r°; Kan 165–74).

I hardly know whether this should seem a marvel, since he [St Paul] attributes something of folly to God also: 'The foolishness of God is wiser than men' [I Corinthians 1:25]. Moreover the exegete Origen opposes your being able to make this refer to the opinion of men—in which category is [I Corinthians 1: 23], 'and unto the Gentiles, foolishness'.

Here we are plunged into the thick of important texts of the New Testament, texts which Erasmus permanently and seriously associated with the doctrine of Christian folly—which for him was not only that divinely inspired wisdom of the Christian which seems foolish to the wordly-wise.

Erasmus does not bother to point out the ambiguity of the Vulgate reading—*sapientius est hominibus* is ambiguous, as Augustine noted (*De Doctrina Christiana* II. xxii. 55f.). It can mean 'wiser to men' as well as 'wiser than men'. Such questions he prefers to treat in his *Annotations* (*LB* 6. 665CD). It is a feature of the *Moria* that Erasmus, despite his veneration for the Greek New Testament, normally sticks to the text of the Vulgate whenever he can, a practice which makes his allusions more accessible to the reader of his day.

When he does depart from the Vulgate in the *Moria,* either the allusion is made carelessly or else a point of some importance is at stake. But his formal citing of the Vulgate's words often hides the fact that his understanding of the texts is conditioned by the Greek originals.

The ambiguity noted by Augustine is of minor importance: the context makes the meaning perfectly clear. More vital to an understanding of the *Moria* is the fact that Folly's interpretation of this and other Biblical folly texts is supported by the exegesis of Origen. For Erasmus Origen was not the hopelessly marred heretic he was for many of his contemporaries. His extant writings he held in the highest esteem at this point in his career.[1] Origen's platonising tendencies were well fitted to please Erasmus. And indeed few if any of the ancient fathers—none indeed that I know at first hand—could supply more ammunition to a man looking for authority to support a particular conception of the theme of the folly of the Gospel.

One of the reasons why Erasmus and others can so successfully develop the theme of Christian folly is that the Christian religion did seem particularly stupid and absurd to both the Jewish and the Gentile worlds in which it first appeared. Two millenia of existence, marked by long periods of dominance, have blunted this stark fact. For Jews and for Gentiles the three basic doctrines of Christian belief were not merely unlikely, unproven or distasteful: they were daft. These doctrines are the Incarnation, the Crucifixion and the Resurrection of the body. They seemed more absurd to sophisticated pagans than even the discredited legends and myths of their own traditional pantheons; to educated Jews, the first two especially seemed both blasphemous and insane. That God, conceived monotheistically and transcendentally, should take man's nature upon himself—don, that is, the flesh of man and live really and truly as a man—flew in the face of all mature philosophical and religious assumptions. That this God-Man should then allow himself to be legally executed as a criminal by the properly constituted political authorities, seemed even more insane. It was precisely because of this that early heresies tend either to strip Christ of his deity or else to make the Incarnation and Crucifixion into a divine charade, with an exclusively divine Christ only pretending to be a man and only pretending to die upon the Cross.

Defenders of the doctrines of the Incarnation, the Crucifixion and the Resurrection of the body in such a hostile intellectual atmosphere tended to insist on the 'foolishness' of what they preached. The wisdom of this world was dismissed as being indeed incompatible with that of God, who did indeed prefer to work in ways which are not only silly but absurd and insane by the standards of Athens, Jerusalem, Alexandria or Rome.

[1] Cf. D. P. Walker, 'Origène en France' in *Courants religieux et humanisme . . .*, *Colloque de Strasbourg 1957*, Paris 1959; E. Wind, 'The revival of Origen', in *Studies in Art and Literature for Belle da Costa Green*, Princeton, 1954; A. Godin, THR, *L'Homéliaire de Jean Vitrier*, Geneva, 1971.

On the other hand the intellectual vigour of Greek philosophy during the early centuries of Christianity led to the introduction of some of its main concepts into the very heart of Christian thinking. This happened as early as Origen; the adoption of Christianity as the Imperial religion by Constantine the Great in the fourth century accelerated the process. By the sixth century neo-Platonism had so contaminated Christian thought that the works of Dionysius, whose doctrines are not really compatible with some fundamental Christian assertions, became ascribed to Dionysius, the Areopagite converted by St Paul during his visit to Athens. They were accorded a place of great importance, being thought of as a special revelation from St Paul entrusted to a chosen disciple. In theory the Pseudo-Dionysian corpus was subordinate to Scripture: in practice the Judaeo-Christian biblical writings were often interpreted in its light. In mediaeval times Thomas Aquinas cites him in the same breath as Aristotle and the Bible; this led Thomas to accord an important place to neo-Platonic teachings within his influential scholasticism. Ficino revered Dionysius; John Colet venerated him; St François de Sales never doubted his authority as St Paul's disciple and the patron saint of France.

As neo-Platonism lent its colour to Christianity, God the Father became conceived of more and more in terms of the inaccessible, transcendent Deity of philosophical paganism. Such a concept was not of fleeting concern. W. Chalmers Smith's famous hymn—

> Immortal, Invisible, God only wise,
> In light inaccessible hid from our eyes,

is pure Dionysian doctrine; and he died as recently as 1908. The French translation of Dionysius which Mgr Darboy, an archbishop of Paris, published in 1932, is preceded by a long and nasty introduction passionately defending Pseudo-Dionysius' authenticity and attacking both the good faith and morals of those who have ever doubted it (*Saint Denys L'Aréopagite: Oeuvres, traduites du Grec*, A. Tralin, Paris 1932).

The absorption of neo-Platonic and Platonic ideas into Christian philosophy led to their becoming not the enemies but the allies of Christian folly. In the process folly risked becoming something very different from the madness of a God who decided to become a man and be crucified. Instead of centring on the folly of the Incarnation and of the Cross, there was a tendency to make Christian folly consist in an overwhelming awareness of the invisible and spiritual world which lesser men ignore or deny.

Erasmus' predilection for the earliest Christian writers exposes him to these tendencies, but it does not lead him simply to replace Christian assumptions by Platonic or neo-Platonic ones. He is more inclined to syncretise the two together, without, however, temporising over the fundamentals of the Incarnation, the Crucifixion or the Resurrection. What is remarkable is that he should have seen through the error of those who so grossly antedated Pseudo-Dionysius. That suggests a high degree of philosophical and historical insight. It also enabled him to bypass one of the major sources of ecstatic doctrine and so to reach back to something more authentically Platonic and, perhaps, more authentically at home in the first Christian centuries.

These varying influences all contribute to the special nature of Erasmus' concept of folly. The early pagans sometimes found the concern of Christians for the poor, the needy, the weak, the backward and the unintelligent to be very odd indeed. Christians could seem, by several different standards, to be acting as madmen. So too could Jesus, Paul and those who followed them. And when judged against the standards of philosophy, God's plan for the redemption of mankind could be made to seem an act of divine lunacy. Both God the Father and God the Son, as Christians conceive them, can be thought of as mad.

Very influential in the development of such powerful paradoxes was Erasmus' beloved Origen. Erasmus was attracted by Origen's interpretation of the folly of God as something quite different from the rather obvious fact that Christianity seemed daft to unbelieving Jews and Gentiles, though it is that as well. The question is, where in Origen's works did he come across it? By no means all of the works which we can read so easily in the *Patrologia Graeca* were readily accessible when the *Moria* was created. On the other hand, writing to John Colet in December 1504, Erasmus was already claiming to have read most of the extant works of Origen with great profit.

Erasmus saw Origen as, in some respects, the greatest of the ancient fathers. But he was aware of his heresies. Towards the end of his life when he came to restate yet again some of the doctrines of the *Moria*, he was moved both to sympathise with Origen's lapses—he wrote so much—and to stress that the cause of his downfall lay in his Platonism (*LB* 5. 432B—in his very personal commentary on the 38/39th psalm). Erasmus also convinced himself in the end that Rufinus (whose Latin renderings are the only sources we have of some of Origen's *Homilies*) had hopelessly perverted his doctrines (*LB* 8. 435F). But that Origen remained for so many of his contemporaries a dangerous and potentially misleading author probably explains Erasmus' reticence in citing him directly on questions of Christian folly, once the *Moria* had been attacked. Since he does not tell us what Origen said, nor in what work he said it, we have to look for it ourselves.

The fullest and clearest exposition of Origen's conception of the true nature of Christian folly is to be found in his eighth *Homily on Jeremiah*. (In St Jerome's Latin translation, which was for long the only source, it is numbered fifth.) Origen develops at some length the theme of all human wisdom being but folly when compared to the ineffable wisdom of God. He does this when expounding Jeremiah 10:14: 'Every man has been made a fool by wisdom (*Infatuatus—stultus—est omnis homo ab scientia*) (*PG* 13. 345f.). He naturally associates this text with I Corinthians 1:20 and 21: 'Hath not God made foolish the wisdom of the world? For seeing that, in the wisdom of God, the world through its wisdom knew not God, it was God's good pleasure through foolishness of the things preached to save them that believed.' This is, inevitably, a text that Folly is soon to cite herself.

Origen gives to this text an important and profound meaning. It is this teaching that Erasmus appears to be referring to obliquely and which he subtly develops in the following pages. Origen stresses that this text does *not* mean merely that God's wisdom seems foolishness, but rather that all the wisdom which God actually vouchsafes to man is only, as it were, his own 'foolishness'. Yet this divine fatuousness is greater than the greatest of all human wisdom. Even the wisdom of Paul, who only saw through a glass darkly (I Corinthians 13:12) is to be reputed folly when compared to celestial wisdom as it is, to that perfect knowledge *(gnōsis)* which is God's. Eventual access to this perfect knowledge is vouchsafed to man through God's baby-talk, so to speak, through that 'foolishness' which is all of God's wisdom that man can take. Such foolishness is the wisdom of God revealed, in ways that man can grasp, in the Bible. The highest manifestation of that foolishness—that divine Wisdom made intelligible to man—is Christ: God made man.

Erasmus several times explains this conception of the folly of God. The self-emptying of God in folly is a theme of two of his later works, both commentaries on the psalms: Christ's appearance in the form of a man was equivalent to the simple stammering sort of speech used by parents to their babes (*LB* 5. 382AB); when the Scriptures talk about God's anger, joy, hatred—impossible emotions in an impassible God—it is similar to the lisping speech affected by nurses and mothers talking to their little children, hoping to make them understand at least something (*LB* 5. 511EF). The same Origenesque theme appears in the *Enchiridion* (*LB* 5. 8F): 'The divine Wisdom lisps to us and, like a dutiful mother, accommodates his words to our *infantiam*' (to our childish inability to speak or think in an adult fashion).

As Origen puts it, using a concept often echoed by Erasmus, we are strengthened by Jesus' weakness; so too we are made wise by God's folly (*apo tou mōrou tou theou*); through it we may ascend in the spirit to the wisdom and power of God, Jesus Christ our Lord (*PG* 13. 343C–348A).

These descriptions of Christ as the wisdom and power of God derive from Philippians 2:7. What Erasmus also took this verse to mean will soon explain much of what is to follow in the *Moria*.

Origen takes the most arresting of ways to make his point:

If every man is made a fool by knowledge, and Paul is a man, then Paul was made a fool by knowledge—'For we know in part, and we prophesy in part' [I Corinthians 13:9];—he was rendered a fool by knowledge, seeing 'through a glass' [I Corinthians 13:12, *per speculum*], seeing a small portion [*nunc cognosco ex parte*, 'Now I know in part'] and, if it may be said, only just recognising that part (PG 13. 343–4CD).

The point is rammed home by Origen with clarity and fervour: Paul's and Peter's knowledge, at its best, was no more than the folly of God, his silliness as it were. Origen is conscious of speaking boldly: God, on descending to the world, 'emptied himself' (Philippians 2:7); yet it was this 'emptying' of God—the technical word for which is now *kenōsis*—which for men is wisdom itself, 'Because the foolishness of God is wiser than men' (I Corinthians 1:25). Paul, a wise man having the authority of an apostle, dared to say that all earthly wisdom—in himself, in Peter and the rest of the apostles, and including that which comes down from God to this world—is but God's foolishness. Compared with God's wisdom as it really is, what is revealed to man, within the limits of man in this world, is indeed merely God's folly. 'But this silliness of God is wiser than men. Which men? Not foolish men merely, but wise men.' (The words Origen uses are *mōros*, foolish and *sophos*, wise.)

The whole development of the theme of folly by Origen in this *Homily on Jeremiah* would be a strong draught of theology for one about to embark on the last serious pages of the *Moria*. Origen, indeed, does not believe that St Paul, in declaring that 'the foolishness of God is wiser than men', was simply saying the same thing as is meant by I Corinthians 1:23: 'We preach Christ crucified, unto the Jews a stumbling-block, and unto the Gentiles foolishness.' He meant that revealed wisdom—the mere 'foolishness' of God—surpasses all human knowledge, yet is as nothing when compared with the wisdom of God awaiting the spirit of man in the life to come. Did Erasmus already know the *Homilies on Jeremiah* in Greek at first hand? Naturally St Jerome's translation of this Homily was widely studied by the Latin fathers. From 1503 onwards some of Origen's Homilies were available in print, from Aldus of Venice, but those on Jeremiah were not printed before 1513.[1]

One work of Origen's certainly was known to Erasmus and he invited comparisons between it and the *Moria*: the *Homilies on the Song of Songs* (extant in the Latin translation of Rufinus). There we can read words which lend themselves to Folly's interpretation of the folly of God within a kenotic context:

What was Christ *not* made for our salvation? We were empty: he emptied himself, taking on the form of a slave. We were a people foolish and lacking wisdom: he was made the foolishness of preaching so that the silliness of God might be wiser than men. We were weak: the weakness of God was made stronger than men (*PG* 13. 49A).

Quid enim pro nostra salute non factus est? Nos inanes, et ille exinanivit semetipsum formam servi accipiens. Nos populus stultus et non sapiens, et ille factus est stultitia praedicationis, ut fatuum Dei sapientius fieret hominibus. Nos infirmi, infirmum Dei fortius hominibus factum est.

The more straightforward interpretation of the theme of Christian folly—the kind represented by the words 'unto Gentiles foolishness'—Erasmus, like anyone else, could find textually and clearly in his New Testament, in the Latin as clearly as the Greek. He could also have found it in many a Christian writer spanning the gap from patristic times to his own: it was a commonplace among the Latin Christians as well as the Greeks.

Although Erasmus certainly makes Origen's theology of the folly of God central to the *Moria*, one may note that, apart from the brief but important allusion to Origen in that work itself, he only once again specifically alludes to a relevant folly text of Origen in any edition of the *Moria*. This allusion occurs in an important marginal note added in late 1516. Nevertheless he continued to make unacknowledged borrowings from Origen until the end of his life (see below, p. 238). Erasmus accepts the kenotic view of Christ's manhood. This can be seen from his brisk little annotation of Philippians 2:7 (*LB* 6. 867F, note 11). He polishes up the Vulgate words *exinanivit semetipsum* ('he made himself void, empty'), preferring *inanivit seipsum* ('he emptied himself out'). The original word, *ekenōse*, he takes to mean here that Christ 'made himself most humble and nothing' (*humillimus et nihil*), sharply rejecting the opinion of those who hold that Christ only gradually, or little by little (*pauxillum*) lowered himself from the Godhead. He adds:

[1] Copy in BL at *3805.g.15(2)*. For the manuscript tradition one can still consult with profit E. Klostermann's *Die Überlieferung der Jeremiahomilien des Origenes*, 1897.

'In what manner he may be said to be *diminished* or *emptied* is not relevant to my purpose at this point' (*non est hujus instituti persequi*). I think he would have developed it in terms of the folly of God as expounded by Origen, but was untypically moved by discretion. On 17 March 1517, Jerome Dungersheym, who studied Greek at Dresden with Richard Croke, wrote a courteous but troubled letter to Erasmus on this very subject (*EE* II no. 554). Erasmus's reply has not survived. But there can be little doubt about his answer. It was about this question of Christ's kenosis that he quarrelled with Faber (Lefèvre d'Etaples) over the meaning of Hebrews 2:6. For Erasmus this text means that the Father made Christ, 'for a while, lower than the angels'. In a very long footnote to the New Testament he defends this doctrine with a display of vigour and erudition, including fifty-seven numbered arguments. (*LB* 6. 985C–991E). The whole point is to stress God's kenosis in Christ, a Man among men.

In the *Moria* Erasmus introduces this theology with an allusion to Origen by name: *Porro Origenes interpres obsistit* . . . ('Moreover the exegete Origen opposed . . .').

This fact remains vital and he never struck out the reference. Nevertheless in the *Annotations on the New Testament* he omits all mention of Origen when explaining I Corinthians 1:25:

Paul calls the preaching of the Cross the foolishness and weakness of God, either because it seems foolish and weak to impious men, or because, compared with the ineffable wisdom and power of God, it is in some way foolish and weak. Just as 'all the justice of men is as a woman's soiled menstrual rag' [Isaiah 64:6], so the entire wisdom of mortal men, if compared to that unthinkable heavenly wisdom, can be called a certain kind of folly—*stultitia quaedam*.

(It is interesting that one of the very few changes that Erasmus made to the full climax of the *Moria* was to insert an *aliqua* before *stultitia* at the beginning of 'chapter 66'. From 1523 onwards we are dealing not with plain folly but a 'certain kind' of folly.) Erasmus was often called upon to defend the arresting phrase, the 'foolishness of God'. He does so in the *Annotations*; with reference to Christ and the teaching of the apostles:

There is no reason to detest the expression 'foolishness of God', *stultitia Dei*, which did not horrify Augustine. In his hundredth and second letter he wrote: 'This foolishness of God and their foolishness of preaching draw many to salvation'. If God lowered himself to our weakness to make us strong, what is there new if he should lower himself to our foolishness, making wise men out of fools? (*LB* 6. 665DE).

On many occasions Erasmus found opportunities for defending or expanding such ideas, sometimes when one might least expect it. This applies to some of his very latest works, showing that Christian folly as Origen and others revealed it to him remained a powerful element in his version of the philosophy of Christ. One could cite, for example, his Paraphrase of Luke 1:45 (*Magnificat*): 'He hath showed strength with his arm: he hath scattered the proud in the imagination of their hearts:'

So God, wishing to cast down the pride of wisdom and earthly power through his Son made humble, stretched forth the strength of his arm and made foolish the wisdom of this world; he cast down and broke the power of this world, showing that even when he had lowered himself to the maximum, he was yet stronger than the highest point of all human power; he showed that what seemed foolish in him was wiser than the wisdom of this world, however marvellous . . . (*LB* 7. 293B–D).

The same kenotic interpretation of Christ's redemptive action and of God's folly is found in the paraphrase of I Corinthians 1:25, a text central to the *Moria*: 'Because the foolishness of God is wiser than men.' For this very reason it reads like a commentary on the *Moria* and certainly throws light upon its meaning:

God in a way cast himself down from his eminence towards our lowliness; he came down from his wisdom to our folly; and yet what seemed foolish in him surpasses the entire wisdom of the world; and what seemed weak in him was stronger than all human strength . . .

5. The wisdom of the world

The *Paraphrase of Luke* dates from 1523 and the *Paraphrase of I Corinthians* from 1519 (cf. *EE* III. no. 916, Introduction). Yet the association of ideas is the same as in the *Moria* of 1511. Erasmus goes straight on, in the *Paraphrase of Luke*, to condemn those who trust in their own wisdom and in their own strength and who 'oppose their necks to God'. Such men God scatters in the imagination of their hearts.

In the *Moria* this point is made paradoxically, by means of a parable which can puzzle readers not used to the techniques of such a mode of preaching. Folly expressed no surprise that God's foolishness should be greater than men, nor that he should prefer the fools of this world. Do not even worldy monarchs suspect and dislike the most sagacious (*cordati*) of their subjects? Julius suspected Brutus and Cassius, yet had no fear of the drunken Mark Anthony; Nero suspected Seneca; Dionysius, Plato. Yet they delighted in the stupider and simpler men. 'In the same way Christ always loathes and condemns those *sophoi* who trust in their own sagacity.' What is arresting is not that Brutus,

Cassius, Seneca and Plato should be condemned for their trust in human wisdom, but that Christ should apparently be compared to such a tyrant as Nero. This is in the spirit of the parable, where everything is ignored except its theological application, which normally comes at the end. It is a commonplace of exegesis that detail must not be pressed. (Maldonatus says much to good effect in his *Commentarii in Quattuor Evangelistas*, Venice, 1597: tome I, several references s.v. *parabola*; tome II, 219Dff.; etc.) In Luke 18:1–8, Christ himself explained the ways of God in terms of an *unjust* judge . . .

Erasmus has some pertinent things to say about parables in *Ecclesiastes, or How to Preach*, 1535: Scripture hides its meaning under a contemptible appearance, behind which appears the wisdom of God, which is visible to the eyes of the spirit. The Holy Ghost mixed absurdities in his revelations which, taken literally, do not hang together. This incites our minds to leave the literal meaning and forces it to look for what is hidden behind the words.

The same doctrine expounded here in the *Moria*, that those so-called philosophers who rely on proud human knowledge are fundamentally opposed to the folly of the Gospel, is frequently made by Erasmus in a less paradoxical form. He does so, for example, in his paraphrase of I Corinthians 1:12, ('Now each one of you saith, I am of Paul; and I of Apollos; and I of Cephas; and I of Christ'):

Thus from among those who follow the foolish wisdom of this world, one boasts of Pythagoras, another of Zeno, another of Epicurus, another of this author or that one; and they each fight for their own against the other (*LB* 7. 861B; cf. also the paraphrase on I Corinthians 3:4).

Origen had made much the same claims as Folly in *Contra Celsum*, rejecting Plato, the Stoics, the Peripatetics and the Epicureans in the name of Christian folly. But Origen takes care to underline that Plato, for example, is condemned for his wrong psychology. What the Scriptures reject is that form of wordly wisdom which is full of erroneous opinions (*PG* 11. 679–80).

In the *Moria* Folly goes on to make her point more cogently, with direct appeals to Scripture:

Testatur id Paulus haud quaquam obscure cum ait: *Quae stulta sunt mundi elegit deus*, cumque ait, *deo visum esse per stulticiam servaret mundum, quandoquidem per sapientiam restitui non poterat*. Quin ipse idem satis indicat clamans per os prophetae: *Perdam sapientiam sapientium, & prudentiam prudentium reprobabo*.

Paul testifies to this in no obscure fashion when he says, 'God chose the foolish things of the world' [I Corinthians 1:27]; and when he says, 'It seemed good to God that he should save the world through folly, when it could not be restored through wisdom' [I Corinthians 1:21]. Christ himself points this out clearly enough, proclaiming through the mouth of the prophet, 'I will destroy the wisdom of the wise; and the prudence of the prudent will I reject' [Isaiah 29:14, as cited I Corinthians 1:19]. (Scheurer, G6rº; Kan, 175).

It is possible that these texts also—all obvious ones to choose—were read by Erasmus in a context of Christian folly when he was studying his Greek fathers. In the course of several important developments of the theme of folly Origen calls upon many of these scriptural commonplaces of Folly's—cf., apart from his *Homilies on Jeremiah* (PG 13. 343ff.), the *Contra Celsum* (PG 11. 679ff.) and the *Commentary on Romans* (PG 14. 859ff.).

It would be unscholarly to assume that Erasmus somehow knew them all before the manuscripts were identified and published; but he certainly knew some of them and claimed to have read most of them.

Origen is the only commentator mentioned by name in these pages of the *Moria*. But he had no monopoly of the theology advanced by Folly. An attractive development of the theme Christian folly, opposed to the wisdom of this world, may be found for example in Chrysostom's fourth Homily (on I Corinthians [18–20]), which ends with the words just cited and translated above. Erasmus may have drawn on this Homily, but if so he goes beyond it. For Chrysostom folly is, above all, that simple Christian faith which overthrows the wisdom of the pagan philosophy: 'God cast out Plato not by means of another, more learned philosophy but through an ignorant fisherman.' The victory was all the more splendid because of this (PG 61. 33).

The use Folly makes of the verses of Scripture exploited at this point need not have posed much difficulty to a sixteenth-century mind. They are largely of the same kind as the ones which Johannes Viguerius cites later in his *Institutions of Natural and Christian Philosophy*. There, in a section specifically devoted to distinguishing between true and false wisdom (*sapientia*) and good and bad folly (*stultitia*), he assembles the same kind of texts as figure in the *Moria* of 1511. Evil folly, he says, is known in the Bible as fleshly, worldly, earthly, diabolical, 'of this world' (or 'age': *saeculum*). The texts he cites are Jeremiah 4:22, 'They are wise so as to do evil'; I Corinthians 3:19, 'The wisdom of this world is foolishness with God'; I Corinthians 1:19, 'I will destroy the wisdom of the wise: and the prudence of the prudent will I reject.' The two other texts he quotes are rather mangled. 'Thy wisdom (*sapientia*) deceiveth thee', which he attributes to Isaiah 47, is presumably a reference to Jeremiah 49:16, 'Thy pride (*arrogantia*) deceiveth thee'; similarly, what he cites as 'the wisdom (*sapientia*) of the flesh is death' is clearly Romans 8:6, where it is not the 'wisdom of the flesh' but its *prudentia* which is death. This is a reminder that Folly's rather cavalier attitude towards some of her scriptural authorities—in 1511 only—is by no means an isolated phenomenon.

As for the wisdom that the Scriptures oppose to good Christian folly, 'which is contempt for earthly things', Viguerius maintains that 'Christ, who despised earthly and wordly things, was called a fool (*dicitur fuisse stultus*): Solomon, speaking in his name (*in ejus persona*) declared 'I am the most foolish of men' (Proverbs 30:2). He further illustrates the meaning with two more verses of Scripture only: I Corinthians 1:25, 'The foolishness of God is wiser than all men' (Viguerius himself adds the word *all*), and I Corinthians 3:18, 'If any man thinketh he is wise among you in this world, let him become a fool that he may be wise' (J. Viguerius *Institutiones ad Naturalem et Christianam Philosophiam*, 1565, p. 130r°).

Viguerius' examples are obvious enough. But the authorities he marshalls do contain one text the import of which in Erasmus might easily be overlooked. Erasmus also cited Proverbs 30:2: 'I am the most foolish of men.' He gives it as Solomon talking in his own name. That it could also be taken as one of those many examples of an Old Testament character speaking words, the meaning of which only becomes apparent when they are seen as anticipating Christ, is not without importance. Erasmus rarely loses the opportunity of reminding his readers that Christ seemed foolish, indeed mad, to those who judged him with the wisdom of this world. He may or may not have that in mind in quoting Proverbs 30:2: he certainly has it in mind in the pages which are to follow, and he certainly accepted, as an exegete, the Christian assumption that Christ often spoke through the mouths of the Old Testament authors. Folly has just quoted from Isaiah 29:14, a text cited by St Paul in I Corinthians 1:19. Erasmus does not make her attribute the words 'I will destroy the wisdom of the wise' to Isaiah or to Paul. For Folly these words were those of Christ in person, who proclaimed them through the mouth of the prophet. No Old Testament text can be lightly assumed not to have a possible reference to the *ipsissima verba* of Christ. All that the Jews of old wrote was inspired directly by the Holy Ghost. That is why Erasmus, who sometimes treats the unspiritual meaning of Old Testament writers as being no more credible than myths out of Homer, reads the full philosophy of Christ into the very same texts. The Old Testament is like the Sileni of Alcibiades (*Adages* 3.3.1). These Sileni were ugly boxes containing god-like images. Alcibiades compared the physically ugly Socrates to just such a Silenus. So too, the Old Testament: to Erasmus it often seemed ugly and even laughable. But not when one opened the Silenus and found the divinity which was treasured inside. And of all the Sileni, Christ was by far the greatest.

The texts which Erasmus attributes to Folly in this part of the *Moria* naturally appear in other of his works. As one might expect, he paraphrases I Corinthians 3:18–19 in ways designed to strengthen the case for Christian folly (*LB* 7. 868F.f.). We might note, in the light of Folly's condemnation of the proud pagan philosophers a few lines earlier, that in his paraphrase he specifically includes among those who are wise with worldly wisdom not only those who excel in the Mosaic law but also those who excel in philosophy. Such worldly wisdom contributes nothing to salvation, merely making men puffed up, harsh and unteachable. Some of the terms he uses in his Paraphrase on I Corinthians 3:18–9 textually recall what he wrote in the *Paraphrase of St Luke's Gospel* to explain *Magnificat* (*LB* 7. 293B–D), where Christian folly is accorded a place of great importance. Such repetitions of words, phrases and ideas are a feature of Erasmus' writings; they remind us that he often preached the same message, in season and out of season—in the *Moria* as much as in his technical theological works and in his works of *haute vulgarisation*.

6. Children . . . or fools?

So far Folly's use of Scriptural commonplaces has been whimsical but not particularly erudite—the vital debts to Origen apart. The next sentence changes matters:

Rursum cum patri agit gratias, quod salutis mysterium *celasset sapientes, parvulis* autem, hoc est stultis, *aperuisset* (Scheurer G6r°; Kan 176).

Again, when he [Christ] gives thanks to the Father that he should have 'hidden the mystery of salvation from the wise' and have 'revealed it to little children'—to fools that is.

For those who only knew their Vulgate this allusion to Matthew 11:25 and Luke 10:21 must have seemed perverse or even irreverent. At first sight it is by no means obvious what Folly is offering other than a piece of special pleading. Where is folly seriously to be found in the words of Christ, 'I thank thee, O Father, Lord of heaven and earth, that thou didst hide these things from the wise and understanding and didst reveal them unto babes'? In fact Folly's glossing of *parvuli* ('little children', 'babes') to mean 'fools' (*stulti*) shows that Erasmus, even when citing the Vulgate, took the Greek as normative. Folly's gloss only makes sense in the light of the original text. What he says later shows this.

Erasmus was moved to defend what he wrote here. He does so more than once. First we may note that he interpolated a sentence of explanation into the 1514 *Moria*:'Nam graece pro *parvulis* est *nēpiois*, quos opposuit *sophois*' ('In the Greek, for *parvuli*, 'little children', there is *nēpioi*, whom Christ contrasts with the *sophoi*'). For those with little or no Greek that was not very helpful! It might even have been taken as wilful blinding with science. But a glance at the first edition of his *Novum Instrumentum* soon dispels such an idea. For there Erasmus actually translates *nēpioi* by *stulti* in the text itself. In one of the holiest parts of the Scriptures, Christ, in Erasmus' great translation, spoke not of 'babes' or 'little children' but of 'fools': 'I thank thee Father . . . that thou didst hide these things from the wise . . . and didst reveal them unto *stulti*.' The *Annotations on the New Testament* twice explain why, elaborating on the bald statements of the *Moria* of 1511 and 1514. In both cases one can see that Erasmus is directly defending what he wrote in the *Moria*.

This is how he comments on Matthew 11:25 in his *Annotations*:

Parvulis. The word is *nēpiois*, which has the sense of both fool and infant, that is, one who, by fault of his age has as yet no understanding. [Erasmus is exploiting the fact that the basic meaning of *nēpios*, like *infans*, is dumb, speechless.] He does not say *mōrois*, as Chysostom also comments. [*Mōros*, dull, stupid, foolish, is of course the strong punning word for fool, dolt, which gives the Greek title to the *Morias Encomion*.] But here, 'to fools', *stultis*, suits better, so as to be set against, 'to the wise,' *sapientibus*.

There is no reason why anyone should object to the noun *stultus*, fool, since Paul openly says that 'God chose the foolish things—the *Mōra*—of this world'. Here he calls *sapientes* not those who are truly wise, but those who seem wise to the world. So, too, he calls *stulti* not those who are truly foolish, but those who are foolish to the world. Nevertheless, we have preferred the interpretation of some critics over and above our own judgment (*LB* 6. 62 E).

The last sentence alludes to the fact that, in the second edition of his own Latin *New Testament*, Erasmus restored the word *parvulis*, not daring, apparently, to retain the translation *stultis* by which he shocked some of his readers in 1516.

The following note to Matthew 11 stresses the point that *nēpioi*, being contrasted to both *sapientes* and *prudentes*, means 'simple babes unable to talk (*simplices infantes*) who, because of their age, are neither strong in learning nor know how to use things'. (*LB* 6. 62F. no. 38.)

Not content with this defence of what he wrote in the *Moria* of 1511, and which he strove to explain with the additional sentence of 1514 and defend with his *Novum Instrumentum*, Erasmus again returns to the subject in his annotation on Luke 10:21 (where the relevant words of St Matthew's Gospel are repeated verbatim):

Parvulis: *nēpiois*, which here should preferably be rendered by *stultis* ('to fools') or *insipientibus* ('to the foolish', 'to the unwise'), in order to make the contrast with *sophois* ('to the wise') which comes before—unless, that is, this expression should seem a little too harsh (*duriusculus*). However I have treated this elsewhere (*LB* 6. 274E).

Is Erasmus on the defensive? Few passages show how closely interconnected were the *Moria* and the wider world of his scholarship than this apparently innocent claim of Folly that wisdom had been hidden from the wise God revealing only 'to babes, that is, to fools'. The furore caused by the appearance of *stultis* in the *New Testament* can be easily imagined. Stunica (*López Stuñica*) attacked Erasmus with vigour. He received a reply in kind in the *Apology against Stunica* (1521). Erasmus defends his rendering by citing Jerome's advice to translate the sense, not the words as such. Stunica had suggested (quite correctly, I think) that Erasmus had chosen to render *babes* by *fools* in his Latin *New Testament* in order to bolster up the theme of the *Moria*, a work which, incidentally, he speaks highly of. Erasmus snarls back that he hopes he has treated folly more dexterously than Stunica treats Evangelical wisdom. He denies, with both classical and biblical examples, Stunica's contention that *nēpios* means 'fool' only in a good sense, while *mōros* allegedly means 'fool' only in a bad one: as for *mōros*, Paul used it in a good sense (I Corinthians 1:27), 'God chose the *foolish things* of the world') and (I Corinthians 1:25), 'Because the *foolishness* of God . . .' Indeed, 'only a little earlier Paul had contrasted the *foolishness of preaching* with the *wisdom* of scribes and philosophers'. So Paul did not shy away from the word *mōra*. 'Just as there is a double meaning to *wisdom* in the Scriptures, so too there is to *folly*. Both those who are praised and those who are condemned are called sometimes *nēpioi*, sometimes *mōroi*.' Christ condemns the wordly wise. 'Similarly he calls his disciples fools, *stulti*, not because they are really foolish but because they were considered foolish against the wisdom of this world.' To translate *nēpiois* by *parvulis* or *infantibus* here is to weaken the contrast. Moreover the disciples were not really babes, only babes in wickedness. 'In my judgment *stulti* is a better translation than *parvuli*. And yet, in the second edition [of the *Novum Instrumentum*] I restored *parvuli*, as though divining that there was to arise a Stunica, calumniating me over this word' (*LB* 10. 298–9).

Later works of Erasmus prove that he had changed a word, not his mind. He yielded to pressure. But he did not really give way. That is shown in his *Paraphrases* and in other annotations. The words of Christ to the Father are rendered thus in the *Paraphrase of St Matthew's Gospel* (11:25; *LB* 7.68EF):

I give thanks to thee, Father, who art the Lord of heaven and earth, by whose wisdom all things are governed, that this heavenly philosophy thou hast hidden from those who are puffed up and exalted with worldly wisdom and prudence, and hast opened it to the weak, the humble and to those who, in the opinion of the world, are fools—*stulti*.

Similarly for I Corinthians 3:1–2; where the Vulgate reads *tanquam parvulis in Christo* ('like little ones in Christ') Erasmus renders this in his *Novum Instrumentum* by 'like babes in Christ', *ut infantibus in Christo*. He points out—again—that the Greek word used here, *nēpios*, means *infans*, a child—weak, foolish (*stultus*) and lacking in prudence, especially because of his age.

The same point is made in the *Paraphrase of St Luke's Gospel* (10:21) (*LB* 7. 376BC), though there he prefers the words *idiotae* ('common uneducated men') and *insipientes* ('the foolish'). To many readers, both today and in the sixteenth century, the more modern meaning of *idiot* inevitably hovers about the classical one, even when they know it to be irrelevant. It is the word Erasmus applies, a few lines later in the *Moria*, to the original apostles. He had good authority for doing so.

7. Harmless animals. Socrates. The Holy Ghost as Dove

The next sentence or two of the *Moria* can be taken more in one's stride. The meaning is fairly straightforward; the paradoxes and whimsicalities of the last few sentences are laid aside. But there are fine points made which could easily escape attention.

Huc pertinet quod passim in evangelio Pharizeos & scribas, ac legum doctores incessit, vulgus indoctum sedulo tuetur: quodque parvulis, mulieribus ac piscatoribus potissimum delectatus esse videatur. Quin & ex animantium brutorum genere, ea potissimum placent Christo, quę à vulpina prudentia quam longissime absunt, eoque asino maluit insidere, cum ille (si libuisset) vel leonis tergum impune potuisset premere. Ac spiritus ille sacer *in columbae specie* delapsus est. Pręterea cervorum, hinulorum, agnorum, crebra passim in divinis literis mentio. Adde quod suos ad immortalem vitam destinatos, *oves* appellat, quo quidem animante non est aliud insipientius, vel Aristotelico proverbio teste *probateion ēthos*, quod quidem admonet ab ejus pecudis stoliditate, sumptum in *stupidos & bardos* convicii loco dici solere (Scheurer G6r°–v°; Kan 176–7).

Relevant to this is the fact that frequently in the Gospels Christ upbraids the Pharisees, the Scribes and the doctors of the law, but carefully watches over the unlearned multitude—and also that he seems most to have delighted in little children, women and fishermen. Indeed, amongst the species of brute beasts, those most please Christ who are as far removed as possible from fox-like prudence; and so he preferred to sit on the back of a donkey, whereas (if he had pleased to do so) he could, with impunity, have bestridden the back of a lion. And the Holy Ghost descended in the form of a dove. Moreover, in the sacred writings roes, young harts and lambs are frequently mentioned. Add to which the fact that he calls his own, who are destined to eternal life, *sheep*; no animal is so silly—witness the Aristotelian proverb, *Sheepish ways*, which he warns us used to be employed as an insult against the dull-witted and the stupid, because of that animal's obtuseness.

The word *hinulus*, which gives translators some difficulty, I have rendered as *young harts*. It is an allusion to the six occasions where it is used in the Vulgate (Proverbs 5:19; Song of Songs 2:9; 2:17; 4:5; 7:3; 8:14). The traditional English translation is 'young harts'. More recent translators seem to prefer 'gazelles'.

The proverb 'Sheepish ways' is explained in the *Adages* (3.1. 95). (*Ovium mores*). What is interesting in the explanation is not the list of classical examples of similar usages but Erasmus' last sentence, where he calls upon Origen, in a context of folly—something he never does in his *Annotations*:

Referring to this, Origen, expounding Leviticus, interprets the sacrifice of a sheep as the correction of foolish and irrational desires (*affectuum stultorum & irrationabilium correctionem*).

I doubt if Erasmus is using it with that sense in the *Moria*; but his deliberate association of it with Origen in the *Adagia* is not without importance. (In the part of the *Second Homily on Leviticus* which Erasmus is alluding to, Origen is expounding a theme dear to him and to Erasmus: St Paul's distinction between 'animal' and 'spiritual' man: *PG* 12. 413Bff.)

More easy to overlook is the force of his adjectives *stupidi* and *bardi* applied by implication to Christians who are judged foolish by the worldly wise. The humour here is very fine and quite untranslatable.

Erasmus has just lambasted those pagan philosophers whose wisdom led to pride, not to the ways of God. But it would be a gross error to believe that he—in a book written in elegant Latin and full of whimsically learned allusions—was actually opposed to humanist erudition, or that he condemned those of the ancient philosophers whose wisdom led towards Christ not away from him. High on the

list of such good men was Socrates. The adjectives *stupidi* and *bardi* are
in fact an important allusion to him. *Bardus* (stupid, dull), is a very rare
word indeed. Its best-known, and perhaps only generally known, use
is that made by Cicero, who tells us that Zopyrus the physionomist
dared to condemn Socrates on account of his odd appearance, applying to him the same two adjectives that Folly uses here: 'Zopyrus said
that Socrates was *stupidus* and *bardus*' (*De Fato* 5.10).

A humanist reader can be expected to have recognised and savoured
the Ciceronian allusion as readily as an educated Englishman would
recognise and savour an allusion to a similarly arresting phrase in
Shakespeare. In other words, Christians, when called such names by
the wordly wise, can take comfort in the fact that the good and pious
Socrates had also had exactly the same terms applied to him. Readers
of Erasmus' great essay on the adage 'The Sileni of Alcibiades' (3.3.1)
will not be surprised to find Socrates hinted at in the *Moria* as a human
prototype of aspects of the divine Christ: Socrates' folly was not
without analogies with that of Jesus. Both were Sileni: figures hiding
divine wisdom within unpromising exteriors. So, too, readers of
Cicero's *De Fato* would not be surprised to find Socrates selected for
praise in a book which sharply attacks the arrogant doctrines of the
Stoics. Erasmus' predilection for the Platonic philosophy on account
of its consonance with Christianity is already clearly stated in the
Enchiridion (*LB* 5. 7f.). In this he is following Augustine (*De Doctrina
Christiana* 2. 40, 60)—indeed there we are told to take over 'what is
true and conformable to our faith': the Platonists hold such truths 'as
unjust possessors, almost'. In the *Ratio Verae Theologiae* we are
reminded that 'you will find in the life of Socrates things which closely
conform to the life of Christ'. But Christ alone harmonises the discordant philosophies of men (*LB* 5. 92 B).

Certainly Socrates' life conforms to Christ's in that both were called
fools by misguided men.

Another reminder that Erasmus was writing as a scholar even when
drawing on such uncomplicated Biblical texts as those invoked here, is
proved by the allusion to Matthew 3:16, where we learn that the 'Spirit
of God', at Christ's baptism, was seen 'descending as a dove'. Folly
uses the term, *in columbae specie* (under the form of a dove), whereas the
Vulgate reads *sicut columbam* (as, or like, a dove). Here was a case in
which Erasmus simply could not accept the careless rendering of the
Vulgate. In his *Annotation* on this verse (*LB* 5. 22C) he rejects the
Vulgate translation, carefully avoiding attributing it to Jerome by
name: 'The interpreter renders this rather obscurely. He seems to say
that the Holy Ghost came down as a dove does (*more columbae*),

whereas what it means is that he came down in the form of a dove (*specie columbae*). The paraphrase of this verse of Matthew's Gospel also keeps the word *species*—*visibili specie columbae*, 'in the visible form of a dove' (*LB* 7. 17E). Now *specie columbae* is the translation to be found in Rufinus' version of Origen, *On the Song of Songs* (*PG* 13. 184C). Wherever one turns the way leads back to Origen.

In 1514 Erasmus saw wider propaganda possibilities in the choice of a dove to represent the Holy Ghost in a form visible to men's eyes. It could be briefly considered here, since it underlines how Erasmus continued to associate the *Moria* with ideas defended in his technical theological works as well as his evangelical propaganda generally. In 1514 Erasmus expanded the phrase in which the Holy Ghost came down *in columbae specie*. From then on the text reads: 'in the form of a dove, not of an eagle or a bird of prey' (*non aquilae aut milvii*). This forms part of Erasmus' anti-war propaganda which first reached its widest audience precisely in the *Moria* of 1514. In the *Adages* of 1515 Erasmus added the proverb 'The beetle searches for the eagle' (*Scarabeus aquilam quaerit*, 3. 7.1). A simple reading of that passionate plea against the actions of men of power who act like rapacious, war-like eagles suffices to explain the interpolation of the contrast with the eagle in the *Moria*. As for the *milvius*—that bird of prey, the kite, which will triumph with rattlesnakes, jackals and wolves in the terrible day of God's vengeance described by Isaiah (34:1–15), it remains for Erasmus a powerful contrast to the self-revelation of the Holy Ghost in the form of a dove. When explaining David's cry in Psalm 55/54:6, 'O that I had wings like a dove', Erasmus stresses that he did not yearn for the wings of an eagle, a vulture or a *milvius* . . . (*LB* 5. 421D). But in 1511 he was content to remind his readers that the Holy Ghost chose to appear in the form of the most peaceful and guileless of birds.

8. *Christ as fool: a sacrificial Lamb*

The next sentences in the *Moria* bring us on to the central theme of Christ as a fool. As such they form an important preparation for the ecstatic climax:

Atqui hujus gregis Christus sese *pastorem* profitetur, quinetiam ipse agni nomine delectatus est, indicante eum Johanne: *Ecce agnus dei*: cujus rei multa fit & in Apocalypsi mentio. Hec quid aliud clamitant, nisi mortalis omnis [1514, more clearly, *mortaleis omneis*] stultos esse, etiam pios? Ipsum quoque Christum, quo nostrae stulticiae subveniret, cum esset sapientia patris, tamen quodam modo stultum esse factum, cum hominis assumpta natura, *habitu inventus est ut homo*, quemadmodum & *peccatum factus est*, ut peccatis mederetur. (Scheurer, G6v°; Kan 177.)

Yet Christ declares himself to be the shepherd of this flock; he delighted indeed in the name of lamb, when John pointed him out, saying, 'Behold the Lamb of God' [John 1:29 and 36], of which matter much mention is made in Revelations [chs 5, 6, etc.]. What else do these things proclaim, but that all men are fools, even the devout; and that Christ himself, so as to help our foolishness—even though he was the Wisdom of the Father [I Corinthians 1: 24, 30; Colossians 2:3; Luke 11:49]—yet became in some way a fool when, taking to himself the nature of man, he was 'found in fashion as a man' [Philippians 2:8]; just as he was 'made sin' to remedy sins [II Corinthians 5:21].

Here we have the full statement of the kenotic interpretation of Christ's redemptive action, expressed in the terms which Origen first expounded. God 'emptied himself' on becoming a man (Philippians 2:7): although sinless he became very sin itself (II Corinthians 5:21); though being no less than the Wisdom of God, he became 'in some way a fool'.

The salutation of Christ as the Lamb of God by John the Baptist is given a commentary in the *Annotations* (LB 6. 344E–345C). Erasmus explains that John recognised him not merely as a lamb, but as the Lamb destined for slaughter—the Lamb of whom Isaiah prophesied (53:7) when he said, 'as a sheep before the shearers is dumb'. The following note shows that Erasmus, when annotating this part of St John's Gospel, was studying Origen and Augustine as well as Aquinas, but as usual he makes no mention of any specific folly texts of Origen here.

Folly links this salutation of Christ as the Lamb with Paul's statement to the Philippians (2:8) that Christ 'was found in fashion as a man' (*habitu inventus ut homo*). The connexion between these two verses of Scripture was a lasting one for Erasmus: he makes it again in his *Paraphrase of John* 1:29ff. John the Baptist was enabled to recognise Jesus, with unshakable certainty, as the Lamb of God, but only because of the descent of the Holy Ghost in the form of a dove; for Christ presented himself as an ordinary man among a crowd of men; he came to be baptised, as though he were 'guilty of sin' (*peccatis obnoxius*); John was not led to recognise Jesus as Messiah by his *habitus corporis* (the fashion of his body)—his human form—nor by human conjecture: only the sign from God provided the proof (LB 7. 508F–510A).

The importance of this stressing of the ordinary human form of Christ, is that it derives from the kenotic text of Philippians 2:7: it was by being 'found in likeness of a man' that Christ despised his being 'in the form of God', took 'the form of a slave' and 'emptied himself' on behalf of men (Philippians 2:6–7).

The final emptying of Christ was the act of becoming 'in some way a fool' in order to save men, this despite his being in reality the Wisdom of the Father. The expression 'Wisdom of the Father' as applied to Christ is not strictly Scriptural: it is a sort of gloss, a theologically more precise way of rendering I Corinthians 1:24, where Christ, in the context of divine folly, is presented as 'the power of God and the wisdom of God' (*Dei virtutem et Dei sapientiam*). That Erasmus is alluding, yet again, to this great folly chapter, I Corinthians 1, is certain; his *Annotations* make that clear. Glossing I Corinthians 1:23 he asks rhetorically, 'What do you seek, O Jew? A sign; here is the power of God. And what do you seek, O Gentile? Wisdom; here is the Wisdom of the Father everlasting' (*LB* 6. 665–C). The same texts are associated in the moving paraphrase of I Corinthians 1:18–25. '. . . we preach what at first sight seems foolish and lowly . . .' Yet those who are brought to faith by grace realise that the 'lowly crucified Christ is the power of God, the Wisdom of God, so that those Jews desire signs no more who have found a greater one in Christ, and those Greeks no longer seek wisdom, having once and for all found Christ, the fount of all wisdom. God in some way cast himself down from his height to our lowliness; he descended from his wisdom to our folly . . .' Among the saintly Christians who guided Erasmus towards such a doctrine was St Bernard of Clairvaux (see below, p. 44).

The combination of the twin ideas of Christian folly and Christ as the revealed, lowly Wisdom of the Father remained for Erasmus a source of spiritual strength, enabling him to preach unwelcome truths even to kings. In December 1523 he sent his *Paraphrase of St Mark* to Francis I of France by Hilaire Bertolph, a friend later to become also a friend of Rabelais. In his dedicatory letter Erasmus condemns kings who 'pillage, cast down, cast out, burn, oppress and kill the poor and the lowly'. Such kings 'accuse Christ, who is the Wisdom of the Father, of folly—he who poured out his precious blood to save such as they' (*EE* 5, p. 354).

The idea of Christ becoming a fool to save man is in accord with Origen's teaching. Like Erasmus Origen reads such a meaning into Philippians 2:7.

Erasmus taught this doctrine when he translated I Coronthians 2:3 with the words *stultitia Dei* (the foolishness of God), and *infirmitas Dei* (the weakness of God). The traditional renderings *quod stultum est Dei* and *quod infirmum est Dei* do not really change the sense much, but his version sharply juxtaposes the name of God to both weakness and folly. Erasmus explained this kenotic theology in terms of folly in his annotation on I Corinthians 2:3. He hints at it in his paraphrase of I Corinthians 1:18–20; he is quite explicit in the paraphrase of I Corinthians 1:25 (cited above, p. 25). Yet, although in the *Moria* he alludes to Origen by name in this context, he never does so again, even in his numerous and detailed replies to his critics. It was, I think, one of the cases where to have attempted to shelter behind Origen's authority may have made matters worse. We have to await his last, lengthy exposition of the doctrine of Christian folly towards the end of his life to find the name of Origen coupled, critically, with the foolishness of Christ and his followers (see Appendix A). In his replies to his critics Erasmus, in matters of folly, is more likely to cite Augustine than Origen—for obvious reasons. In his note on I Corinthians 25, he can show that Augustine had used the words 'the foolishness of God' in his 102nd letter (*LB* 6. 665E). But his sheet-anchor is St Paul himself. When Sutor, a quarrelsome theologian of the Sorbonne, accused him of blasphemy by attributing foolishness to God, Erasmus replied: 'There is indeed one blasphemy [in the *Moria*], but it is common to me, the apostle Paul and the holy fathers, who attribute foolishness to God with the same figure of speech (*trope*) as I used myself' (*LB* 9. 805DE, *Against the Drunken Ravings of Peter Sutor*, 1525). Whether it is really right to speak of a trope to explain the kenotic doctine of folly is not at all certain. But one can sympathise with Erasmus' impatience. The Scriptures go so far as to say that Christ was 'made to be sin on our behalf' (II Corinthians 5:21). This is at least as arresting as talking of the foolishness of God, but centuries of familiarity had dulled the impact of the one, while the other was new with the newness most valued in the Renaissance—an old doctrine rediscovered and given new life.

9. *Ignorant disciples and the folly of the Cross*

The pages preparing for the final climax of Folly's encomium draw rapidly to a close, all Lucianesque irony now being laid aside. A gentle humour remains to sweeten the bitter lesson of man's nullity. But Christ who became sin to save men from sin is not a matter about which Erasmus feels moved to jest. The cure of sins was preached we are told, by the 'folly of the Cross', spread by uncouth and ignorant disciples:

Neque alia ratione mederi voluit quam per stulticiam crucis, per Apostolos idiotas ac pingues . . . (Scheurer G6v°; Kan 177).

Nor did Christ wish to cure [sinners] by any other system (*ratio*) than through the folly of the Cross, through ignorant and rough Apostles . . .

The use of the word *idiotae* to describe the apostles is arresting but entirely Biblical. Peter and John are called *idiōtai* (ignorant) in Acts 4:13: 'Now when they beheld the boldness of Peter and John, and had perceived that they were unlearned (*agrammatoi*) and ignorant men (*idiōtai*), they marvelled.'

In Erasmus' own *Novum Instrumentum* the word *idiotae* is retained in its Latin guise, as it is in the Vulgate. The word *idiota* is one which arrogant men will also dare to apply to Christ. Paraphrasing the order to love the Lord God with all our hearts, Erasmus stresses the spiritual nature of Christ's commands. Those who sport their magnificent titles consider Christ an *idiota*, an ignorant common man. They did not understand that 'evangelical wisdom does not consist in an abundance of reading—in *multitudine litterarum*—but in the purity of the spirit (*in sinceritate spiritus*) (*LB* 7. 252C–E).

Pinguis (fat, and hence dull, doltish, stupid) is not applied to the Apostles in the Bible. (Indeed, it is not found in the New Testament at all, outside Revelations 18:14, where it has a different sense: *pinguia*, 'things that are dainty'.) It is not an obvious word to apply to the Apostles. I suspect that Erasmus chose *pinguis* because of associations with the adage '*Pingui Minerva*' (1.1.37), which is used adverbially to mean unskillfully, rudely, artlessly, roughly. Erasmus explains that it is applied to what is rather uncouth (*inconditius*), rather simple (*simplicius*) and, as it were, unlearned (*quasi indoctius*). As such it could be a vivid way of rendering the term *agrammatoi*, 'unlettered', which is applied to John and Peter by the crowd in Acts. Outside the *Moria* Erasmus clearly prefers to use the Scriptural word *idiotae* when talking of the rough simplicity of the apostles (cf. for example, *LB* 5. 279F; 7. 61CE; 10. 1695D).

The term 'folly of the Cross' (*stultitia crucis*) is even more arresting. If it were not for the fact that Erasmus left it unchanged in later editions, one might almost suspect it of being a slip of the pen. Erasmus is loosely alluding to I Corinthians 1:18, but there we do not find the expression the 'folly of the Cross'. It is the 'word of the Cross' (*verbum crucis*) which is 'to them that are perishing *stultitia* (foolishness)'. Nevertheless, Erasmus still attributes the term 'folly of the Cross' to St Paul in the letter to Martin Dorpius (May 1515; *EE* II, no. 337, line 497).

Erasmus' expression could very well suggest that Christ's death on the Cross was an act of divine foolishness, in the Origenistic sense. I suspect that that is what it does mean. If so, it is a sense from which he later drew back. Indeed, it is a sense he rejects in his *Annotations*, as far as I Corinthians 18 is concerned.

On I Corinthians 1:17 he insisted that *en sophia logou* should not be translated, as in the Vulgate, by *in sapientia verbi* ('in the wisdom of the word') but by *in sermone erudito* ('in learned speech'). Similarly for verse 18, which balances it. The Latin expression *Verbum crucis* could be taken as an allusion to Christ, the Son of God, the *Word* crucified on the Cross. This is not the sense of the Greek, which is still talking of reason or speech (*ho logos gar ho tou staurou*). What is being contrasted is the learned speech of the worldly-wise and the simplicity of the preaching of the theme of the Cross. In preaching the doctrine of the Cross what is required is simple (*simplex*), not complicated (*compositus*) nor artificial (*fucatus*). Such style belongs to philosophers and rhetoricians (*LB* 6. 664CD).

This is the sense that Erasmus chose to bring out in his *Paraphrases* (*LB* 7. 862AB): 'The Cross of Christ seems a lowly and mean thing (*humilis et abjecta res*), yet it conquered all the greatness of the world . . . The rough and simple speech by which we preach Christ crucified seems a somewhat foolish and unlearned thing (*stulta quaepiam & indocta res*). But to whom?' And the rest of the context stresses the folly of the Gospel in terms of the wrong judgments of the wordly-wise. Again in the *Antibarbari* (1520) Erasmus returned to the same themes. He believed there was a need to defend even the kind of learning which the apostles did not have, against the lazy ignorance of unworthy monks. In the *Antibarbari*, to reject all learning in the name of Christian simplicity is to act like a Frenchman who was silly enough to prefer to go naked than wear good English cloth, or an Englishman who preferred to remain thirsty, rather than drink good French wine (*LB* 10. 1695D). Scholarship has a rightful place as a subordinate ally of modern Christian fools. Erasmus' position is really quite clear and consistent: pagan writers have much to teach Christians, when read as pagans (Cf. *EE* 8, p. 31, lines 232f.; to Peter Tomiczki). But following a current of thought which ran strongly right through the Renaissance, he did not think of certain pre-Christian Gentile philosophers as pagans at all but as forerunners of Christianity. Plato, perhaps, or Socrates certainly, can be thought of as being close to Isaiah or David: as inspired writers preparing the world, with their veiled wisdom, for the ultimate revelation in Christ. This belief, which can be justified from the writings of such early Christian writers as Justin Martyr and Clement of Alexandria, appealed to many Renaissance humanists. It was not an airy-fairy mystic but a hard-headed, brilliant and honoured legal scholar, Guillaume Budé, who stated as a matter of undoubtable fact that when Plato wrote of the *logos* he manifestly referred to Christ (*Opera*, 1557, 243, 14). Erasmus could never think of Socrates or certain other pre-Christian philosophers, who were both wise and good and who adopted a morality where humility reigned supreme, as other than *Sileni*, in some way resembling the greatest *Silenus* of all, the Godhead veiled in flesh in Christ.

10. *Examples of wise lack of care: boys, flowers, sparrows*

To return to the *Moria*, the simplicity which the rough and simple apostles preached was the special kind of foolishness which Christ carefully inculcated. The 'folly of the Cross' was preached through ignorant and rough apostles:

quibus sędulo stulticiam praecipit, a sapientia deterrens, cum eos ad *puerorum, liliorum, sinapis & passerculorum* exemplum provocat, rerum stupidarum ac sensu carentium, soloque naturę ductu, nulla arte, *nulla sollicitudine* vitam agentium.

to whom he earnestly commended foolishness, discouraging them from wisdom, when he appealed to the example of boys [Matthew 18:3 etc.], lilies [Matthew 6:28, etc.], mustard seed [Matthew 13:31, etc.,] and little sparrows [Matthew 10:29 etc.]—things which are silly and lacking in sense, living their lives as nature leads them, without art, without cares' [Matthew 6:28 etc.].

These examples of guileless innocence are not advanced without careful erudition. When Erasmus says that Christ used the example of 'boys', *pueri*, he was consciously departing from the Vulgate. In Matthew 18:3 Christ insists that, unless men become 'as boys' (or 'as little children') they will not enter the kingdom of heaven. The Greek is *hōs paidia*, 'like little boys', which in the *Annotations* (but not in the *Novum Instrumentum* itself) Erasmus translates as *sicut puelli*, using a rarish diminutive variant of *pueri*. He does this because the Vulgate's *parvuli*, ('little ones') does not adequately convey Christ's sense: it could apply, says Erasmus, to pygmies. Christ is using 'boys' in order to bring out 'that innocence and simplicity' which are typical of childhood (*LB* 6. 94DE). Erasmus' ideas on children seem to have been based largely on hearsay.

Similarly, when Erasmus proposes the example of the lilies of the field who live *nulla sollicitudine*, 'without cares', he is calling upon the context in which the lilies are mentioned by Christ (Matthew 6:28, Luke 12:27). In both cases, they are cited to deter his followers from being anxious—*quid solliciti estis*, 'Why are ye anxious? Consider the lilies of the field . . .'

The fuller sense of the injunction to live *nulla sollicitudine*, 'without cares', is probably to be found in the parable of the sower, for there it is precisely the seed that fell among thorns which was overwhelmed with the anxiety, the *sollicitudo*, of this world (Matthew 13:22). But the meaning is also vital to Matthew 6 as Erasmus understood it. The Vulgate reading of Matthew 6:27 did not satisfy him: there Christ asks, Who can add a single cubit to his stature by 'thinking' *(cogitans)*? The original word is *merimnōn*, which means not by 'thinking' but by 'being anxious'; Erasmus comments in the *Annotations* (*LB* 6. 38, no. 54), 'it is not just *cogitans* but *anxie et sollicite cogitans*' (not just 'thinking' but 'thinking anxiously and with care'). The word is the participle of the verb which is frequently rendered *sollicitum esse* (to be uneasy, troubled in mind, anxious). These comparisons which Christ made with boys, lilies and the mustard-seed are, for Erasmus, all designed to condemn human *sollicitudo*, 'anxiety' about the future.

The theme of *sollicitudo* is continued in the next sentence, for it is important to Folly's argument: the followers of Christ should not be prudent men and women, anxiously taking care for the morrow:

Praeterea cum vetat *esse sollicitos*, qua essent apud praesides oratione usuri, cumque interdicit ne *scrutentur tempora vel momenta temporum*, videlicet ne quid fiderent suae prudentiae, sed totis animis ex sese penderent (Scheurer G6v°; Kan 178).

Also when he forbade them to be anxious about what speech they would use before the governors [Matthew 10:18–19; Mark 13:9–11; Luke 12:11–12] and when he prohibited them from searching the times or the moments of time [Acts 1:7; cf. I Thessalonians 5:1], lest they should rely on their own foresight, but rather depend on him with all their hearts.

The *Annotations* on Matthew and Mark show how vital was the distinction which the Vulgate was blurring. Matthew 10:19 must not be rendered, as the Vulgate does, *nolite cogitare* ('do not think'): 'In Greek it is *me merimnēsete*, that is, "be not anxious *(anxii)* or *solliciti*" (full of disquiet or care). The Lord is not telling them to cast away thought, *(cogitationem)* but anxiety *(sollicitudinem)*' (*LB* 6. 201, no. 9). Erasmus similarly corrects the Vulgate reading of Mark 13:11: *Nolite praecogitare*, 'Take no thought beforehand'. It does not mean that. It means 'Be not anxious beforehand' *(ne ante sitis solliciti sive anxii)*.

Erasmus underlines Christ's injunction to his disciples to 'be not anxious' because anxiety would stop them from having such faith that they could 'depend on him with all their hearts'. This is no passing form of words for Erasmus. He takes up the theme, in the same context, when paraphrasing Matthew 10:17–19. The witnesses of Christ will be dragged before the rulers and justices: before so many, they will be so few; before so many powerful men, so weak and

unarmed; before so many learned men, so simple (*idiotae*). Yet what is
to be said before these potentates is not a matter for anxiety: 'To think
anxiously of such a matter does not belong to one who entirely
depends upon divine help' (*LB* 7. 61C–E). The *Paraphrases* make much
the same points when expounding the relevant parts of Mark (*LB* 7.
254C–D) and of Luke (389C–E). In both cases the stress is on the
avoidance of *sollicitudo*: Christians must not be anxious. They must
trust in God with all their hearts (*totis animis*).

The phrase *totus animus* is Biblical, best known, perhaps, from the
psalms (e.g. Vulgate 118, 2, 10, 34, etc.) and from the injunction 'to
love the Lord thy God with all thy heart and with all thy soul and with
all thy mind and with all thy strength' (Mark 12:30; Luke 10:27). That
may be relevant here. More certainly relevant is Erasmus' belief that it
is the few, the weak, the defenceless, the *idiōtai*, who, avoiding anxiety, entirely rely on divine help.

11. *St Bernard has the last word*

This part of the *Moria* ends suddenly and forcefully, but not quite
without whimsicality:

Eodem pertinet quod deus ille orbis architectus interminatur, ne quid *de arbore
scientiae* degustarent, perinde quasi scientia foelicitatis sit venenum. Quamquam Paulus aperte *scientiam* veluti *inflantem* & perniciosam improbat, quem
divus Bernardus opinor secutus, *montem* eum in quo *Lucifer sedem* statuerat,
scientiae montem interpretatur. (Scheurer G6vº; Kan 178–9.)

To the same end tends the fact that God, that Architect of the world, forbade
with menaces that any should eat of the tree of knowledge [Genesis 2:17, 19],
as if knowledge were the poison of happiness. Anyway Paul condemned
learning as something which 'puffeth up' [I Corinthians 8:1] and is destructive. St Bernard follows him, I think, when he interprets the mountain on
which Lucifer established his seat [Isaiah 14:12–13] as the mountain of
knowledge.

With the allusion to St Paul's condemnation of knowledge as something that puffeth up, Folly makes a light and fleeting return to banter.
In I Corinthians 8:1, St Paul only says what he says about 'knowledge'
after having claimed, in the very same verse, to 'have all knowledge'.
The point at issue is, in context, that knowledge is a source of conceit
and arrogance when divorced from Christian love. Of course Erasmus
knows this perfectly well and that is what, in context, Folly means too.
Erasmus makes just these points in his *Annotations* (*LB* 6. 783D),
referring the reader, as often, to Augustine's work *Against Faustus* (15.
8), where the matter is 'elegantly treated'. It was sudden shifts of tone

such as this which obviously put some of the readers of the *Moria* into a state of confusion: but it really ought not to have done so . . .

In some ways the greatest surprise of this last sentence before Erasmus embarks on the theme of ecstasy is the allusion to St Bernard. He appears twice in these closing pages of the *Moria*, being cited later indirectly as a pious man so rapt in contemplation that he heedlessly drank oil as though it were wine. Even when he particularly disagreed with his scholarship, Erasmus was not moved to dispraise such a good and holy man as Bernard was. Few mediaeval exegetes are mentioned in the *Annotations on the New Testament* other than to condemn them. St Bernard is one such exception. In the note on Luke 1:28 ('Hail, full of grace') Erasmus shows little sympathy for those who fail to realise that 'full of grace', *kecharitōmene*, means *gratiosa* ('made graceful or charming'). He refuses to be impressed by St Bernard's enthusiastic philosophising on the phrase, as though it applied uniquely to Mary. But he nevertheless specifically includes him among those theologians who are 'learned and pious men' (*LB* 6. 223D–F). If St Bernard has a fault, it is a tendency to make jokes on Scriptural texts! (*LB* 5. 129 A). Most important of all, perhaps, Bernard is one of the few authors Erasmus ever allows to present a favourable view of the monastic life, as lived by devout and ascetic contemplatives. Such men receive the ultimate reward of seeing God's face, their soul panting for heaven and refreshed with spiritual delights (*LB* 5. 492f.). How could the author of the *Moria* not find a place of honour for so saintly a man, who, more by nature than by art, was *festivus et jucundus* ('merry and full of jests') (*LB* 5. 857C)?

There are several good reasons why Erasmus should have selected St Bernard for high honour in the *Moria*. First, he was a good, charitable, pious, learned and occasionally jesting ecstatic. Has anyone who has read him ever doubted his sincerity? The *Dictionnaire de la spiritualité* (p. 2114), writing of course from its own point of view, insists that his experiences of ecstasy were 'incontestably authentic'. That he thought them to be so certainly shines through his life and works. And he was early enough to be quite unmarked by mediaeval scholasticism, earning the reputation of being 'the last of the fathers'.

There is much in St Bernard's language about ecstasy which is foreign to Erasmus: there is a monkish, convent-centred element in his conception of ecstatic charity which represents so much of what Erasmus loathed in the religious orders of his own day. It is partly Pseudo-Dionysian in conception, though not in style or terminology. It also affords a much larger place to the passionate language of Bridegroom and beloved than Erasmus does in the 1511 *Moria*. On the other hand, when Erasmus later felt the need to explain the soul's distraction in terms of Origen's *Commentary on the Song of Songs*, that very fact brought him closer to St Bernard (see below, p. 185; and cf. *PL* 184, *In Cantico sermo* no. 31, 162C). The ecstasy, the *mentis excessus*, which preoccupies Folly in the *Moria* is close to that which St Bernard had personally experienced (cf. *PL* 184: *Sermons on the Song of Songs*, especially Sermon no. 7; *De Peregrino* 183Cf., and 52; *De excessu qui contemplatio dicitur* 1029Df., etc.). By alluding to St Bernard at the very end of that part of Folly's oration which leads straight on to the praise of ecstasy, Erasmus was reminding his readers of the great tradition which Bernard represented.

Another reason for citing St Bernard is that he lends strong support to the praise of Christian foolishness. He is, in fact, a source—an important one too. In some ways, Folly's allusions to St Bernard are as meaningful as her reference to Origen: both help to establish the savour of the foolish ecstasy that Folly so wittily praises. That St Bernard and Origen should come together in the *Moria* is perhaps what one ought to have expected. Bernard knew some of Origen's works and drew upon him. He makes use of his *Homilies on the Song of Songs* (the earliest example of the interpretation of that book in terms of Christian ecstasy). These he knew in the translations of Jerome and Rufinus. He also made use of at least one homily of Origen on Leviticus. That he was acquainted, directly or indirectly, with the writings of Origen's disciple, Gregory of Nyssa, is accepted by scholars (E. Gilson, *La Théologie mystique de Saint Bernard*, Paris, 1947, 27f.).

According to Folly, St Bernard, under the influence of St Paul, interpreted Lucifer's mountain [in Isaiah 14:12–13] in much the same way as Christians traditionally interpret the tree of the knowledge of good and evil in Genesis 2. Isaiah 14 is a major passage of the Old Testament; it tells of the dreadful fate awaiting evil men when the Day of the Lord shall come to punish the world for its wickedness, and when the king of Babylon shall be derided and overthrown:

How art thou fallen from heaven, O Lucifer ! [. . .]
And thou saidst in thine heart, I will ascend into heaven ; I will exalt my throne above the stars of God; and I will sit upon the mount of congregation (*in monte testamenti*.)

It is this mount that St Bernard interprets as a symbol for that proud, worldly knowledge which puffeth man up. He does so in his fourth *Sermon on the Lord's Ascension* (*PL* 183. 310CDf.). The sermon is worth reading right through for students of the *Moria*. So much of Folly's theology is there. Christ, for St Bernard as for Erasmus, is 'the power and the wisdom of God' (309D) who 'emptied himself'; what he suffered, he suffered willingly and in full knowledge; human learning is but a spark against such brilliant light. But as St Paul affirms (Ephesians 4:10), 'it is the same Lord who descended as he who ascended'. Christians likewise must learn to 'descend' into selflessness: 'But woe unto us, if we shall have wished to follow him who says, "I will sit in the mount of congregation" ' (*PL* 183. 309–10). Such followers of Lucifer are lost in worldly desires. For the mount of Lucifer is like the tree in the garden of Eden (Genesis 3:5). Such things, such knowledge, are vanity (Psalm 4:3). St Bernard then develops the theme of Christian folly, drawing upon the same texts which Folly has just used and, moreover, interpreting Christ's folly in the spirit of kenotic theology:

Do you not know that God chose the weak things of the world to confound the strong, and that God chose the foolish things of the world to confound the wise [I Corinthians 1:27]? The fear of a threatening God does not call us back, a God who will 'destroy the wisdom of the wise and reject the prudence of the prudent'; neither does the example of the Father, nor, finally, our own sense of the experience of hard necessity, to which we are bound by the mad appetite for knowledge . . .

Yet we are clearly warned (I Corinthians 1:19), 'I will destroy the wisdom of the wise, and the prudence of the prudent will I reject'. We must learn to follow God's example, and come down from our heights:

The Most High came down from the mountain of power, having clothed himself in the weakness of the flesh; he came down from the mountain of knowledge, because it pleased God to save them that believe by the foolishness of preaching [I Corinthians 1:21]. What can seem weaker than his tender body and babyish limbs? What seems more unlearned than the little one who knew only his mother's paps? What weaker than him whose limbs were all pierced by nails and all of whose bones were counted? [Psalm 22:18, Vulgate.] See how far down he came, he who gave over his soul to death and who restored that which he took not away [Psalm 68:5, Vulgate]; how much he emptied himself of wisdom. (*PL* 183. 309–10.)

This last phrase is an echo of the principal kenotic text, Philippians 2:7, accommodated to the theme of Christian folly. For St Bernard as for Erasmus, when God emptied himself, taking the form of a servant, and being made in the likeness of man, he came from the loftiest heights, emptying himself of his divine wisdom.

It is fitting that the *Moria* should find words of praise for Bernard as well as for Origen. Folly is deeply indebted to both of them.

CHAPTER THREE

Christian Ecstasy

It is not an arbitrary act on our part to interpret the final pages of the *Praise of Folly* as a praise of ecstasy. The readers of the Froben *Morias* would have required strong reasons for *not* doing so. The notes of Listrius added successively to these editions have largely been ignored by later editors. That is a pity. They underline that the *Moria* is concerned with ecstasy. Moreover, Erasmus' letters to Dorpius and Martin Lypsius specifically explain the end of the book in terms of ecstasy. These points will become clear as this study progresses.

Ecstasy is a phenomenon to be found in many religions as well as in many philosophies of a mystical bent. Some idea of the richness and the variety of the ecstatic tradition in Christianity can be gleaned from the well-documented articles in the *Dictionnaire de la Spiritualité* or in the *Dictionnaire de Théologie Catholique*. Naturally many of the mediaeval authors mentioned there were unknown to Erasmus. Naturally, also, many authors he did know are interpreted in the light of scholarly insights dating from recent times. The articles *extase* in both these dictionaries are nevertheless a good starting-point for anyone who wishes to get a quick idea of a tradition of major importance to Christian thought. There is no need to cover that ground again here, but some definition of terms is necessary, if the end of the *Moria* is not to be misunderstood.

Ecstasy in one form or another is a feature of the Old Testament as well as the New. Early Christian writers almost to a man knew their Old Testament in the Greek Septuagint translation rather than in the original Hebrew. So, too, did many Jews of the diaspora. There they found the noun *ekstasis* and the cognate verb *existēmi* ('to be ecstatic') used many times. But when ideas are translated from one culture to another, the words used to render the foreign concepts risk encouraging associations of meaning quite unknown to the words in the original languages used to represent those concepts. That happened in the case of *ekstasis*. Ecstasy is a Greek word for a Greek set of ideas; its roots are in Greek philosophy and in Greek paganism. It was used to translate Hebrew experiences of quite a different type. Inevitably, those who read the Old Testament mainly or always in Greek, soon began to read into their Bibles meanings additional or alternative to the ones which *ekstasis* was meant to convey. These meanings sometimes have nothing at all to do with what the old Jews wrote about and experienced in their relationships with God.[1]

Christian writers went one stage further: they associated together those texts of the Old Testament where *ekstasis* and *existēmi* appear with those passages of the New Testament where the same words may be found. It further encouraged Greek-speaking Christians and some Greek speaking Jews to interpret the ecstatic phenomena mentioned in their Bibles by the light of systems of thought more at home in Athens or Alexandria than in Jerusalem. An accessible mine of information on such matters is Kittel's *Theologisches Wörterbuch*, 1954, which was done into English in 1964.

For centuries before Erasmus, ecstasy had come to mean the state of a Christian who had been raptured outside himself, his soul 'leaving his body' in the process. Exactly how, and to what extent, the soul left the body is not always clear. St Augustine made a sharp distinction between the soul's being actually caught away physically (as it were) into heaven—in which case the body was left as dead, in fact actually dead—and those ecstatic raptures in which the soul despite its 'leaving the body' in fact remained in some way in the body, in the sense that it remained alive (*De Genesi ad litteram*, cited below, p. 197). Both states are referred to as the soul being *extra corpus* ('outside the body') or as the ecstatic person being *extra se* ('outside himself'). It is on the whole wise to assume that an author is referring to an ecstasy in which the body is not left dead, or as though it were dead, unless he explicitly says the contrary.

The Old Testament phenomena rendered in Greek by *ekstasis* and its cognates by no means imply any departure of the soul from the body—real or apparent. It is especially a state of amazement or stupor caused by fright—even fright from natural causes. It more characteristically refers to the terror felt for God or for his judgments. On one occasion (Genesis 2:21) it is the deep sleep sent by God upon Adam, when woman was created out of his rib.

Christians did not abandon such conceptions of ecstasy; they added some Greek ones to them. And these Greek conceptions eventually almost took over—so much so that Daniélou could assert that Christian ecstasy *always* implies 'a going out of oneself' (*Gregory of Nyssa: From Glory to Glory*, p. 33). This is overbold. But Daniélou more than

[1] See Redpath and Hatch, *Concordance to Septuagint*, 1898, for the various LXX occurrences of *ekstasis* etc., and the Hebrew words they represent.

atones for this in his *Origène* (Paris, 1948, pp. 295f.) and more fully, in his *Platonisme et théologie mystique* (Paris, 1944, pp. 261f.), both of which give useful and full details of what ecstasy was understood to be.

Christian notions of ecstasy do owe much to Platonic thought and to Greek thought generally. So too do those of Jews contemporary with New Testament events, as can be seen from the writings of Philo of Alexandria (20 B.C.–A.D. 55). From the earliest Christian times both Jewish and Christian experiences were widely interpreted in terms of Greek ideas which were not infrequently foreign to the actual experiences of the Biblical Jews and sometimes foreign to the experiences of the very first Christians who were, of course, mainly Jewish. But the fusion of Greek, Hebrew and Christian concepts of ecstasy occurred very early, already in New Testament times. Erasmus is not the author of such a powerful syncretism of Jewish, Christian and Platonic notions, which characterise his theology of ecstasy! It already abounded in the early fathers to whom he turned for guidance. Such fathers found ecstasy of various kinds all over the place in their Bibles: in the Psalms, in the Gospels, in the writings of St Paul, in the lives of Peter, Paul and the other apostles, as well as in the journey of Abraham and the love-poetry of the *Song of Songs*.

For those on the look-out for ecstatic commonplaces, it is essential to read the Septuagint or the Vulgate, not only the Authorised Version. Many texts of major importance to patristic writers on ecstasy do not seem to call forth their reflexions at all, unless one turns to the actual versions of Scripture which they used. For example, David 'said in his haste, All men are liars'—but not in the Greek or Latin, where his outburst is an insight attributable to ecstatic revelations. For the Greeks, David said what he did *en tē ekstasei mou* ('in my ecstasy'). For the Latins, David's cry was made either *in excessu meo* ('in my ecstasy') or, for those who had access to the version of the Psalms made from the Hebrew, *in stupore meo* ('in my amazement'). Commentaries or allusions to this psalm (115/16:11) in patristic writers normally stress the ecstasy in ways which seem strange to those using other versions.

There is no question of trying to define in this study what were the actual experiences which the author of the 30th psalm, say, or St Luke or St Paul were striving to convey. On points such as these I am quite unqualified to speak and simply follow the standard sources, when, that is, I am not directly following patristic authors at first hand. What matters is what such experiences meant to Erasmus, when seen through the interpretative prisms of Origen, Chrysostom, 'Athanasius', Augustine and others of those early fathers in whom he sought help in understanding the spiritual truth which, in the Scriptures, is often veiled in metaphor, parable or myth, or embodied in carnal literalness.

In classical Greek *ekstasis* means a displacement or a casting down of a thing from its normal place or state. From this literal meaning it took on the sense of a form of acute distraction, brought on by a strong emotion such as terror or astonishment. Under the influence of such an ecstasy a man or woman might be vouchsafed visions from God or the gods. The verb *existēmi*—to put something out of its place—similarly acquired the meaning of 'to astonish' or 'to amaze'.[1]

Greek writers, as well as seeing ecstasy as a confusion of mind or spirit brought on by passions, also used it for a kind of madness, *ekstasis manikē*. This is a transport in which an alienated person is possessed by a god, who endows his host with prophetic powers. Such persons may seem mad or drunk. *Ekstasis manikē* was further conflated with those various kinds of natural and divine *mania* (which the Latins called *furor*) to be found described by Plato in the *Phaedrus*.

Mania is used by Plato for these good, divinely induced forms of madness during which the soul leaves the body, or at least strives to do so. When *mania* of this kind was fused with *ekstasis* the force of the combined ideas was to prove of the greatest importance to neo-Platonic and the Christian doctrine. From such rich semantic confusions arose that particular conception of ecstasy so prized by Hellenising Jews, by Christians and by their rivals in the neo-Platonic schools of late antiquity. It was also appreciated by heretics.

A most useful text to read in order to understand how Jewish and Greek views of ecstasy were fused together is Philo's *Who is the Heir of Divine Things?* This first-century text (usually known by its Latin rather than its Greek title as *Quis rerum divinarum heres*) is the earliest extant treatise to incorporate fully Greek notions of ecstasy into the interpretation of the Jewish Bible. Philo does so in such a way that scholars agree that he did not invent such an interpretation but was codifying an already established practice.

Philo distinguished four sorts of ecstasy in the Old Testament: (i) madness; (ii) astonishment and amazement caused by fear; (iii) a stupor found in God-given rest or sleep; and finally (iv) the kind of inspired prophetic madness such as befell Abraham in Genesis 15:12 where we read that, about sunset, a trance (LXX, *ekstasis*) fell upon Abram, as a 'great, dark terror' (*phobos skoteinos megas*) came upon him. In *Who is the Heir?* Philo took the vital step of explaining such an

---

[1] Liddell-Scott-Jones's *Lexicon* and J. H. Thayer's *Greek-English Lexicon of the New Testament*, based on Grimm's Wilke's *Clavis Novi Testamenti*, can supply detailed references.

ecstasy in pagan Greek terms, as a state produced by the soul's temporarily leaving the body as it rises to contemplate higher things:

Who then is the heir? Not that way of thinking which abides in the prison of the body of its own free will, but that which, released from its fetters into liberty, has come forth outside the prison walls, and if we may say so, left itself behind.[1]

Philo therefore urges his own soul (*psychē*) to leave his body, his senses and his power of speech, so as to 'issue forth' on its spiritual quest. He partly bases his case for this on a metaphorical interpretation of LXX Genesis 12:1.

And the Lord said to Abram, Go forth out of thy land and of thy kindred and out of the house of thy father, and come into the land that I shall show thee.

Throughout this part of *Who is the Heir?* Philo emphasises the soul's joy at leaving the body. This joy is specifically likened to the frenzy which seizes persons possessed, such as the Corybants of Greek paganism. The mind is driven onwards by a mad love of heavenly things, drawn, indeed, upwards to heaven by its very love. The ordinary world is perceived by the sense; but the mind can discover a higher world belonging to the order of invisible truth (*Who is the Heir?* 75). The spiritual man, whether he is of priestly line or not, holds life in the body to be a sojourning in a foreign land; only when he can live uniquely in his soul does he feel like a dweller in his true fatherland (*Who is the Heir?* 82). So the true spiritual sense of the strange phrase of Genesis (LXX) 15:5, 'He led him out outside' (*exēgagen auton exō*) is not mere tautology. Philo saw this text as a veiled allusion to the soul's being led out from the prison-house of the body and the senses. The double use of 'out' (*exēgagen: exō*), properly understood, refers to the soul's leaving its body in *ekstasis*. In such an ecstasy a man is 'led out of himself', out of trust in his own knowledge to a trust in God (*Who is the Heir?* 85). This is not *ecstasy* as the old Jews thought of it. It is ecstatic rapture—the soul's being snatched out of the body and ravished up towards the godhead by the power of a great emotion—especially love. It is, moreover, a case of 'possession'.

In other words, ecstatic rapture is being read back into Genesis by Alexandrine Jews at the very time that the events portrayed in the Gospels were running their course and the New Testament itself was slowly being composed among Christians who were open to both Jewish and Greek influences at one and the same time.

[1] *Quis heres* XIV. 68: Loeb IV pp. 316–17; cf. p. 279 of the Analytical Introduction.

The term ecstasy by now had acquired a wide semantic field. It could apply to madness; to a prophetic state akin to madness; to a God-induced stupor; to a state akin to drunkenness; to the often visionary amazement produced by religious fear or awe; and it could also apply to a state of spiritual possession during which men or women are transported out of themselves, especially by a rapture induced by love of God.

All these senses are known to Erasmus and used by him in ecstatic contexts—except that he studiously avoids any suggestion of Dionysiac 'possession'. Two are more important than the others. It will be necessary to refer to them several times. The first is the ecstatic amazement produced by fear and awe—major Biblical examples are the confused amazement of the disciples at the Transfiguration or Peter's vision of the tablecloth laden with food. The second is the real or apparent transporting of the soul out of the body; the principal New Testament example is St Paul's rapture to the third heaven, which he mysteriously relates in II Corinthians 12. (No Christian interprets this as a case of possession.)

Erasmus would have found variations of these themes in many of the fathers, including Origen and Augustine. Whether or not he had access to a manuscript of Philo before writing the *Moria* is not certain. He did not have a Philo to hand when preparing his *Paraphrase of St Luke* (first edition, 1516, p. 306), but that does not mean he had not read him. The contrary may seem to be implied. But directly or indirectly Philo's ideas were known to all who knew their early fathers. Philo enjoyed a great and lasting place of honour among Christians, summed up in the Greek saying, duly collected and explained by Erasmus (*Adagia* 2. 7. 71): *Either Plato philonised or Philo platonised*. Such an epigram means much more to Renaissance syncretists than might at first strike the eye. This is made very clear, for example, by Sigismund Gelenius in his edition of *All the Lucubrations which can be Obtained of Philo the Jew, that Most Eloquent Writer and Highest Philosopher, Made Latin out of the Greek*, 1561. Gelenius insists that Philo has at least as much right to be welcomed by Christians as Plato, Aristotle or Averroes. More in fact. He was of exemplary piety in his own religion, which was then in its declining old age. He wrote when the light of the Gospel was not yet widely spread (and so certainly cannot be blamed for remaining in the old religion). For Gelenius, it is much more probable that Plato philonised than that Philo platonised. Did not Plato in fact learn his doctrines from Moses? (This was a commonplace of Renaissance scholarship which made the Jewish period in Egypt under Moses into the means by which revealed religion was taught to both the Egyptian and the Greek philosophers.)

All agree, he asserts, that Plato travelled to Egypt. There he learned not only from Egyptian priestly authors but had access to Jewish truth as well. Such ideas were commonly held by fathers of the early Church. Among Christians of all periods Philo's reputation stood high. The authorities whom Gelenius assembles as testimonies to Philo include Eusebius in his *Ecclesiastical History* and St Augustine in his treatise *Against Faustus the Manichean* (XII. 2). As for St Jerome, did he not include him in his *Catalogue of Ecclesiastical Writers*? He specifically mentions *Who is the Heir?* and ends his eulogy of him with an allusion to the Greek proverb, stressing that there is 'much similarity between the meaning and eloquence of Philo and Plato' (Philo, *Lucubrationes*, ed. Gelenius, Basle, 1561, dedicatory letter to the protonotary Johannes a Balma).

Any Christian humanist, let alone a scholar like Erasmus who admired St Jerome, is likely to respect a philosophical theology deriving in part from Philo. And yet, on vital points Erasmus differs both from him and the theology he represents. In early Christian times, too, the soul-departing ecstasy which Philo attributed to Abraham was held in deep suspicion by most Catholic theologians. Abraham's ecstasy, in Philo's conception, was a case of divine possession. It was essentially Dionysiac in conception: Abraham's *nous idios*, his own mind, was driven out by the divinely infused Spirit. Such an ecstatic is an enthusiast. For Christian theologians, including Origen, Clement of Alexandria and Basil, such an ecstasy was to be kept at arm's length: it was too reminiscent both of pagan prophets and of the charismatic abuses of the heretical Montanists. Modern scholars agree that Philonic ecstasy cannot be found in Origen, who accepts a departure of the spirit outside the body but not the departure of the man from himself, as his *nous idios* is replaced by the Spirit of God.[1]

It was Gregory of Nyssa who reacclimatised in orthodox circles the kind of ecstasy in which a man went out of himself, *exō heautou*. This became possible once Montanism had collapsed. But even for Gregory such an ecstasy was not a driving out of man's own mind by the divine Spirit; the spirit or mind of man was thought of as soaring aloft to God.

Christian forms of ecstasy were parallel to, but different from, those which are characteristic of Plotinus and the neo-Platonists. For Plotinus ecstasy consists in the abolition of the individual soul and its fusion into the One; as such it is an anticipation of the final release of the soul from the body at death, when it is absorbed into the One for ever. There is much in this that Christians cannot accept. But there

[1] See J. Daniélou, *Platonisme et Théologie Mystique*, Paris, 1944, especially ch. 3, pp. 259ff. and the works mentioned there, above all Lewy's *Sobria Ebrietas*, Giessen, 1929.

was also much which was found deeply congenial. Echoes of Plotinian themes and language can be found in many later Christian mystics, including St Bernard, St Bonaventura and Meister Eckhart. Traces of the language—but not the concepts in their neo-Platonic form—are apparent in the *Moria*. Few mystic writers escape them entirely—supposing always they wished to escape them.

But for Gregory of Nyssa, and others before Pseudo-Dionysius, ecstasy is a suspension of natural life, while the soul is vouchsafed a beatifying contemplation of divine reality. It is no less than a foretaste of eternal bliss, mediated by the eucharist. And that eternal bliss will only be enjoyed to the full when immortality in the body is man's individual lot at the resurrection. That is the Shibboleth: no Platonist or neo-Platonist can accept an individual immortality lived in the resurrected body: no Christian can deny it.

Of course, non-Christian neo-Platonic mystics such as Plotinus exerted a great influence during the Renaissance, when Ficino and others drew eclectically and enthusiastically upon both Christian Platonists and pagan neo-Platonists. Erasmus placed Plotinus high among non-Christian writers. But an author so sensitive to nuance and to the finest points of doctrine such as Erasmus shows himself to be could not have fallen into neo-Platonic heresy by following Plotinus rather than Christian authorities. Any subsequent mystic may use a terminology reminiscent of Plotinus. Erasmus may have gone more deeply into Platonist—as distinct from neo-Platonist— ways of thought than he later held to be wise or even orthodox. That may be suggested by what he wrote in one of his last works (see *LB* 5. 432AB). But in the *Moria* this was not under the influence of Philo the Jewish Platonist of Alexandria, of Plotinus or Pseudo-Dionysius; it was under the influence, direct or indirect, of such fathers whom he recommends to the reader in the *Enchiridion*—Origen, Ambrose, Jerome, Augustine—or of those Greeks whom he turned to for spiritual and scholarly guidance, such as Basil, Gregory of Nyssa, Nemesius, and Theophylact. All these fathers are in varying degrees indebted to both Plato and Philo. The one who most closely recalls aspects of Philo's conception of ecstasy is perhaps Ambrose. The one least likely to lead Erasmus astray in matters of ecstasy was Origen: the Montanist heresy, which gave a large rôle to divine possession in ecstatic rapture, made Origen, Basil and many of the earliest fathers deeply suspicious of any form of ecstasy which was combined with spiritual possession. Origen avoids the term *ekstasis* and even sees the devil at work in St Peter when he babbled in ecstatic amazement (see below, p. 213). In other areas of theology Origen's platonising heresies were not hidden snares: they were public knowledge, encouraging

Erasmus to read him at times with considerable caution. What is striking is how little Erasmus owed to the one author who could have muddied the distinction between the early, orthodox platonising of the older fathers of the Church and neo-platonising heresies or near heresies: Pseudo-Dionysius. Between the *Enchiridion* and the *Moria* Erasmus had learned to treat him with caution, even at first with suspicion.

Pseudo-Dionysius dominated western mysticism. His fusion of Platonic and Christian love led him not only to value highly the soul-departing ecstasy of enraptured men but also to treat Christ as an ecstatic lover of the Christian soul. His concept of ecstasy is open to a fully Philonic and classical, pagan, Dionysiac interpretation: the passionate lover of God is so enraptured that he is outside himself, his own mind living in Christ while Christ's spirit lives in him. The text in which Pseudo-Dionysius saw the clearest allusion to the mutual ecstatic love of Christ and man was Galatians 2:20: 'I live: not I, but Christ liveth in me.' It is found over and over again in ecstatic contexts whenever Pseudo-Dionysius is being read. It is a commonplace of Platonic philosophy that lovers live not in themselves but in the one whom they love, their souls departing from their bodies and entering that of the beloved, in a mutual exchange (*Phaedrus*, 244C–265B). The fact that Erasmus also makes his ecstatic love partly depend on such a Platonic concept must not blind us to the vital fact that he rejects the interpretation put on to Galatians 2:20 by the neo-platonising antedated saint. For Pseudo-Dionysius the love of Christ and man is a reciprocal ecstasy. Both are outside themselves: Christ lives in man and man lives in Christ as lovers who are both 'outside themselves': for him, that is what St Paul meant by 'Christ liveth in me'. Such an idea Erasmus finds abhorrent. He never expounds it, not even when treating Galatians 2:20 directly in the *Annotations on the New Testament* or in the relevant paraphrase. His silence is deafening. This is no accident. To be concerned as Erasmus was with ecstasy, and yet never once cite Galatians 2:20, can only be a conscious act of rejection. (He does cite it of course in non-ecstatic contexts: cf *LB* 5. 1301DE.)

Erasmus never mentions, either, that spiritual darkness which, according to Pseudo-Dionysius, awaits the soul enraptured toward the God who is Light. Such a darkness is a constant theme of spiritual writers from Gregory of Nyssa and Pseudo-Dionysius onwards. Not to allude to it is to wish to reject it. Commonplaces such as that occurred to anyone writing in the tradition of Platonico-Christian ecstasy. Some would even maintain that an ecstasy without spiritual darkness is inauthentic.

In practice many followers of Pseudo-Dionysius quietly dropped the Philonic overtones. The love remains in some ways Platonic, but it is conceived as a one-way enrapturing of the human soul into the godhead of Christ. Not infrequently St Paul's cry 'Christ liveth in me' is cited as though he was saying, 'I live in Christ.'

That, with significant modifications, is closer to Erasmus' concept of ecstasy, though he rarely sees the soul as living in Christ: the raptured soul is caught up towards the Father.

Much more successfully than most, Erasmus finds strong Christian authority for interpreting ecstasy as a divinely induced insanity. Either directly or indirectly he owed at least something to Gregory of Nyssa. This kind of Christian *ekstasis manikē* is induced by the souls striving to leave the body; to think otherwise is to open the way not to ecstasy but to diabolical possession.

Pseudo-Dionysius was not a recent discovery in the West. For Erasmus there was no aura of Renaissance freshness about him despite his being admired by John Colet. A principal commentator on Pseudo-Dionysius was Thomas Aquinas, the arch-scholastic whom Erasmus constantly criticised. The text of Galatians 2:20 on which Pseudo-Dionysius centred his ecstatic doctrine appears again and again in the mouths of the mediaeval ecstatics. This already applies to great writers such as Hugo of St Victor (*PL* 196. 1222B–D), after whom—partly because of Aquinas, no doubt—the influence of Pseudo-Dionysius grew even more dominant among ecstatic authors, major and minor alike.

A quick means for a modern reader to see how the Dionysian theme was handled is to read Aquinas' *Summa Theologica* 2^a 2^{ae}, 175, especially art. 2.[1]

Pseudo-Dionysius was a major influence on Ficino. The same applies, though with different emphases, to high-Renaissance Catholic theologians such as St François de Sales, who is worth quoting here not so much for himself (interesting though he is) but because he so elegantly sums up a thousand-year-old tradition:

Ecstasy is called rapture [*ravissement*] because through it God draws us and raises us up to him; and rapture is called ecstasy in that, by it, we come out of ourselves, remain out of ourselves and above ourselves, in order to unite ourselves to God (*Oeuvres*, Paris, 1669, 1, col. 423).

Like so many others he divides ecstasy into two major types, that

---

[1] The English version of the Blackfriars, (tome XLV, London and New York, 1970) translates Aquinas' *raptus* by 'ecstasy'. This is rather confusing: while all raptures are ecstasies, not all ecstasies are raptures. Generally speaking, rapture is a higher boon than ecstasy, but some do use the words interchangeably. The translation is freer than one might prefer and there are many misprints, but it remains useful.

caused by amazement (*admiration*) and that caused by rapture. In his account of the second kind he is deeply indebted to Pseudo-Dionysius' love-induced ecstasy:

Whence it follows that ecstasy and rapture depend totally upon love, for it is love which brings the understanding to contemplation and the will to unity—in such a way that one must conclude with the great Saint Dionysius that Divine love is ecstatic (*que l'amour Divin est extatique*), not permitting that the Lovers should belong to themselves but to the Beloved object. That is why that wonderful apostle St Paul—being in the possession of this love Divine and being made a participant in its ecstatic force—said through his divinely inspired mouth: *I live; not I, but JESUS CHRIST lives in me*. And so, like a true lover who has come outside himself unto God (*sorty hors de soy en Dieu*), he lived his own life no more, but the life of his Beloved, as being sovereignly lovable (*Oeuvres* i, col. 428–9).

It is tempting to leave the main thread of the argument and to try to resume here the ecstatic theories of Origen and other fathers with long excursuses into later and by no means irrelevent mystical theologians of both the Christian East and West. It is best to avoid such a temptation; otherwise this study would be endless. It is wiser to let a few of them speak for themselves insofar as they are quoted to explain particular thoughts and words as they occur in the closing pages of the *Moria*. But it would be easy to find verbal and conceptual parallels between the *Moria* and a great many earlier writers on ecstasy.

Above all, it may be stated quite categorically that ecstasy conceived as a *mentis excessus*, a departure of the mind from the body, as a rapture (*raptus*) by which the soul of man leaves, or seems to leave, the body, living *extra se*, as a soaring of the soul aloft toward a union with God, was a commonplace of mediaeval mysticism, known to literate Christians through some of the most widely studied writers. Erasmus uses this traditional language; even when he is most consciously going back to his earliest Christian and pre-Christian authors, he employs a terminology which St Bernard, say, or St Bonaventura would have recognised as in many ways their own.

One convenient way to understand ecstasy is to read Augustine preaching to a country congregation on the 30th (31st) psalm. His sermon serves to remind us how Church fathers could find ecstasy in places where we might not find it today. He also makes with admirable clarity that confusion of, and distinction between, the ecstasy of amazement and the ecstasy of rapture which will prove so important for the understanding of the *Moria*. In the Latin text used by Augustine the superscription of the 30th (31st) psalm reads *In finem, psalmus ipsi*

David ecstasis (Towards an End: a psalm of David's ecstasy). Another version differs only in form of words, not meaning: *In finem. Psalmus David pro exstasi*. The words *In finem* ('towards an end') were taken to mean, as Augustine briefly remarks, that the psalm had particular, often hidden, reference to Christ, the End towards whom Christians tend. (Erasmus believes this too. The Hebrew term actually means 'Dedication'.)

There are two sermons of St Augustine devoted to explaining this psalm. Both tackle the meaning of the word *ecstasis*. In the first sermon it is a matter of a rapture, an *excessus mentis*, produced by dread (*pavor*) or by a revelation (*CCSL* 38, p. 186). In the second, Augustine uses *excessus* as the approximate, single-word rendering of the Greek word. It is then interpreted as having either of two meanings: (i) a state induced by dread, or (ii) a rapture induced by a spiritual concentration directed towards higher things (*intentio ad superna*). 'In such an ecstasy were all holy men to whom the hidden things of God surpassing this world were revealed.' St Paul experienced 'this *mentis excessus*, this ecstasy', when he said of himself [II Corinthians 5:13] 'For whether we are beside ourselves (*mente excessimus*) it is unto God; or whether we are of sober mind, it is unto you.' He shows that the psalm can be properly interpreted with the *ecstasis* being taken as dread just as well as rapture (*CCSL* 38, pp. 191–4).

This explanation of St Augustine's was destined to be widely disseminated; it figures in the *Glossa Ordinaria*. (I have used the Lyons, 1589 edition; p. 394.)

The next to last word can be left with Guillaume Budé. His *Commentaries on the Greek Language* are a mine of scholarly information. He devotes much space and learning to explaining *ekstasis*, the cognate verb *existēmi*, as well as *mania*. For Budé it is repeatedly a question, where ecstasy is concerned, of people being out of their minds (*mente alienari*), bursting outside themselves (*extra se erumpere*), of losing control of their minds (*exire a potestate*). His main preoccupation is with a verse of St Luke's Gospel (24:22): 'Moreover, certain of our company *amazed us*', when they told the strange news of the empty tomb and Christ's resurrection. (The verb used for 'amazed us' is *existēmi*: *existēsan hēmas*'.) To explain the force of this word he draws upon writers, classical and Judaeo-Christian, including Plato and Pseudo-Dionysius. From Plato he cites key passages of the *Phaedrus*. The kind of ecstasy which Plato describes he then applies directly to Christian mystics: 'With these words Plato describes those whom we call "enraptured in ecstasy" (*ecstasi correptos*)—something which often happens to certain holy men who, having quite forgotten themselves (that is to say, their body and its desires), are entirely given over to contemplation, being as though called forth from their body and its cares (*velut a corpore ejusque curis avocati*).' From Dionysius he cites—naturally—the passage which includes Galatians 2:21, 'I live, but not I; Christ liveth in me.'

Almost all the erudition and presuppositions of Erasmus, as far as ecstasy is concerned, can be paralleled in Budé. We can be sure that at least one reader fully understood the implications of the *Moria*: Budé himself. So, too, could anyone who had read the relevant parts of the *Commentarii Linguae Graecae*.[1] Budé is referred to, from time to time, in the following pages. It is no exaggeration to say that, for those who can read his condensed Latin and heavily ligatured Greek, he is an ideal guide to the meaning of the closing pages of the *Moria*.

Yet there is a dimension missing from him which is a source of spiritual depth for Erasmus: the mystical itinerary which Erasmus found in his Old Testament under the guidance of Origen and Ambrose.

The 33rd chapter of the book of Numbers lists the wanderings of the Children of Israel on leaving Egypt and their various *mansions* (the places where they rested). These were interpreted by Origen (*PG* 12. 796BC) and by St Ambrose (*PL* 17. 29cf.) as various stages on the mystical road to God. Both Origen and Ambrose interpreted the mansion called Terah (Vulgate *Thare*) as the ecstasy of amazement.

Erasmus was not unaffected by this. His *Enarratio* on the 22nd (23rd) psalm sees the soul's journey in just such terms. Christ 'leadeth me beside the still waters':

As soon as our soul has been restored by such waters, it conceives the fervour of the spirit and turns away from the pleasures and conveniences of this world. Then the Shepherd leads it through the paths of righteousness, through the forty mansions of the Children of Israel. In rapturous joy (*alacriter*) it reaches the land flowing with milk and honey (*LB* 5. 341BC).

Its goal is the House of the Lord, where it remains for ever.

These mansions are normally numbered forty-two. According to St Ambrose (*On the Forty-Two Mansions of the Children of Israel*) it is the forty-second which is Terah.

Folly in the *Moria* is explained as an ecstasy of that kind. By doing this, Erasmus is taking up and developing the implications of what he wrote in the *Enchiridion* (*LB* 5. 8D); there he uncovered veiled allusions to ecstasy in the twelve fountains which refresh pilgrims on the stages of the forty mansions of the Children of Israel. (*Numbers*

---

[1] *Opera*, 1557, reprinted Gregg, second impression 1969, IV, cols. 66off. and 1050f.

33:9 and context.) As so often in Erasmus, this ecstatic interpretation of a *locus classicus* takes us back beyond Augustine or even Ambrose to the authority who was for him the most bountiful fountain of all spiritual allegory: Origen.

CHAPTER FOUR

The Climax in Ecstasy (I)

1. *Minor additions to the end of the* Moria

The praise of ecstasy in the closing pages of the *Moria* seems virtually untouched, compared with the many and long interpolations made elsewhere in 1514 and, less, in later years. Such changes as there are are very significant.

After 1514 Erasmus became more aggressive. He does concede, by adding an *aliqua*, that he is dealing with 'a certain kind' of folly, not just plain folly (1522 *Moria*), but he inserts an *inquiunt* ('so they say') in the middle of a sentence in which Folly had gently conceded that the ceremonies of the Mass are not to be despised in themselves (1516 *Moria*).

From 1516 Erasmus was forced to be prudent, though only about ecstasy. All the 1514 additions, with all their biting satire, are maintained. But the ending was modified. He softened an allusion to 'Moria's part' which had made Folly akin to Mary Magdalene. He had added notes attributed to Listrius to the first Froben edition: he added more during 1516. Both the notes themselves and their dating are highly suggestive. So is an apparently unimportant correction of an allusion to I Corinthians 2:9. Most important of all, he quietly cut out eight words. (All these points will be mentioned later.)

Nevertheless the climax of the praise of ecstasy remains, in its essentials, unchanged. Only under the force of necessity did he make even slight concessions. What he wrote for the *Moria* of 1511 is what he still wanted to say in 1515–16. Much of Erasmus' difficulties over the *Moria* arose from this fact. He could not, and would not, change what he wanted to say. He was prepared to defend it; prepared too to explain it. In the course of his explanations he shifted his ground. But what he wrote, in More's house no doubt, for this part of the *Moria*, where wit, laughter and Lucianesque mockery largely give way to ecstatic joy, stood as a corner-stone of his spirituality.

For him, ecstasy was a form of madness. So much so that few could tell the two things apart. On that he would not budge.

2. *Natural fools and Christian fools*

Folly, in order not to go on for ever, cuts matters short. Christianity is akin to foolishness. Both natural fools and Christian conduct show this to be so. The humour is now gentle, quiet, serene, giving way, when appropriate, to a mood of deeply emotive zeal and piety.

Ac ne quae sunt infinita persequar, utque summatim dicam, videtur omnino Christiana religio quandam habere cum stulticia cognationem, minimeque cum sapientia convenire, cujus rei si desyderatis argumenta, primum illud animadvertite, pueros, senes, mulieres ac fatuos, sacris ac religiosis rebus praeter caeteros gaudere, eoque semper altaribus esse proximos, solo nimirum naturae impulsu. Pręterea videtis primos illos religionis authores mire simplicitatem amplexos, acerrimos literarum hostes fuisse. Postremo nulli Moriones magis desipere videntur, quam ii quos Christianae pietatis ardor semel totos arripuit, adeo sua profundunt, injurias negligunt, falli sese patiuntur, inter amicos & inimicos nullum discrimen, voluptatem horrent, inedia, vigilia, lachrymis, laboribus, contumeliis saginantur, vitam fastidiunt, mortem unice optant. Breviter ad omnem sensum communem prorsus obstupuisse videntur, perinde quasi alibi vivat animus, non in suo corpore, quod quidem quid aliud est quam insanire? (Scheurer G6v°–H1r°; Kan 180–1)   *clu 6/6*

Lest I should chase after matters which have no end—and to sum up briefly —it seems that Christianity certainly has some kinship with folly, while having very little in common with wisdom. If you want confirmation of this, turn your attention first to the fact that children, old men, women and the simple-minded find more joy than others in sacred and ritual matters. They are, therefore, always nearest the altars—under the sole impulse of nature, no doubt. Besides, those who first laid the foundations of religion embraced simplicity to a marvellous extent, and were very bitter enemies of learning. Finally, no cretins seem more void of understanding than those who are once seized by the fire of Christian piety: for they pour out their own wealth, overlook wrongs, allow themselves to be deceived: they make no difference between friends and enemies and withdraw from pleasures with horror; they feed on fastings, vigils, tears, toil and insults; they show distaste for life, desiring only death—in short they seem to have been completely dazed in regard to ordinary intelligence, just as if their soul were living elsewhere, not in its own body. And what is that, then if not to be mad?

There are several nuances here which are difficult to render in English. There is, for example, the use of the word *religio* in apparently two different senses, with *religiosae res* in another. I have done my best to translate what seems to be the appropriate shade of meaning, but I could well be wrong. And the kind of sustained play on words represented by the repetition of the term is utterly lost. Normally in this study *insania* is rendered by 'insanity', the same applying to its cognates. I really prefer mad, madman, etc., but *insania* allows word-play on *sanus* (sane, healthy); when that is so, I use *sane* and *insane*—a poor compromise , since the English term *sane* lacks the accompanying idea of 'sound health'.

The general import of the passage presents less difficulty. Christian ritual attracts the weak and foolish; and that is quite natural. The first apostles were simple and illiterate men, hostile to erudite wisdom—by this time we realise that the contrast is with the learning of worldly-wise philosophers and legalists. The Christian who is burning with the zeal of piety is so selfless and Christ-like that he seems a fool, ignoring the rule of ordinary human prudence. But behind this simple *résumé* lie several important undertones.

The end of the *Moria* is steeped in Platonic assumptions. This applies not only to some of the most mystical parts of Folly's peroration but to the light-hearted, yet paradoxically provocative, assertion that 'children, old men, women and simpletons' are more susceptible to religious ritual than are men in their prime. This quip is an ingenious extension to women and simpletons of an idea attributed to Plato during the Renaissance. Montaigne refers to it in his sceptical defence of Catholic doctrine, the *Apologie de Raimond Sebond*. Plato, for Montaigne, was a 'great soul'; yet he was but a pagan for all that and 'great with human greatness only'. So he too was led into error, asserting that 'children and old men are more susceptible to religion, as though it was born of our weakness and drew its strength from it' (*Essais* II. 12; Bordeaux edition II, p. 151).

Erasmus and Montaigne are making different points, but they are alluding to the same, allegedly Platonic belief.

More specifically and authentically Platonic is Erasmus' unrelenting concern with the reality of the unseen and the unreality of the things of this world.

Folly's emphasis is not on what is but what seems to be. This is shown by the verb *videre* being used no less than four times, three of them with the same construction, which strikes me, at least, as Ciceronian: *videtur . . . videntur . . . videntur*, ('it seems', 'they seem'). What lies behind this foolish-seeming, superficial view of the Christian life is to occupy Folly for the rest of her speech.

Another parallel emphasis is on the extreme foolishness or madness apparently displayed by Christian men in their burning zeal. Such Christians seem *desipere*, 'to act as though devoid of understanding'. Erasmus is alluding fleetingly to a well-known passage of Cicero's *On the Nature of the Gods* (I. 34. 93–4): in the eyes of the Epicureans, Socrates was not the father of philosophy but a mere Attic buffoon (*scurra Atticus*). The greatest of the wise men are said by them *disipere*,

delirare, dementis esse ('to be void of understanding, to rave, to be mad').
Yet such men perceived something of the nature of the gods; if they
did not, then nobody did . . . Erasmus comes to the climax with the
seeming madness of the Christian man—the *quasi* underlines the
seeming—and is at pains to use the strongest of terms to rub this
home. Such men are thought not just to be mad, but madder than
moriones. This word is a rare one.

Erasmus would have liked it, since it derives from a Latinisation of
the Greek *mōros* which gave its name to his book. He would have read
it in Augustine, who points out that those whose unlettered stupidity
(*fatuitas*) makes them little different from the brute beasts are popularly called *moriones* (*PL* 33 Augustine 2, Epistle 166; 728, 17). This is
Erasmus' meaning without a doubt; he is soon to use the verb *ob-*
stupesco; when he repeats it a little later, he links it with *obbrutesco*, 'to
become as stupid as a brute beast'. But whatever other associations the
verb may have, it is important that its ecstatic meaning should not be
allowed to be weakened or lost, not least in the *Moria*.

Obstupesco chiefly means 'to be astounded, struck with amazement';
the primary meaning is 'to be benumbed or senseless'. Erasmus, who
has a predilection for it in certain ecstatic contexts, was influenced in
this by his reading of Origen on the 'mansion' *Thare*, extant only in
Rufinus' Latin version. At this point Rufinus was obliged to go over to
a paraphrase:

Then comes *Thara*, by which is understood *contemplatio stuporis* [a state of
contemplativeness induced by shock and amazement]. We cannot express by
one word in Latin what the Greeks call *ekstasis*—that is, when, because of
wonder at any great thing, the soul is amazed (*cum pro alicujus magnae rei
admiratione obstupescit animus*). That is the meaning of *contemplatio stuporis*:
when, because of its acknowledgment of great and wondrous things, the
mind is thunderstruck and stunned (*cum in agnitione magnarum et admirabilium
rerum mens attonita stupet*) (*PG* 12. 796BC).

St Ambrose makes the same points. The mansion of the ecstasy of
amazement he calls by the Vulgate's name of *Thare*. He cites many
examples from the Old and New Testaments. They serve to recall to
mind that *stupor* is a scriptural word for this amazement; so is the verb
obstupesco.

Erasmus uses the verb in ways which cause some difficulty. Here
the Christian fools are said to seem to be struck with amazement or
numbness *ad omnem sensum communem*. The words 'common sense' are
a well-known source of difficulty, since *communis sensus* rarely implies
what modern usage would tempt us to infer; but one of its meanings is
that plain, every-day wisdom 'without which a man is foolish or

insane' (*NED*, s.v. *Common sense*). It had such implications in Renaissance usage. That is the force of the term here, as can be seen from
Erasmus' paraphrase of John 10:20, where Christ's enemies exclaim,
'he hath a devil. He is mad' (*mainetai*: 'insanit'): 'For many were saying
what they had said before more than once, whenever Christ revealed
their secret counsels and whenever he said or did anything surpassing
human power: "He is a daemonic, and, he is mad".' The next phrase in
the Gospel is, 'Why listen to him?' (*quid eum auditis?*). Erasmus renders
this by: 'The things he says are lacking in common sense (*carent sensu
communi*). What is the use of listening to him?' That is what one would
expect them to say of Christ, who was for them a raging lunatic, quite
lacking in plain, everyday wisdom.

The meaning of the words *ad omnem sensum communem* imply that
the Christian fool appears to lack the minimum intelligence of the
ordinary sensible man. The problem is, how exactly to fit the phrase
grammatically to the verb *obstupesco*. It is not easy to resolve. Folly
seems to be saying that the burning zeal of the Christian man may seize
him so violently (*arripere*) that, in his amazement, he looses all feeling
where common prudence is concerned. Erasmus certainly associated
it with the amazement which seizes a man who discovers the spiritual
truth hidden within the Silenus of Christ and the Scriptures. Much
later, in 1530, when again expounding the theme of Christian folly, he
tells of the joys which, under grace, will come to his readers if he
succeeds in revealing the hidden spiritual sense of the 33rd psalm:

> ... dum ... expandimus Silenum ... animi vestri ... obstupescent ad
> divinae sapientiae contemplationem (*LB* 5. 371).

while we unfold the Silenus, your souls will be amazed into contemplation of
divine wisdom.[1]

Similarly in *De Ratione Concionandi* Erasmus tells how 'you may be
increasingly amazed—*magis et magis stupescas*—as you discover the
divine spiritual wisdom hiding beneath the contemptible surface
appearance of parts of Holy Writ (*LB* 5. 870Af.). The sense of *obstupesco*
here is similar, but despite the parallel construction with *ad*, the sense
of the passage in the *Moria* is different. In the *Moria* the amazement
leads to a numbness which neglects common prudence. In the later
passage, the amazement leads towards the contemplation of the wisdom
of God. In both cases the Christian man is struck with astonishment,

---

[1] The verb *obstupesco* was used throughout the Christian centuries with precisely
this sense of the ecstatic 'amazement' produced by a spiritual confrontation of the Old
and New Testaments (cf. Appendix A. *ad fin.*).

an astonishment which, in the *Moria*, makes him seem mad to the ordinary run of mortal men. In this the Christian can find a prototype in Socrates. The adage 'The Sileni of Alcibiades' contains a sustained though slightly veiled defence of the *Moria* and its theology. Among many, many points of similarity, one might note that Socrates is said to have seemed like a fool, because of his constant jesting: he was a perpetual joke, in this not unlike a cretin (*nonnullam habebat morionis speciem*), Erasmus again using the word *morio*. Socrates appeared to be a *morio* at the very time when worldly-wise fools, *stulti*, were actually affecting wisdom *ad insaniam* 'to the point of madness'! (*LB* 2. 770F). Yet he it was who proved to be the sane one, with his love of the spiritual and the invisible: the real fools were the worldly-wise. But to such men Socrates—or Christ—will always seem a crazy fool.

This point is one which Erasmus insists upon. Like Socrates, the Christian fool seems quite insane, not merely silly. This is the drift of 'The Sileni of Alcibiades' as well as of Folly's closing pages. In the *Moria* this madness is described in terms which dominate the rest of the book. It is, we are told, as though the soul had left the body, living elsewhere. Here is the first clear use of this ecstatic formula. In a context where *seeming* is dominant, such ecstasy is talked of in terms of apparent madness: *quod quidem quid aliud est quam insanire* ('And what is that, then, if not to be insane?'). This rhetorical question will be answered. What Erasmus writes here and elsewhere shows that he is not indulging in overstatement simply for the sake of literary effect.

Folly is about to carry her argument into deeper meanings of Christian madness. The selfless conduct of the Christian fool, as Folly has just described it, is in itself an ecstasy, an apparent departure of his soul from its body, leading to an apparently insane selflessness. St François de Sales, although writing over a generation later, makes this so clear that he is worth quoting to clinch the matter: this kind of ecstasy—without which, he writes, other ecstatic experiences are at worst false and at best dangerous—is *l'extase de l'œuvre et de la vie* (that form of ecstasy which manifests itself in good works and in a selfless way of life). Such an ecstasy makes a man or woman to live a life 'which is in every way outside of and above our natural condition'. Some virtues are in accordance with natural reason: not to steal or to do no murder; to say one's prayers or to honour one's father and one's mother. But to leave all one's goods, to embrace poverty, opprobrium, martyrdom, chastity, going against the current of a hostile world—that is to live above the level of ordinary humanity:

That is not to live in ourselves but outside ourselves (*hors de nous*) and above ourselves.

No one can do this 'unless the Father draweth him' (John 6:44):

And so this kind of life must be a perpetual rapture (*ravissement*) and a perpetual ecstasy of act and work (*une extase perpétuelle d'action et d'opération*) (St François de Sales, *Oeuvres* (1669) I. 431).

It was no new thing to insist that the true ecstatic differs from the self-indulgent, pietistic, would-be mystic. He must live in close, practical, sustained and selfless charity with his neighbour. Richard of St Victor—who was as convinced as Erasmus that ecstasy (*mentis excessus*) was a 'sort of foolishness'—was equally convinced that the man who was vouchsafed a rapture (an *excessus*) lives in charity with his neighbour (*PL* 196. 121 6D). Similar doctrines are found most widely taught by spiritual writers—by Meister Eckhart and Henry Suso among others (*Dictionnaire de la Spiritualité*, 2134). In this—and indeed in his general conception of ecstatic rapture—Erasmus was heir to a long tradition, which partly shaped even his reading of the fathers. Not infrequently, this more perfect life of the charitable ecstatic is interpreted in monastic or semi-monastic terms by mediaeval writers: there is, of course, no hint of that even in the *Moria* of 1511.

3. *The madness of Christ: an excursus*

Folly has not pulled her punches. The extreme terms she has just employed, not without a confident smile, emphasise an important aspect of Erasmus' teaching on ecstasy. The person who has been vouchsafed an ecstatic experience, and who lives his life accordingly, does not just seem odd or a bit silly: people take him for a lunatic. This fact is not allowed to be forgotten: words subsequently used keep the idea before our mind: *insanire* (Kan 181); *insanire . . . sanum . . . sanus . . . insaniam* (Kan 182); *insaniae genus . . . meram insaniam . . . insaniam . . . delirantem* (Kan 183); *insanire* (Kan 186); *furorem . . . furor* (Kan 187); *extra se . . . extra sese*; and, strongest of all, *quoddam dementiae simillimum*, 'something most closely like dementedness' (Kan 188). Other less obvious expressions keep this flame burning bright throughout the closing pages of the *Moria*.

Folly's jesting is as constant as that of Socrates. The humour keeps hovering in the background, but it is almost as self-effacing as the smile of the Cheshire cat by the time Folly at last develops the full theme of Christian madness.

The insistence on insanity in these final pages does not come like a bolt out of the blue. Much earlier in her declamation Folly playfully distinguished between the various forms of *insania*, using words and whole phrases which are repeated here in the climax. We were told of two types of insanity, one hellish, the other a great gift of the gods—an *insania* which is blessedly happy (*felix*) and joyful (*jucunda*). And both kinds of madmen find the other kind insane (Kan, 'chapter 38', pp. 69-72; Scheurer D2v°ff.) The kind of insanity which Folly finally praises is a kind of Christian joy.

In the climax of the *Moria* we are dealing with that special kind of *insania* which makes an élite of Christ's disciples seem mad, above all to the many who insanely love this world. Such followers of Christ have been granted the boon of ecstasy. Their master had also been taken for a maniac. Erasmus' Christ is not a gentle Jesus, meek and mild, dressed up in cleanly laundered bathrobes. And nothing can be farther from his conception of Jesus' relation to his family than the excruciating words still bellowed out at carol services by parents and children alike: 'Christian children all must be, Mild, obedient, good as he . . .' Erasmus' Christ is a person of the godhead who emptied himself for the redemption of the world. At best he might seem no different from ordinary men. At worst he seemed a raving lunatic—not least to his relatives—and that in the presence of his mother and brethren.

Erasmus brings home the reality of Christ's misprised manhood in many of his works. It underlies the whole kenotic conception of Christ's person and mission. As such it is implicit in the *Moria* and in authors such as Origen to whom Erasmus turned for guidance. Explicitly we meet this theology in unexpected places and with unexpected directness in some of Erasmus' most important theological writings. For those who thought like Erasmus, Christ was indeed not accepted as a prophet in his own country. On the contrary, his nearest and dearest relations took him for a lunatic.

In later works—in contexts where the *Moria* is rarely out of sight—the madness of Christ is arrestingly brought to the mind of the Christian reader. To give a few examples here will avoid later misunderstandings.

St Mark tells us what happened when Christ came home to his own province to teach the good news of the kingdom:

Then he cometh home. And the multitude cometh together again, so that they could not even eat bread. And when his family heard it, they went out to lay hold on him: for they said, He is beside himself (Mark 3:19-21).

The crucial words for Erasmus are in the last two clauses. People said,

'He is beside himself', and his family went out 'to lay hold on him'. He interprets these words within the fuller context of St Mark's account, during which the people blasphemed saying, 'He is possessed by Beelzebub' (3:22). Moreover, when his mother and brethren came, they stood outside, not caring, or daring, to go within the house; instead of going indoors 'they sent in to him, calling him'. Others passed on the message:

And they say unto him, Behold thy mother and brethren without seek for thee. And he answered them and saith, Who is my mother and my brethren? And looking round on them which sat round about him, he saith, Behold my mother and my brethren! For whoever shall do the will of God, the same is my brother, sister, and mother (Mark 3:29-35).

The original form of the accusation 'He is beside himself' appears in Erasmus' Greek text as *exestatai*, with, as a variant, the normal reading today *exestē*. In his *Annotations* he explains *exestatai* as *mente captus est* ('he is robbed of his mind')—meaning to be mad or beside oneself (*LB* 6. 162F). Erasmus' explanation brings out the accusation of madness more clearly than the Vulgate does, where *in furorem versus est* can certainly mean 'he is raging mad' but could also imply passions such as those of anger.

Christ's kinsfolk, seeing his apparent frenzy, came out to Jesus to seize him. Erasmus' allusions to this are so startling as to trouble some readers.

First one might look at the *Annotations on the New Testament*. The Vulgate reads, anodynely: *exierunt tenere eum* ('They came out to hold him'). In his *Novum Instrumentum* Erasmus renders the Greek much more satisfactorily: *exierunt ut manus injicerent in eum* ('They came out to lay hands upon him'). He glosses this verse in such a way as to bring out the madness: '*kratēsai auton*, that is, *ut comprehenderent eum*' ('to seize him hostilely: to arrest him'). For that is the duty of members of a family (*agnati*), if anyone should begin to be of a disturbed mind (*commotae mentis esse*).'

But it is in two other works that Erasmus makes the violence and tragedy of the scene really vivid. These works span thirteen years of his life. The first is the *System of True Theology* (January 1518). The second dates from his closing years: the mystical commentary on psalm 33 (34), which was published in 1531.

In the *System of True Theology* Erasmus shows that Jesus was not simply confronted with polite incredulity when he came into his own country to preach. He quotes from Matthew to show that local opinion was scathingly dismissive: 'Is not this the carpenter's son? Is not his mother called Mary? Are not his brothers James, Joses, Simon and

Judah? Are not his sisters here among us? Where did he get all this from!' (Matthew 13:54). Erasmus then adds this comment:

And again, elsewhere, his kinsfolk prepare to cast him into chains, saying, as we read in Mark 3 [21]: 'He is raging mad'—*in furorem versus est* (*LB* 5. 114E).

The poignancy of Jesus' rejection by his own family and childhood friends is evoked in greater detail in 1531, in that profound commentary on the 33rd psalm (which is studied in Chapter Six of this book):

. . . We hear that his kinsfolk prepared chains to fetter him saying, 'He is raging mad' (*LB* 5. 382BC).

The Pharisees even accused him of being diabolically possessed (John 8:48).

That is what the Christian fool must expect. These people who would have chained up Christ like a lunatic were not mere strangers; they were his *agnati* or *cognati*; they were, that is, members of his own family. Clericus is moved, against his normal practice, to place a footnote at this point in the *Opera Omnia*, stating that the allusion is clearly to Mark 3:20-1, but that chains are not mentioned there. But they are, if read as Erasmus read these texts, with the help of his chosen commentators. In the *Paraphrases* this passage is explained in ways which link the accusation of madness levelled against Christ with the theme of the *Moria*: the members of Christ's own family knew Jesus' mother, his earthly father Joseph and all his family. They though that they knew him to be, in other ways, no different from themselves:

And so, because they were members of his family they thought it was their duty, according to the laws of men, to restrain him with chains (*vinculis coercerent*), as one who was weak in the head (*mentis impotens*) and seized by a spirit. *For they said, He is beside himself.* For those who, despising all earthly things and even life itself, embrace the heavenly philosophy with all their heart, seem mad (*insani*) to those for whom nothing is pleasant but the earthly and perishable (*terrenum ac caduca*). He who pours out his inheritance for the poor is mad (*insanit*) in the opinion of the man who places the defence of his life in riches. The man who, for the Gospel, willingly exposes himself to exile, poverty, imprisonment, torturing and death, in hope of eternal blessedness, is a lunatic (*furit*) for the man who does not believe that, after this life, there is a more blessed one for the pious. He who spurns the honours of princes and of the people to obtain glory with God, is mad (*insanit*) for those who really are mad (*insaniunt*) . . . (*LB* 7. 183DF.).

Erasmus wrote his *Paraphrases* with the help of the commentaries of Theophylact. He says so specifically in his prefaces. It is Theophylact who explains their emphasis on chains intended to restrain a raving Christ. In his exposition of the passage of Mark 3:20–2 he tells how Christ's family came out and, thinking he was a demoniac, would *desmēsōsin* him—they came out, that is, to fetter him as a madman. *Desmeuō* means 'to restrain with *desmata*' (chains or bonds).

Both Erasmus and Theophylact use here the verb applied to the demoniac who had to be physically restrained in Luke 8:29: 'He was kept under guard and bound (*edesmeueto*) with chains and fetters.' By choosing to use this verb to explain the actions of Jesus' family setting out to restrain their lunatic relation, the pathos of Christ's situation is dramatically and emotively enhanced. Neither Theophylact nor Erasmus play down the apparent madness of Christ: if anything they play it up.

In the Renaissance—and not only in Italy—the Italian expression *matto da catena*, 'mad enough for chains', was widely used and widely understood. In the eyes of his family, such a madman was Christ. The Paraphrase of Mark 3:21 explains that Christ allowed this to happen, so that his disciples should not find it a stumbling-block, if they should hear their own families levelling such accusations against them (*LB* 7. 183EF).

4. *Christ's apostles: drunken madmen*

Folly, emphasising the way in which pious men live an ecstatic life of self-less charity, asked the question: 'What is that, then, if not to be mad?' This madness—this *insania*—of Christ's followers is, in Erasmus' later writings, anchored in the apparent madness of their divine Master. For, whilst Erasmus' concept of ecstasy includes self-less charity, it is by no means to be limited to it.

By an association of ideas dating from classical and early Christian times, it was easy for Erasmus to pass from madness caused by the soul's leaving, or apparently leaving, its corporeal prison, to mad antics resembling those of drunken men, and then on to St Paul's own appearance of madness before a wise and learned judge:

Quo minus mirum videri debet, si Apostoli *musto temulenti* sunt visi, si Paulus *judici Festo* visus est *insanire*.

And so it should not seem a marvel if the Apostles seemed to be drunk on new wine [Acts 2:13], or if Paul seemed insane to Judge Festus [Acts 6:24].

The emphasis is still on seeming (*videri . . . sunt visi . . . visus est*). The reality was otherwise. This Erasmus brings out in his Scriptural works. Of particular relevance, since it links the sneer about drunkenness levelled at the apostles, when they were filled with Holy Ghost at Pentecost, to the accusation of diabolical madness made against Christ, is the paraphrase on the relevant passage of Acts (2:13). The great importance of this episode within Erasmus' scheme of Christian folly is shown by his taking no less than forty-four lines of the Clericus edition to expound, in one consolidated paragraph, Acts 2:13: 'But others mocking said, 'They are filled with new wine (*musto pleni sunt isti*).' For Erasmus, those who mocked in this way were disciples of those Pharisees who said of Jesus, 'He hath a devil' (*LB* 7. 668cf.). He adds that the kind of drunkenness which puts you out of your mind—*ebrietas vehemens*—is very like 'raging madness' (*furor*). The words used here need to be pressed closely. In the *Moria* as well, *vehemens* is not used simply with the meaning of 'vehement' but with full regard to its apparent etymology (*veho*, bear away + *mens*, mind). (See below, p. 220). A man who is *vehemens* appears to be 'mindless' in a strongly active sense. Similarly *furor*, 'raging madness', is often used, both in the *Moria* and in the *Paraphrases*, with the sense of mad-seeming ecstasy. In his exposition of Acts 2:13, Erasmus makes a sustained comparison between drunkenness and the ecstasy induced by the Spirit. Christ at the marriage of Cana in Galilee changed the water of the Mosaic law into the heady new wine of his spiritual religion. Of course actual drunkenness and ecstasy are different things, but there are close similarities.

As Erasmus asserted in 1526, when defending the spiritual doctrines of the *Enchiridion* in his *Praestigiarum Libelli cujusdam Detectio*, Christ, by changing the water into new wine, produced a draught which 'made spiritual souls drunk: *animas inebrians spirituales*' (*LB* 9. 1561D–citing the fifth canon of the *Enchiridion*).

Ordinary drunkenness *(vulgaris temulentia)* produces four effects: it brings out the secrets of the heart; it leads you to forget past ills; it rejoices the soul and adds strength *usque ad vitae contemptum*, 'to the point of despising life'. (At this point Erasmus echoes the very words we can read in his *Detectio*—a reminder of how interconnected his works are.) Finally, it makes fluent speakers out of those who are normally little able to speak in public. Erasmus invites his readers to see whether Christ's new wine did not produce similar effects on the apostles. It did. And it enabled them, without human help, to confront judges (*praesides*), kings, councils, prisons and tortures. (The link with Paul before Festus is still in his mind.) And it made fluent preachers out of *piscatores et idiotae*, 'fishermen and simpletons . . .' (*LB* 7. 668cf.).

A contrast between the tasteless (*insipida*) law of Moses and the new heady wine of Christ's spiritual doctrine is a frequent theme of Erasmus' most serious Scriptural writings (cf. Paraphrase on John 2:11,

(*LB* 7. 516CD)). An influence on Erasmus here was, I think, Chrysostom, who makes similar points in his *Commentary on Acts*. Erasmus
certainly translates him in a way which links the new wine's effects to
those of folly: 'Others said they were out of their minds (*dementes*),
saying, They are full of new wine' (*LB* 8. 214E; cf. ibid., CD). Erasmus'
bold comparison of ecstatic madness with drunkenness most certainly
owes something directly to Greek patristic writers, for whom it was a
powerful association of ideas. Gregory of Nyssa uses it in his *Commentary on the Song of Songs* (*PG* 44. 989CF.; cf. Daniélou, *From Glory to
Glory*, pp. 238f.). In his *Exposition of the 22nd (23rd) Psalm*, (1530)
Erasmus points out that the apostles' drunkenness was a holy and
sober one, a *sobria temulentia*: they only seemed really drunk to those
who were excluded from the joys of Christ's table (*LB* 5. 344C). The
alliance of the words *sober* and *drunkenness* in the context of ecstasy
shows that Erasmus was heir to an idea which goes back to Philo the
Jew.[1] It is particularly important for Gregory of Nyssa. It found its
way from the Greeks to the Latins. Origen does not use this term,
though, like Erasmus, he associates and contrasts religious ecstasy
with drunkenness (*methē*). The terms the Greek fathers used, *nēphalios
methē*, 'sober drunkenness', is important enough to merit a section to
itself in Daniélou's *Platonisme et Théologie Mystique*, 274f.; (cf. *From
Glory to Glory*, pp 238f.). As the years went by Erasmus owed more,
not less, to such authorities. They reinforce the teaching of the *Moria*
and contribute much to his other writings. Naturally, in the paraphrase on Acts 26:24–5, Erasmus brings out the full force of Festus'
accusation of madness against Paul: the point does not need to be
laboured, but once more, Paul did not seem to be mad in any light,
ironical sense. To Festus he seemed quite insane. Festus took St Paul's
references to his vision and to the resurrection as signs of crazy
wanderings (*deliramenta*): too much study had 'snatched away his
sanity' (*sanam mentem arripuit*). In the *Paraphrases* Paul replies with
dignity and with significant puns:

I am not insane, most excellent Festus. Insanity is to deviate (*delirare*) from the
truth because of a defect of the mind. I am sober; I tell of 'things which are
true'; which to know is *sanitas* ('sanity and health') (*LB* 7. 764BC).

This paraphrase is connected by Erasmus with this part of the *Moria*
as is shown by the words employed. Not only do we have the
reference to sobriety (which almost seems to be dragged in, if the
associations are not recognised), but there is St Paul's talk of 'things

[1] See H. Lewy, *Sobria Ebrietas*, in *Zeitschrift für neutestamentliche Wissenschaft*, Beiheft
IX, 1929.

which are true'. Such 'things' occupy Folly in the lines which immediately follow.

5. *The philosophy of Christ: an exercise in dying*

We have now reached that part of Folly's dense oration in which seeming gives way to spiritual reality. Folly—and Erasmus—believe, every bit as certainly as Plato, that it is the invisible things which really are; as such they are able to be appreciated by man's soul, which is akin to them. Visible and tangible things, akin to the body, share in the body's changeableness, temporariness and eventual dissolution. The spiritual man distrusts them (cf. *Phaedo* 79A–80E, etc.). As far as possible, he avoids the body and separates his soul from its grossness and heaviness (*Phaedo* 67A; 82Df., etc.).

The ensuing parts of Folly's oration are composed of arguments, allusions and authorities so closely interconnected that any dividing of them up for purposes of study becomes even more arbitrary than it has been so far. Folly is now in full flight of her exposition of that Platonico-Evangelical 'philosophy of Christ' which was so dear to Erasmus' heart. The unity of these pages is built around a fusion of Platonic concepts with Scriptural authority. At this juncture there is, above all, one Scriptural text which was fundamental for Erasmus as it had formerly been for Origen. The text itself is not alleged until a little later on, but may be noted at the start. The authority concerned is again St Paul, this time in Philippians 4:8: 'We look not at the things which are seen, but at the things which are unseen. For the things which are seen are temporal, but the things which are not seen are eternal.' These words are open to a Platonic interpretation.

In Erasmus' version of the philosophy of Christ this doctrine of St Paul's is permanently associated with the reality of the spiritual over and above the material, as well as with the truths which Plato sought to convey in his myth of the men bound in a cave, delighting in shadows.

Such themes are now to be embarked upon by Folly.

Sed postea quam semel *tēn leontēn* induimus, age doceamus & illud, foelicitatem christianorum, quam tot laboribus expetunt, nihil aliud esse, quam insaniae stulticiaeque genus quoddam. Absit invidia verbis, rem ipsam expendite. Jam primum illud propemodum Christianis convenit cum Platonicis: Animum immersum illigatumque esse corporeis vinculis, hujusque crassitudine praepediri, quo minus ea quae vere sunt contemplari fruique possit. Proinde Philosophiam definit esse *mortis meditationem*, quod ea mentem a rebus visibilibus ac corporeis abducat, quod idem utique mors facit (Scheurer H1r°; Kan 182).

But after we have once 'donned the lion's skin', let us teach you this too: that the happy state which Christians seek with so many labours is none other than a kind of insanity and foolishness. May the words not offend; rather weigh the thing itself. First of all, Christians and Platonists virtually agree that the soul is submerged, bound in the chains of the body, by the grossness of which it is impeded from contemplating and enjoying things which really are. Next, philosophy is defined as 'practising death', because it leads the mind away from visible and bodily things—both of which death does.

Folly is now going to be shameless—'donning', in a Greek idiom, 'the lion's skin'—parading magnificently about in the borrowed clothes of a preacher (*Adages* 1. 3. 66).

Folly's contention that Christians and Platonists agree on many things is a commonplace since St Augustine's *City of God* (8. 9) and *De Doctrina Christiana* (*CCSL* 32. 2. 40. (60)). Erasmus, with characteristic preference for the authentic over the derivative, does not produce a mere reflexion of the 'Platonism' of Ficino and his school, although his ready Christianising of the basic Platonic concepts may well owe much to his influence. On the whole, however, Erasmus goes back to Plato himself, guided in his interpretation by patristic authors as well as by Cicero, whose *Tusculan Disputations* are particularly important.

It was always a source of strength to Erasmus to have Augustine behind him—in order to regret, for example, that Aristotle, the god of the scholastic philosophers, had been allowed almost to drive out his superior Plato. He uses Augustine's authority to lament the neglect of so good a platonising father as Origen, 'easily the prince of theologians' when it came to eliciting the spiritual meanings of Scriptural allegories (*Enchiridion*, *LB* 5. 7F; 29F, etc.). Erasmus' respect for Plato and his philosophy was no passing fad, destined to fade away as he grew older and wiser. It reappears in his last works as cogently as in the *Moria*. His repeated praise of Socrates is intimately connected with this sustained respect for Plato's spiritual insights. Socrates was, for Erasmus, an inspired, spiritual man who pointed the way to Christ. In the *Ratio Verae Theologiae*, immediately after noting yet again the degree to which Platonic philosophy agrees with that of the Christians, Erasmus praises Socrates for the way in which his life conformed by anticipation to that of Christ—though it is the divine Christ, of course, not the human Socrates, who provides the harmony to otherwise discordant human wisdom (*LB* 5. 92B).

For the understanding of Erasmus' thought this sustained concern for the philosophy of Plato as both a companion to, and an anticipation of, Christian concern with the primacy of the invisible world is an important matter to keep in mind. Insofar as Erasmus was in any way led astray from strict evangelical doctrine it was under the influence of

Plato and his interpreters. For Plato, the body is essentially gross, clogging the soul in its yearnings to aspire upwards to the truth and beauty of God. At times Erasmus confounds this Platonic view of the body with St Paul's condemnation of 'the flesh'. But 'the flesh' for St Paul does not primarily mean the body: it mainly means all aspects of human life which are in opposition to the spiritual. This is a distinction which Erasmus knew, of course, very well. Indeed, it is central to his thought. In later works he takes care to make it with admirable clarity. In the *Moria* he does not always do so. Nor did a multitude of platonising Christian writers always do so, from the earliest times until his own.

Among many works which encouraged this confusion between the body and the flesh were the old Latin translations of Origen; but the tendency was too widespread to put all the responsibility on to them or, indeed, on to Origen himself. By semantic confusions such as these traditional Christianity became lastingly contaminated with Platonism. The doctrines of many sixteenth-century reformers—especially perhaps the Calvinists—were in part a conscious reaction against this. For Erasmus, on the contrary, this centuries-old syncretism was something to treasure. Indeed, for him this *was* Christianity, provided that the guiding light, first and last, was not Plato, nor even Socrates, but God made man in Christ. And on one point Erasmus was never tempted to adopt the language and thought of Plato. For Plato, for the pagan neo-Platonists and for the followers of Pseudo-Dionysius, it was divine beauty which sets the soul soaring aloft. It never is for Erasmus. For him the goal towards which the aspiring soul yearns is the goodness, purity and oneness of God, in whom the soul finds unspeakable joy, as well as communion with his neighbours.

Folly is about to explain that the happiness which Christians seek with so many labours 'is a kind of insanity and folly'. The terms used are specifically Platonic, a reminder that Erasmus is evoking memories of Socrates here, especially as portrayed in the *Phaedo* and the *Phaedrus*. Both these works talk of the body in terms of contempt which are a constant danger to Christian orthodoxy.

It is in the *Phaedrus* that Plato makes the distinction between the two main categories of madness (*mania*), the one being connected with illness, the other with divine enthusiasm. Souls, when they leave their bodily prison—for whatever reason—produce similar effects.

According to Folly, the soul is weighed down, bound by 'the chains of the body' (*corporeis vinculis*). The general allusion is to a Platonic commonplace, that the body (*sōma*) is the grave-stone (*sēma*) of the soul (*Gorgias* 493A). But Erasmus does not make that honoured pun.

He is thinking more specifically of what Socrates said (*Phaedo* 67CD) about the purified soul of the 'maniac' philosopher separating itself as far as possible from the body, living both now and hereafter freed from the body 'as from fetters' (*hōsper ek desmōn*). He is also, I think, recalling what Cicero wrote under the influence of Plato in the *Tusculan Disputations*. Cicero develops the theme of the body being the soul's prison by using the metaphor of a soul 'in chains': when a man dies, his soul will be liberated *ex his vinclis*, 'from these chains'; such souls are to be thought of as being 'released' (*soluti*), since they had long dragged out their existence *in compedibus corporis*, 'in the shackles of the body'. The tone of Cicero in the *Tusculan Disputations* (I. 30–1) is that of Folly. He is almost certainly a source. But the theme itself was a commonplace throughout late classical and mediaeval Christianity, including the western Church. Few writers were more appreciated in the west than Boethius. It is in his *Consolation of Philosophy* (II. 83f.) that the mind of man, his *mens*, is enjoined to free itself from its earthly prison (*terreno carcere*), rejoicing in heavenly things and despising those of the world . . .

Folly does not assert that Christianity is plain madness but 'a certain kind of insanity and folly'. The distinction is that made by Socrates, duly adapted to Christian theology. The madness that Folly is praising is that good *mania* which Socrates saw as a divine favour. Erasmus took care to soften the effect of his paradoxical language: 'May the words not offend: weigh, rather, the thing itself.' But the words *did* offend; he had to point out that he had taken steps to avoid such offence. He vainly took the same precautions, using the same words, *Absit invidia verbis*, in 'The Sileni of Alcibiades', where the spiritual doctrine of the *Moria* is restated on the basis of the same scriptural text (*LB* 2. 773Bf.).

Typically, Erasmus introduces a markedly evangelical corrective to any temptation to interpret Socrates' thought in purely meditative, philosophical or monastic terms. Contemplation is highly honoured. It is indeed indispensible. But, for Erasmus, Christians do not mainly seek the blessedness of Christian joy in cells or studies; they seek it—in a phrase redolent of St Paul's own life—'with so many labours', *tot laboribus* (cf. II Corinthians 6:5; 11:23; I Corinthians 15:10, etc.).

By freeing itself from the chains of the body, the soul, we are told, will be able to 'contemplate and enjoy' *ea quae vere sunt*, 'things which really are'. Erasmus permanently associated this doctrine with II Corinthians 4:18: *non contemplantibus nobis quae videntur sed quae non videntur*, ('We look not at the things which are seen, but at the things which are not seen'). Folly's ensuing argument is dominated by what

Erasmus believed those words to mean. Before tackling that question it would be useful to look at what he wrote in that most famous of his writings, the *Paraclesis* ('Exhortation') which, from 1516 onwards, accompanied editions of his *Novum Instrumentum*. He asks rhetorically: What is 'the philosophy of Christ, which Jesus himself called "being born again"'? It is the *instauratio bene conditae naturae*, 'the repairing of human nature, the foundations of which have been well laid'. The phrase contains a sustained architectural metaphor. Human nature after the Fall of man became like a ruined building; Christ restored it to its original well-founded goodness.

Although nobody taught this more perfectly (*absolutius*) nor more efficaciously than Christ, nevertheless many things can be found in the books of the pagans (*Ethnici*) which agree with his teachings. [. . .] In many parts of Plato Socrates taught that an injury was not to be thought an injury; also, that since the soul is immortal, we should not weep for those who, having confidence in a life well lived, migrate hence to a happier life; and above all, that the soul is, by every means, to be led away from bodily affections towards things which really are, since they cannot be seen (*ad ea . . . quae vere sunt, cum non videantur*) (*LB* 6. sig. *4).

The pagans whose teachings conform in many ways to Christ's definitive teachings include Socrates, Diogenes, Epictetus.

Some strange interpretations have been put upon these words of Erasmus by those who have not recognised how they are intertwined with his Scriptural piety and erudition. Erasmus is not denying original sin; nor is he limiting the rôle of Christ in the redemption of mankind to his expounding of an admittedly higher version of Greek philosophy. Christ's redemptive work is not at issue here; it is his moral teaching and his insistence on the reality of the spiritual world as against the material. There are elements of the thought of Plato, Diogenes and Epictetus which do indeed conform to the philosophy of Christ: but it is Christ alone who achieved the actual *instauratio*, the restoration, of human nature, to the state in which it was well founded by God when man was created, and which will be man's in the world to come. Meanwhile, Christians have a foretaste of this in the new life they lead on earth.

One of the authors who led Erasmus towards such thoughts was Origen, who repeatedly preaches the reality of the invisible in contrast to things which are merely passing and visible. The text of St Paul which especially gives authority to such a philosophy—for Origen as for Erasmus—is precisely, II Corinthians 4:18. Part of this has just been quoted. It continues: *Quae videntur, temporalia sunt, quae autem non videntur, aeternae sunt*, 'The things which are seen are temporal, but the things which are not seen are eternal.'

For Origen the soul, by God's desire, is drawn away from the visible towards the invisible and the spiritual—the *invisibilia ac spiritalia*. Origen then cites II Corinthians 4:18, going on to show that the soul, being incapable of grasping the naked wisdom of God as it really is, does the best it can in this world, with the help of the 'examples, traces and likenesses' of that wisdom in 'visible things' (Origen, *On the Song of Songs*, trans. St Jerome, *PG* 13. 181BC).

This text of St Paul's underpins all the argument which is to follow in the *Moria*.

If that is so, why did Erasmus apparently change *ea quae vere sunt*, 'things which truly are'—things, that is, which really exist—to *ea quae vera sunt*, 'things which are true'? The short answer is: he did not. Both Clericus and Kan do indeed read *vera* for *vere*—'true' for 'truly'. This has inevitably resulted in its being the standard reading of subsequent editions, translations and studies. It is nevertheless not a change that we can attribute to Erasmus' own pen. *Vere*, not *vera*, is the reading of all editions up to and including that of Froben 1515/16 and is repeated in the Aldine edition of the same year. *Vere* is maintained in the overwhelming majority of subsequent editions (including the Froben texts of 1521, 1522 and 1532). *Vera* was clearly an Italian reading—a misprint no doubt. It is repeated, for example, in the Venice edition of 1525 procured by B. de Vitalibus. What Erasmus himself wrote—and what he subsequently stuck to, was *ea quę vere sunt*, 'things which truly are'. The curious effect of the change to *vera* in Italian editions is to associate the phrase with Philippians 1:8: 'whatsoever things are true.' If this is a chance result from a misprint it is in some ways a happy one. But, at best, such an association of ideas is secondary. Erasmus is concerned less with 'things which are true' than with those spiritual realities which *vere sunt*, which unlike the deceptive would-be realities of this transitory world, have a true, a real, existence.

The phrase *ea quae vere sunt* clearly puzzled some readers. What were these things which 'truly are'? Erasmus answered a query on this precise point on 21 June 1520, in reply to a letter from George Halewin, a respected scholarly nobleman who published an adapted translation of the *Moria* in French.[1] Erasmus' reply restates in full the doctrine expounded in the *Moria*:

The part that puzzles you in the *Moria*—in what sense I say that some things really are (*quaedam vere esse*)—will become clear if you recall Plato's fable about the cave and those who were born in it, who admired shadows as real

[1] P. Vidoue, Paris, 1520; copy in BL, *90. h. 15*; cf. *EE* 3, no. 739.

things. Any things whatsoever which are grasped by the senses do not truly exist (*vere non sunt*), since they are neither everlasting (*perpetua*) nor do they always have the same mode of existence (*neque eodem modo sunt*). Only those things really are which can be grasped by the attention of the mind (*contemplatione mentis*). Plato impresses this upon us in many places; Aristotle also testifies to this in his books of *Metaphysics* (*in libris rerum ultramundanarum*). So too Paul, in II Corinthians 4: 'We look not at the things which are seen, but at the things which are unseen' (*EE* 4, no. 289).

The rest of the letter remains relevant, but to quote it now would complicate matters by anticipating later problems.

There is no comment of importance on 'whatsoever things are true' in the *Annotations*. But this verse of Philippians 4:8 is paraphrased in such a way as to bring out the contrast between those things which delight or terrify the world, from which Paul wishes his followers to be free, and those 'things which are true'. Christ's followers must 'with all their souls be vigilant to enrich themselves with the virtues which commend them to God'. Such things include 'whatsoever things are true and opposed to pretence'.

Folly sees the soul as being 'immersed in the body, held down by 'bodily chains'. True philosophy consists in 'leading the mind away from visible and bodily things'. In other words (we are told) 'to philosophise' is to 'practise dying'. Socrates—as every literate reader knew—defined philosophy as 'practising death', since it temporarily detached the soul from the body, so anticipating its final departure (*Phaedo* 80DE; cf. 67D, 68B, 82D–83A, etc.). Socrates was, of course, an ecstatic, passing long periods rapt in thought, his body motionless and abandoned to itself, while his soul was winging its way aloft, contemplating goodness, beauty and truth. Not surprisingly, therefore, his definition of philosophy as 'practising death' makes it into an ecstatic rapture, in the Greek sense of the soul's temporary departure from the body in a kind of divine madness. This detachment from the body arises out of the soul's kinship with things which are invisible and eternal, divine, immortal and wise (*Phaedo* 80A–81A).

The words which Socrates uses for 'to practise' and 'practice' are *meletaō* and *meletē*: in other words, by means of philosophy, a man can be said to 'practise' dying as a recruit may 'train' for war or a budding orator for public speaking.

Folly's term *mortis meditatio* is a successful attempt to convey this meaning. She is soon to use the verb *meditari* with the same sense of 'to practise'. Every time it occurs it is used with this sense. To translate or interpret Folly's terms as though they implied meditation is to weaken Erasmus' thought to the point of parody, making nonsense of some of the most important themes of the *Moria*.

The choice of words is important. The obvious term to use was not *meditatio* but *commentatio*, the word which Cicero employs in that part of the *Tusculan Disputations* which Erasmus is partly following (I. 30). For Cicero, philosophy is a *mortis commentatio*. But *commentatio* is too passive, too cerebral for Erasmus; it means 'a diligent meditation' on something, a 'careful preparation' for something by study. Erasmus, like Socrates, saw true philosophy as something much more active, something much more akin to the training soldiers undergo before a decisive battle. That is what *meditatio* means.

Erasmus delighted in applying to Christianity the ancient patristic term 'the philosophy of Christ'. The full force of that phrase must be seen in the light of the Socratic definition of philosophy.

This conception of true Christian philosophy is already to be found in the earliest edition of the *Enchiridion* (1503/4) which was published by Theodoric Martens of Antwerp in a collection of *Lucubratiunculae*.

Since Socrates in Plato's *Phaedo* thought that philosophy was nothing other than a practising of death (*mortis meditatio*)—that is to say that the soul leads itself away from bodily things knowable to the senses, betaking itself across to those things which are perceived by reason not by the senses—he certainly seems to be in agreement with the Stoics (*Lucubratiunculae*, 1503/4, E6vº; *LB* 5. 14F).

By the time he came to write the *Moria*, Erasmus was far less inclined to give the *beau rôle* to reason except when used of the spirit. He was also more inclined to separate the admired and inspired Socrates from the human arrogance of the Stoics. But it was probably this earlier belief that Socrates and the Stoics were in agreement on this point which explains his adopting the term *mortis meditatio*. Despite the fact that he uses it in contexts of Christian Platonism, the phrase itself is Senecan.

The Stoic Seneca suffered from asthma. In one of his *Moral Epistles* (54.2) he tells us, with a certain ironic detachment, that Roman doctors (noticing no doubt how close the soul was to leaving the body during an asthmatic attack) jokingly called it a 'practising of death'—*meditatio mortis*.

It is probable that this idea, expressed in this form of words, was one of the real debts Erasmus owed to Ficino, despite the fact that it was only marginal to Ficino's Platonism, whereas it is central to his own. Ficino touches on this idea in the *Theologia Platonica* (bk 16, ch. 8):

What [Ficino asks] does speculative philosophy do, other than to summon reason away from the senses? As Plato says, this entire study of philosophy is a practising of death—*totum hoc philosophiae studium, ut inquit Plato, est meditatio mortis.* Indeed, death is the freeing of the soul from the body; it is not terrifying to philosophers . . .

As far as I know, Ficino does not return again to this form of words: Erasmus does, more than once. In both authors *meditatio* is used with the established classical sense of practising not of meditating.

It was with this sense that it entered into the language of the Latin Fathers through Erasmus' much admired Jerome. (*PL* XXII, 598, epistle LX, *Ad Heliodorum*).

As the years rolled by, this conception of the Christian religion as a philosophy, conceived as Socrates understood the term and as Folly spoke of it, became even more firmly anchored in Erasmus' thought. The best commentary on this part of the *Moria* is what he wrote towards the end of his life in his deeply pious treatise, *On Preparation for Death* (1534). There is no sporting irony now: Erasmus, an old man, is preparing himself for death. He writes with a sustained intensity, returning to the same themes which Folly treats in the *Moria*. And this time he takes care to avoid all ambiguities:

'The things which are seen,' says Paul, 'are temporal: the things which are unseen are eternal'. . . Plato thought that the whole of philosophy was nothing other than a *meditatio mortis.* He called it a *meditatio*, that is, a preparation and, as it were, an exercise for death (a *preparatio* and an *exercitatio ad mortem*), no different from that of the *tyro* ('the recruit', or 'the novice') about to fight the enemy, who exercises himself for the encounter. There is no saying more salutary than this one, provided that what was said philosophically by a philosopher be interpreted by Christians in a Christian sense (*LB* 5. 1295DE).

There are eternal truths to be found in purely human writers, he adds, but no state of blessedness. The Christian does not spend his time contemplating Platonic ideas: he fixes his attention on those good things which, through Christ, are promised by God to the elect. Such things are visible to men only through the eyes of faith.

6. *The prophetic gifts of the insane*

Itaque quamdiu animus corporis organis probe utitur, tamdiu sanus appellatur, verum ubi, ruptis jam vinculis, conatur in libertatem asserere sese, quasique fugam ex eo carcere meditatur, tum insaniam vocat. Id si forte contingit morbo vitioque organorum, prorsum omnium consensu insania est. Et tamen hoc quoque genus hominum videmus futura praedicere, scire linguas ac literas, quas antea nunquam didicerant, & omnino divinum quiddam prae se ferre. Neque dubium est id inde accidere, quod mens a contagio corporis paulo liberior, incipit nativam sui vim exercere. Idem arbitror esse in causa, cur laborantibus vicina morte, simile quiddam soleat accidere, ut tanquam afflati prodigiosa quędam loquantur (Scheurer H1r°–v°; Kan 182).

Thus, as long as the soul uses its bodily organs aright, a man is called sane; but, truly, when it bursts its chains and tries to be free, practising running away from its prison, then one calls it insanity. If this happens through disease or a defect of the organs, then by common consent it is, plainly, insanity. And yet men of this kind, too, we find foretelling things to come, knowing tongues and writings which they had never studied beforehand—altogether showing forth something divine. There is no doubt that this happens because the mind, a little freer from polluting contact with the body, begins to use its native powers. The same cause, I think, explains why something similar befalls those who travail close to death, so that they speak prophetically, as though inspired.

It was natural for anyone taking Plato as a starting-point to associate closely together the insanity of those who are mentally ill and those good forms of insanity vouchsafed by God (cf. *Phaedrus* 244). Socrates insists that insanity (*mania*) is a blessing, where its origins are divine; but he makes no fundamental distinction between the mechanics (so to speak) of the various sorts of insanity. All share many characteristics in common.

An excellent help towards understanding how a Renaissance reader could interpret both the *Phaedrus* and the *Moria* where insanity is concerned is the section of Budé's *Commentaries on the Greek Language* devoted to explaining Socrates' term *mania*. Budé shows how deeply interconnected Platonic and Christian (including Pseudo-Dionysian) notions of *mania* were. By *mania* the Greeks included ideas which, says Budé, are better distinguished in Latin. In Latin, he writes, following Cicero (*Tusculan Disputations* 3. 4–5), we can distinguish between that form of *insania* which is widely used to mean folly (*stultitia*) from that form of raging madness known as *furor*. (Budé, *Opera Omnia* 4. 1050. 38f.) This is a distinction which Folly deliberately blurs in order to make her Christian paradox more effective. But the distinction between the man who is *sanus* (sane, in good health) and the man who is *insanus* (insane, in bad health) is an age-old one. Erasmus uses it more than once. Commonplace though it was, he may have owed it chiefly to Cicero. (A danger here is that, since Satan is the Ape of God, diabolical possession has most of the characteristics of divine ecstasy. Only experts can be certain which is which.)

Folly is not now comparing and contrasting a vicious insanity and a pious one. She is drawing comparisons between natural, constitutional madness and a divinely induced one. These forms of madness closely resemble each other in their outward manifestations and in their strange prophetic powers. In other words, while an unbridgeable gulf separates diabolical insanity from Christian madness, only fine distinctions can separate the madness of the Christian fool from the madness of the medically insane. Both, as Socrates saw, can be prophetic; both can be seen as blessings sent to man by the gods (*Phaedrus* 244AE).

The reason why the medically insane closely resemble ecstatic Christian fools is because, in both cases, the soul is striving to leave the body. Since in both cases, though from different causes, the soul is trying to break out of its bodily prison, in both cases also the madness produces similar results. Folly's assumptions are those of Socrates, for whom prophesyings and similar strange phenomena arise from the soul's entering into a closer relationship with divine reality as it leaves its body temporarily behind (*Phaedrus*, 244A–245C, etc.). As Folly puts it (in language which echoes Socrates' definition of philosophy as 'practising death'), in the case of both these kinds of insanity, the soul, 'having broken its chains, tries to be free and practises *(meditatur)* running away'. So even the medically insane may foretell the future or have strange powers to read or speak languages which they have never studied.

Folly explains this in terms of the mind's freeing itself from the contact—or contagion—of the body (*a contagio corporis*). The phrase is one Erasmus probably took over from the *Tusculan Disputations* (1.30) where certain souls are said to have *minima corporibus contagio*, 'only a minimum polluting contact with their bodies'. But Erasmus is not merely playing a Platonic or Ciceronian game. Folly's ideas became even more widely held as the Renaissance ran its course. Readers of Rabelais (a great admirer of Erasmus) will recognise many of these traits in that most philosophical of all comic books, the *Tiers Livre de Pantagruel* (1546). There, the simple-minded judge Bridoye and the real-life court fool, Triboullet, are both true 'maniacs', the judge charismatically insane, the court fool both naturally and prophetically so. But I have studied them elsewhere (*Rabelais*, 1979).

In his scholarly religious writings, Erasmus makes many of Folly's points over again. This is so, for example, where he paraphrases Romans 8:21, which reads: 'Because the creature itself also shall be delivered from the bondage of corruption unto the glorious liberty of the children of God.' In the paraphrase of this verse we are told that Christians are 'freed' by Christ from all 'contagion of mortality' (*liberati . . . ab omni mortalitatis contagione*), a freedom which takes them away from what is gross (*crassus*) and carnal (*carnalis*), and brings them to what is spiritual and immortal (*LB* 7. 803, vv. 21 and 23).

The persons whose souls are freed from restraint in this way do have the gifts which Folly attributes to them in the *Moria*. Erasmus shows that he believes this in other of his writings. The attentive reader will notice that the *insane* fools of the *Moria* are closely parallel to charismatic fools mentioned elsewhere. The disciples at Pentecost seemed 'vehemently drunk'. Such a mind-enrapturing drunkenness is very much like the raging madness known as *furor*:

And it may happen that a man in his *furor* may speak various tongues which he has never learned. And no *furor* is characterised by people being able to understand everything you say (*Paraphrase of Acts* 2:13; *LB* 7. 668CD).

It is true that the crowd were mocking the apostles. 'But nothing prevents you from sometimes telling the truth in jest'—*jocando vera dicere*. The echo is, of course, Horatian.

Erasmus also uses similar terms when paraphrasing Christ's words in John 16:9. Christ asserts that the Holy Ghost 'when he is come, will convict the world of sin—because they believe not on me'. Among the manifest signs of the Holy Ghost which the worldly-wise refuse to acknowledge is the fact that 'those who believe on me, having received the Holy Ghost, speak in tongues unknown'—*linguis ignotis* (*LB* 7. 620F). (Erasmus does not interpret the 'tongues' spoken by the apostles at Pentecost as the gibberish of charismatic glossalalia. The 'tongues' were languages the apostles themselves did not know.)

As for the prophetic powers of those about to die, the idea was a commonplace among writers, both pagan and Christian, ever since the *Phaedrus* (244B–245B).

All this prophetic insanity Folly attributes to the soul's bursting out of its bodily chains, seeking to assert its freedom, 'practising running away from the prison of its body'. These ideas remain dear to Erasmus to the end of his life. They are dominant in parts of the *On Preparation for Death*, where Erasmus is moved to bestow the surname of 'the Philosopher' on Plato, not, as the scholastics did, on Aristotle. This is particularly important when philosophy interpreted as 'practising death' is integrated into the full philosophy of Christ.

Practising death is practising for the true life. This not only confirms what the Philosopher promises, that the soul, being less weighed down, may make its departure from its bodily home, but also, that, being transported by the joyful ardour of the spirit (*alacritate spiritus*) as from a dark and irksome prison, it may leap into blessed freedom and into that truly loveable light that knows no darkness (*LB* 5. 1295F).

The body, being corruptible, weighs down the soul. That is what David meant when he sang, 'Bring my soul out of prison (*de carcere*) that I may give thanks unto thy name' (Psalm 141/2:8).

The normal Vulgate reading of Psalm 141/2:8 is *educ de custodia*, 'Bring out of custody' or 'out of its guard-house'. Erasmus follows the far less common Latin version translated directly from the Hebrew: *educ de carcere*, 'bring out of prison'. That phrase fits Plato's terminology like a glove. Erasmus, like many other Renaissance writers, preferred it for that very reason. He also used it to link David and Aristotle with Christ: Aristotle, 'a philosopher of great reputation', declared that, 'of all terrible things, death is the most terrible'. But the celestial Philosopher taught us, not only with words but with convincing examples, that man does not perish with the death of his body. He is drawn asunder. His soul (*anima*) is led out as from a most troublesome prison (*velut e molestissimo carcere educi*), while his body is destined to live again in glory' (*LB* 5. 1993–4).

Erasmus at times integrates this concept with that of man's two-fold resurrection: in his summary of St Paul's Epistle to the Romans, for example, having noted that glorious final resurrection of which Christ's is the forerunner, he then describes that first 'resurrection' of Christians in this world, by which we are 'brought back to life again' from former sins, 'advance from virtue unto virtue, in this respect, as far as it is licit to do so, practising future immortality (*hac parte quoad licet futuram immortalitatem meditantes*. *LB* 6. 549–50).

To return to the *Moria*, Erasmus still remains indebted to Cicero. To use, as he does, *demigrare* ('to migrate', or 'to emigrate') for the action of the soul on leaving the body is a conscious Ciceronianism. In classical times this usage was possibly confined to Cicero who, moreover, uses the word just before alluding to Socrates' definition of philosophy as a preparation for death (*Tusculan Disputations* 1. 30–1). Erasmus liked the word *demigrare*, using it for example in the *Paraclesis*, prefixed to his *Novum Instrumentum* (1516). It comes in a passage where those pagan philosophers are praised who do have insights into Christian truth, including the fact that the souls of the pious *demigrant* (emigrate) to a happier life (*LB* 6. sig. *4).

Cicero realised that intense joy closely resembles madness. It was this realisation which gave to the word *alacritas*, which appears in the passage of Erasmus just cited, a meaning which goes beyond its basic sense of lively, joyful activity. Its secondary meaning is rapture, or transport of delight. The Christian religion, as Folly presents it, leads to joy beyond compare. Such a joy can be tasted, already in this life, by enraptured Christian fools. Folly's philosophy of Christ finds room for Cicero at this point too. The verb she uses for the soul which is 'rushing out' of its irksome prison is *gestio*, (*ex carcere gestiens*). *Gestio* means 'to use passionate gestures', 'to throw oneself about for joy'. Is there an echo, here too, of the *Tusculan Disputations* (4. 16)? I think so:

There is an avid desire that is always seeking after something, an *inanis alacritas* (inane joyful transport) and a happiness which throws itself about (a *laetitia gestiens*). They do not differ much from *amentia* (a 'mindless madness').

Erasmus was not a future editor of Cicero for nothing. Of course Cicero, an *ethnicus*, did not think much of such joys which disturbed the tranquillity of the philosophical mind. There are times, too, when Erasmus values highly such a *tranquillitas animi*. But not when praising the ecstatic joy of the chosen Christian fool and comparing him to the wise man as Plato described him in a famous myth. As Erasmus wrote on the 4th Psalm, the Christian drinks a spiritual wine. Its effect is such that, even in the midst of his afflictions, 'his soul throws itself about with spiritual joy' (*spirituali gaudio gestiat*) (*LB* 5. 287E).

7. *Pious insanity: Plato's mythical cave*

Rursum si id eveniat studio pietatis, fortasse non est idem insaniae genus, sed tamen adeo confine, ut magna pars hominum meram insaniam esse judicet, pręsertim cum pauculi homunciones ab universo mortalium coetu tota vita dissentiant. Itaque solet iis usu venire, quod juxta Platonicum figmentum opinor accidere iis, qui in specu vincti, rerum umbras mirantur, & fugitivo illi qui, reversus in antrum, veras res vidisse se praedicat, illos longe falli, qui praeter miseras umbras nihil aliud esse credant. Etenim sapiens hic commiseratur ac deplorat illorum insaniam, qui tanto errore teneantur, illi vicissim illum, veluti delirantem, rident atque ejiciunt (Scheurer Hɪvº, Kan 183).

On the other hand, if this happens because of pious zeal, it is not the same kind of insanity, perhaps, but near enough to it for most men to judge it to be pure insanity—especially when a few little fellows, by their whole life, disagree with the mass of all mankind. And so there happens to them the same as befalls those who, according to Plato's myth, are bound in a cave, marvelling at the shadows of things: a runaway comes back into the cave, declaring that he has seen the real things themselves, and that those people are very mistaken who believe nothing but the wretched shadows to exist. Because of this, that wise man pities, and weeps over, the insanity of those who are held in such an aberration. They, on the other hand, laugh at him as a man deranged, and throw him out.

Zeal for piety (*studium pietatis*) produces a madness so close to that of the medically insane that most men think it is the same.

Folly then compares the Christian madman to the enlightened man in Plato who strove in vain to convince his purblind companions of the spiritual realities. The allusion is to one of Plato's most powerful and influential myths, related at the beginning of the seventh book of the *Republic*. Folly has already alluded to this myth once, in 'chapter 45'

(Kan 91; Scheurer E 4r°). On the first occasion Folly with her tongue in her cheek, pretends to believe that men who are content with the shadows are at least as well off as the wise man with his spiritual realities. It was the same with Thomas More's first wife: he gave her imitation jewels telling her that they were the real thing. She was just as happy! (Scheurer E3v°–4 r°; Kan 91). But then, More was a *facundus nugator*, an eloquent jester. In a similar state to More's wife is the typical Englishman who eats rotten fish thinking it tastes like ambrosia. Sadly, Erasmus later saw fit to cut out the word *Britannus* as apparently too offensive to ichthyophagic Britons.

But at the climax of the *Moria* the time for such jesting is over. The myth is now used straight, to show how the spiritual man will always have the multitude against him.

The myth of the cave in Plato was, for Erasmus, one of most vital of Greek spiritual insights. Any feeling that one might have that it was appropriate for use in a literary work but not in works of serious theology is dispelled as one reads one's way through the Erasmian corpus. Ficino also gave an important place to the myth of the cave. But Erasmus' emphasis is very different. A useful and quick way to distinguish Erasmus' platonising Christianity from Ficino's, and to free it from any confusion with it, would be to compare the realities which the two men believed to lie behind the shadows which delude ignorant, carnal men. Naturally, since both are Christianising the same myth, they have much in common. But for Erasmus, these realities are divine realities foreshadowed in the truths of Scripture, spiritually understood; the guide to understanding them and enjoying them is also their end: God, as revealed in Christ and working in man through the Holy Ghost. For Ficino, the cave is inextricably intertwined with the *Prisca theologia* (of which there is no trace in Erasmus); the emphasis is rather on that 'ancient theology' which Hermes Trismegistus and others somewhat ambiguously revealed to antedated men of old.[1]

Plato's wise man, freed from his fetters in the cave, saw the spiritual realities. On his return, he tells his fellow troglodytes that they have been taken in by mere shadows. He is not believed. His fellows laugh at him, not least because, on leaving the spiritual light and returning to the darkness of the cave, his eyes, still dazzled by what he has seen, can no longer see properly the shadows his fellow-men mistake for reality (*Republic* 515D–516A).

[1] Cf. Ficino *Opera omnia*, Basle, 1576, reprinted, Bottega Erasmo, Turin, 1959: II. 837–59; III. 1408ff., etc. (For a scholarly view with a different emphasis, see P. O. Kristeller, 'Erasmus from an Italian Perspective', in *Renaissance Quarterly*, XXIII, no. 1, Spring 1970, pp. 9–14.)

Folly adds a Christian dimension. As she relates the myth, the others laugh at the spiritual man, judging him to be 'deranged' (*delirantem*). He does not laugh at them in return; he weeps over their insane delusions. This is a powerful development of the myth. When Folly first related it, light-heartedly, both parties in the cave laughed at each other. Not so now. The man who really knows spiritual reality is moved to tears of pity by the crassness of his fellow men.

The Platonic cave makes its first Erasmian appearance in the *Enchiridion* (*LB* 5. 40B). It is briefly applied to the majority of men who, bound in the fetters of their passions, admire shadows as though they were the truest of things. Much later, in the *Commentary on Psalm 38* of 1532, it plays a central part in the theology of Erasmus' exposition of the spiritual meaning of the psalm. Erasmus sees both the patriarch Jeduthun of the psalm and the apostle Paul as examples of men who ventured out beyond the cave. And, in 1532 as in 1511, his wise men convict the majority of the world of mere insanity, on account of their preoccupations with shadows (*LB* 5. 453AB).

The verse of Scripture in which Erasmus saw this doctrine most clearly expounded was I Corinthians 7: 31: *praeterit enim figura hujus mundi*: 'For the fashion of this world passeth away.' He himself preferred to render the Greek not by *figura* but *habitus*. In the *Annotations on the New Testament* he points out that the original Greek word, *schēma*, may be translated by *habitus* (state, condition) or by *figura* (fashion, structure). Theophylact is quoted to make the point that nothing in this world is solid; this world only knows the *species*, the 'seeming show', of good and of evil (*LB* 6. 690F).

Apart from specific references to the cave as such, references to its shadows are frequent in Erasmus' writings. The man who is taken in by them remains a wordly madman even when Erasmus sets about paraphrasing Christ's Beatitudes (Matthew 5).

Christ said: 'Think not that I came to destroy the law and the prophets. I came not to destroy but to fulfil.' For Erasmus this fulfilment consists in the superseding of the fleshly, gross Mosaic Law, which has served its purpose, by revealed spiritual truth. Light banishes the shadows. It is foolish (*stultum*) to believe that the life to come will be like the present; it is mad (*insanum*) so to delight in the shadows that you despise real things (*res veras*); so to cling to the imperfect, that you disdain the perfect; so to embrace the carnal that you scorn the spiritual; to be so attached to the earthly, that you neglect the heavenly (*LB* 7. 28C–29A).

8. *'Things which are seen', and the soul's rapture towards 'things which are not seen'*

Itidem vulgus hominum ea quae maxime corporea sunt, maxime miratur, eaque prope sola putant esse. Contra pii quo quicquam propius accedit ad corpus, hoc magis negligunt, totique ad *invisibilium rerum contemplationem* rapiuntur (Scheurer H1v°; Kan 183).

Similarly the crowd marvel at things which are most corporeal; they think they are almost the only ones to exist. Pious men, on the contrary, most neglect whatever is closer to the body: they are entirely caught up in 'contemplation of things which are not seen' [II Corinthians 4:18].

Doctrines such as these Erasmus seldom, if ever, expounds without the support of Scripture. The key text now is, at last, quite specifically, II Corinthians 4:18: *non contemplantibus nobis quae videntur, sed quae non videntur*, ('while we look not at the things which are seen, but at the things which are not seen'). This, as St Paul goes on to explain, is because the things which are seen are temporal; but the things which are not seen are eternal. A major influence on Erasmus, leading him to interpret this verse as one of the foundation-stones of his teachings about the reality of the spiritual world is Origen, who develops this theme with particular clarity in the *Homilies on the Song of Songs*. Rufinus in his translation uses the word *corporalia* for 'things of the flesh' and *spiritalia* for 'things of the spirit'. Erasmus later suggested that his meaning in part of Folly's peroration could best be understood by interpreting what he wrote there in the light of what Origen says in that work (see below, p. 184; *PG* 13. 97AB; 189C, 190C, etc.). The parallels which can be drawn between the spiritual doctrines of the *Moria* and those expounded by Origen are indeed very numerous. The debt of Erasmus is clear. It was openly acknowledged.

When George Halewin was puzzled by the teaching of the *Moria*, Erasmus referred him to II Corinthians 4:18 (*EE* 4, no 1115, 10f.). And when, in *On Preparation for Death*, Erasmus again introduced Plato's definition of philosophy, he immediately preceded it by this same verse of Scripture (*LB* 5. 1295E). There is no note at this point in the *Annotations on the New Testament*—the Greek poses no problems. But the *Paraphrase*, as one would expect, develops the doctrine of Erasmus both briefly and cogently: bodily afflictions are light and passing things when accepted for Christ and the Gospel. They nevertheless bear the weight of ineffable glory, making us worthy of the highest joy and bringing the reward (*praemium*) of eternal life. 'Sustained by this hope, we consider that life in the body is nothing, hardly noticing the things which can be seen by the eyes of the body, but rather only those things which can be seen by the eyes of faith.' The things which can be seen are neither true goods nor true evils; nor are they eternal, 'whereas the things which are seen by the eyes of faith are true and, so, eternal' (*LB* 7. 932AB).

In 1514 Erasmus was to praise faith itself for being, above all, a solid hope grounded on things unseen. This insight was to prove one of the most important of his whole career: cf. his annotation on Hebrews 11:1.

The final word in the sentence under discussion is worthy of special mention. Those who are entirely given over to the 'contemplation of things which are not seen' are said to be enraptured: *toti rapiuntur* (they are entirely 'caught up'). The verb is a very strong one, implying a ravishment like a seizure. The men and women who contemplate the spiritual realities can expect to be snatched away from themselves. It is a word which belongs to the language of ecstasy. When St Paul was 'caught up to the third heaven', the Vulgate uses this verb (II Corinthians 12:2 and 4). Similarly, St Paul tells how, in the Last Day, 'the Lord himself shall descend from heaven with a shout', the dead shall be raised, while 'we that are alive, that are left, shall together with them be "caught up", in the clouds, remaining with the Lord for ever' (I Thessalonians 4:16). Again, the verb is *rapio*. And the same verb is used for the physical rapture of Philip, who was bodily transported by the Spirit of the Lord from Gaza to Azotus (Acts 8:39).

This verb, with its powerful ecstatic overtones, is one which Erasmus often affects. Only a few examples must suffice, but many could be found. Indeed, *rapi*, 'to be caught away', is one of those key words to which Erasmus returns again and again, reminding his readers of the soul-enrapturing effects of the deepest Christian piety. In the paraphrase of John 16:9, Erasmus includes in the signs which ought to convince the sinful and the faithless that Jesus is indeed the Christ the facts that idolatry has been overthrown, that God is worshipped with true piety, that bodily advantages are held to be nothing, and that men 'are entirely caught up towards heavenly things' (*totos ad coelestia rapi*). Such are the effects of the Spirit (*LB* 7. 620F).

In the paraphrase on Romans 8:5 the contrast is made between those who have 'things which are fleshly' in their hearts, and those in whom Christ dwells. The latter, leaving aside fleshly matters, are 'caught away' to the things of the spirit (*LB* 7. 800ff., especially v. 5). Similarly, in the Commentary on the 14th psalm, the progress of piety comes to a climax in rapture: 'For on the road of piety there is a race. . . . The apostle said [I Corinthians 9:24], "Even so run, that ye may attain." The Christian who *walks*, goes forward; he who *stands*, perseveres in the good, ready against the snares of the Devil; he who *runs* is

the man who, with great joy and great fervour of spirit, is caught away
to pious things' (*LB* 5. 301E).

9. *God, the* Simplicissimus: *have as though you had not*

Nam isti primas partes tribuunt divitiis, proximas corporis commodis, postremas animo reliquunt, quem tamen plerique nec esse credunt, quia non
cernatur oculis. Ediverso illi primum in ipsum deum, rerum omnium simplicissimum, toti nituntur, secundum hunc, & tamen in hoc, quod ad illum
quam proxime accedit, nempe animum, corporis curam negligunt, pecunias
ceu putamina prorsus aspernantur ac fugitant. Aut si quid hujusmodi rerum
tractare coguntur, gravatim ac fastidienter id faciunt, *habent tanquam non
habentes, possident tanquam non possidentes* (Scheurer H1r°; Kan 183).

The crowd attribute the first place to wealth, the next to what is useful for the
body, and relegate the last to the soul. Many do not believe that it exists, since
they cannot see it. Unlike them, pious men entirely strive, first of all, towards
God himself, who is most absolutely One. And then, after him, yet in him,
they emphasise what comes as close as possible to him: the soul. They neglect
looking after the body, despising money as so many nutshells and running
away from it. If they are forced to deal with such things, they do so cautiously
and with distaste, 'having as though they had not, possessing as though they
did not possess' (I Corinthians 2:29–30).

We are still being treated by Folly to a sermon based on St Paul's
letters to the Corinthians. The theology is expressed in terms which
remind us how much Erasmus was indebted to traditional philosophical concepts, many of them Platonic, which had for centuries become
embedded in Christian thought. The contrast is made between
isti—the *vulgus hominum*, the crowd—and the Christian élite. In classical Latin the word *vulgus* often comports an accessory notion of
contempt for the multitude. This accessory feeling of contempt is also
contained in the *isti* (those) which harks back to the *vulgus hominum* of
the previous sentence. For Erasmus the 'crowd' does not mean the
great unwashed: it includes among others the men of worldly power,
the cynically successful as well as the arrogant, ignorant, scholastic
theologians of the Sorbonne. Nevertheless this sentence may evoke
echoes of Cicero's intellectual snobbery rather than of Christian
humility (cf. *Tusculan Disputations* 3. 26. 63).

Spiritual men invert the order of priorities of the majority of gross
and physical men. For them, the soul and its concerns are in what is by
far the highest category; the body and its preoccupations find a poor
second place; riches are banished to a despised third. The spiritual man
strives towards God, so fulfilling St Paul's injunction (I Corinthians

2:29–30) 'to have as though they had not; to possess as though they did not possess'. The goal of the spiritual man is God, conceived as *Simplicissimus*.

This title of *Simplicissimus* dominates what is to follow. English translations have let their readers down badly here, using such terms as 'the purest of all existences', 'the most spiritual of all things', or 'who is absolute purity'. Yet *Simplicissimus* is a technical term for Christian theologians, who took both it and the idea it conveys from Plotinus and the neo-Platonists generally, for whom God is the Most *Simplex*, the most uniquely and totally One. But for neo-Platonists God was often thought of as being beyond mind, in which there is already multiplicity. For Erasmus God the Father is Mind at its most absolute. In the *Commentary on the Second Psalm*, Erasmus contrasts the lot of men, subject to the passions, with God the Father, 'who is always serene (*tranquillus*) and unmoved (*immotus*)'. God is free from all affections of the soul; how much more so therefore, from those of the body:

God is Mind (*Mens*); but Mind uniquely so (*simplicissima*); in no wise can he be called a body, unless you use that term for anything that subsists in its own nature (*LB* 5. 212F).

Erasmus returns to the same theme in his *Concio* (sermon) *on the Fourth Psalm*: the Jews of old whose minds were fixed on the letter of the law could not lift up their hearts to the spiritual meanings; in Christ they saw no more than what can be perceived with the eyes of the flesh. The disciples themselves were rather like this, until the Holy Ghost set their hearts soaring aloft to heavenly things. The Greek philosophers were in a similar state; being above all concerned with creatures and angels, they saw what little they did see of truth through a cloud. And much less did they understand the *simplicissima natura* of God; and insofar as they did, it was of no avail, since they did not worship him for what he is. (*LB* 5. 246B.)

In *De Ratione Concionandi* (1535), a work in which Erasmus deals sympathetically with the *Celestial Hierarchies* (without, however, attributing the work to the Dionysius converted in Athens by St Paul), he explains the term *Simplicissimus* with considerable precision. The supreme Monarch of all, we are told, is God alone; his nature cannot be comprehended by men or even angels. No words can describe him, no mental images represent him to our minds; he informs all things, embraces all things, while remaining, himself, *incomprehensus*—neither understood nor in any way limited.

He is *simplicissimus*: there is no wisdom in him, no power, no goodness, no knowledge, no mercy, no love: but in him all this is a uniquely undivided essence (*haec omnia in illo simplicissima est essentia*). If you compare any created things with him, however sublime, they are nothing. He alone really is, who is in himself unchangeable, having no end.

The Persons of the Godhead in no wise affect this supreme unity of God.

It is not detrimental to the *simplicissima natura* of God, when we hear that it is divided into three Persons, the Father, Son and Holy Ghost, since there is one and the same undivided essence in all three, and God is therefore One (*LB* 5. 1073Af.).

The Father is uniquely and absolutely One (*simplicissime est simplex*): unlike the Son and the Holy Ghost he never manifested himself in any way, neither as man (as the Son did) nor as a dove (as, in another sense, the Holy Ghost did).

Whether the whole of this negative neo-Platonic theology is to be read back into the *Moria* is doubtful, but these are the concepts hovering around the term *simplicissimus*. Such ideas help to explain the extraordinary force of what Erasmus wrote of Christ and his foolish apostles in the *Antibarbari*—an early work not published until after the *Moria* (Basle, 1520): our religion did not arise out of the philosophers, the orators, the dialecticians or the mathematicians; 'it was born from Christ, the *Simplicissimus*, and spread by foolish apostles (*ab idiotis apostolis*)' (*LB* 10. 169.5D).

There is here, I believe, a deeply pious pun, juxtaposing Christ as *Simplicissimus* with the apostles as *idiotae*. *Simplex* in Latin also means 'simple'—in the sense, still current among country folk at least, of simple-minded, foolish, backward. In Latin it can be applied to a man who is ingenuous and without guile. In the *Moria* too it may well comport such a half-suggested secondary meaning: the complicated, successful men of the world will always reject as 'simple-minded' the followers of the *Simplicissimus*.

The term *Simplicissimus* applied to God is so widely used in Christian theology that it would be most misleading not to recognise its force. At the same time, it would be even more misleading to attempt to place Erasmus in a specific school of thought on the strength of this word alone. Vives gives an excellent and non-partisan explanation of the force of the word in the section *De Prima Philosophia* of his treatise *De Disciplinis*. (I have used the Lyons, 1551, edition, pp. 465f.) It is the Oneness of the Godhead which is stressed by the word. God is *simplex*: single, uncompounded, unmixed. He is indeed uniquely so; hence *Simplicissimus* is applied to him alone, whereas an angel, like the human mind, is only *simplex*, even though unmixed. This Oneness radiates from God; that is why every single thing is one: there is only one author of all things, one created universe, one human race, one Son of God, one Christ, the Master, Restorer and Saviour of the one fallen humanity.

But, while it would be wrong to attempt to place Erasmus into a school on the strength of the word *Simplicissimus*, it is a term one expects to find in the context of Christian ecstasy. For centuries the term had been most widely diffused in precisely such a context—naturally so, given the profound influence of neo-Platonic ideas on Christian concepts of ecstasy. Erasmus was not an admirer of St Bonaventura, laughing at such titles as the Seraphic Doctor given to him by his followers. But he is very close indeed to Bonaventura's conception of ecstasy. God for St Bonaventura is absolute purity precisely 'because he is *simplicissimus*; he is *simplicissimus* because he is, in the highest sense, One' (*Collationes in Hexaëmeron*, no. 20: *Opera*, Quaracchi 1891, tome 5, col. 426, 6). It is union with this *Simplicissimus* which the soul strives for in ecstasy (ibid. tome 1, p. 41: *Commentary on the First Book of the Sentences of Peter Lombard*, dist. 1, art. 3. quaest. 2).

Ideas such as these Folly is about to expound.

10. *St Paul's tripartite man and the* Summum Bonum

Sunt & in singulis rebus gradus multum inter istos diversi, principio sensus tametsi omnes cum corpore cognationem habent, tamen quidam sunt ex his crassiores, ut tactus, auditus, visus, olfactus, gustus. Quidam magis a corpore semoti, veluti memoria, intellectus, voluntas. Igitur ubi se intenderit animus, ibi valet. Pii quoniam omnis animi vis ad ea contendit quae sunt a crassioribus sensibus alienissima, in his velut obbrutescunt atque obstupescunt. Contra vulgus in his plurimum valet, in illis quam minimum. Inde est quod audimus nonnullis divinis viris accidisse, ut oleum vini loco biberint. Rursum in affectibus animi, quidam plus habent cum pingui corpore commercii, veluti libido, cibi somnique appetentia, iracundia, superbia, invidia; cum his irreconciliabile bellum piis: contra vulgus sine his vitam esse non putat. Deinde sunt quidam affectus medii, quasique naturales, ut amor patris, charitas in liberos, in parentes, in amicos, his vulgus nonnihil tribuit. At illi hos quoque student ex animo revellere, nisi quatenus ad summam illam animi partem assurgant, ut jam parentem ament non tanquam parentem (quid enim ille genuit nisi corpus? quamquam hoc ipsum deo parenti debetur) sed tanquam virum bonum, & in quo luceat imago summae illius mentis, quam unam summum bonum vocant, & extra quam nihil nec amandum, nec expetendum esse praedicant. Hac eadem regula reliqua item omnia vitae officia metiuntur, ut ubique id quod visibile est, si non est omnino contemnendum, tamen longe minoris faciant quam *ea quae videri* nequeunt (Scheurer H2r°–v°; Kan 183–5).

In all these things there are many levels, widely differing from each other. To begin with, although all the senses have some kinship with the body, some of them are more gross than others, such as touch, hearing, sight, smell, taste. Others are farther removed from the body, such as memory, intellect and the will. It is the direction of the soul's striving which gives it its strength. The pious, precisely because all the force of their soul strives towards things which are most alien to the grosser senses, are as stupid as beasts and amazed in bodily matters. (The crowd are strongest in such things, weakest in the spiritual ones.) Hence what we hear has happened to holy men: they drink oil instead of wine. The same applies to the passions of the soul: some, such as lust, the desire for food and sleep, anger, pride and envy, have more to do with the gross body. With these the pious wage a war which allows of no appeasement, whereas the crowd think there is no life without them. Then there are certain passions which are intermediate, and, as it were, natural—such as love for one's father, affection for one's children, relations, friends. The crowd attributes not a little to these. But the pious take care to pluck them from their mind—except insofar as they rise up towards the highest part of the soul, so that they do not love their parent just because he is their parent—what did he beget, apart from the body? And even that is owed to God as parent. They love him as a good man, in whom may shine forth the likeness of that Supreme Mind whom they call the Supreme Good, outside of whom they declare, nothing is to be loved, nothing desired.

By this they also regulate all the other duties of life, so that whatever is visible—even if it is not entirely to be despised—they everywhere treat as being far less important than those 'things which cannot be seen'.

The declamation of Folly has now reached the very foundations of Erasmus' thought. The ideas are not difficult to grasp and they are expounded with great precision.

The structure of Erasmus' moral thought (here and in all his moral writings) is based on a classical commonplace, often associated in the Renaissance with Stoic philosophy but in fact of the very widest currency. It was normal to divide all passions and all actions into three categories: those which are good in themselves; those which are bad in themselves; those—very numerous—which are neither good nor bad in themselves but which can be rendered either good or bad, depending upon man's own attitude towards them. Passions and actions in this last category are often considered to be intermediate between those which are good or bad *per se*. They are variously known as *adiaphora*, or 'things indifferent'. Folly's plea is for the good man to hold fast to the good, to reject the bad, and then so to treat the *adiaphora* that their potential good is realised. The Stoic associations of these ideas often encouraged Renaissance moralists to assume that these 'intermediate', 'indifferent' things become good when treated with 'indifference', that is, negligently. By not making one's happiness or one's ultimate good depend upon them, a man can use them aright in this world. For example, a man may be married; that is neither good nor bad in itself. If he is passionately enslaved to his wife, neglecting his duties to God, the state, his friends, his studies, his avocation, in order to please her, then it is bad. Similarly, celibacy can be a source of pride. Such a moral system was read into St Paul, who wrote (I Corinthians 7:29):

> But this I say brethren, the time is short, that henceforth, both those that have wives be as though they had them not, and those that weep, as though they wept not; and those that rejoice, as though they rejoiced not; and those who buy as though they possessed not; and those who use the world as though they used it not; for the fashion of this world passeth away. But I would have you to be free from cares.

Folly has just alluded to this: pious men use the world *gravatim* (with caution) and *fastidienter* (with distaste) 'having as though they had not, possessing as though they possessed not'. Erasmus has abandoned the Vulgate here. In the Vulgate, the contrast seems to be between those who *use* the world and those who *abuse* it. (The parallel verbs are *utor* and *abutor*.) Erasmus will have none of this, employing *uti* in both clauses in his *Novum Instrumentum* and glossing the second as *vehementer utantes* (using to mindless excess). And when, in the previous verse, St Paul wished to spare men 'the tribulations of the flesh', Erasmus, in a phrase textually recalling the *Moria*, refuses in his *Annotations* to allow this to refer to the matrimonial cares often emphasised by a gamophobic celibate clergy: 'Paul,' he says, 'in his usual fashion, is using *flesh* to mean that which is *pinguis et crassus* (dull and gross), going away from the purity and simplicity of the Holy Spirit' (*LB* 6. 689F–690CE).

Two of the greatest Renaissance exponents of this theology of 'indifference' based on St Paul are Erasmus and Rabelais. (The *Tiers Livre de Pantagruel* makes it into the standard of wise Christian conduct. So did others.) But Erasmus, much more than Rabelais, encourages the wise Christian to spiritualise the *adiaphora*, drawing them away from the body towards the spirit and judging them not by the momentary standards of a fleeting world but by the changeless standards of a Triune God, who revealed himself uniquely in Christ, while still enlightening men through the promptings of the Holy Spirit.

The life of man is lived in the body. All our senses are in some way connected with it, some, however, more than others. Erasmus' platonising tendencies lead him to take it for granted that the body exerts a deleterious effect upon the higher parts of man. For him 'the body' comes very close to being what St Paul meant by 'the flesh'. The only body Erasmus' Christian will ever be truly at home with is his own spiritualised body which he will receive at the resurrection (*LB* 5. 246A).

It is taken for granted that the physical senses—touch, hearing, sight, smell, taste—should be treated with care by the pious man, who, as far as he can, concentrates on the higher ones—memory, intellect, will. The same applies to the passions of the soul. Those that are closest to the body include lust, pride and so on. The pious man avoids these, of course; indeed he wages an unceasing war against them. All his strivings are towards God, the Supreme Good. By such a standard he judges those passions which occupy a middle position. Is it good, for example, to love one's father? Not in itself; not if you simply love him as *parens*, the man who begot you. A 'parent' merely begets the body—and even that, only as an agent of God. What one must do is to love him not as a *parens*, 'begetter', but as a good man who shows forth some likeness of God. (God, of course, is the *Father*.) For outside of God, the Supreme Mind, the Supreme Good, nothing is to be loved; all that we do love should be loved in him. (To render Folly's *parens* here as 'father' is to confuse the whole issue and to coarsen Erasmus' thought.)

Anyone who came to the *Moria* from the *Enchiridion* would have noticed that Folly is saying, with a greater sense of *nuance*, much the same things as Erasmus had expounded in that early work:

Therefore the spirit makes us into immortals (*deos*); the flesh, into beasts; the soul (*anima*) into men. The spirit makes us pious; the flesh impious; the soul, neutral. The spirit seeks after heavenly things; the flesh after delights; the soul after things which are necessary. The spirit carries us away to heaven. The flesh lowers us down to hell. Nothing is attributed to the soul. Whatever is carnal is bad. Whatever is 'animal' is intermediate and indifferent.

Erasmus has taken the standard division of actions and passions, making them conform to a division of man which he owes to St Paul: man is spirit, soul and body. Each of these parts of man corresponds to one of the categories: the good belongs to the spirit, the bad to the flesh; the *adiaphora*, to the soul. The explanation concentrates on the *adiaphora*. The example which is given in the *Enchiridion* corresponds to the one given in the *Moria*: it is not so much virtuous to love your parents, brothers, children, friends, as wicked not to do so. Christians must do at least as well in such things as the Gentiles do under the promptings of nature. Where love of one's parents is concerned, the soul is solicited both by the flesh and by the spirit. The spirit says: 'The parent to be preferred is God; to one's earthly parent one owes but the body; to God one owes everything' (*LB* 5. 19E–20D). Similarly, in *De Ratione Concionandi* true 'parents' are said to be not those who merely beget the body but those who form the minds of their children and instruct their souls in piety (*LB* 5. 1081EF).

Clear though these ideas are, they caused some confusion. But nobody who could understand the *Moria* at all would have been puzzled by such a routine term as *Summum Bonum* (the Supreme Good). Eternal life in God is the Supreme Good for Christians—a Supreme Good infinitely more satisfying than any good imagined by the pagan philosophers; that is a commonplace at least since Augustine who compares and contrasts Christianity with its pagan rivals on just this subject. (It is theme of book XIX of the *City of God*.) There is no need to invoke Ficino or others to explain this particular term, though they do, of course, use it in similar circumstances. The *Summum Bonum* is God, or, from another point of view, the beatitude awaiting the Christian in the next life, when he will be as one with him. God, as the *Summum Bonum*, is also the goal of the ecstatic. For the soul—using 'soul' not in the special Pauline sense just noted, but in the wider sense (also found in St Paul) of the higher part of man—can be satisfied only by union with God. University men had long been used to such ideas. For example, students of St Bonaventura's commentary on the *Sentences* of Peter Lombard knew this quite well—and who had not at least some knowledge of such a work in the late fifteenth century and the first half of the sixteenth century? Bonaventura taught that no finite good can satisfy the soul; for the soul can imagine something greater than the finite. Therefore nothing finite can ever be its *Summum Bonum*. 'So God alone must be enjoyed, because he is both the *Summum Bonum* and the Infinite' (dist. 1, art. 3, quaest. 2, in *Opera Omnia* 1, Quaracchi 1882, p. 41, col. 1). And St Bonaventura goes on to state that it is precisely because the soul was born to perceive the Infinite Good who is God, that it can only find its rest and joy in him.

Christians, and not only platonising Christians, frequently used *Mens*, the Mind, for God in this sense. Just as the spirit of man is often called the mind (*mens*) by Christian theologians including Erasmus, so too, God, who is Spirit, was frequently spoken of in philosophical terms as *Mens* or *Suprema Mens*. It is in his Sermon on the 4th psalm that Erasmus condemns the inadequate notions of the pagan philosophers who never truly worshipped God as God: 'For God is the Eternal *Mens*, to be worshipped therefore with a pure mind' (*LB* 5. 246A; cf. *LB* 7. 529CD, on John 4:24. The *spirit* of man is also often rendered by *ratio*, 'reason'; cf. *LB* 5. 175A).

It was a commonplace that the Christian must live by the standards of God not by the foolish standards of wordly-wise men (cf. *City of God* XIV. 4, etc.). But Erasmus gave a twist to his ideas which some of his contemporaries found hard to grasp. This was because he sought some of his terms in the writings of Origen. To make his meaning clearer, he appended a note to the undated [1515] *Moria*. (It was the last Listrius footnote of all until 1516.) The note is attributed to Listrius, but the hand of Erasmus is visible here, nowhere more clearly. In Kan it has been misplaced and truncated, making little sense.

What Erasmus felt obliged to explain was his expression 'the highest part of the soul'. He does this by expounding St Paul's tripartite conception of man, in the light of what he had read in Origen. So against the phrase the *highest part of the soul* we find the following note:

That is, the spirit. For Paul and Origen his interpreter say that there are three parts of man: the highest, by which we cleave to God and divine virtues, is called the *spiritus*. The middle part, which embraces the things we call *adiaphora*, they call the *anima* (the soul). The third is irrational (*bruta*); it lets in pleasures and all the bilge-water of the vices; this they call the flesh (*caro*).

What Erasmus calls the highest part of the soul (*summa animi partem*)—the spirit—is therefore what theologians such as Bonaventura called the *supremum animi*—the *mens* (*In 2 Sentences of Peter Lombard, dist. 26, art. 1, quaest. 5*, in *Opera*, Quaracchi, II. 642B). The Christian man lives according to his highest nature, the spirit (or *mens*). He shuns his basest nature, the flesh. All things which the pagan philosophers called *adiaphora* belong to the domain of the soul, the *anima*, in this particular sense. The Christian raises such 'animal' things to the rank of the spiritual by treating them aright.

For some readers this may seem to make confusion more confounded. Many readily think of man as body and soul, with the soul (*animus* or *anima*) being the highest there is in man. But the two ways of dividing man are both scriptural. Erasmus, of course, accepts both of them, often in the same passage. He does so here, at this point expounding the tripartite division of man, despite a general assumption of the double division (body and soul). His authority for the triple division is St Paul—not in all of his epistles but in I Thessalonians 5:19–23:

Quench not the spirit; . . . hold fast that which is good; abstain from every evil. And the God of peace himself sanctify you wholly; and may your *spirit, soul and body* be preserved entire, without blame, at the coming of our Lord Jesus Christ.

This text is explained in the *Annotations* of 1516 (*ad loc.*); Tertullian and St Jerome are quoted, the latter to point out that St Paul divides man into spirit, soul and body. But no mention is made of Origen. This silence is interesting. Earlier Erasmus thinks of the division as being at least as much Origenistic as Pauline.

That Erasmus owed primarily to Origen the importance he attached to St Paul's division of man into three parts is certain. Among other things, it is advanced with copious allusions to Origen in the *Enchiridion* (caput 7; *LB* 5. 15–20), where the sources, which are not given in detail, include Origen's commentaries on Romans 1:4–17 (*PG* 14. 847– 68). Moreover there was absolutely no need for him to mention Origen at all beside St Paul in the footnote to the *Moria*, if this were not so. Paul's triple division of man is so fundamental to Origen's whole system of theology that it would be difficult, perhaps impossible, to attribute its influence on Erasmus to particular parts of one particular work. Origen himself was aware that it was a constant theme of his teachings. When he expounded it yet again in his commentary on Romans 9:23 (*PG* 14. 1226AC—only the Latin translation is extant), he alludes to it as something that *saepe jam diximus* ('I have often said already'). But it is worth noting that Origen sometimes links such ideas with the theme of Christian folly. He does so, for example, in the second *Homily on Leviticus*, in which case also only the Latin translation survives. Origen points out that what St Paul calls the 'animal man' is one who, even when not given over to vice, has nothing spiritual within him (*non . . . habet aliquid in se spiritale*): 'That is what the apostle Paul himself says of him: "Now the animal man perceiveth not the things of the Spirit of God; for they are foolishness unto him, and he cannot understand them, because they are spiritually judged. The spiritual man, however, judgeth all things [I Corinthians 2:14]."' The animal man cannot do this: the disciples at Pentecost could—those of whom it was said, 'They are full of new wine' (*PG* 12. 413Df.).

There is no need to believe that Erasmus affected the Origenistic triple division exclusively on the strength of this one passage; but it could easily have been a factor of special importance in the development of his theology between the *Enchiridion* and the various versions of the *Moria*. Yet this reference to Origen in the note to the Froben *Morias* is unique (apart from the earlier allusions in the *Enchiridion*). On several later occasions where Erasmus mentions the tripartite division of man, he attributes it (quite reasonably) to St Paul alone, omitting all reference to Origen. This omission of Origen's name even from the Annotations on I Thessalonians (5:19–23) and the numerous other allusions to the theme apparently arose out of a tardy realisation that Origen had pushed his interpretation of St Paul beyond the frontiers of orthodoxy. It was far safer therefore to cite St Paul by himself. Nothing that St Paul authorises can be heretical. Origen believed, on

the strength of Matthew 10:28, that only the body and soul of unredeemed sinners were condemned to perdition, the spirit being
exempt. The text of Matthew reads, 'And be not afraid of men which
kill the body, but are not able to kill the soul; but rather fear him which
is able to destroy both soul and body in hell.' Origen concluded that
the body and soul of the sinner are destined to be separated from his
spirit and condemned, 'while "the spirit" which does not belong to
him, "returns to God which gave it" [Ecclesiastes 12:7]' (Origen,
Commentary on Matthew, PG 13, col. 1691B, on Matt. 10:28). Such an
idea is abhorrent to later orthodoxy. It is no doubt so as to detach
himself from such heretical associations that Erasmus omits some
expected allusions to Origen. Similarly, when glossing the words
'every soul' (*omnis anima*) in Romans 13:1, he stresses that it means
'every man', absolutely. This reminds us that he did not take the
tripartite division to apply to all of Paul's allusions to the soul, even
though, in this case, no heresy would be involved if it did:

Origen philosophises about this, asserting that soul (*anima*) here means man
with regards to that part which is lower than the spirit, just as flesh is used for
the lowest part of man; so *anima* is to be understood to apply to a man who is
not entirely pure from the things of this world, and therefore must rightly
obey those who govern the affairs of the world. That seems to me to be more
wordy than true (*argutius quam verius*) (*LB* 6. 634. 1). (He is alluding to what
Origen wrote on Romans 9:25; *PG* 14. 1226AC.)

Erasmus clings throughout his life to Paul's triple division. But he
never uses it exclusively, nor as a normative way of interpreting the
term *soul* wherever it occurs in Scripture in general and St Paul in
particular. And he never gives any grounds for thinking that the spirit
of even an unrepentant sinner would return to God, while his soul and
body were banished to eternal damnation (but cf. Theophylact, below
p. 139).

Nevertheless the footnote in the *Moria* is puzzling where the text
itself is clear. St Paul and Origen are talking of parts of *man*, not parts
of the *soul*. Yet this division of man is used in the *Moria* to explain the
term 'the highest part of the soul'. Erasmus has jumped a stage in his
argument, for he believes that not only man has this tripartite division,
but so does everything else. He uses St Paul's three categories in two
ways: to apply to man as an individual person and, where appropriate,
to apply to divisions within his individual soul. This is by no means
evident from the Listrius footnote. But once Erasmus had dropped the
associations of Origen, attributing the doctrine solely to St Paul in I
Thessalonians 5:23, it became an integral part of his own theology,
applying to man as a whole, to his soul and even to the sacraments. It is

likely to pop up at any time, even where, as in this part of the *Moria*, the sacraments are ostensibly being talked of in terms of the simpler double division of body and spirit (or body and soul).

Close to the *Moria* in matters of detail are several passages in Erasmus' works of Scriptural exegesis. When expounding psalm 22/3 Erasmus condemns those who allow their minds to become cold to the things of the spirit. The prophet David warned against this when he said (psalm 22/23:3): 'He restoreth my soul.' The Vulgate version, *animam meam convertit*, 'he turns my soul about', is the sense that Erasmus plays on:

For Paul divides the soul (*anima*) of man into three parts: into the flesh, which inclines to earthly things; the spirit, which strives towards heavenly things; and the soul (*anima*) in the middle which is turned now one way now the other. Of this kind are natural affections: care for one's own safety, love for one's wife, love for one's parents or children, affection for neighbours and friends. Such things are common to us and to pagans, partly, indeed, with brute beasts. Such affections turn the soul towards the spirit, provided that they are applied to the spirit, so that those whom we love, we love in Christ, and so that, should it be necessary, we would prefer to abandon them than to draw away from the love of Christ. If, on account of them, we are drawn away from God's commandments, then our soul is already turned towards the flesh. In order that the whole man may be aglow with the spirit, our Shepherd must turn our soul towards himself (*LB* 5. 341AB).

This quotation is not an isolated echo of the theology expounded in the *Moria*. Such ideas are for Erasmus, in the strictest sense of the term, an essential part of the philosophy of Christ. This can be seen from the words which he puts into Christ's own mouth in the long paraphrase of Matthew 5:20 ('If thy right hand offend thee, cut it off'). Since Christ in the *Paraphrase* says what he says in the first person, he sounds like a philosopher who has just read his Origen. Erasmus' Christ is careful to state that he does not want anyone actually to amputate a limb: nor is any part of the body bad in itself; what is condemned is misuse of the body. Christ tells us that he is really talking about the soul (*animus*), anyway:

I am talking of the members of the soul: for the soul also has harmful members, which it is pious to cut off as quickly as possible. When you have amputated a limb from the body, apart from the pain there is the additional loss that, once you have cut if off, it can never be restored. But cut off the harmful members of the soul—such as hate, anger, lust, ambition, avarice—then not only is the soul not mutilated but, once you have cut off its unnatural and harmful parts, it is more complete. And perpetual pleasure follows upon the brief trouble of cutting them off. I will explain myself more fully, so that you may know what I mean. The passions (*affectus*) are the members of the soul. There are some passions which, by their very nature, lead towards impiety, such as anger, hatred, malice, coveting other people's goods. If any one of these begins to put forth shoots in the soul, it is to be cut off at once. It will be cut off more easily and more safely if you do it as soon as the evil is born. There are also passions which are in no wise bad in themselves but which, at times, may lead you away from that which is best: such are love for your country, love for your wife, your children, your parents as well as other relations or friends; there is also care for your reputation. If these members help the man who is hastening towards evangelical perfection, there is no reason to cut them off. My teaching does not fight against the natural affections: it restores nature to its former purity. However, if it should chance to happen that your love for your parents, wife or children should at any time hinder you from applying yourself to evangelical piety, drawing you back to the world, then cut away that harmful dutiful affection . . . (*LB* 7. 31F–32C).

What is being cut away is a *pietas*, a dutiful affection. But even such apparently good things may be turned more towards the body than the spirit. These ideas—identical to those expounded by Folly—must have been vitally important for Erasmus to make Christ wordily philosophise this way. He temporarily forgot that Christ avoided technicalities, preaching his doctrines to simple and uncouth men. What would the *idiotae* have made of all this?

Erasmus is obsessed by this theme. This study is not an anthology of all the passages in Erasmus' other writings where similar or identical themes are treated, so I must stop somewhere. But one more must be mentioned. Everything indicates that these ideas, already rooted in the *Enchiridion* took on a new urgency for Erasmus about the time that the *Moria* was first conceived and written, growing in intensity during the gestation of the 1514 *Moria*, the additional adages of 1515 and the *Novum Instrumentum* of 1516. As already suggested, the long and profound essay 'The Sileni of Alcibiades', which was included in the *Adages* (3. 3. 1.) from 1515 onwards, has an especially close relationship to the theology expounded by Folly, stressing as it does divine folly and seeing Socrates as a pointer to the supreme folly of Christ. The doctrines being studied at this point reappear in detail in 'The Sileni of Alcibiades'. The grossness of the body is presented as the source of the trouble besetting the spiritual man. This notion is applied to 'the body' but especially to 'the flesh'. Both Socrates and St Paul contribute to this. Socrates was a joke to the unphilosophical: yet when one opened the Silenus one found in him divinity (*numen*) rather than mere humanity. In the *Phaedo* he was shown jesting on his death-bed. It was as though, having drained the hemlock, he had taken a medicine, 'already feeling the benefit of health (*sanitas*) as he went out from his body, whence all the ills of the soul spring and sprout forth' (*LB* 2. 771AB). With these terms Erasmus is again making serious play on *sanus* (sane, healthy) and that good insanity which is death. The soul in death leaves the earthly body behind, as it strives to do in the practising of philosophy.

The Christian is contrasted with the worldly-wise because of his respect for things which cannot be seen with the eyes of the body; the body and its affairs are either neglected entirely by such a pious man or placed last in his consideration (774D). St Paul's division of man is cited again (as the flesh, the soul and the spirit), and the same conclusions are drawn from it (774Ff.). The worldly man, rejecting Paul's repeated counsels 'prefers gold to learning, an ancient family to an honourable one, bodily endowments to those of the soul, ceremonies to true piety, the decrees of men to the precepts of Christ, the mask to the truth, shadows to realities, the counterfeit to the natural, the merely passing to the solid, the momentary to the eternal' (775A).

These are ideas which Erasmus connects with the 'passing frame' of this temporary world, which the spiritual man uses as though he used it not, precisely because it has no lasting value.

Erasmus had a message to preach. He preached it untiringly.

The influence of Origen is real and profound—he is named in 'The Sileni of Alcibiades' as well as in the *Enchiridion* and the *Moria*. But Erasmus believed that the heart of the philosophy he was expounding was, at base, the very stuff of what he had learned as a boy, before he had read a word of Origen. If he was correct in this belief, then he remained for ever true to something he had learned from the Brethren of the Common Life. He was irritated by those who cast doubts upon the orthodoxy of such basic teachings. This can be best seen from his scathing replies to the adverse criticisms and the condemnations of Noël Béda, who had drawn up a seemingly endless catalogue of the errors he claimed to have found in Erasmus' writings. At the time Béda was a man of power, the head of the Sorbonne and the leading, though very shrouded, light of the powerful Collège de Montaigu. His later disgrace and banishment were unthinkable events, hidden in the future (1533–5). The book in which Erasmus counter-attacked this powerful enemy was published in Basle in 1527 under the title of *Supputationes Errorum Natalis Beddae*. In it he 'reckons up' all of Béda's errors and replies to them. In his 177th article of condemnation, Béda had criticised a passage of the paraphrase on I Corinthians 15:45. The original says, (citing Genesis 2:7): 'The first man Adam became a living soul. The last Adam became a life-giving spirit.'

In his paraphrase, Erasmus uses terms identical to those found in the

Moria. The body which is buried is *crassus* (gross) and *piger* (sluggish), and so, in life, it was often a burden to the soul. Christ's salvation consists in spiritualising both the soul and the body. The paraphrase then explains this idea:

This gross and earthy body we receive from the originator of our race, that former Adam who, being made out of clay, was under the penalty of earthly passions. But, truly, there is a second Adam, the originator not of our birth but of our rebirth; since he has a heavenly origin, he was free from all polluting contact [all *contagio*] with earthly desires. We read in Genesis that the first Adam was created so that he might live for the good of his soul (*anima*)—but in such a way that the soul, being as it were bound to the gross body, may do nothing except through the organs of the body or, at least, through something material. But, after him, the Second Adam was vouchsafed to man; since he was conceived by the Holy Spirit, the life he imparts to his own is not this gross one, which has much in common with the beasts, but a life spiritual and divine (*LB* 7. 910D–F).

The sting in Erasmus' reply to Béda is in his assertion that he is really repeating what he had learned as a schoolboy. And yet the syndic of the Sorbonne claims to find him censurable!

At this point we are called back by Béda to the memory of what I learned when I was fifteen years old: whether the soul (*anima*) can, while it is in the body, do anything at all without the assistance of the body.

In his biting explanation of such allegedly elementary matters for the illustrious, aggressive, censorious syndic, Erasmus rather confusingly uses both *animus* and *anima* to mean the soul, while also using *anima* to mean the middle part of the *animus*. But apart from that his account is clear enough, though quite technical. It would serve just as well for a footnote to the *Moria* as it does for a reply to Béda's ignorant condemnations. First he asserts that the entire body is the instrument of the soul. He then postulates two sets of powers or affections within the soul—'or, as some call them, senses'. There are the external ones, such as sight, hearing, taste, smell, touch. Then there are the internal ones, such as to love, to hate, to be angry, to covet; further, there are ones which are internal to these also, such as imagination, memory and recollection. These ideas are explained with detailed reference to Aristotle, including quotations from books 1 and 3 of *De Anima* (cf. 1515 *Moria*, X2v°). And Erasmus throws in Béda's teeth the scholastic maxim 'There is nothing in the mind which was·not first in the senses'. That the soul uses the senses of the body and that, while it is bound to the body, it is impeded by bodily affections, he supports by citing the

Wisdom of Solomon [9:15]: 'For the corruptible body weigheth down the soul, and the earthly dwelling presseth heavy on a mind thinking many things.' Erasmus reminds Béda that he is dealing primarily with the affections which can lead a man to sin and which are shared with the brute beasts. It is probable that it is the same substance within man which feels, desires, remembers and understands. Nevertheless the word animal (from *anima*) is used for the affections which we share in common with the beasts. Similarly, the power of understanding is called *logos*. Since he is replying to the Greekless Béda, Erasmus insultingly explains even the most elementary terms:

So the power of understanding is called *logos* (that is, *ratio*), or *nous* (that is, *mens*), a term we often render by the word *sensus*. And, indeed Paul divides the affections of men into three parts, the soul, the flesh and the spirit. He calls those men 'animal' who are led by their human affections [I Corinthians 2:14], and the body which is exposed to harm from these affections he calls 'animal' [I Corinthians 15:44–6]. James [3:15] similarly calls 'animal' such wisdom as lacks the spirit of God but which is puffed up by faith in human reason; and Jude calls men *animales* who are void of the spirit [1:18–19]. A censor ought to weigh carefully what I was treating, against the tenor of what I was talking about. And he ought not to be ignorant of the language of the Holy Scriptures.

All Béda did was to think of Aristotle, who wrote dubiously about the soul! After citing the actual words of his paraphrase, Erasmus concludes: 'You see how far I am from what Béda dashed in to attack' (*LB* 9. 685c–687a).

In Erasmus, the word *soul* can mean several things. In the *Moria* and in many other of his works it often means what it means in St Paul in I Thessalonians 5:23. That text is vital to the economy of man's salvation which Folly is about to expound. When man is restored by Christ to his pristine state, the spirit redeems the soul; the soul the body. This applies to some extent and in different degrees to both of the resurrections available to man: the sacramental resurrection of the Christian to a new life in this world: and, definitively, to the final resurrection of the complete man at the end of the world.

The full scriptural force of Erasmus' teaching risks being partly hidden from English readers. Such terms as *animalis homo* correspond to what in English is usually called the 'natural' man—that is the translation usually adopted in the Authorised Version. Both 'natural' and 'animal' risk misleading modern readers, but the term 'animal' is preferred in this study, where it is always used in Erasmus' scriptural sense. The term 'natural' now evokes no echo at all of 'soul' and so is even more inadequate than 'animal'.

Erasmus did not keep such ideas in a special category reserved for a philosophically minded élite. His Christ expounded them to the simple faithful in the *Paraphrases*. So too did he in his would-be elementary *Catechism on the Creed* (1533). There we read that 'the eye of faith' above all stretches forth towards Christ. 'Charity has, as it were, two eyes, the right reaches forth to God, the left turns aside to one's neighbour; the one, loving God above all things as the *Summum Bonum*, the other cherishing his neighbour on account of God' (*LB* 5. 1135). And God the Father, is, of course, presented as the *Mens* towards whom the spirit—or *mens*—of man must strive (*LB* 5. 1143D).

The Origenesque flavour of the theology is recalled by the last phrase of the passage quoted at the beginning of this section:

. . . so that whatever is visible . . . they everywhere treat as being far less important than those 'things which cannot be seen'.

Here, yet again, we are given an echo of II Corinthians 4:18: 'We look not at the things which are seen, but at the things which are not seen.' Erasmus is careful to correct the Vulgate at this point in his *Novum Instrumentum*. When, in the same verse, St Paul explains why the Christian attaches importance to 'the things which are unseen' he stresses that 'the things which are seen' are merely passing phenomena. The word he uses is *proskaira*. The Vulgate renders this as *temporalia* ('belonging to time', 'temporal', 'lasting but a time'). Erasmus rejects this for *temporaria*, which more sharply contrasts them with eternity. He points out that it is the word the Gospels apply to the seed which is choked by the thistles of worldly cares in the parable of the Sower (*LB* 6. 765F, 31). The paraphrase of this verse brings out the full contrast between 'momentary' afflictions and that highest ever-lasting joy which can be man's reward (*LB* 7. 923AB).

Folly gives her rule as one which must govern the whole of the Christian's morality: 'By this rule they regulate all the duties of life.' In no part of the *Moria* is the identity of views with the doctrine of the *Enchiridion* more evident or more important. Folly is repeating the rule with which the Christian knight arms himself at the outset of the fifth canon of the *Enchiridion*:

We will add a fifth rule, as a reserve; you should establish perfect piety in one thing only: you should always strive to advance from things which are seen (which are normally either imperfect or intermediary), to things which are unseen . . .

The Scriptures dominate the Christian man's search for the things that are unseen; but so too does Socrates, approached as a Silenus. The

Scriptures themselves, we are warned, also have their 'flesh' and their 'spirit'. God hates what is *pinguis et crassus*, stolid and gross. Here again we have that significant alliance of words, found not only in the *Enchiridion* and the *Moria* but in many other places, including the *Annotations on the New Testament*. For example, when explaining the words *tēi sarki* in I Corinthians 7:28, Erasmus notes that they mean 'of, or in, the flesh', Paul often using the term 'flesh' for what is *pinguis et crassus* (*LB* 6. 689F). So too, the sacraments of the Church have inner spiritual meanings, but are effected by religious actions marked by liturgical ceremonies.

The Christian must be on guard against the seductions of 'the flesh', not least when piously approaching the sacraments themselves. To be content with what is *pinguis et crassus* in baptism or the eucharist is to render them ineffective. Ceremonies are in themselves indifferent; they are often pernicious unless they serve spiritual ends. Neither baptism nor the Mass can be reduced to superstitious attachment to their ceremonial aspects. Similarly, too, with Holy Writ. The letter may kill when the spirit is in the allegory, absolutely or primarily. The guides which the Christian takes to help him to understand the allegories and obscurities of Scripture are not his own conjecture, but (in the *Enchiridion*) Dionysius on *The Divine Names*, St Augustine in *De Doctrina Christiana*, and Origen. St Paul is Erasmus' principal guide—he does not say so specifically at this point: that is assumed. But Origen is highly praised indeed in the *Enchiridion*, being closely associated with Christ and St Paul:

It was the apostle Paul who, after Christ, opened up certain streams of allegory, followed by Origen, who in this part of theology easily occupies the first place.

Moderns cannot compete with the ancient fathers; they were enlightened by Platonic philosophy: moderns are hampered by Aristotelian scholasticism.

Only a withdrawal from Dionysius—and that a real but a partial one—separates this doctrine from what Folly proclaims as the guiding rule for Christian fools in the *Moria*. Pseudo-Dionysius played an important part in Erasmus' early attachment to the spiritualising of Christian doctrine. Even when he was no longer an authority to quote in the same breath as Origen or Augustine, he was but partially eclipsed: he was never totally blotted out.

All this philosophical theology has not taken us away from the main thread of Folly's concern with ecstatic piety. On the contrary, it is about to be reinforced.

Meanwhile, with a return to strong words, we are told how spiritual men are 'as stupid as beasts' (*obbrutescunt*)—a verb implying a loss of bodily sensation as they rapturously concentrate on 'invisible realities'. Such men are so intent on higher things that they may absentmindedly drink oil from their lamps as though it were wine. This rather cryptic activity is vaguely explained by 'Listrius' in a note as something which happened to St Bernard while he was meditating on Scripture. Erasmus' story of oil drunk absentmindedly as though it were wine is a somewhat garbled memory of what was told of St Bernard in at least two accounts of his life. The closer of the two is that of Galfridus, a monk of Clairvaux who later became its abbot. Galfridus tells of St Bernard's inner beauty, and how it resulted in an emaciated body and a neglect of physical things. Such natural fire as he had was entirely consumed in meditation and study. He was so free from the temptations of the palate that he had virtually lost all power to distinguish foods by their taste. 'Once, when oil was given him to drink in mistake for wine', he was quite unaware of what had happened. Only by chance was it known that he had drunk the oil, when the signs of it were noticed on his lips (*PL* 185. 303C–304D). Similarly, William of Saint-Thierry relates in another account of his life how Bernard, in the course of an illness, was attended by a brutally negligent doctor. The saint was so 'absentminded' that for several days, without knowing it, he ate lard instead of butter. He also drank oil as though it were water. (He could only taste water at best.) Erasmus' general judgment rings true of what is told of Bernard's otherworldliness. William lays great stress on the saint's spiritual abstraction: when he was rapt in contemplation Bernard scarcely allowed enough scope to his bodily affections for him to remain in contact with ordinary men. Not only had he tamed his carnal desires; he had virtually benumbed his senses. 'When wholly absorbed into the spirit, with all his hope directed towards God and his memory entirely occupied with spiritual endeavour (*intentio*) or meditation, then, seeing he did not see, hearing he did not hear. When he ate he tasted nothing. He had virtually no bodily feeling at all' (*PL* 185. 238BD).

Such is the ideal Christian man whom Folly is setting before us and against whose standard lesser men may compare themselves. The word that William of Saint-Thierry uses for St Bernard's spiritual endeavour, *intentio*, is cognate with the verb that Erasmus uses when Folly asserts that the *animus* of man is most strong 'in those things towards which it spiritually strives' (*ubi se intenderit*). The term is a technical one in Christian Latin, including mediaeval and Renaissance religious writing, and is so used by Erasmus. It has nothing to do with 'intention' or 'inclination' in any current modern sense. It implies a stretching forth of the soul, the spirit or the mind away from the body towards the higher truths to be found in heavenly things. The *New English Dictionary* (s.v. *intention*) provides an excellent and relevant quotation from Thomas à Kempis as translated into English about the middle of the fifteenth century (*Imitation of Christ* 3.30): 'Nevere to relesse the soule fro *intencion* of hevenly thinges.' This meaning partially lingers in the 'intention' for which a eucharist may be celebrated.

St Bernard, like the ideal Christian man of Thomas à Kempis and Folly, keeps the soul's 'intencion' on 'heavenly thinges'. This is emphasised by the Listrius footnote, which explicitly states that the saint mistook oil for wine when he was meditating *intentissime*, 'with the maximum spiritual endeavour'. A man who does this neglects the body. Indeed, at the highest level such a man is an ecstatic, his spirit abandoning its body while he 'stretches out' towards things eternal and invisible—things despised by 'animal' man. William of Saint-Thierry was especially well-placed to appreciate this. The *Dictionnaire de la Spiritualité* (p. 2115) sees him as in some ways indebted to the last, faint glows of Plotinian influence. And he, too, appreciated the tripartite views of man—in his case, the division is into the carnal, the reasonable and the spiritual; for him, saintly endeavour consists in the cultivation of the spirit above all else.

Such links with the ecstatic tradition form an important strand in Folly's account of Christian folly. For St Bernard was not a typical, ignorant, aggressive, lay-about monk of the kind which Erasmus believed the majority of his contemporary religious to be. He is picked out for particular praise in the letter to Paul Volz, dated 14 August 1518 but prefixed to the July 1518 and subsequent editions of the *Enchiridion*. Together with St Benedict he is held up as an example of a man who withdrew from a world where ambitions reigned and where charity was growing cold, in order to practise a pure and simple Christian life (*EE* 3, no. 888, lines 512ff., including variant H).

Erasmus' piety becomes far less bookish, far warmer and far more at home in the western tradition because of this discreet place of honour reserved for St Bernard of Clairvaux. On the whole the western Church of his day was not yet ready to appreciate the unadulterated force of the theology of the Greek fathers, though such influence was growing. Thomas More appreciated it as superior to the Latin variety, and texts and translations were regularly being published. St Bernard, precisely because he was the 'last of the fathers', is a bridge over which Erasmus could lead his readers towards a warmer appreciation of a theology, lack of contact with which had impoverished the western Church almost to the point of spiritual dessication.

11. *The Body and the Spirit of the Sacraments*

Ajunt autem & in sacramentis, atque ipsis pietatis officiis, corpus & spiritum inveniri. Velut in jejunio non magni ducunt, si quis tantum a carnibus coenaque abstineat, id quod vulgus absolutum esse jejunium existimat, nisi simul & affectibus aliquid adimat, ut minus permittat irae quam soleat, minus superbiae, utque ceu minus jam onustus mole corporea spiritus, ad coelestium bonorum gustum fruitionemque enitatur (Scheurer H2v°; Kan 186).

They say too that a body and a spirit may be found in the sacraments and in the actual duties of religion. In fasting, for example, they do not think it is very important if anyone should abstain from meat and from dinner—for the crowd that *is* fasting, absolutely—unless it frees them somewhat from their passions, so that they allow less scope than usual to anger, less to pride; so, too, that their spirit, being less burdened by the weight of the body, may strive upwards towards a taste and enjoyment of the good things of heaven.

Rather disconcertingly Erasmus passes abruptly from the tripartite division to a simpler double one, body and spirit. This makes a sharp contrast between the unredeemed literalness of carnal man and the spiritual insights of the Christian fool. In the *Enchiridion* it has a section to itself: '*Chapter 6: On the Inner and the Outer Man; and on the Two Parts of Man According to the Holy Scriptures*'; it immediately precedes the chapter on the 'Origenistic division' of man into spirit, soul and body (*LB* 5. 15E–20E). The contrast between the flesh and the spirit is based on St Paul (including Galatians 5:16–17 and Romans 8:13).

This doctrine is given pride of place in the paraphrases of Romans 8 and Galatians 5. For Erasmus, ceremonial and ritual observances—even those celebrated during the most venerable sacraments of the Church—have no value whatsoever when divorced from the spirit. The full shock of this doctrine—which again owes much to Origen—can only be felt when one recalls that many of his readers had been schooled to believe, as a matter of fundamental faith, that the actual performances of ritual observances constituted an efficacious sacrament, *ex opere operato*. In the paraphrase of Romans 8:9, Erasmus spells his doctrine out where baptism is concerned, speaking directly in the name of Paul: 'You are spiritual, provided that you live in such a way that the spirit of God deigns to live in your hearts. A man is baptised; but that pertains only to the flesh, unless he drink the spirit of Christ and be inspired by the Holy Spirit. We are joined to Christ by the spirit, not by ceremonies . . .'

The continuity of Erasmus' doctrine as expounded by Folly is shown in the paraphrase of Galatians 5:15. This was the text of Paul cited in the *Enchiridion*; it underlies the passage of the *Moria* which concerns us now. St Paul wrote: 'Walk by the spirit, and ye shall not fulfil the lusts of the flesh.' The spirit is contrary to the flesh, 'But if ye are led by the spirit, ye are not under the law.' The law, for Erasmus, here as always, means not only the law of Moses, but Christian observances which he believes to be like it.

. . . Take care to live your life by the guidance of the spirit. If you do, you will refrain from the things which the lusts of flesh entice you towards. A man is one person but has a gross, heavy body and a heavenly, immortal spirit. So, too, in one Law there is a gross element which we call the letter and, opposed to it, a heavenly element we call the spirit. Similarly, in the soul of man there is a force calling him towards honourable things and another force opposed to this, akin to the body and the letter, urging us to an opposite mode of life. Between these two there is a ceaseless war, as the flesh resists the spirit: the spirit, the flesh (*LB* 7. 963D–964AB).

This last sentence recalls the actual words of the *Moria*, in which the pious wage 'perpetual war' against the fleshly passions of the soul. But, more clearly than Folly's oration, the paraphrase reminds the reader that, in this sense, the 'flesh', too, is as invisible as the spirit.

Such links with both future and previous works help readers to keep constantly in mind that the *Moria* is not a light-hearted piece of writing of a man taking a holiday off from his principal concerns. Indeed, the germ of this part of the *Moria* is to be found, textually, in the fourth canon of the *Enchiridion*, where it is pointed out that even learning is indifferent in itself, only being good when it leads towards God, the *Summum Bonum*. (At this point the influence of the ninth book of *The City of God* seems particularly strong.) Christian folly is a minor theme in the *Enchiridion*, but even there it is the guide to proper fasting, certainly; Christ must be our sole aim:

'The time is short,' as the Apostle said, and it remains that those who use this world be as though they used it not' [I Corinthians 7:29–31]. This state of mind the world, I know, laughs at as foolish and hardly sane. Yet truly, through this folly alone it pleased God to save those that believe [I Corinthians 1:21]. 'Because the foolishness of God is wiser than man.' [I Corinthians 1:25]. Apply this rule to everything you do (*LB* 5. 26CD).

Fasting is specifically given as an example.

The literal insistence on fasting—or indeed on any physical or ceremonial aspect of the Christian sacraments—Erasmus saw as mere Judaïcising—a sub-Christian, carnal way of approaching God. For him Christ came to fulfil the Law and the Prophets of Israel by spiritualising observances which, under the old dispensation of unredeemed Israel, were essentially and intentionally carnal, at least for all but the most spiritually enlightened of men of olden times. The majority of the Christians of his day, including great magnates of the Church, most monks and many of the humble worshippers, still clung pharisaically to the mere fleshly body of the Church's teaching, ignoring the way of the Spirit revealed to man in Christ. So at least Erasmus believed. For him, traditional Christianity was turning Christ's religion into a neo-Judaic legalism. That is the theme of his massive paraphrase of Christ's teachings in Matthew 5, when Christ already began 'to act as a teacher of the heavenly philosophy' (*LB* 7. 23A). Christ in Matthew 5:17 declared, 'Think not that I come to destroy, but to fulfil.' In the paraphrase Christ is made the mouthpiece of Erasmus' spirituality: he has not come, he says, to burden the law of Moses with additions (*additamentis*) or with the petty constitutions of men (*humanis constitutiunculis*). As light banishes shadows, so he has banished the imperfections of the law, which has served its purpose. The law had its own honour in its own time, but now 'what the law foreshadowed figuratively (*typis quibusdam*) is now made manifest (*repraesentatur*)'.

The law hedged around the desires of man with a fence of carnal ceremonies and precepts. This was to stop them from sliding down into every kind of vice and to make them more able to receive the teachings of the Gospel; that perfection has now been revealed. Even though the law was carnal and gross it was useful for making men acknowledge their sin: now grace is vouchsafed, without ceremonies, washing sin away . . . It is foolish to think that the future will be like the present; foolish so to delight in shadows, that you cast away the things which are true; so to cling to the imperfect, that you despise the perfect; so to embrace the things of the flesh, that you shrink from the things of the spirit; so to be attached to earthly things, that you do not heed the heavenly (*LB* 7. 28C–29B).

Christ adopts the full doctrine of Folly when Erasmus paraphrases the commandment in Matthew 6:16, 'Moreover, when ye fast, be not like the hypocrites, of a sad countenance . . .'

You have been told how far your almsgiving ought to be from the almsgiving of the Pharisees, and your prayers from their prayers. Now hear how far your fasting ought to be from theirs, if you wish it to be pleasing to the Father and fruitful to you.

And the faithful are told by Christ that, in fasting too, they must value the invisible things far more highly than the visible, no matter what the crowd, the *vulgus hominum*, may think (*LB* 7. 38BE).

In the *Moria* as in the *Paraphrases* Erasmus remains true to the teachings of the fifth canon of the *Enchiridion*. If anything, there is, in the *Moria*, an even sharper awareness of the division between flesh and spirit, the transitory and the permanent, the unreality of things which are seen and the reality of those things which are not seen, but really *are*.

To some readers this sharp division between invisible reality and visible unreality may have seemed neo-Platonic. It does indeed recall the teachings of Plotinus, who believed that true philosophers would ascend from matter to soul: from soul to mind, from mind to God, the undivided One. The Greek fathers are far from being uninfluenced by such teachings. They were also spread in the West by the works of Pseudo-Dionysius. In both patristic times and in the Renaissance the direct or indirect influence of Plotinus or of vaguely Plotinian concepts was not negligible; to judge from the interpretations of nineteenth- and twentieth-century scholars, few Christians escaped them entirely, when they turned from the fading pageant of the world to the unchanging spiritual realities. But the main influence on Erasmus was again Origen, supported by some of the early fathers, including Augustine, both of whom he praised so unequivocally in the *Enchiridion*. For Erasmus, the New Testament is uniquely normative. He cites it directly or indirectly many times on nearly every page. But so it was for Luther, as it was later for Calvin. The message that Erasmus read in it, with such passionate certainty that he confidently puts his own teaching directly into the mouth of Christ and the apostles, is not one which even an earnest student of the Bible would necessarily find there without the aid of those platonising Greek fathers he chose for his guides. But the New Testament forms the solid structure of his teachings. That is why it is so serious whenever his scriptural allusions pass unnoticed. The passage that is to follow is firmly founded on scriptural authority. Erasmus has chosen his texts with care; they are basic ones indeed, not casually selected passages pressed into reluctant service to make a different point. The principal guide that Erasmus takes to lead him through the scriptural labyrinth remains his beloved Origen.

When the Sorbonne censured his theology of fasting as expounded in *On Eating Flesh* and in the *Paraphrases*, Erasmus retorted—as he could have done for the *Moria*—that his theology of fasting was the same as to be found in Origen (*LB* 9. 833B). The belief that the Christian, born again in this world, puts off the sordidness of the body and so lives that he gives less place to anger and to misfortunes, free from impure loves and free from a preoccupation with money, is a constant theme of Erasmus' writings, governing even the texts he chose to translate—such as St Basil's treatise *On the Holy Spirit*, 1532 (*LB* 8; cf. 510F–511A, etc.). He taught so often, and so consistently, his doctrine of the primacy of the spiritual over the fleshly, of moral regeneration over ceremonial or merely literal observances, that one can understand his anger when his critics simply refused to understand. After explaining, yet again, what he meant to the syndic of the University of Paris, Erasmus was moved to exclaim that he could even put up with ignorance of Latin—let alone Greek—provided he did not have to accept such scholastic enthymemes as: 'I, Béda, do not understand the proper use of language: therefore Erasmus is wrong in matters of faith.'

12. *The Holy Communion: arising to the new life in unity*

Similiter & in synaxi, tametsi non est aspernandum quod cerimoniis geritur, tamen id per se aut parum est conducibile, aut etiam perniciosum, nisi id quod est spiritale accesserit, nempe hoc quod signis illis visibilibus repraesentatur; repraesentatur autem mors Christi, quam domitis, extinctis, quasique sepultis corporis affectibus, exprimere mortales oportet, ut *in novitatem vitae* resurgant, utque *unum cum illo, unum* item *inter sese* fieri queant. Hec igitur agit, hec meditatur ille pius; contra vulgus sacrificium nihil aliud esse credit, quam adesse altaribus, idque proxime, audire vocum strepitum, aliasque id genus cerimoniolas spectare. Nec in his tantum quae dumtaxat exempli gratia proposuimus, sed simpliciter in omni vita refugit ab his quae corpori cognata sunt, ad aeterna, ad invisibilia, ad spiritalia rapitur (Scheurer H2r°; Kan 186).

Similarly in the Communion. Although the ritual is not to be despised, nevertheless it is, in itself, of little profit, even harmful, unless it bring nearer that which is spiritual—especially that which is represented by these visible signs. What is represented is the death of Christ. Mortal men, having tamed, destroyed and, as it were, buried their bodily passions, ought to imitate this death, so that they may rise again 'to newness of life', able to be 'one with him' and 'one with each other'. These are the things which the pious man does; these are the things which he practises. The crowd, on the contrary, believe that the sacrifice consists in being near altars—as close as possible—hearing the yelling voices and gazing upon other ritual trivialities. Not in such things alone, which we only put forward as examples, but quite simply in all his life, the pious man flees from those things which are akin to the body, and is caught up towards the things which are eternal, invisible and spiritual.

(i) *Arising to the new life*

Erasmus is now touching upon the central mystery of the Christian faith. In that too he saw a body and a spirit. And the body—by which he means above all the ceremonies as such and the mere act of being present at the sacrifice—he sees as potentially pernicious and at best, at

this level, indifferent. That is not because he has a low view of the
Mass. On the contrary, it is because he has so exalted a one, as exalted
as did Origen in particular and the Greek fathers in general.

It is a curious fact that traditional, orthodox, ecstatic mysticism in
the west gave hardly any place at all to the eucharist. Since Gregory of
Nyssa the Greeks did: Erasmus' debt to the Greek fathers is a real one.
For him as for Gregory and others it is the chosen vehicle for man to
form an ecstatic union both with God and his neighbour as a foretaste
of heavenly bliss.[1] One of the reasons why Edward Lee condemned
the *Moria* was that he believed Folly's doctrine of the union of the soul
with God to be dangerously tainted with heretical Germanic mysticism. He may well have been led to this conclusion by the importance
attributed to the Mass in this mystical process.

Folly refers to the Mass by the Greek name *synaxis*. It means 'a
bringing together', especially of Christians assembled at the Communion. From thence it took on the meaning of the Communion
service itself. Erasmus also uses with respect and affection the term
eucharistia, but there are times as in the *Moria* where *synaxis* better suits
the finer points he wishes to make. It was not from motives of
pedantry or elegant variation that Folly talks here of *synaxis* not
eucharistia. The difference between the two words—which are not
mutually exclusive—is a vital one. As Erasmus wrote in his treatise
How to Worship God (Basle, 1524), the word *synaxis*, though perhaps
less authoritatively correct than the word *eucharistia*, is widely used by
the Greeks with the meaning of *conciliatio* (a word implying the
uniting of men in one bond or union of kindly feeling). This is
precisely what, for Erasmus, the Mass 'represents':

And so the proper name given to the Mass is the eucharist, although the
Greeks say *synaxis*, that is the *conciliatio*, since there is also represented the
bond of love between all of Christ's members, whence the Latins also call it
communio (*LB* 5. 1102D).

The Communion means a mutual participation, a fellowship on the
part of Christians.

One can only admire Erasmus' boldness—rashness even—in taking
on so many enemies at once. His terms were bound to shock and
annoy. Some were destined to be misunderstood—as, one would have
thought, the most ordinary prudence on his part should have foreseen.
For many of his readers even the word *synaxis* was troublingly exotic.
The terms with which he rejects the validity of the ceremonies of the
Mass in themselves are scathing. Such ritual observances are not

[1] Cf. J. Daniélou, *Platonisme et Théologie*, Paris, 1944, especially p. 245.

merely *cerimonia* but *cerimoniolae*, trivial little ritual nonsenses. Far from being in a mood for compromise, even the one concession that *is* made—that the ritual ceremonies 'are not to be despised'—is weakened in 1516 by the insertion of an *inquiunt*, 'so they say'. As for the singing of the Masses, so highly developed in the late mediaeval and Renaissance Church, Erasmus dismisses as so much yelling. This is not a piece of comic or satirical hyperbole appropriate to the *Moria* but destined to be expressed more circumspectly in more serious works. This same *vocum strepitus*, this 'yelling of voices', is also the subject of a long and biting note in the *Annotations on the New Testament*, on I Corinthians 14:19, dating from 1516 and so reinforcing the doctrine of the *Moria*. Erasmus contrasts St Paul, 'who preferred five words of edification to ten thousand words in the spirit' with the Church of his day, given over to singing and yelling at the expense of preaching true piety. English Benedictines come in for particular censure with their senseless fauxburdons. Truly spiritual singing and dancing are moderate and circumspect. But St Paul prefers sound preaching even to that, though it has its proper place.

Erasmus breaks off his long note suddenly: it is better to get on with his allotted task 'than to deplore these things, doubtless in vain' (*LB* 6. 731C–732C).

Erasmus' concept of the Mass was opposed to some of the basic intellectual assumptions of the scholastic theologians. That we would expect. He also took up a stand which set him apart from some major humanistic teachings. But not all his quarrels were with intellectuals. He had no time, either, for the kind of simple piety which led many of the faithful to seek places in church nearest to the altars. He rejects such things as being on a par with the 'yelling of voices'. This makes the crowd, the *vulgus*, like the natural fools whom Folly mentioned earlier, who are attracted to altars as are superstitious boys and old men. And it is in a context of scorn that he chooses to use, twice, the verb *repraesentare*, which hostile critics could wrongly take to mean that he thought of the Mass as merely symbolic. *Faute de mieux* I have translated this literally as *to represent*. It has several meanings including a suggestion of symbolic representation, without any necessary corollary that the Mass is 'merely' a symbol. To those who disliked his choice of words Erasmus could have countered that the Scriptural basis of what Folly says is clear beyond peradventure from the important allusions which she makes to it.

Erasmus' doctrine of the Mass is Origenistic. The Mass is a sacrifice, but there is not the slightest hint that it is an efficacious sacrifice in itself, a valid sacrifice *ex opere operato*, even when ignorantly mumbled by a drunken priest who duly performs the ritual, or attended by a

gross and fleshly man who fails to seek the spiritual reality it represents. Nevertheless, the pious man *is* brought nearer to spiritual reality
through the Communion. By faith he concentrates on those spiritual
realities which are represented by the visible actions; they bring him to
the Real Presence.

The word *repraesentare* was not lightly chosen. As it embodies a
concept central to Erasmus' eucharistic theology, it is a term which he
repeatedly returns to. In the *Paraphrases*, when expounding the New
Testament texts where the Lord's Supper is mentioned, Erasmus uses
the term *symbolum*; in some cases (as in the major exposition of the
doctrine of the Mass in the paraphrase of I Corinthians 11:25) this is
coupled with the verb *repraesentare* (*LB* 7. 897B; 133EFf.; 260D; 450F).
One of the reasons why he is impatient with those who attack each
other with hatred over what he calls the 'eucharist or *synaxis*' is that
hatred is, by its very nature, opposed to love; yet it is Christian love
that 'we represent in this mystery' (*LB* 7. 849–50: dedication of
Paraphrases on the Epistles to the Corinthians, 5 February 1519). The
term, though frequently to be found in Erasmus, was not unique to
him. John Colet uses it in his explanations of Dionysius' doctrines
(*Two Treatises on the Hierarchies of Dionysius*, ed. J. W. Lupton, London, 1869, p. 211; III. 3); J. Viguerius uses it to explain Aquinas'
eucharistic doctrines in the *Institutions* (Antwerp, 1565, p. 159; XVI. 2).
In the context of eucharistic theology *repraesentare* is a technical word.

But the term was open to misunderstandings. Lutheran reformers
later seized on it as proof that Erasmus did not believe in the Real
Presence; he was accused of believing in his heart of hearts that the
Mass was no more than a solemn, symbolic commemoration of
Christ's dying sacrifice. Erasmus was stung to make sharp replies to
such unfounded accusations. This was no prudent after-thought. In
the passage we are considering now he calls the *synaxis* a sacrifice
(*sacrificium*), though one the crowd fails to understand with spiritual
insight.

In *Detectio Praestigiarum Libelli Cujusdam* (Basle, 1526), dedicated 'to
all lovers of truth', Erasmus defends his conception of the eucharist
from the smear of sacramentarianism. He was shocked, irritated and
bitter, calling on all lovers of truth to weigh his words with care.
Erasmus cites a long passage from the fifth canon of the *Enchiridion* in
which the term *repraesentare* is also used of the eucharist. He restates,
yet again, his doctrine of the body and the spirit to be found in all
things, denying that this could possibly imply any doubts about the
Real Presence.

In the eucharist there are elements which affect the eyes, touch, smell and the palate: there are words which strike the ears; there is the physical reception perceived by the senses. There is certainly no hope of salvation in these, unless men are drawn towards 'those things which cannot be seen'. Such things are partly of the nature of a gift; partly of congruency; partly of example. Of the nature of a gift are faith and the other gifts of the Spirit which are imparted by means of the visible elements. Congruent are the things which correspond to the visible signs of the sacraments, just as in marriage is represented the ineffable joining of the divine nature with human nature in Christ as well as the undivided fellowship of the mystical body, which is the Church, with Christ its head. Of the nature of example is the signifying in the eucharist of the immense love of Christ towards the human race, for the saving of which he gave himself over to death, so that we might respond to the Redeemer by loving one another. There is signified the closest of fellowships between Christians, just as one bread is made up of many grains and as wine flows from many grapes, or as eating and drinking together is the symbol of friendship and fellowship (*LB* 10. 1562BD).[1]

Erasmus is adopting an interpretation of the eucharist to be found in Origen and which is current among the Greek fathers. The best study on this is probably still Daniel Huet's (*PG* 17, *Origeniania* 1076Dff.; also *PG* 13, 948ff., especially notes 35–47). Daniel Huet insists that, on this matter, Origen's teaching is all but identical with Augustine's. He may well be right. As Huet points out, Erasmus was accused of perverting Origen's texts dealing with the Mass, but he did not.

Folly now expounds Erasmus' version of the Greek doctrine with the aid of the Scriptures.

She is putting forward in a few densely packed phrases a doctrine of the *synaxis* in which those who partake of it in faith rise as from the dead to the new life, being then in a communion of love with Christ and with each other.

In Christian teaching (especially in the west since Augustine but, of course, the Greeks had it earlier in their own language) there are two resurrections, not one. (An important *locus classicus* is Origen, writing on Romans 5:15–17: *PG* 14, 1047CD.) The first is the resurrection of the soul: this is produced by Christ, here and now in this world. The follower of Christ to whom is vouchsafed the forgiveness of sins, lives henceforth not for himself but the risen Christ. This is the 'resurrection of mercy'. The second resurrection is that of the body at the

---

[1]The reader who has to rely on the text in the Lug. Bat. *Opera Omnia* should note that Clericus has inadvertantly dropped the *non* from *ea quae non videntur,* so making nonsense of the argument; in the original there is no doubt whatsoever about the reading: the pious man seeks salvation by drawing the sacraments 'towards things which *cannot* be seen'—*Detectio Praestigiarum Libelli cujusdam, ficto authoris titulo, cum haec inscriptione, Erasmi & Lutheri Opiniones de Coena Domini*, Nuremberg, J. Petreius, 1526, leaf b1v°. Copy in British Library.

Judgment. The wicked who are condemned at the Judgment are those whose lives were wicked after their first resurrection, that 'resurrection of souls which is here and now'. Such men have 'not risen to the new life' (*City of God* 20. 7).

Baptism is the sacrament by which the Christian first passes through symbolic death to newness of life. But so too for the other sacraments. In fasting, for example, it is no good simply abstaining from food 'if your soul does not restrain itself from depraved desires'. And the same applies to all the sacraments of the New Law of Christ: baptism, the eucharist, unction . . . (*Praestigiarum Libelli Cujusdam Detectio*, 1526: *LB* 9. 1562B). For Erasmus' spiritually pious man it is the communion which is the Christian's renewed means of resurrection. Holy Communion represents the death of Christ. The pious man buries his fleshly sins, dying, as it were, in Christ. He then 'rises again into newness of life'. This 'newness' of the Christian man and his way of life appears in many places in St Paul (II Corinthians 5:17; Galatians 6:15; Ephesians 4:23–4; Colossians 3:10). In Romans 7:6, St Paul reminds us readers that we were delivered from the Mosaic law, so 'that, being dead wherein we were held, we should serve in newness of spirit, and not in the coldness of the letter'. But the key text, for Erasmus as for St Augustine, is Romans 6:4: 'So also we might *walk in newness of life*' (*en kainotēti zōēs peripatēsōmen;* in the Vulgate, *in novitate vitae ambulemus*). The *Moria* echoes this textually. But one should note that Folly does not use the scriptural verb 'to walk' in the new life; the verb used is *resurgere*, 'to rise again': *ut in novitatem vitae resurgant*. The new life of the Christian is, as it was for Augustine and as it was for Origen and for many others such as Theophylact, a resurrection here and now in this world.

This aspect is underlined by Folly. The communion represents both death and new life; Christians must imitate or express this death by 'taming, destroying and, as it were *burying*' their bodily passions. In this way they 'rise again into newness of life'. It is probable that Erasmus took this idea, too, from the Greek fathers. Theophylact, resuming a long Orthodox tradition, links Christ's death in the flesh and his subsequent resurrection with the Christian's dying to sin and rising again to a new mode of life (*PG* 124, 410Df. On Romans 6).

This emphasis on death and resurrection derives from the context of Romans 6:4, where St Paul is talking of baptism. From earliest times baptism was conceived as a death (symbolised by the plunging of the convert below the surface of the water) followed by a resurrection into that 'newness of life', by which the Christian 'walks' in God's ways. It was precisely this baptismal context which encouraged Christians to see the 'walking' which St Paul talks about as a resurrection.

Theophylact uses language which could only reinforce Erasmus' theology, especially (but not exclusively) when he knew him in the original. Theophylact, commenting on Romans 6:4, passes with consummate ease from *peripatēsōmen* ('that we may walk') to the resurrection of the Christian to a new life: Christ died so that 'we too, by another resurrection, may rise again' (*heteran anastasin anastōmen*). And that resurrection is not the final resurrection of the body: it takes place within time, in this world.

This transference to the Communion of terms St Paul applies to baptism is in accordance with the doctrine that all sacraments lead to a communion with God but none more wonderfully than the eucharist (cf. Colet, *Two Treatises*, 1869, III. 1, p. 216).

Erasmus sometimes uses Folly's and St Paul's terms in the context of baptism. That is only to be expected. Naturally we find the theme developed in the *Paraphrases*. But it is likely to crop up anywhere. When writing on the 4th psalm, Erasmus reminded his readers that, 'by being buried (*sepulti*) with Christ, who spent a Sabbath in the tomb, and by abstaining from evil works, we so rise again with him in newness of life' that we do not live a life of concupiscence but of justice (*LB* 5. 239BC). But by writing of the *synaxis* in the same terms as St Paul used for baptism, Erasmus made the act of communion for the spiritual man into a source of spiritual and moral regeneration. Partaking of the bread and the cup, the communicant shares in the death and resurrection of his Lord, so rising, already in this world, to the newness of life which is the philosophy of Christ in action.

Some modern readers of Erasmus feel that, in his interpretation of the Mass, he did go very far towards the sacramentarians, considering it symbolic in a sense which denied the Real Presence, since he left no room for the reality of transubstantiation. Such doubts about his catholicity are not, I think, justified. Certainly he repeatedly and unambiguously insists upon the Real Presence in the *Praestigiarum Libelli cujusdam Detectio* (*LB* 10. 1558–72). What seems, above all, to confuse critics is his terminology and his avoidance of the theory of transubstantiation. He sharply answered the accusations of secretly holding the same doctrines as Carlstadt, who supported Zwingli in conceiving of the Mass as a purely symbolic commemoration of Christ's sacrifice on the Cross and of his glorious resurrection:

If we accept the opinion of more recent theologians, are not the species of bread and wine the symbols of the body and blood of the Lord? Or at least (*sin minus*), are not the consecrated bread and wine symbols of the body and blood of the Lord hidden beneath them? Finally, the body and blood is in some manner exposed there to our sense: are they not symbols of those things which cannot be distinguished except by the eyes of faith?

He had protested in the *Adages* and the *Complaint of Peace* about men fighting each other, and yet sharing the same Communion. This he saw as a scandal:

I call the *receiving* of the body and blood of the Lord the symbol of the mystical body [the Church], joined with Christ its head, and the concord amongst those members. Where then are those alleged words now, which exclude the reality (*veritatem*) of the body and blood of Christ? (*LB* 10. 1560EF).

He challenges the same reader to show where his insistence on spiritual realities over and above mere ceremonial ever implies disbelief in the reality of the body and blood of Christ in the Mass (*LB* 10. 1562Af.). He repeats several times that it is not the elements of the Mass which he calls symbolic: it is something else. He did not ever say 'that the bread is the symbol of the body or the wine the symbol of the blood'. What he calls 'the symbol is the actual consecration and receiving' of those elements at the Mass (*LB* 10. 1568D). Similarly he does not call the bread the sign (*signum*) of Christ's body; what he does do is to call 'the consecration and receiving' of it 'the sign of the covenant (*foedus*) between God and Man' (*LB* 10. 1568E).

Throughout this *Detectio* Erasmus strives, probably successfully, to maintain his orthodoxy. But there is no doubt that he did not like the term *transubstantiatio*, which he studiously avoids, nor the mechanistic theology it can be used to defend. In the *Detectio* as in the *Moria* and in many other works, Erasmus saw no merit at all in a routine act of communion. To be effective the Mass had to be grasped at a spiritual level; the true body and blood contained in the elements had to be so received that they did indeed 'symbolise' a real, effective union of the communinants with God and with each other.

Erasmus' distaste for all that is implied by the scholastic doctrines of transubstantiation must be seen in the context of his time. That doctrine, despite its dominance in theological circles, was not a compulsory article of faith for Roman Catholics until the thirteenth session of the Council of Trent on 11 October 1551. And even then the doctrine had to await the eventual acceptance of Trent as a truly ecumenical council—in 1551 the Gallican Church, for example, was not prepared to do any such thing. Erasmus claimed to accept without question what the Church had incontrovertibly decided under the inspiration of the Holy Ghost. In other matters he quietly used the freedom granted by St Paul (Romans 14:5): *unusquisque in suo sensu abundet*, 'Let everyone be fully persuaded in his own mind' (*LB* 10. 1570B–D). But even here his words are not without an element of prudent ambiguity. What Erasmus embraces 'without discussion' (*citra disceptationem*) are those traditions of the Church which have been, *citra controversiam*, arrived at under the inspiration of the Spirit. But who is to decide what the Holy Ghost has 'without controversy' inspired the Church to make part of her tradition?

Erasmus' whole mode of thought was hostile to what Trent decided on 11 October 1551. That can be seen from his long and pugnacious annotation on I Corinthians 7:39: 'She is freed from the law: let her marry whom she wishes.' Here we find one of his few allusions to transubstantiation—in a highly sarcastic context:

Paul forbade that anyone should be made a bishop who was a recent convert, a brawler or a wine-bibber [I Timothy 3:3]. But today the Roman Pontiff admits to episcopal rank a man baptised yesterday or an acknowledged pirate. The Church defined transubstantiation in the communion (*in synaxi*) at a late date; for long it was enough to believe that the true body of Christ was there, either in the consecrated bread or in some other way (. . . *sive sub pane consecrato, sive quocumque modo adesse verum corpus Christi*). When she looked at the matter more closely, when she weighed it more precisely, she prescribed more definitely (*LB* 6. 696c).

The whole tenor of this long and controversial note is that the Church can modify the doctrines she has established. Would that she always modified them for the better, under the guidance of the spirit . . .

Erasmus, neither in the *Moria* nor in any other of his writings, ever showed the slightest sympathy for that magical view of the Mass which had grown up in the Church. For him the communicant had acted in vain if he did not spiritually perceive the divine truths behind the symbolic actions which were performed, being led on by them to the New Life of Christianity in moral action. And that New Life could be a form of ecstatic folly.

(ii) *One man with Christ: one body with fellow Christians*
Erasmus places the emphasis on the Mass as a *synaxis*. Spiritual communicants become one with God and with each other.

Such expressions sound like the essence of the Christian religion. The doctrine may be vertiginous: the words sound innocuous. But at least one up-and-coming clergyman believed Erasmus was teaching a doctrine rampant among mediaeval German heretics and still flourishing (see below, p. 164f).

Erasmus set about emphasising the scriptural basis of his teaching. There are several ways of being 'one with him' when *him* means God. Being 'one with him' may imply doctrines of unimpeachable orthodoxy: it may also imply a heresy with which no compromise was possible. Doubtless that is why the marginal notes to the *Moria* as published by Froben draw repeated attention to scriptural sources.

That Christians are, or ought to be, one with Christ is taught by St Paul (in Galatians 3:28 for example).

In English Galatians 3:28 reads, 'For ye are all one in Christ.' If this is Erasmus' authority then it is significant that he progressively preferred to interpret this with a sense found in the original Greek, not in the Vulgate.

The Greek reads *heis este en Christo Iesou*: Christians are 'as one man in Christ Jesus'. The Vulgate reading is *'unum* [not *unus*] *in Christo Jesu'*. That implies that we are 'one thing' in Christ. In his *Annotations* Erasmus shows that Jerome, Ambrose and Augustine preferred that meaning, but Theophylact is cited to show that it probably means that all Christians are as 'one man' with their Lord: they are the body; he is the head. He adds that no one should find such a trope in any way shocking (*LB* 6. 816EF). He brings out the same meaning in the *Paraphrases* (*LB* 7. 956C); it also occupies an important place in the *Praestigiarum Libelli cujusdam Detectio* (*LB* 9. 1562Bf.).

Erasmus may have been thinking of other scriptural texts as well, of course. A major source of the doctrine of the unity of Christians with God and in God is John 17:20–3. He paraphrases this to bring out strongly the union of Christians as a body with Christ their head, unified also among themselves in peace and concord (*LB* 7. 629AB). Both in the *Moria* and in many other writings, Erasmus quietly shows that the union of Christians is a double one: with Christ; with each other in Christ. Such teachings, which are those of the *Moria* but made more explicit, are orthodox. Being *unum item inter sese*, 'one also with each other', echoes those numerous verses in Scripture which tell of the unity of men in Christ (cf. John 17:11, 17:21, I Corinthians 10:17, etc.).

Such a doctrine, lying as it does as the very heart of eucharistic theology, is a constant preoccupation of Erasmus. The paraphrase of John 6:58, elaborates the theme that 'whoever eats me, thus joining himself to me by a mystical eating and drinking, so that he be one with me'—*mecum unum fiat*—obtains eternal life. In the prayer that Erasmus wrote *For Those who are about to Receive the Lord's Body*, the pious man prays that he may 'persevere in the blessed society of your mystical body, which you wished to be one with you, just as you and your Father are one, firmly joined together by the Holy Ghost: to whom be all honour and glory' (*LB* 5. 1204B).

(iii) *Practising the philosophy of Christ*

Erasmus' doctrine of the eucharist is refreshing in its insistence both on the communion, the *synaxis*, of the faithful in Christ, as well as on the new life which the Christian must lead. In this he anticipates the invitation in the *Book of Common Prayer*, where you are invited to make your communion if you 'are in love and charity with your neighbours, and intend to lead a new life'. (A modern Anglican paperback liturgy rightly talks of *the* new life, keeping the notion centrally important.) Erasmus, with more sensitivity than the Prayer Book at this point, makes the *synaxis* into the means of love and charity rather than the pre-condition of sharing in it. Living the new life is the constant endeavour of the pious man. It is in fact the sacramental aspect of the philosophy of Christ—that 'practising of death' which Socrates glimpsed and which Christ both taught and rendered possible. By now the full sense of *meditari* has been firmly fixed in the reader's mind. Repetition has seen to that. Folly teaches that the Christian must, in the communion, die to sin and rise again. That is what gives its full force to the sentence which follows upon the assertion of the *synaxis* as the means of unity with Christ and in Christ: *Haec igitur agit, haec meditatur ille pius.* 'These are the things, therefore, which the pious man does: these are the things which he practises.'

But this idea of 'practising death' contained in the *meditari* is also basic to the sacramental doctrine both of Folly and of St Paul—at least as Erasmus paraphrases him on Romans 6:3–5. Paul is made to say:

Christ rose again into the heavens; he sits on the right hand of the Father. Those things which Christ has already achieved are to be hoped for, eventually, for ourselves—provided that we strive after those same things and, as it were, practise them (*aemulemur, ac veluti meditemur*) (*LB* 7. 795B, verse 5).

'Walking in newness of life' is, therefore, a 'practising' of the philosophy of Christ, spiritually achieved through the eucharist, by grace of which the Christian repeatedly dies to his sinful, fleshly nature, soaring aloft to the spiritual realm, which alone pleases God. Here is the practice of Christian dying in action. The pious man, in all things, throughout his life, flies from things akin to the body. He dies to his sins. And then he is enraptured, *'caught away* towards the things which are eternal, invisible, spiritual'.

This is no mere play on words, designed to make the teaching sportingly conform to Folly's concern with soul-departing insanity. It is part of the permanent teaching of Erasmus. The ceremonies of the Mass are of no value in themselves. A man who stops at that level of worship is condemned to remain for ever in the 'flesh of the sacrament'. Yet God 'hates a religion which is *pinguis et crassus*'. (Again we find these twin words 'stolid and gross' which form a leitmotiv in his writings; *Praestigiarum Libelli cujusdam Detectio*, 1526; *LB* 9. 1562A.) Only those Christians who go beyond the carnal find those true things which really are, being spiritual. Indeed, their entire life is a rapture: 'Quite simply, in all his life, the pious man flees from the things which are akin to the body, and is "caught up" towards the things which are eternal, invisible, spiritual—*ad aeterna, ad invisibilia ad spiritalia rapitur*'.

The full force is in the verb. *Rapitur*, 'caught up', belongs to the language of Christian ecstasy.

13. *Two sets of mutually opposed madmen: pious jesting*

Proinde cum summa sit inter hos & illos omnibus de rebus dissensio, fit ut utrique alteris insanire videantur, quamquam id vocabuli rectius in pios competit quam in vulgus, mea quidem sententia. (Scheurer H2v°–H3r°; Kan 186–7)

Since there is total disagreement in all things between these two sets of people, both seem insane to the other. However, the word *insane* more rightly suits the pious, in my opinion, than the crowd.

The previous sentence ended with the pious man 'caught up'. Since rapture is, as it were, a sudden departure of the soul from the body, pious men (who know for certain that carnal men are truly mad to cling to those transitory things which are seen) themselves appear to be mad (*insanire videantur*) to worldly madmen. Indeed, in a higher sense they *are* mad, living their life outside themselves, firmly convinced of the reality of things which are not seen.

The two opposing camps are made up of carnal men and, totally at war with them, spiritually enlightened men. Pious men in their rapture have souls which, here and now, in this mortal life, practise leaving their bodies, caught up by God in the spiritual realities lying beneath the illusory shadows of this passing world.

Such a rapture is not only a cherished grace in itself: it is a foretaste of future bliss.

Carnal men hate the pious, not despite this but because of it. It is not a question of a gentle agreement to differ: the carnal and the pious are opposed in all things.

At least as clearly as in the *Moria*, Erasmus elaborates the same points in 'The Sileni of Alcibiades' (*LB* 2. 778F). The concordance between this adage and the *Moria* is now very close indeed.

But in the *Moria* Folly suddenly makes a marked return to amusing paradox. She suggests that it is not the impious who are rightly to be called insane; it is the pious. Their madness is both real and good. This arresting way of leading the reader on to the account of ecstatic love for God which follows hard upon the paradox could, if read in isolation, trouble even a sensitive and intelligent reader. But there is no excuse for reading it in isolation, though Cardinal Prince Pio da Carpi apparently did.[1]

Folly is harking back to an earlier part of the *Moria* ('chapter 38'). There, as here, the good and the evil forms of insanity are amusingly and allusively compared and contrasted. Evil insanity—not, I repeat that medical insanity which is so strange an ally of ecstasy—is diabolical; but Plato, we were told, rated good ecstatic madness (*furor*) among the choicest of the divine gifts. It was the gift vouchsafed to poets, seers and lovers.

This reference to Socrates in the *Phaedrus* (244A) is now taken up again and elaborated with the help of the Gospel.

[1] Cf. his *Three and Twenty Books against Places in the Various Lucubrations of D. Erasmus*, 1531; copy in the Bodleian Library at *A 8° 12 Th.; fol. lxxxiii, v°f.*

CHAPTER FIVE

The Climax in Ecstasy (II): Rapture

1. *The madness of lovers: St Paul and Plato as linked by 'Athanasius'*

Quodquidem magis perspicuum fiet, si (quemadmodum pollicita sum) paucis demonstraro, summum illud premium, nihil aliud esse quam insaniam quandam. Primum igitur existimate Platonem tale quiddam jam tum somniasse, cum amantium furorem omnium foelicissimum esse scriberet. Etenim qui vehementer amat, jam non in se vivit, sed in eo quod amat: quoque longius a seipso digreditur, & in illud demigrat, hoc magis ac magis gaudet; atque cum animus a corpore peregrinari meditatur, neque probe suis utitur organis: istud haud dubie furorem recte dixeris, alioqui quid sibi vult, quod vulgo etiam dicunt: *Non est apud se, & ad te redi, & sibi redditus est?* Porro quo amor est absolutior, hoc furor est major ac foelicior (Scheurer H2vº–H3rº; Kan 187).

That will be clearer if I demonstrate in a few words—as I promised—that the highest reward is nothing other than a kind of madness. First therefore consider that Plato already dreamed of such a thing when he wrote that the madness of lovers is the most blessed of all. Whoever loves to distraction, no longer lives in himself but in him whom he loves: the farther he can go away from himself and migrate into the other, the more and more he is delighted; and when the soul practises sojourning away from the body, not using its organs properly, that, without doubt, you would rightly call madness. Otherwise what is meant by the popular sayings *non est apud se* ('he is not at home to himself'), or, *ad te redi* ('to have come back to yourself'), or, *sibi redditus est* ('he has been given back to himself again')? But the more unfettered the love is, the greater and happier is the madness.

(i) *Laughter*

One might have expected Folly to lay aside her smiles now and to become passionately earnest. She is about to talk of the joy of the pious who are caught away to God, so having a foretaste of the eternal bliss. In fact, the language and the style become both more intense and more colloquial.

There is not only a similarity of theme between the passage just cited and 'chapter 38': there is a similarity of style and language. The same phrases occur—for example the expression *sibi jam totus esset redditus* (Scheurer D2v°; Kan 71) directly prepares the way for the expression we meet now: *sibi redditus est* (Scheurer H3r°; Kan 187). The idea that a man who has ceased to be abstracted into temporary insanity has been given back, or has come back to himself plays an important rôle in most theories of ecstasy. The phrase is striking enough in itself. The parallel between the two contexts in which it appears ('chapter 38' and 'chapter 67') remains arresting after 1514: it was even more so in the first version of the *Moria*, before a mass of satirical additions had pushed these pages farther apart, somewhat diluting the main argument in the process. Those who knew their mediaeval mystics were quite at home with such terms; they are almost a commonplace.[1]

A further feature linking these two parts of the *Moria* is a kind of comic joy. In 'chapter 38' a major contribution to this happy feeling is made by allusions to actors and acting. At a more refined level the choice of words itself contributes to this feeling, for Erasmus lightens his language with echoes of Terence's comedies. Praising good, happy, divine madness, Folly had said in that earlier 'chapter':

The other form of insanity, which clearly proceeds from me, is far different. Of all things it is most to be yearned for. It occurs whenever a certain joyful wandering of the mind (*mentis error*) frees the soul from anxious cares and sends it back anointed with pleasures manifold (Scheurer D2v°; Kan 70).

The word which Erasmus uses for 'anointed' is *delibutus*. This usage is virtually confined to Terence, who employs it in the comedy *Phormio* (5. 6. 15) where we find the phrase, 'Will it do, if I send you back *delibutum gaudio*, (anointed with joy)?' It is Terentian language which comes to the fore again now. The man who is mad, we are told, *non est apud se* (is 'not at home') since his soul has gone wandering off. This and similar phrases are presented as colloquial expressions (*quod vulgo etiam dicunt*). So they are. They recall several comedies of Terence and the colloquial Latin style which so elegantly characterises them. *Apud se esse* (to 'be at home'; to 'be oneself'—to be sane, that is) is particularly associated with Terence, appearing in the *Phormio* (1. 4. 27) as well as in the *Andria* (5. 4. 34), the *Heautontimorumenos* (5. 1. 48) and the *Hecyra* (4. 4. 85). It also turns up in one of the best-known comedies of Plautus, the *Miles Gloriosus* (4. 8. 36).

[1] For one example among many, see the *Lives of the Fathers*, PL 73. 808A–C, where the phrase used is *reversus ad se*, 'come back to himself'. Such a man, who has 'come back to himself' after his ecstasy, has now, we read, become 'sane' again: *sanus effectus est*.

These happy links between 'chapter 38, and 'chapter 67' are further increased by that essentially serious play on the etymology of *vehemens* which we must consciously note every time it occurs. When jesting earlier, Folly produced what is almost a punch-line: both kind of madmen laugh at each other, but the pious madman laughs more heartily. Indeed, the *major insanus vehementius rideat minorem*—the greater madman laughs at the lesser one *vehementius*': with, that is to say, a greater carrying away of his mind (Scheurer D3r°; Kan 71). The smile still lingers around it, no doubt, but to use it with ecstatic overtones is by no means only comic nor even principally so. Indeed, for centuries *vehemens* and its cognates were used in no other way by writers on ecstasy. It is certainly the sense in which Folly uses it here of the pious man who loses his mind to spiritual realities as his soul soars aloft, enraptured by his love for God.

Folly promises to prove that man's 'highest reward' is a kind of madness. The term Erasmus uses for this reward is *praemium*. Here, once more, is a word taken over from the standard language of ecstasy. (One example may suffice: Bonaventura, *Opera Omnia*, Quaracchi, VIII. p 47.) *Praemium* in this sense is very often to be found in Erasmus' writings. This *praemium*, this reward, is ecstatic union with God, provisionally and temporarily in rapture; permanently in death.

One might have thought that such an awe-inspiring theme would be expressed in sober language or, perhaps, in the passionate poetry of enthusiastic revelation. But that would be to misunderstand the basic tone of the *Moria*. Erasmus prefers to treat it with an undercurrent of light-hearted banter. Later in life he tells us why. He does so in his treatise on how to preach, *De Ratione Concionandi*. There he insists that *jucunditas* (a pleasant, happy style) has an important place in preaching. St Bernard's mind, for example, is characterised by something gentle (*mollis*) and *facetus* (jesting), whereas Hilarius' mind—despite, by implication, his name—is uniformly severe. A similar contrast is made between Hilarion (*not* Hilarius) and Bonaventura. Hilarion is sustainedly jolly (*ubique festivus*) whereas Bonaventura is *tetricus*: forbidding and stern (*LB* 5. 860Af.). Erasmus then proceeds to defend his own light-hearted style in the *Moria*, without however mentioning it by name. Such a style is peculiarly appropriate, when treating of the joys of the elect:

There is another kind of *jucunditas* which the subject-matter itself particularly requires. Matters which deserve happy, festive thankfulness (*laeta gratulatio*) should be unfolded in pleasant words not sad ones—for example, if anyone should undertake to unfold how great is the happiness of the angels and of those pious souls who, in heaven, gaze on the face of the Father, of Christ and of the Holy Ghost; or if anyone would treat what the life of the pious will be after the resurrection . . . (*LB* 5. 860Af.).

There are many links—textual links—between the various versions of the *Moria* and *De Ratione Concionandi*. A good example of the indirect way in which Erasmus later defended his *jucunditas* towards the end of the *Moria* is found not in what he defends but in what he condemns. He comes down heavily against that coarse buffoonery (*scurrilitas*) which leads monks to make puns on the sacred writings while in their cups. (One thinks of Rabelais' Frère Jean.) French monks, we are told, use St Paul's words, 'Are they Hebrews? so am I', as though the text alluded not to *Hebraei* (Hebrews) but to *Ebrii* (*ivres*: drunkards): 'Are they tipsy? So am I.' The implied force of this condemnation lies in the source: II Corinthians 11:22. Erasmus was attacked for using the very next sentence of St Paul, not as a coarse buffoon but as a pleasant jester! St Paul's words, 'I say as a fool, I am more' (II Corinthians 11:23) appear in the 1511 *Moria*, as we saw, loosely cited as 'Are they fools? I am more'. What a contrast there is, he implies, between monkish *scurrilitas* and his own *jucunditas*: between the coarse jokes of drunken buffoons in their monasteries and Folly's happy, pleasant style as she light-heartedly tells of the spiritual reality of ecstatic Christian love, that foretaste of the life which will be that of the pious in heaven, pending and after the final resurrection.

(ii) *The immortal soul: the debt to Plato*

The Folly who now explains her paradox is a platonic evangelical humanist. All the hints are at last spelled out for us: the pious man may rightly be called insane precisely because he is enraptured. His soul, like the madman's, is striving to leave his body. Such a man lives *extra se*, 'outside himself' with joy. In such a state, his soul, in this and other ways just like the madman's, fails to make proper use of its bodily organs. The ultimate cause is not identical to that which produces similar effects in the medically insane, but the immediate cause is closely analogous.

Erasmus is the heir to a long tradition, stretching back through Origen and Gregory of Nyssa to the New Testament read in the light of Greek philosophy. This tradition was particularly powerful whenever Pseudo-Dionysius was being read (without his Pseudo). Within this tradition the love which leads to ecstatic union with God is not that specifically Christian benevolence, that loving goodwill, which goes by the name of *agapē*. And it has nothing to do with 'Platonic love' as popularly understood today. The love of man for God is a passionate desire which shares its name with the love of men and women: it is *erōs*, an erotic love. In the case of the love of true Platonic lovers for each other, their souls leave their bodies and live in their beloved. They die to themselves and live again in the person whom they love. This theme was soon to become a commonplace of European poetry, thanks partly to Ficino's commentary on Plato's *Symposium*. But Folly is not treating of love between human beings. This *erōs* is the love of the Christian for God: his soul too is drawn out of his body, soaring aloft to the supreme Object of his passionate desire. This is no new-fangled Renaissance theme. Such a concept of ecstasy is as true for St Bernard as it is for Gregory of Nyssa; for Aquinas, as it is for Pseudo-Dionysius. In all cases the debt to Plato is incalculable. So, too, is the debt to Philo. Whether Erasmus owed much of a debt to Ficino—especially to his commentary on the *Symposium*—is by no means certain. Ficino muddles together so many types of love which Greek distinguishes between—*agapē*, *erōs*, *philautia* (self-love) and so on—that it is hard to see how he could have made much of an impact on a philologist.

Erasmus' Platonic assumptions become the more important when seen in their wider traditional context.

This Christianising of the Socratic conception of an ecstatic love for God occurred in patristic times. But, as the mediaeval world merged into that of the Renaissance, it found itself at war with a growing Aristotelianism. Some interpretations of Aristotle, reached partly under the guidance of the Arabian scholar Averroes, made such teachings about the soul seem quite unphilosophical to many of the university scholars of western Christendom. By reaction even greater importance was attached to the authority of Pseudo-Dionysius. By reaction also, many turned with enthusiasm to rediscovered texts of Plato and the platonising fathers.

The Platonic element in Christian concepts of ecstasy was reinforced in fifteenth-century Italy, partly in conscious opposition to neo-Aristotelian scepticism about the philosophical bases of the alleged proofs of the soul's immortality. The followers of William of Occam and other troublesome *Britanni* had joined with Paduan Averroists in denying that the immortality of the soul can be proved by philosophy—the philosophy, that is, of *the* philosopher, Aristotle. For such philosophers, the immortality of the soul was a matter of pure revelation, to be accepted, if at all, by faith alone. Philosophically speaking, there was nothing to be said for it.

Scholars such as Petrarch and Coluccio Salutati reacted strongly against this assertion. They found an ally in Aquinas, who despite his Aristotelianism was fundamentally marked by neo-Platonic assumptions. Similarly Leonardo Bruni, without being an out-and-out opponent of Aristotle, translated several works of Plato, including the *Phaedo*, the *Phaedrus*, the *Gorgias*, the *Apology for Socrates*, the *Crito* and parts of the *Symposium*. Tellingly, he dedicated the translation of the *Phaedo* to Pope Innocent VII with the sub-title *On the Immortality of Souls*.

Such tendencies were continued by Valla; by Thomas More's hero Giovanni Pico della Mirandola; massively by Marsiglio Ficino and, right into Erasmus' time, by Pico's nephew, Gianfrancesco Pico. These are a few great names among many which could be cited. The struggle against the Aristotelians led Pietro Barozzi, bishop of Padua from 1487 until his death in 1507, to issue an episcopal condemnation of the Averroists on 4 May 1489. While Erasmus was a young man, in and out of Italy the battle raged.

The *Moria* appeared when the quarrel was reaching a crisis. In between the two main versions of the *Moria*, 1511 and 1514, the matter was debated and, at least for some Catholics, settled, it was hoped, once and for all, by the Fifth Lateran Council, called by Julius II and continued by Leo X. On 19 December 1513 there was promulgated the decree *Apostolici Regiminis*, which not only asserted the doctrine of the immortality of the soul but actually required philosophers—not only theologians—to teach it from their university chairs. If the Fifth Lateran Council had been accepted as ecumenical, that would no doubt have settled the matter. But in many ways the council was a damp squib. The Gallican Church rejected its Catholicity from the start, even though Francis I eventually supported it. And it did not silence Pomponazzi. Nevertheless, *Apostolici Regiminis* rejoiced the hearts of many platonising Christians.[1]

The living soul is so central to Erasmus' theology that one might have expected him to embrace *Apostolici Regiminis* whole-heartedly. But he does not, even though it was promulgated by his papal patron, Leo X. The reasons for his hesitations are suggested by his preface to the paraphrase of Corinthians, in which he speaks scathingly of what is taught in Italy on the subject of the resurrection: in St Paul's day, there were those who denied the resurrection, as though it were not the very basis of Christian hope. This 'snake' is still alive today in some men's hearts despite St Paul's battle against it. (The word Erasmus uses for snake, *excetra*, is very rare. No doubt he took it from Cicero's *Tusculan Disputations* 9. 2. 22.) In Italy, for so many years, there have been

[1] An excellent study of this subject is Giovanni di Napoli's *L'Immortalità dell'anima nel Rinascimento*, Turin, 1963; there are several good and relevant articles in the *Dictionnaire de Théologie Catholique* including one on the Fifth Lateran Council. Especially for later developments, consult H. T. Burns, *Christian Mortalism from Tyndale to Milton*, Harvard U. P. 1972.

public harangues on this theme, 'many believing they have reached harbour if they can teach that Aristotle did not utterly lay aside immortality of souls'. Erasmus' only regret is that St Paul did not speak more fully on this subject (*LB* 7. 854; *EE* 3, no. 916, 270ff.).

Erasmus delights in reminding his readers that Aristotle wrote, at best, ambiguously about the soul. This was a way of getting at Béda and his ilk, as well as putting a distance between himself and certain Italians. His growing commitment to Plato às *the* philosopher, as well as his use, in the *Moria* and elsewhere, of the *Phaedo*, the *Phaedrus,* the *Republic* and other Platonic dialogues, leave his general sympathies in no doubt. The same applies to his ready use of Cicero's *Tusculan Disputations* which was a favourite book among Christian humanists seeking authority to oppose philosophical scepticism about the soul. But he never confuses the mere immortality of souls with the immortality promised Christians at the Second Coming.

Erasmus turns to the *Phaedrus*, Plato helping him to fill the gap in our knowledge left by St Paul's regrettable reticence about the immediate fate of the soul upon the death of believers.

So much is evident. Not so evident, today, is the theological tradition in which this borrowing is set. It is a long one. Christians had long since been able to reconcile the doctrines of the resurrection and of the Platonic immortality of the soul. Erasmus was too sound a philologist not to see that St Paul writes of the resurrection of the dead in terms which by no means always (if ever) imply the immortality of the soul. The Greek New Testament centres its eschatology on the Second Coming of our Lord. The dead will then be raised incorruptible; those who remain alive will be changed into spiritual beings 'in the twinkling of an eye'. In that great day 'our mortal' will put on immortality (I Corinthians 15). The only immortality that St Paul acknowledges specifically is that of resurrected man and of such of the elect as are alive when Christ returns in majesty. These are doctrines which the Vulgate makes less clear, since the translation is somewhat garbled when compared with the best Greek manuscripts.

In I Thessalonians 4, the dead are to be raised before—but only, it seems, just before—the spiritualising of those who remain alive: 'those that sleep in Jesus', the 'dead in Christ', shall 'rise first'. The living Christians are then enraptured: '*caught up* to meet the Lord in the air.'

Erasmus never, I think, confuses his categories: the term 'immortality' he uses above all for the state of the pious after the resurrection, when the bodies of the dead are returned to them. Death is the divorce of body and soul: eternal life is vouchsafed them when body and soul are finally brought together. The soul may not be subject to death: but Christian immortality is not lived eternally in the soul alone.

In his scriptural *Annotations* Erasmus loyally expounds St Paul's meaning. He does not even mention the immortality of the soul in his long, bitter and expanded note on I Corinthians 15:51. The Vulgate reads: 'Behold, I tell you a mystery; we shall all rise again, but we shall not all be changed.' The original Greek, as known to Erasmus, means quite differently: '. . . We shall not all sleep, but we shall all be changed.' This reading (which remains the best attested one) states that those of the elect who remain alive at the day of Judgment will not have to die before they pass into glory. The Vulgate apparently requires all men to die first—including those of the elect who are living when 'the trumpet shall sound'. Erasmus, naturally, translated the Greek according to the plain sense. He was, with virulent unfairness, accused of denying the resurrection, since not all men, he says, are to die before they live again in Christ. His reply is technical and need not detain us here. (Essentially, he shows that the Greek is referring at various times to 'all' the dead, and 'all' those who are still alive at the Second Coming.) But corrections such as these made to texts believed to be infallibly authoritative in their Latin translation were bound to shake ignorant conservatives. They changed alleged certainties into error or, at best, into disputable or probable opinions.

The same applies to the treatise he wrote to defend his annotation on I Corinthians 15:51 against the attacks of Nicolas Egmontanus. St Augustine is cited to show that those who are still alive on that great day are those whose 'souls remain in their bodies'. He is further quoted as asserting that we do not need to know all the details: suffice it to say that, at the general resurrection, 'the bodies of the dead will live again, with the souls they used to have' (*LB* 9. 437B; 440A).

On the vital question of the resurrection of the body Erasmus does not hesitate: it is the basis of Christian hope. When paraphrasing I Corinthians 15, for example, it is a case of the pious living again 'completely', *toti*, once their bodies rise again from the dead. The implication is, no doubt, that they were living incompletely before. The point is not pressed. But in ways such as these the resurrection of the *dead* of the New Testament becomes, in a special sense, the resurrection of the *body* of the creeds.

Erasmus' eschatology conforms to that found in an army of writers from patristic times—especially among the Greeks, whose text of St Paul is so much more authoritative for him than the Vulgate translation. Erasmus does not doubt that the souls of the pious remain alive after death; but he could wish that St Paul had been clearer on this and allied points of disputed doctrine. For the belief in the immortality of the soul leaves several questions unanswered: where, for example, *are* these souls, between death and resurrection? Erasmus would dearly have liked to know on Paul's own authority. When he admitted as much in his preface to his *Paraphrases on I Corinthians* the Faculty of Theology of Paris moved in to condemn him. What Erasmus wrote was calculated to raise the hackles of die-hard Sorbonagres:

Would that Paul had shed more light for us on how the souls exist when removed from their bodies: whether they enjoy the glory of immortality; whether the souls of the wicked are already in torment; whether they are helped by our prayers or other good actions; whether the indulgences of the supreme pontiff free them from punishment immediately. I see many hesitate over such matters or, indeed, dispute about them. That would have been quite unnecessary, if Paul had clearly defined them (*LB* 7. 854; *EE* 3, no. 916, 244f.).

The Sorbonne found such a wish for more enlightenment to be 'dangerous'. They also suspected a 'scandal': was Erasmus suggesting that the Bible does not contain all that is requisite for faith? Anyway, Christ said to the thief on the cross, 'Today shalt thou be with me in paradise': that proves that the souls of the just reign with God after death (Luke 23:43).

Erasmus denied the charges. If it is impious to wish for more enlightenment on such matters, then he must confess to being often tempted. How he would like to know more, for example, about those saints who rose from the dead at the Crucifixion and who were seen wandering about the streets of Jerusalem after the Resurrection (Matthew 27:51–4). This kind of problem tickled his soul. Would that we knew whether they died again; who they were; to whom they appeared. We may not need to know such things: it would be nice to do so (*LB* 9. 849E–853B, proposition no. 33).

Erasmus is a difficult enemy for those who rush in where scholars fear to tread. The Sorbonne theologians had asserted their belief in the immortality of the soul on the basis of specific texts of the Vulgate. In his *Annotations* Erasmus quietly showed how silly they were. He too believed that the soul reigned with God after death, but he would not allow ignorant theologians to reach unwarranted certainties which were no such thing. In the *Annotations* and the *Paraphrases* all the texts which the Sorbonne cited against him are glossed in ways favourable to himself and unfavourable to the Sorbonne. He has a note on those resurrected dead seen wandering about in Jerusalem after Christ's own resurrection. Were they the first-fruits of the resurrection as implied by the Greek as Origen, Jerome and Chrysostom interpreted it? Or did they die again, as Theophylact opines? (*LB* 6. 145C, no. 55). Christ's cry to the good thief is similarly shown to be hard to interpret: how could the thief be with Christ in paradise 'today', while Christ's body was in the tomb and his soul harrowing hell? Theophylact (coldly) attached the word *today* to the previous clause: 'And Christ said to him today: "Thou shalt be with me in paradise".' Theophylact may be prolix at this point, but (as Erasmus adds with a sneer) he holds doctrines 'which do not sufficiently agree with the decrees of today's scholastic theologians'. Does this imply some sympathy with Theophylact's belief that Christ's human spirit (his *mens*) was in paradise, while his soul (his *anima*) was visiting hell? (*PG* 123. 1106C; *LB* 6. 326E, no. 28). In fact Erasmus believed that these worrying resurrected dead who were seen wandering about Jerusalem were living, here and now, with Christ. This is shown by his paraphrase of I Corinthians 15:23. And the paraphrase of the 20th verse shows that he envisaged the general resurrection as the completion of a process already started (*LB* 7. 907E–908B).

But the most suggestive text of all is St Paul's cry in Philippians 1:23, which the Sorbonne had also cited in its criticisms of him. Erasmus did indeed believe that this text threw light on the state of the soul after death. But even here the Sorbonne got it wrong! Erasmus finds the Vulgate rendering to be not above criticism—'I wish to be *loosed* (*dissolvi*) and to be with Christ'—but it will do. Chrysostom, however, interpreted *analuein* ('to loose', 'to depart') as '*methistasthai*, that is *emigrare*, or, to change one's seat'. *Emigrare* is the Ciceronian verb which (as we have seen) Erasmus often affects, since it allows of an ecstatic interpretation: death and ecstasy are both seen as a matter of the soul's 'emigrating' to another place. Now, if St Paul was expressing a wish 'to emigrate' in death, then he was wanting to do, once and for all, what he had momentarily been vouchsafed in his famous rapture (II Corinthians 12). That is precisely the sense which Erasmus reads into Philippians 1:23 when he comes to paraphrase it. St Paul is made to say:

There are reasons why I would prefer to die: others, why I should not refuse to live. Truly, consulting my own soul and balancing my own interests, I can see that it would be better for me to be freed from the tribulations of this life and to be joined more closely to Christ, returning to that ineffable happiness which I once tasted, when I was caught up into the third heaven (*LB* 7. 994E, verse 23).

The soul's rapture is, therefore, a foretaste of heaven. Erasmus does eventually find his authority for that in Paul himself.

That is the doctrine of the *Moria*. Such a theology by-passes all those tedious quarrels about the immortality of the soul based on Aristotle or counter-Aristotelian arguments! Immortality concerns the complete man, body and soul, joined together again in the last days. But that the souls of the pious dead are already with God is shown by what happens to the soul in ecstasy.

If St Paul's rapture is so important a pointer towards such things, we would expect it to have an important place in these last pages of the *Praise of Folly*. We shall not be disappointed.

(iii) *Socratic* mania

Aristotle may be a bad guide for Christians seeking certain doctrines. Plato is less so. From Plato Erasmus now takes over the conception—basic to his argument—that passionate love is a kind of insanity, a *mania*, a *furor*. In the *Phaedrus*, Socrates called the madness of the lover the most happy form of divine insanity during a wide-ranging discussion of the various forms of *mania*. In 'chapter 38' Folly had already alluded to this part of the *Phaedrus* with jesting profundity. Now she applies it to Christian ecstasy.

According to Socrates the lover is insane (*mainetai*), but that does not mean that those who are truly wise do not fall in love. To love is to be insane; but insanity is not always an evil. The greatest blessings come to man through madness, when it is a gift from the gods. Such divine gifts (for Socrates) include prophesying: so much so that the prophetic art should be called *manic* not *mantic*. Etymological fantasies played an important rôle in Platonic philosophy—witness the *Cratylus*.

Men are released from present ills by divine madness. The Muses drive their devotees creatively insane. The man who is inspired to devote himself to spiritual realities is mad—though not in the sense used by the mob. The soul of such a man soars aloft to the divine source of all beauty, borne upwards on the wings of the spirit. In other words his soul—like the ordinary madman's—strives to leave its body.

Socrates places forms of *mania* in four categories: the prophetic, under Apollo; the mystic, under Dionysius; the poetic, under the Muses; the amatory, under Aphrodite and Eros. Of these four, that of the lover is most to be desired (*Phaedrus* 233A–245B; 265A, etc.). Leonardo Bruni, Pico, Ficino and many others had made such matters commonplace among humanists.

Erasmus presents the bare bones of this doctrine with considerable sympathy. This is something that Plato had 'dreamed'. Folly's term *somniasse* may sound pejorative to ears attuned to classical usage. It is not so here. It is probably not even moderately amusing. *Somniasse* implies that Socrates had learned of these mysteries in an inspired dream: it does not mean that he dreamed them up. (Erasmus may be thinking of the end of the *Cratylus* where such terms are used to explain how Socrates learned of the divine 'ideas', so fundamental to platonic philosophy, if it is to claim certainty in a world of flux.)

When expounding these concepts in relation to Christian insanity Folly uses the standard word *furor* to translate *mania*. Such a *furor* is an ecstasy. That is what the word means in context. As such, it finds a place not only in the *Moria* but in Erasmus' works of scriptural exegesis.

From Plato's account of Socrates' doctrines Erasmus omits all reference to the presiding classical deities. He makes no allusion to the other three forms of divine madness—this later proves important. Nor does he ever make the soul of the pious love God for his beauty, first perceived as mirrored in his creation. For a scholar who knew his business that can only mean a conscious rejection of the idea, which is fundamental to Plato, to neo-Platonists and to Florentine Platonists alike. It was one of the many reproaches that Pio da Carpi made against him that he only heard cacophonous yelling where he ought to have perceived the soul-enrapturing beauty of liturgical singing. Cardinal Pio threw the whole weight of Ficinian Platonism against him, *prisca theologia* and all. It left Erasmus saddened, irritated, annoyed, but quite unimpressed (*Three and Twenty Books against Places in the Various Lucubrations of D. Erasmus*, 1531, p. 35 r°f; 73 v°f., etc.).

Whatever Erasmus had once learned from the teachers of such doctrines as Cardinal Pio espoused—if indeed he owed them anything—he is quite different in his emphasis.

It is true that Erasmus agrees with Socrates that the ecstasy of the lover is the most blessed—provided his love has God as its object. But this was no news to Renaissance Christians who had any knowledge of the tradition of their Church. For the better part of a millenium the love of the pious Christian's soul for God had been thought of in terms of Platonic rapture. Erasmus' originality, as far as the West is concerned, consisted in linking this erotic rapture inextricably to Platonic and Christian madness.

(iv) *Erotic rapture. Madness for God, sanity for men. The debt to Theophylact (I)*

Folly's happiness has become an attractive mixture of zeal and serenity. Like a thoroughbred who has finished with canters and skittishness, Folly makes a short, straight, powerful dash for home.

Only one of Socrates' *furores* interests Folly here: the happy erotic madness of the divinely-prompted lover.

The divine, erotic *mania* leads the Christian who is seized by it to love God *vehementer*, so that he lives not in himself but in him whom he loves. Ecstatic love of this intensity is reserved for only a very few;

it is a priceless foretaste of the durable, ineffable rapture which awaits all pious Christian souls in death, as, divorced from their earthly bodies, they live 'absorbed' into the Deity, awaiting the return of their same, but spiritualised, bodies at the final resurrection. Erasmus never explains what the rôle of the resurrected body is.

The general drift of what Folly was saying must have been clear to anyone who had read Pseudo-Dionysius, say, or Bernard, Aquinas, Hugo of St Victor, Bonaventura or, indeed, almost any of the mediaeval mystics. On the other hand the detail or the emphasis may have puzzled some.

The Pauline text which Erasmus sees as lending authority to the madness of the Christian lover is powerful in its implications, since it was taken as fusing together ecstatic love and ecstatic madness. It shows that St Paul loved God not with the mutual rapture of a pair of lovers but with ecstatic folly. Paul would have liked to remain thus mad for ever. His return to sanity was a duty on behalf of his flock. The *locus classicus* is II Corinthians 5:13. It may be rendered into English as: 'For whether we be mad, it is to God; or whether we be in our right mind, it is for your cause.' This text lends itself well to Erasmus' theme; for Folly it has all the advantages: it avoids the theological inconvenience of making man's love for Christ into a mutual rapture of vehement souls; it makes rapture—as in its most orthodox form it most surely is—the privilege of union with God the Father, not with the Son or the Holy Ghost; and it unequivocally shows St Paul's relationship with God to have been an ecstatic form of madness. As such it is a major source of authority for the doctrine of Christian folly. The only one of these points which Erasmus later made a compromise over was the limiting of the rapturing Godhead to the Father. In his glosses—but not in the *Moria*—he introduces the person of Christ in this context, without, of course, compromising the Father's privilege.

In the original Greek, II Corinthians 5:13 establishes the link with ecstatic folly more clearly than the Vulgate does. St Paul wrote: 'If *we are beside ourselves*', or, 'If we are mad (*exestēmen*), it is to God; if *we are in our right mind* (*sōphronoumen*), it is to you.' The contrast is between being mad and being sane. For readers of Plato this contrast between the verbs *existēmi* and *sōphroneō* strongly recalls, within the context of the *Moria*, both the *Phaedrus* (244B) and the *Republic* (I. 331C) where similar contrasts are made between the 'man of sound mind' (the *sōphrōn*) and the one given over to—potentially divine—*mania*.[1]

---

[1] See J. H. Thayer, *A Greek-English Lexicon of the New Testament*, 4th edition, Edinburgh, reprinted 1955, col. 224 (A) s.v. *existēmi* and, especially, col. 612 (B), s.v. *sōphroneō* and the five subsequent entries.

The Vulgate weakens this contrast but does not obliterate it. The element of frenzy in St Paul's statement still filters through. For *exestēmen* ('we are beside ourselves') the best manuscripts of the Vulgate read *mente excedimus* ('we are gone out of our mind'). An alternative reading is *mente excidimus* ('we are deprived of our mind'). For *sōphronoumen* ('we are in our right mind') the Vulgate reads *sobrii sumus* ('we are sober', or 'temperate'), a possible meaning, but one which weakens the balance implied in the sentence itself.

The importance of this text, both for Erasmus in general and for the *Moria* in particular, is best shown by forging ahead a little to the full version of Erasmus' note on this vital verse in the *Annotations on the New Testament*.

The first point that jumps out of the page when we do this is Erasmus' Latin rendering. The Vulgate is puzzling, but not particularly shocking: *sive enim mente excedimus, Deo; sive sobrii sumus, vobis* ('Whether we are gone out of our mind, it is unto God, whether we are sober it is unto you'). The translation in Erasmus' *Novum Instrumentum* allows of no such tergiversation: *nam sive insanimus, Deo insanimus; sive sani sumus, vobis sani sumus*. This outdoes the Greek original in the clarity of its opposition of the two verbs; in other words, Erasmus has not softened but emphasised the contrast between them. St Paul is made to say—with no beating about the bush—that he is 'insane' to God, 'sane' to his followers in Corinth: 'For if we are insane, we are insane to God; if we are sane, we are sane to you.' (There is no genuine hypothetical force in the repeated *sive* ('if' or 'whether'). St Paul is made to mean that he is sane and insane by turns, depending on whom he is dealing with, men or God.)

The relevance of all this to the *Moria* is shown by the two notes on this verse. That on the verb *exestēmen* is short and to the point:

exestēmen: as though you were to say, 'we are enraptured outside ourselves' (*rapti sumus extra nos*)—what is called ecstasy (*mentis excessus*) or rapture (*raptus*). Perhaps what was written [in the Latin] was *excidimus mente* not *excedimus*, giving the meaning: 'if we are mad (*insanimus*): if we are sane (*sani sumus*): if we are wise (*sapimus*): if we are foolish (*desipimus*).' That is explained better by what follows.

'What follows' is the note on *eite sōphronoumen:*

that is, 'if we are sober' (*sive sobrii sumus*). Ambrose reads *sive sanum sapimus* ('if we perceive sanely'), for that is also what *sōphronein* means at times. Greek glosses (*Graecanica scholia*) advises us that to speak wondrous things appertains to the insane (*insanorum esse ingentia loqui*) who have apparently forgotten themselves. Ambrose points out the same. So does Augustine, in several places, including his exegesis on the thirtieth psalm, making *excessus* refer to ecstasy. Several times Augustine reads *excessimus* [in the perfect tense] not *excidimus* [in the present], following the tense of the Greek—although when dealing with passions of the soul it is usual to use the past for the present. In his twelfth book *Against Faustus*, chapter 26, for *sobrii sumus* he reads *temperantes sumus* ('we are moderate').

This last clause shows that more than one interpretation is possible. Nevertheless the allusion to the 'insanity' stressed by the Greek *scholia* reinforces the meaning given by Ambrose, who does indeed, though with a different sense, contrast *sanus* and *insanus*—if, that is, the *Commentary on Corinthians* is by him (see *PL* 17. 312C). The main weight of St Augustine's authority probably also makes the balance tip in favour of ecstatic madness, but less certainly. Erasmus' own rendering leaves one in no doubt whatever about which way he inclined. His note continues in such a way as to clinch the matter:

Theophylact wrote a triple commentary on this: i) [St Paul], he says, 'being about to utter great things, calls it ecstasy' (*de magnis rebus loquuturus, ecstasim vocat*); ii) again, he says, 'if we seem to be insane: if we seem to be sober'; iii) finally, he attributes madness (*insaniam*) to Paul, but a madness which is *erōtikēn*, that is, amatory. For Plato taught that *furor* was of three kinds: that of seers, poets and lovers, the last of which he believed to be the most happy (*felicissimum*). Such a *furor* Theophylact attributes to St Paul, who lived not in himself but in Christ—just as the soul (*anima*) of the lover is not where it animates but where it loves (*non est ubi animat, sed ubi amat*). And Paul, for the sake of his brethren, could wish to be anathema to Christ' [Romans 9:3]. It should be noted that unless you repeat both the verbs, the sentences seem incomplete: 'If we have gone out of our mind, we have gone out to God: if we are of a sound mind (*sanae mentis*), we are sane (*sani*) for you'. For if Paul glories in anything, it pertains not to his own glory but to God's. If he says ordinary things (*mediocria*), he attributes that to the weaker ones, to whose passions and capacity he conforms himself . . . (*LB* 5. 767EF, 3 21).

This account of Theophylact's linking of St Paul's rapturous love with Socratic *mania erotica* is loyally taken over from the manuscript of Theophylact's Pauline Commentaries which Erasmus used. It is now in the Bodleian at *Ms. Auct. E.1.6*, where it was recently identified by Mr R. W. Hunt.[1] The relevant part of Theophylact's commentary on

[1] See his important article 'Greek manuscripts in the Bodleian Library from the collection of John Stojković of Ragusa', in *Studia Patristica* VII, ed. F. L. Cross: *Texte und Untersuchungen zur Geschichte der altchristlichen Literatur*, Band 92, Berlin, 1966, pp. 75–82. Mr Hunt saved me months, perhaps years, of fruitless search.

II Corinthians 5:13 which Erasmus transcribed in the *Annotations* appears on leaf [79 v°]. The text also appears, correctly transcribed, in Liddell's edition of Theophylact (London, 1636, p. 365) and in Migne (*PG* 124. 852D–853A).

The ecstatic implications of this text of St Paul's were recognised in patristic times. Gregory of Nyssa exploits it much as Erasmus does, linking it with the theme of sober drunkenness and with Festus' accusation of madness levelled against St Paul (Daniélou, *From Glory to Glory*, pp. 238f.). Whether Erasmus knew of this at first hand I cannot say. Anything written by Gregory of Nyssa was widely read among patristic authors and their Renaissance students. Erasmus later spoke of Gregory in the highest terms.

(v) *Erotic rapture: the debt to Theophylact (II): confusion with Athanasius*
The twin glosses on II Corinthians 5:13 which appear in the *Annotations* are so rich in their allusions that they merit a book in themselves. The light they throw upon the *Moria* is very great, showing how Erasmus wanted the insane ecstasy which Folly eulogised to be interpreted.

The *Annotations on the New Testament* were published in 1516. If the second note, just transcribed, had appeared there in its entirety, just as it does in the *Opera Omnia*, we would be justified in attributing Folly's development of Christian ecstasy in terms of erotic *furor* principally to the influence of Theophylact. This Greek-Orthodox Archbishop of Achrida exerted such a fundamental influence on Erasmus' theology in all his New Testament studies, including the *Novum Instrumentum*, the *Annotations on the New Testament* and the *Paraphrases*, that there is nothing in itself improbable about this. What *is* puzzling, is the general neglect of Theophylact by Renaissance scholars: he is one of the most vital of the channels through which Greek theology poured into the receptive west.

But the note is not fully developed in 1516. The allusion to Theophylact and what follows it does not appear until 1527. Does this mean that the citing of Theophylact's authority is purely and simply an afterthought? I think not. I believe Theophylact exerted a profound influence on Erasmus long before he knew who he really was. The question is a complicated one.

Erasmus may not have had access to the original text of Theophylact until 1514, when he arrived at Basle. There he found two volumes, one of which contained Theophylact's commentaries on the Gospels, the other (among other things) his commentaries on the Pauline epistles. The first of these volumes is still in Basle, in the university library at *A.III.15*. The second is the manuscript *Ms. Auct.*

E. 1.6 of the Bodleian Library, which Mr Hunt's scholarly vigilance recently identified.[1]

When Erasmus came across these volumes he believed that they were the work of a certain Vulgarius. It is under the name of Vulgarius that Theophylact appears, in company with Origen, Chrysostom, Cyril, Jerome, Cyprian and Augustine—after Cyril and before Jerome—on the title page of the *editio princeps* of the *Novum Instrumentum* (Basle, 1516). He does not appear in the epistle dedicatory to Leo X. Whenever Erasmus cites him, he calls him Vulgarius, until the 1519 edition of the *Annotations*. It was during the printing of the volume that he realised his error. Despite his being placed between Cyril and Jerome, Erasmus already realised in 1516 that he was a comparative modern: (*recentior*) but, he added, he was not negligible (*haud aspernandus*).

It is helpful to study these two manuscript volumes of Theophylact at first hand. Both are in a remarkable state of preservation, bearing the labels and pressmarks they had in the fifteenth century. The label of the volume in Basle, containing the Gospels, reads (with abbreviations): *Vulgarius Archiepiscopus Super Evangelia quatuor* followed by the original pressmark *Gr. 27* (Graeca: 27). Moreover, on the verso of the flyleaf is written (in a fifteenth-century hand) *wlgarius archiepiscopus super ewangelia*. Erasmus ought, out of sheer prudence, to have read with greater care the not excessively ligatured title on page one of the manuscript, where the name *Theophylaktos* does appear; he apparently took it as an adjective, though what sense he gave to it is not clear.[2]

The volume containing the commentaries on the Pauline epistles—the one now in the Bodleian—also helps explain Erasmus' error: the original label on the cover is still there also. It too bears the original pressmark *Gr. 27*. The name *Theophylactus* is, except for a few final letters, illegible. The next words—*Vulgarij (?) Episcopi Expositiones* —mean, no doubt 'The Commentaries of Bishop Vulgarius'. In the Dominican Library these two volumes were catalogued under that name. *Vulgarius*, doubtless with the sense of *Bulgaricus*, the Bulgarian, is an appropriate way of referring to Theophylact: orthodox Christian theologians from Bulgaria known to the west were not ten-a-penny.

Erasmus first used the manuscripts of Theophylact precipitously and carelessly, perhaps only exploiting them a month or so before his

---

[1] Cf. André Vernet, '*Les manuscrits grecs de* Jean de Raguse († 1443)', in *Basler Zeitschrift für Geschichte und Altertumskunde*, tome 61 (1961), pp. 75–108, especially p. 88, nos. 27a and 27b; to be completed by the study of Mr Hunt.

[2] Jortin deals unsympathetically with this confusion in his *Life of Erasmus*, 1760, tome 2, pp. 230f. He is very misleading, making no reference to the Vulgarius label or to the inscription on the flyleaf.

Novum Instrumentum appeared in 1516. He made amends later, adding a great many notes inspired by Theophylact in later versions of his *Annotations*.[1]

But Erasmus did not wait until he could read 'Vulgarius' in Greek. He first knew Theophylact in Latin. And he knew him under the name of St Athanasius. It was under the vast prestige of that great and right-thinking saint that the Italian scholar Persona, or Porsena, had published his Latin version of Theophylact's *Ennarationes in Epistolas Sancti Pauli* (V. Han, Rome 1477).

One can imagine the magnetic attraction this volume must have had for a young scholar such as Erasmus, devoted as he was to Origen. When Nicolaus Beraldus dedicated his own re-edition of Porsena's Theophylact—still under the name of Athanasius—to Bishop Michael Bodetus in 1519, he hoped that Athanasius would become as widely read as Origen now was. He evoked great names on the title-page, including that of Angel Politian. He also reprints Erasmus' *Paraclesis* as a preface.[2] This not only gives 'Athanasius' humanist credentials but links him—without permission—with Erasmus' own authority. (Neither Porsena not anyone else ever gives any reason for ascribing the work to Athanasius.)

Erasmus certainly knew and used the Porsena translation. He tells us he suspected the work not to be authentic before he eventually collated Porsena's translation with the original. But this statement, once more, does not appear in the 1516 *Annotations*, being added in 1527 (*LB* 5. 555EF). In other words, whatever his suspicions were, he did not know Porsena's *Athanasius* to be inauthentic, either when composing the *Moria* or when preparing his *Novum Instrumentum*. Part of Erasmus' bitterness on this subject, which encouraged him to believe that Porsena had deliberately deceived his public and his pope, doubtless arose from his being himself taken in (cf. *Annotation* on I Corinthians 12:27: *LB* 5. 721F. Once more this is an addition to the 1516 footnote, dating from 1527.) One of the ironies of fate is that enemies of Erasmus such as Stunica continued to try and squash him with Pseudo-Athanasius' authority long after Erasmus himself showed who he really was. (*LB* 9. 311DE, *Apology against Stunica*; cf. also his *Apology against Sanctius Caranza*, *LB* 9. 409D.) Throughout the Renaissance, scholars were misled by Porsena. Miles Coverdale, in his

---

[1] Dr A. Rabil, the only author whom I know to be aware of the importance of the various additions to the *Annotations*, counted thirty supplementary allusions to Theophylact in the glosses on Romans in the 1527 edition: *Erasmus and the New Testament* 1972, p. 116.

[2] *Athanasii Episcopi Alexandrini Sanctissima Eloquentissimaque Opera*, Jean Petit, Paris; privilege dated, 19 June 1518; text dated *Pridie Idus April*, 1519 Roman style.

Apologie to the Christen Reader prefixed to his English Bible of 1535, still believes that Vulgarius was an ancient Greek, mentioning him in the same breath as Origen (sig. † 4 v°). Moreover, the edition of 'Athanasius' published in 1522 by Knoblouchus of Strasburg is so faulty as to be totally unreliable (copy in British Library at *1221. l.21*). What students made out of that garbled text is anybody's guess. It contains dozens of misreadings per page. To this day, many important libraries still attribute these works to St Athanasius, without a word of warning. No wonder that, throughout the Renaissance, many cited him with awe as an ultimate authority. A generation after Erasmus, Peter Martyr Vermigli thought little of him; but then he was an exceptional scholar and knew who he really was. (*Defensio doctrinae . . . de . . . Eucharistiae Sacramento, adversus Stephani Gardineri . . . Librum sub nomine M. Antonii Constantii editum*, London, 1562, p. 75.)

Erasmus once believed that his linking of Socratic and Pauline ecstasy in the *Moria* had the authority of St Athanasius behind it.

(vi) *Erotic rapture: the debt to Theophylact (III): Socratic rapture according to 'Athanasius'*

Porsena's translation of Theophylact is not a literal one. It leaves things out; it puts things in; it is sometimes nearer to a loose explanatory paraphrase than to a close work of translation. That is what makes it interesting to compare it, in its own right, with what Folly says in the *Moria*. I have used the copy in the British Library at IB 17343. The gloss on II Corinthians 5:13 is to be found on l4r°. In the margin someone has written in a sixteenth-century hand the two relevant Greek verbs, *exestēmen* and *sōphronoumen* (in capitals, without accents) and noted that the word *gar* (for) has not been translated, adding the comment (in Latin): 'Here indeed he calls *extasim* what elsewhere he calls *dementiam* (madness).' It is tempting to think this marginal comment had some connexion with Erasmus, as it closely mirrors his preoccupations, but there are no grounds that I know of for doing so. The Latin is dense. I translate it as literally as possible and apologise for the awkwardness:

Sive mente excedimus deo: sive sobrii sumus vobis. 'Whether,' he says, 'we prophesy something great, whether we have gone out of our mind'—what elsewhere he calls folly—'we do it for God's sake,—lest, if you were to think too little of me, you should suffer punishment and destruction for your contempt of me. If we speak about ordinary and humble matters, we do so in order that you might learn humility.' Or, in another way: 'If anyone suspects that we are out of our mind'—that is, are raging mad—'we expect our reward for this from God; we were accused of this; if indeed anyone thinks we are being abstemious, let him seize the advantages of this our abstaining.' The saying can be understood another way, namely: 'If, seized by raving, we have gone out of our mind, we are insane for God's sake, so that we may make you more commendable to him.' For Paul was seized by the dementedness of a mighty love—if we can call it *dementia*. Anyone aroused by such passion would, as a lover, without a doubt, be dying for God; such a man lives in him with whom he has fallen in love; and so, as someone caught up out of himself, he would be entirely carried away by God. He would not lead his life for itself but as a contemplation of him whom he has so long pursued with such a love. And so he says, 'If we have gone out of our mind, it is to God'—that is, for God's sake.

(The same hand which wrote the marginalia has stricken out the final verb of the penultimate sentence, *insectaretur*, which implies pursuing someone with railing words, replacing it by *prosequeretur*, which allows of the notion of a more honourable pursuit.)

Here then, in a work which Erasmus certainly read, is St Paul's love conceived as foolish insanity (*dementia*), as a *mania* (*furor*), as a form of folly (*stultitia*). Such a passion leads man to rave (*furere*); he may indeed be seized (*arreptus*) by *furor*. And such a madness is interpreted in terms of that Platonic love by which a lover is so 'caught up' (*raptus*) that he is outside himself (*extra se*). A man in that state may be said to be insane (*insanire*).

Anyone reading those words and believing that they loyally conveyed the opinion of St Athanasius could justifiably believe that Pauline rapture and Socratic, manic, erotic ecstasy were one and the same thing.

(vii) *Erotic madness: a strange distortion of the text of Theophylact*
The Greek Church has always allowed a place of importance to divine folly—Dostoïevsky's *Idiot* is more at home in Russian Orthodoxy than in western Catholicism. This perhaps explains why both Porsena's translation and Theophylact's original give a larger place to Christian folly than Western commentators usually do. To list the cases where this is so would take us too far from the *Moria* and so must be resisted. But in at least one case Erasmus was so disposed to find Christian madness in his Greek sources that he read into Vulgarius a meaning which can by no means whatever be justified. (The discrepancy was pointed out by Jortin in his *Life of Erasmus*, II 1760, p. 230, though he does not see its implications.) Erasmus so misread and mistranscribed the gloss on Luke 11:53 that he makes Christ appear as a fool when Theophylact does not. In Luke 11 the Scribes and Pharisees ply Jesus with questions. Theophylact explains that, when many people pose questions in this way to one man, 'he cannot answer them

all (*pasin*), so to simple folk (*tois anoētois*) he appears to be in difficulties'. Erasmus leaves out the *pasin* and transcribes *tois anoētois* as *tou anoētou* which, as Jortin tartly adds (p. 230), results in a sentence which 'is not even Greek'. And so Erasmus makes his authority say that a man in the position that Jesus was in 'cannot reply, presenting the appearance of a fool, because he is stuck', *speciem praebet stulti, quod haereat*, (*LB* 6. 281, 35).

What is disturbing, is that Erasmus realised he was saying something quite startling, yet he never even checked, let alone subsequently corrected, his transcription or translation. Is it conceivable that he did not reread it, when returning to Theophylact for further matter to work into his *Annotations*? He claimed to be following the interpretation 'of the Greek exegetes'. And he prefaced the remarks just cited with a scholarly claim to be trusted: 'In case anyone does not have enough faith in me, I give below the actual words of Theophylact' —originally, of course, 'of Vulgarius'. What he printed and reprinted several times was a perversion of the text of his manuscript, the correct reading of which (as given also by both Liddell and Migne) can be checked in Basle, on leaf [128] of *Ms. A. III. 15*. There is a doodle in the margin—a pointing finger—which indicates the continuation of this very passage. It is almost certainly Erasmus' own handiwork. Both the word *pasin* and the words *tois anoētois* are perfectly legible even today. So there is absolutely no question whatsoever of Theophylact's having stated that Christ at this juncture, presented 'the appearance of a fool'. He did not do so. Erasmus read that meaning into him. He could have corrected his error. He did not.

Far from Erasmus being shocked by the notion that Christ may have presented the appearance of a fool, he made him do so when there is no evidence at all to support his contention—even though he said there was.

(viii) *Erotic madness: the debt to Theophylact (IV). Conjectures about the Grocyn-Linacre manuscript*

It is certain that Erasmus knew some of Theophylact's ideas, believing they were authorised by St Athanasius. Others he knew, thinking they were authorised by a certain Vulgarius. But are we to assume that Theophylact, known to be such, had no influence on him at all? Were both the 1511 and the 1514 texts of the *Moria* written when Erasmus was in a state of utter confusion over the interlocking pieces of a jigsaw puzzle made up of pieces labelled Athanasius and Vulgarius?

On the whole, the answer must be, yes. But he could well have known of Theophylact at first hand when he was in England. Grocyn possessed a manuscript of Theophylact's commentaries on the four

Gospels—not, alas, on the Pauline epistles as well. This passed into the hands of Linacre. Erasmus moved in the same circles as these men. He was known to have a passion for Greek theology. It is by no means impossible that he read it or, at least, heard of its contents.

The first President of Corpus Christi College, Oxford bequeathed the manuscript to his College library. It is still there. I first heard of it during the Thomas More Exposition in London (1977/8) from J. R. Trapp's entry in the Catalogue. Dr Trapp kindly sent me a xerox of a photo of the title-page. This Corpus Christi Theophylact clinches matters. If Erasmus had read this manuscript, or if he had informed talks with Grocyn, Linacre, or someone else who had, then the main lines of Theophylact's thought would have been known to him. Not, however, the linking of Socratic and Pauline concepts of divine erotic mania. To know of that, access to the commentaries on St Paul was quite indispensible. Where and when Erasmus first read Theophylact on St Paul, knowing whom he was reading, I do not know. It was probably long after the *Moria* was written and revised. It is probable that Erasmus, when first writing the *Moria*, believed that his linking of Socratic and Pauline concepts of ecstasy was supported by the authority of St Athanasius; later, when revising the *Moria* for the 1514 edition, he may still have done so. About 1515 or 1516 he had almost certainly come to the conclusion that these ideas were supported by 'both' Athanasius and Vulgarius. Later Theophylact joined these two, making a trinity of authorities. But eventually scholarly patience triumphed. Erasmus realised that he was dealing with one authority only: Theophylact, archbishop of Bulgaria.

This must have represented not only a shock but a great disappointment. To link together Socratic *mania* and Pauline insanity, believing you are following St Athanasius is one thing; to do so realising that you are merely following Theophylact of Bulgaria is another. Some time during his stays in England—some time, that is, before his final departure in 1517—the seeds of doubt, however small, may have finally been sown.

(ix) *Erotic rapture: a link with tradition*

In his note on II Corinthians 5:13, Erasmus not only cited Theophylact's identification of Pauline madness with the erotic *mania* of Socrates, he goes on to link it with a major Catholic tradition: 'St Paul,' he writes, 'lived not in himself, but in Christ.' This reverses the Pauline assertion (Galatians 2:20): 'I live; yet not I but Christ liveth in me.' In his note on this verse (*LB* 6. 811 § 31) Erasmus gives a broad hint of an ecstatic interpretation, pointing out succinctly that Paul changes subject 'as though he had forgotten himself' (see below,

p. 205). In the *Paraphrases* (*LB* 7. 951CE); Christ's 'living in me' is interpreted in terms of that immortal life which, thanks to the Spirit, the
Christian in some sense lives here and now. Nothing, apparently,
would make Erasmus accept the love of Christ and a man as a mutual
rapture in the manner of Pseudo-Dionysius, or as a driving out of the
individual soul by the divine spirit in the manner of Philo. He knew
what he was doing, since he proceeds to quote a scholastic maxim
often connected with Galatians 2:20. The soul of Paul, says Erasmus,
in his gloss on II Corinthians 5:13, like the *anima* of all lovers, 'is not
where it animates but where it loves' (*anima non est ubi animat, sed ubi
amat*). This famous phrase which does not occur in the *Moria* but is
implied there, links the ecstatic love explained in the *Annotations* and
praised by Folly, with a millenium and a half of Christian mysticism.
The standard expression is *Verius est anima ubi amat quam ubi
animat*—the soul, that is, more truly belongs where it loves than where
it simply animates. The expression was coined by St Bonaventura
(*Soliloquium* II. 2, no. 12, in *Opera* VIII, Quaracchi 1898, 49, col. 1).
Bonaventura took the notion over from St Bernard, where it is less
memorable since it is applied to the *spiritus*, not the *anima* (ibid. note 5);
so in St Bernard there is no play on the words *anima* and *animat*. As
Bonaventura coined it, it is one of those powerful expressions which
was so widely used that its source was sometimes lost to view;
Aquinas even attributed it to St Augustine. In the history of mysticism
the idea which it embodies constitutes a bridge by which Platonic
rapture passed through Pseudo-Dionysius to Bernard, Bonaventura
and mediaeval mysticism generally, then on to high Renaissance
ecstatics like John of the Cross, as well as to a scholarly saint like
François de Sales.[1]

In ways such as these Erasmus gently pointed out to his public what
the *Moria*, with its ecstatic love, implied: it was like the rapturous love
that Theophylact, Bernard, Bonaventura and so many others wrote
about; it was in the same tradition—but it was *not* that championed by
Pseudo-Dionysius.

2. Peregrinari: *the sojourns abroad of the wandering soul*

When the soul loves *vehementer*, it migrates (*demigrat*). Such a soul
(*animus*), whenever it practises sojourning away from its body—*cum*

---

[1] A most useful study is that of Jean Orcibal, '*Une formule de l'amour extatique de
Platon à Saint Jean de la Croix et au Cardinal de Bérulle*', in *Mélanges Gilson*, Toronto and
Paris, 1959, pp. 447–63. Cf. also N. J. Perella, *The Kiss, Sacred and Prophane*, California,
1969, pp. 90f. I was kindly put on to this latter study by Dr Sears Jayne; that in turn put
me on to Jean Orcibal, so considerably expanding my examples of the Bernard-
Bonaventura formula.

... *a corpore peregrinari meditatur*—does not use its bodily organs aright. And Folly adds the comment that you would, without any doubt, call such a phenomenon by the name of *furor*.

Here we have both Socrates and Cicero as aids to understanding St Paul. Cicero called Socratic *mania* by the name of *furor* in many places, including his treatise *On Divination* (1. 31. 66) where we are told that *furor* is usual when the 'soul, drawn away (*abstractus*) from the body, is violently agitated by divine instigation'. As for the phrase *animus peregrinatur* ('the soul sojourns abroad' or 'wanders away' from its home), it is found in Cicero's *On the Nature of the Gods* (1. 20. 51).

These usages are important. They set the tone. Much more important is what St Paul said in II Corinthians 5:8: 'We are confident, willing to sojourn away from the body and to be present with the Lord.'

The phrase 'to sojourn away from the body' (*ekdēmēsai ek tou sōmatos*) is translated in the Vulgate by *peregrinari a corpore*. These are the very terms used by Folly, for whom the soul practises *a corpore peregrinari*, 'to sojourn away from the body'. The same verb is used in the same sense in II Corinthians 5:6: 'Therefore we are always confident, knowing that while we are at home in the body, we are sojourning away from God' (*peregrinamur a Deo*).

In Christian usage the notions enshrined by the words *peregrinatio* and *peregrinari* are ambiguous, richly and seminally so. In one sense man is a pilgrim precisely because his soul is living abroad on earth, away from its true home in the heavens. In another sense, the human soul was made to be at home in the pure bodies which Adam and Eve received in Paradise; life in a post-Lapsarian sinful body is a *peregrinatio* back to original innocence; any strivings towards sinlessness or purity are a journey towards one's home. In yet another sense, any living away from God is a banishment, an exile; any striving towards communion with God is also, therefore, a striving to reach home. The sense which is of primary importance to the *Moria* is yet another one: the soul is above all a pilgrim when it practises leaving its body, sojourning abroad from its home in the body—seeking its other home in God.

The word *peregrinari* is not easy to translate into English by one word or phrase. I have nevertheless usually rendered it by 'to sojourn abroad' (or, 'away from'), partly in order to bring its meaning close to the Greek original, *ekdēmeō* (to go abroad; to emigrate, to live abroad), partly to evoke memories of a principal translation of the term in the Authorised Version, from which it has entered the English language. It should be remembered, however, that its usage in II Corinthians 5:8 with *ek tou sōmatos* ('out of the body') gives to this verb the special

sense of the spirit, or the soul, 'emigrating' from its body to 'live
abroad' in ecstasy. To enter more freely into this meaning—which is a
very widespread one—a convenient way would be to read St Bernard's seventh sermon *De Tempore* entitled *De Peregrino, mortuo et
crucifixo (PL* 183, col. 183cff.), where the ideal pious sojourner on
earth is shown as being dead to the world, crucified with Christ and
'caught away to the third heaven', as St Paul was.

II Corinthians 5:6–8 is associated by many mystics with the notion
of rapture—so much that the word *peregrinari* as Folly uses it can be
said to have definite ecstatic overtones. Ever since Augustine's *De
Doctrina Christiana* (1. 3. 3 and 2. 7. 11) it has been used that way,
associated with Philippians 3:20: 'Our usual abode'—or 'our inter-
course'—'is in heaven' (*nostra autem conversatio—hēmōn gar to
politeuma—in caelis est*).

One quick way to check how those interlinked Scriptural verses
may be used in ecstatic contexts is—for those who have access to the
work—to read Bartholomew of Medina's *Expositio in I^a II^ae Angelici
Doctoris* [i.e., of Thomas Aquinas], Salamanca, 1588, pp. 302f. Bartholomew explains that ecstasy may resemble madness (*insania*); that
it makes a man be outside himself (*extra se*); that it is caused by love. He
goes on to explain that, when Paul speaks sublimely, he calls it
'ecstasy' or 'madness', as, elsewhere he calls it 'folly' (*insipientia*). Paul
wishes to 'sojourn away from his body' (*peregrinari a corpore*) so as 'to
be present with God'. How could such a man fail to be 'outside
himself' with loving madness (*insania amatoria*)? And Bartholomew of
Medina, like so many others, sees this in terms of Pseudo-Dionysius'
interpretation of St Paul's cry: 'I live; yet not I; but Christ liveth in me.'

The word *peregrinatio* which in classical Latin means living abroad,
travelling to foreign parts, changing one's abode, has to Renaissance
ears a secondary sense of pilgrimage. Man, because he lives abroad
away from God, yearns either to return home to him in the rapture of
death, or at very least to be with God, even while sojourning on earth
away from him. Life is analogous to the journey of a pilgrim to a holy
sanctuary. Important light is thrown on this part of the *Moria* by the
adage (4. 10. 74) *Man's Life is a 'peregrinatio'*:

Socrates in Plato's *Axiochus* cites this saying as being commonly repeated by
everyone—though this dialogue is placed amongst the spurious ones, seeming to be the work of a Christian man who wanted to imitate Plato. This
judgment is frequently found in the Sacred Books [of the Bible]: life is an
exile, a temporary dwelling (*incolatus*), a sojourning abroad (*peregrinatio*).
However the Platonic Socrates tells that the souls of men had fallen down
from heaven, preparing their return there by the study of philosophy.

This, duly Christianised, is in the main the sense in which Folly and others use the theme of life as a *peregrinatio*: it is a life in which the pious man practises the philosophy of Christ which leads his soul back towards heaven.

These juxtapositions of classical and Christian themes may seem innocent enough. But they are potentially dangerous, in that the Socratic doctrine just cited fully accepts the pre-existence of souls before birth. Christian orthodoxy came to reject this—though it is by no means certain that Augustine always did. Bound with the manuscript of Theophylact on the Pauline Epistles now in the Bodleian, Erasmus would have read Nemesius of Emesa's treatise *On the Nature of Man*. (He would have been all the more impressed, no doubt, since the manuscript ascribes the work to St Gregory of Nyssa.) This Christian Platonist also accepts the pre-existence of souls, though not without *nuances*. But in 553 the Council of Constantinople condemned the doctrine of the soul's pre-existence as Origenistic.[1] I do not think that Erasmus was ever seduced into accepting such heterodox ideas: but in the *Moria* he was indiscreet enough not to make this as clear as a prudent man might think desirable.

Erasmus paraphrases II Corinthians 5:6–8 in such a way as to bring out the theme of the soul's migrating from the body in order to live with God (*LB* 7.923Ef.). A more striking exposition of the theme is to be found in the *Commentary on the 38th Psalm* (*LB* 5. 464D–F). There one can see not only how vital this notion of the soul's *peregrinatio* remained for Erasmus, but also how vital it became for him to avoid certain Platonic associations while expounding others. His starting point is psalm 38 (39): 13: 'For I am a stranger (*advena*) with thee: a sojourner (*peregrinus*).' Erasmus has to take care to show that he does not accept that Platonic view which makes the souls of men exiles in the sense that they have been sent back to earth from their home in heaven, so as to live in other bodies. Ambiguity on such points needed to be avoided. This Erasmus now does.

All men, whether they recognise it or not, are strangers and sojourners, though not all men are sojourners 'with God'. Indeed, these two things seem to be opposed to each other: to be 'with God' and to 'sojourn away from God'. And they *are* opposed, unless man's substance is a double one. Those who are connected with the earth by their bodies but have their hearts in heaven are truly sojourners and strangers 'with God'. Our homeland (*patria*) is there. Our wishes sigh for it; but our outer man sticks here. The most blessed Paul was this kind of sojourner—he who wrote to the Corinthians

---

[1] Useful details in R. T. Wallis, *Neo-Platonism*, London, 1972, pp. 102f.

saying: 'The things which are seen are temporary, but the things which are not seen are eternal. For we know that if the earthly house of our tabernacle be destroyed, we have a building from God, a dwelling not made with hands, eternal, in the heavens' [II Corinthians 5:6–8]: 'We are therefore always of good heart and know that, whilst we are in the body, we sojourn away from God: for we walk by faith not by appearance; we are of good courage, I say, and are willing rather to be absent abroad from the body (*peregre abesse a corpore*) and to be present with God.' [Erasmus is echoing his own *Novum Instrumentum* not the Vulgate. The Annotations *ad loc.* support his meaning here; cf. *LB* 6. 766B; Ff.] Paul said he was a sojourner because, though he was turned towards the earth by his body, he was turned towards God by faith and hope. As a sojourner he despised the things which are temporary and which can be seen with the eyes of the body; he hastened towards the things which are eternal, which can be descried with the eyes of faith [cf. II Corinthians 4:18]. For this reason, the more a man is but a sojourner here, the happier he is (*hoc est felicior*). The children of this world live here entirely: how they grieve when they must emigrate from the body! What complaints they utter!

The words used here, especially the scriptural allusions and such phrases as *hoc est felicior*, make this passage directly relevant to what Folly is now saying. Both the *Moria* and this psalm commentary are appealing to II Corinthians 4 and 5. Then, with an untranslatable play on words, juxtaposing *exsilio* (to spring forth) and *exsilium* (exile), Erasmus adds:

The pious man who has learned from Christian Philosophy to sojourn away from the body—so far as it is allowed—*springs forth* rejoicing from *exile* to his homeland (*LB* 5. 464E).

At pius qui per Christianam Philosophiam didicit a corpore, quatenus licet, peregrinari, gaudens *exsilit*; nimirum ab *exsilio* in Patriam.

Through love of God the pious man leaves his body behind, as far as it is allowed, no longer being 'at home' there as he leaps in ecstasy towards that homeland where his Father reigns and from which, throughout this earthly life, he knows himself to be an exile. But one notices a prudence in this text which is lacking in the *Moria*: the sojourning away from the body is now pursued only *quatenus licet*, 'as far as it is allowed'.

Erasmus felt inclined to enter a further caveat. This use of *peregrinus* and *peregrinari* could evoke associations with those Platonic doctrines which were certainly not orthodox nor, by any stretch of the imagination, able to be made conformable to orthodoxy. He goes straight on to add the following:

In order to emphasise that this life is a sojourning abroad, David did not think it was enough to say 'I am a stranger' (*advena*), but added that he was a sojourner (*peregrinus*).

Erasmus then appeals to the words which the Septuagint uses for these terms.

Paroikos (=*advena*) is one who migrates into a foreign house. *Parepidēmos* (=*peregrinus*) is one who migrates amongst a foreign people. Let there occur to no one's mind Plato's dream about souls falling down from heaven and being allotted other bodies.

Erasmus is correct: *parepidēmos* is used in the Bible to show that Christians merely sojourn here on earth: heaven is their home. But why this sudden warning against Plato's doctrine of the migration of souls? One likely explanation is that the proverb 'man's life is a *peregrinatio*, a *parepidēmia*' is best known from the *Axiochus*. The *Axiochus* follows Plato in making man into an immortal soul entombed in a body which it yearns to leave behind once and for all, and to return to the heaven from which it came.[1] But that is not the whole story. Erasmus realised that his enthusiastic linking of Platonism with Christianity needed defending on several fronts, since it could be taken by hostile critics as suggesting sympathy for a serious heresy, making the spirit belong to heaven in a sense which could be taken—however unjustly—as excluding the earthly body, seen as a permanent and eternal evil as it was for neo-Platonists. The *Moria* is in fact close to the theological position of St Augustine. There is no temporising about the resurrection of the body: the body, duly spiritualised, is what brings immortality. Later Erasmus defends his position by citing, more than once, the Wisdom of Solomon (9:15): 'For the corruptible body weigheth down the soul, and the earthly dwelling presseth heavy on a mind thinking many things' (see below, p. 182). This is an excellent example of how he meets direct or implied criticism. He by no means always replies openly and aggressively: he quietly plugs the gaps and dots his *i*s. St Augustine cites this verse twice in the *City of God*; the second time he quotes it (13:16) to defend the doctrine of the resurrection and to show that Platonic doctrines of the body are really in accord with Christian teachings—if only they were properly understood . . . Augustine does this by showing that it is not the body as such, but the post-Lapsarian *corruptible* body which weighs down the soul. The body became corruptible as a result of sin.

---

[1] Cf. *Axiochus* 365Bf.; Rudolph Agricola renders *parepidēmia* here by *peregrinatio*: cf. *Platonis Opera*, ed. & trans. by Ficino, *et al.*; edition used, Lyons, 1560, p. 729C.

Nevertheless, the separation of the soul from its body is penal, whereas neo-Platonists wrongly believe that it is in release from the body as such that the soul finds eternal bliss. Christians believe that immortality consists in the reunion of the soul with the body rendered incorruptible. This is the achievement of Christ's redemption.

For a platonising Christian such as Erasmus, Wisdom of Solomon 9:15 is a sheet anchor, firmly set in the orthodox platonising of Augustine himself.

3. *The body and the soul swallowed up in victory. The homeland of the soul in heaven. Happy madness*

Ergo quaenam futura est illa coelitum vita, ad quam piae mentes tanto studio suspirant? Nempe spiritus absorbebit corpus, utpote victor ac fortior. Idque hoc faciet facilius, partim quod jam velut in suo regno est, partim quod jam olim in vita corpus ad hujusmodi transformationem repurgarit atque extenuarit. Deinde spiritus a mente illa summa mire absorbebitur, quippe infinitis partibus potentiore, ita ut jam totus homo extra se futurus sit, nec alia ratione foelix futurus, nisi quod extra sese positus, patietur quiddam ineffabile a summo illo bono, omnia in sese rapiente (Scheurer H3r°; Kan 187–8).

What then will that life in heaven be, which pious minds so zealously sigh for? Surely the spirit will swallow up the body, as being the victor and the stronger. And it will do this all the more easily, partly because it is already in its own kingdom as it were, partly because, formerly, in this life, it will have purged and fined down the body for such a transformation. Then the spirit will be wonderfully swallowed up by that Supreme Mind who is infinitely more powerful. And then the whole man will be 'outside himself'—and will be blessed for no other reason than that, being placed outside himself, he will be granted something which cannot be uttered, by that Supreme Good, catching up all things into himself.

(i) *The swallowing up of the animal body*

Ecstasy may be thought of as a foretaste of the life to come, during which the pious man will live united with God, happily outside himself until the resurrection of the body in the last days.

The spirit—the highest part of man—will swallow up (*absorbebit*) its body, being, as it were, both the stronger and the victor. The spirit, in its turn, will be swallowed up by God, the Supreme Mind.

Of all the ideas to be found in the *Moria*, those contained in the passage just transcribed and translated are among the most difficult to grasp. Not that Erasmus is unclear; not that he does not return over and over again to the same themes; but his terms of reference are perhaps deliberately obscure. And his use of the verb *absorbere*, 'to swallow up', can seem very misleading.

One of the many gulfs separating Christianity from neo-Platonism is their opposing concepts of the rôle of the spirit. For Christians the spirit is the highest element in the trinity of spirit, soul and body. It is not normally thought of as a separate entity; it was identified with the mind (the *nous* or *mens*). Classical pneumatologies place the spirit much lower: their hierarchy normally consisted of mind, soul, spirit, body. In neo-Platonic philosophies, the religious strivings of men consist in attempting to free the mind from the bad influences of its lower companions; at the same time the harmony of man may be achieved by giving each part its due by emphasising those better, more refined aspects of it which make it nearer to its more highly placed neighbour. This means in practice giving very little to the body, while carefully cultivating the higher qualities of the *spiritus* and the soul.

Erasmus follows St Paul and places the soul—when used in a triple context of spirit, soul and body—where the neo-Platonists place the spirit. This can lead to some real ambiguity, since all the interconnected classical meanings of these terms were still very much alive in the Renaissance. By stressing as Erasmus does the need for the pious man to spiritualise his soul and for the soul to spiritualise the body, he risks giving rise to the belief that he accepted the neo-Platonic doctrine of the astral body. This astral body is connected with the *aether*; it is the aetheric vehicle which the soul acquires when, following Platonic doctrines of its pre-existence, it descends from the *aether*, through the various spheres, into the earthly body of man, where it lies imprisoned. In the course of its descent, the astral body becomes impure and gross. The pious neo-Platonic philosopher knows that he must strive to repurify it, cleansing it of its heavy earthiness and making it as aetheric as possible. Should he not succeed in doing so, his astral body, made heavy by its impurities, will, when he dies, drag the soul down to some lower form of reincarnation.[1]

Erasmus never uses these terms. But it would be possible for readers to believe that he thought of the after-life as being lived by the *Mens* clad in a spiritual, aetheric body. His repeated insistence on the need for the soul (when conceived as the intermediary between spirit and body) to turn itself towards the spirit and to shun the body except insofar as it makes it more 'soul-like'—more 'animal' that is—almost irresistibly recalls assumptions current amongst neo-Platonist thinkers. That he could indeed be understood, or misunderstood, in his

[1] See D. P. Walker: (1) 'Ficino's *Spiritus* and Music' in *Annales Musicologiques*, I, 1953, pp. 131–50; (2) 'The Astral Body in Renaissance Medicine' in *Journal of the Warburg and Courtauld Institutes*, XXI, 1958, p. 119ff.; and (3) *Spiritual and Demonic Magic from Ficino to Campanella*, London, Warburg Institute, 1958.

sense is suggested by one of the major modifications he made to this passage in 1515/16. It is discussed later.

These neo-Platonic undertones need to be remembered, even though the general terms of reference remain those of II Corinthians 5—at least insofar as the important terms 'victor' and 'swallow up' are concerned.

The verb *absorbere* might seem perversely hyperbolical, since Erasmus apparently uses it to mean *to transform* rather than *to swallow up* in a strict sense. He has taken it over from the New Testament, where it occurs only four times; of those four occasions, only two are relevant here. The first, which continues the same series of scriptural commonplaces, is II Corinthians 5:4: *ut absorbeatur quod mortale est a vita*, 'so that what is mortal may be swallowed up by life'. This passage is frequently associated with I Corinthians 15:54, where the same verb occurs: *Absorpta est mors in victoria* 'Death is swallowed up in victory'. Folly's assertion that the spirit is not only stronger but victorious (*victor*), shows that Erasmus, too, made this association. In other words, he saw the triumphant spirit as mirroring the religion of Christ, that *Lex Christi* which is 'spiritual, the begetter of life, more efficacious and victorious' (*efficacior et victrix*); it frees us from sin and death (*Paraphrase* on Romans 8:1–2: *LB* 7. 800EF).

II Corinthians 5:4 expounds a doctrine dear to Erasmus. This earthly body is only a tabernacle—a tent in which the soul must temporarily dwell until its camp is struck at death. Yet the eternal life promised men will be lived in that same tabernacle: the body rendered spiritual and permanent at the resurrection.

II Corinthians 5:4 reads—in the Revised Standard Version (the Authorised Version is now hardly intelligible):

For while we are still in this tent (*en tō skēnei*), we sigh with anxiety; not that we would be unclothed, but that we would be further clothed, so that what is mortal may be swallowed up by life.

Erasmus explains the Biblical meaning of 'tabernacle' (*skēnos*) in his annotation on this verse (*LB* 6. 766BC).

Folly's doctrine is that the spirit will eventually 'swallow up' the body—something which will be more easily achieved if the body has already been purged and chastened in this life. The general allusion is to I Corinthians 15:44: 'It is sown an animal body (*corpus animale*): it is raised a spiritual body (*corpus spiritale*).' But Erasmus gives it a twist of his own.

The interpretation which Folly places on these mysterious doctrines is consonant with Erasmus' acceptance of St Paul's tripartite division of man in I Thessalonians 5:23. This can be seen from the paraphrase of this verse:

But may God himself, the author of peace and to whom are pleasing the agreement and harmony of all men in honourable matters, grant that you may be entirely holy and unharmed, that your *anima* may accord with your *spiritus*, your body with your *anima*, and that your *spiritus* itself may accord with God, lest there should be anything blameworthy within it, and that you may persevere in this holiness until the coming of our Lord Jesus Christ (*LB* 7. 1026C).

Here we have a hint of Folly's doctrine of the spirit, working down through the lower parts of man. It harmonises with what Erasmus took I Corinthians 15:49 to mean: 'And as we have borne the image of the earthly [in Adam], we shall also bear the image of the heavenly' [that is, of Christ, the Second Adam]. The *Annotations* make the following comment:

We bore the image of the earthly Adam by sinning and dying: we shall bear the image of the Second Adam by living innocently; and we shall in some way (*quodam modo*) imitate his immortality, for here [on earth] there is the beginning of it and a kind of practising for it (*initium ac meditatio quaedam illius*) (*LB* 6. 740D–F).

How this is achieved is shown, in terms directly relevant to the *Moria*, in the paraphrase of I Corinthians 15:44: the body, which is soon to be born again through the resurrection has been—

in some way transformed into the soul to which it had adapted itself by applying itself to piety; so that, just as our soul obeys the Holy Spirit, being caught away and, up to a point, transformed into him, so our body, submitting to the soul, is purged (*repurgetur*), casts off its grossness and is fined down (*extenuatum*) into such a body as may be very like the mind (*LB* 7. 910Cf.).

Here we have the same verbs as in the *Moria*: *repurgare* and *extenuare*. And here too we have both the soul's rapture and the accommodation of the body to the soul (equated with the *mens*, the mind, the *nous*). Later in the century, J. Viguerius, in his *Institutions of Christian Theology* makes similar points. As a careful and scholarly theologian he avoids the dangerous ambiguities which Erasmus had allowed himself to write. He points out that 'when the Apostle says that the body will arise as a spiritual body, he does not mean that the body is a spirit but that it entirely and completely accommodates itself to the spirit (*nec . . . voluit dicere quod corpus sit spiritus, sed quòd plenè & completè subserviet*

Spiritui). Just as our body is now said to be an animal one on account of its 'animal' functions, it will be called spiritual on account of its spiritual functions—'that is, by completely and perfectly serving the spirit' (*Institutiones*, 1565, p. 135).

This is fine so far as it goes. But does it go far enough? What Erasmus avoids repeating in his later works is the force which Folly gives to the verb 'swallowed up'. The *Annotations* do not deal with this verb. The paraphrase of II Corinthians 5 does not help much either, but we do find there the doctrine of the soul's leaving the body, expounded as usual with the help of the verbs *emigrare* and *demigrare*: pending the resurrection, Christians' souls join God, being torn (*divulsi*) from their bodies. But neither the verb *absorbere* nor the word *vita* (life) are given a specific explanation, not even when we come to the verb itself as used by St Paul—*absorpta est*—when death is 'swallowed up' in victory. With a noteworthy economy of words, Erasmus simply reminds us that St Paul is quoting from Hosea.

In the *Paraphrases* Erasmus emphasises that II Corinthians 5:4 is concerned to teach the doctrine of the immortality of the body at the resurrection:

If we groan meanwhile, burdened by the body which is exposed to so many ills, it is not because it is a happier thing in itself to depart (*emigrare*) from it, but because we hope that this body will be restored into a better state (*in melius restitui*), mortality being given immortality through the resurrection. We are not despoiled of our body, which we put off for a time, but shall be better clothed in the same, receiving it back eternal instead of perishable (*quod pro caduco recipiemus aeternum*). There is no reason why we should lack faith, however unlikely it might seem that, in place of a mortal body, there shall rise an immortal one, free from all ills (*LB* 7. 923DE).

Are there signs of a drawing-back from a position which seemed too Platonically soul-centred to suspicious critics? The resurrected body is given a place of proper prominence. But so it was in the *Moria*. The emphasis has changed slightly, but not theology; (cf., in the *Colloquies*, the *Epicurus*).

At all events, the choice of the adjective *caducus* ('inclined to fall', 'fleeting', 'perishable') to apply to the body is interesting. In Cicero too it is used for the 'perishable' body (e.g. *On the Nature of the Gods* 1. 35. 98), being contrasted with the immortal soul. It was axiomatic for Cicero that everything human was *mortale et caducum* except the soul (*Republic* VI. 17). For Erasmus, in conscious opposition to such doctrines, the body is only *caducus* in this world; in the next it puts on that immortality which Classical thought would reserve for a soul alone. In fact, as often, Erasmus may have been influenced both in vocabulary and doctrine by Origen. When expounding the philosophy of

Christ in the *Homilies on the Song of Songs* as translated by Rufinus, Origen explains that divine philosophy teaches us that 'all things visible and corporeal are *caduca et fragilis*—perishable and easily broken'. The Christian philosopher despises them and 'as it were, entirely rejecting the whole world, strives towards the things which are invisible and eternal'. Origen adds that the *Song of Songs* tells us how to do so; and that work unambiguously teaches the resurrection of the body, the spiritualised companion in eternity of the soul (*PG* 13. 75CD).

(ii) *Puzzlement over the swallowing-up of the soul*

Absorbere did seem to cause some puzzlement and hostility. At least three sources show that readers of the *Moria* were sometimes ill at ease with Folly's contention that the spirit of the pious man, having spiritualised his *anima* and his body, will be 'wonderfully swallowed up by that Supreme Mind'. Before thinking about that question, it is convenient to deal with the more basic one of what Erasmus' words may be taken to mean. Folly describes the *Suprema Mens* as being *infinitis partibus potentior*. This should not be translated by some such phrase as 'more powerful than its infinite parts'—does that mean anything at all? Folly is asserting that the Supreme Mind is 'infinitely more powerful'. The expression *infinitis partibus* is modelled on the Ciceronian usage *omnibus partibus*, meaning 'in all respects', 'altogether' (cf. *De Finibus* 51. 31. 91). This is not a minor point: scholastic writers on ecstasy were understandably preoccupied by the problems posed by a finite soul loving a God who is not merely good but supremely so; not merely great, but infinitely so. Such an unequal love implies that the soul will be swallowed up by the Infinite who is God. In what way the finite soul is 'swallowed up' is squarely faced by theologians such as Bonaventura.

In two important letters Erasmus felt obliged to explain what he meant by the verb *absorbere*. The first of these letters is addressed to Martin Dorpius; it was written towards the end of May 1515 and subsequently printed with the *Moria*. An original touchy reply to Dorpius' gentle and courteous, though somewhat naïf, criticism was suppressed by Erasmus, who realised that he had dashed it off too hastily. Thomas More similarly suppressed a caustic defence of the *Moria* which he himself had written (*EE* 2, letter 347, preface; cf. *LB* 3, col. 1892, letter 513).

In his explanation of ecstasy for Dorpius' benefit, Erasmus wrote:

In order to make what followed concerning the joy of holy men more easy, I prefaced it with the three Platonic *furores*, of which that of lovers is the most fortunate, being none other than a form of ecstasy (*ecstasis quaedam*). The ecstasy of the pious is none other than a kind of taste of the future blessedness (*beatitudinis*) by which we shall be entirely swallowed up into God, being in him more than in our very selves. Plato uses *furor* to mean what occurs when anyone, caught up out of himself, is in him whom he loves and enjoys him (*fruitur*) (*EE* 2, no. 337, 486ff.).

There we have the full statement of ecstatic rapture with the key words *ecstasis*, 'swallow up' and 'caught up' (*raptus*). But as an explanation it is calm, confident and serene. Erasmus merely restates what Folly had said, with more attention to his readers who found his allusions hard to grasp.

(iii) *Beghards and Turlupins*:
the soul not absorbed like water in a wine-barrel

The second letter on this subject was written to Martin Lypsius on 7 May 1518. In more than one passage of this letter a careful reading will show that Erasmus is now on the defensive. The reason for his bitterness is that even a man such as Edward Lee, who was in touch with Thomas More, could interpret the end of the *Moria* in terms of real heresy. Powerful enemies had ranged themselves against him, some in print. Erasmus reacted by explaining his teachings with great precision, changing some of his emphases in the process. The letter to Martin Lypsius is an elaborate reply to criticisms of the *Moria* and other works made by Lee (*EE* 3, no. 843, preface). In the part that concerns us for the moment Erasmus comments as follows:

Lee then goes on to nibble away at what I wrote about the ecstasy of the pious, which Plato calls a holy *furor*—that is a kind of taste of future blessedness by which we shall be swallowed up into God, being in him rather than in ourselves. Then he casts up against us I know-not-what Turlupins or Beghards who taught that the soul is swallowed up by the Divinity just as a tiny drop of water, when put into a barrel of wine, is swallowed up by the wine, and that everything will be as it was before the creation of the world. What are such ravings of Turlupins and Beghards to do with me? I said that the soul was swallowed up by God because it is totally caught up into him by love; the soul is more where it loves (*amat*) than where it animates (*animat*). It is so caught up that it is made perfect (*perficitur*), not that it vanishes (*evanescat*) (*EE* 3, no. 848, 90, line 617f.).

Erasmus' expanded Annotation of II Corinthians 5:3 now comes into its own. In his *Novum Instrumentum* he translated this verse in such a way as to bring out St Paul's insanity, his ecstatic soul-departing union with God in rapture. Lee is not suggesting that Erasmus showed sympathies for early platonising universalists such as Origen or Gregory of Nyssa. Origen, it is true, held that the divine purpose embraced the emancipation of the soul from its corruptible body, its return to

God and the ultimate restoration of all creation, including the Devil. (This doctrine of the *Apokatastasis* is based on Acts 3:21 where we read of the 'restoration of all things': *hē apokatastasis pantōn*.) Gregory of Nyssa, who taught some of the same doctrines, cited Origen as his authority. And Origen believed that the souls of men existed before they entered their bodies. But one would be hard pressed to find evidence of a sympathy for any of these doctrines in any of Erasmus' mature writings, let alone the *Moria*.

What then do Lee's accusations of heresy imply? Certainly not conscious or unconscious Plotinianism. Only those who knew little or nothing of the traditions of Eastern and Western mysticism could have seen Plotinian neo-Platonist ecstasy necessarily lurking behind Folly's use of such terms as *Simplicissimus* or the One for God, or the verb *absorbere* applied to the enraptured soul. They are quite at home in St Bonaventura—which is precisely why Erasmus cites his memorable jingle about the soul in the *Annotations*. And he is right. The question of the soul's being 'swallowed up' merits a specific explanation by St Bonaventura in his *Commentary on the Sentences of Peter Lombard* (*lib. I, dist. 1, art. 3, quaest. 2*, in *Opera*, Quaracchi, 1, p. 41). Bonaventura not only admits the possibility of the soul's being swallowed up into God: he insists upon its necessity. Blessedness is to be enjoyed in God alone (*fruendum est ergo solo Deo*) because he is the highest and infinite good (*summum bonum et infinitum*). Indeed, 'because the soul is born to perceive the Infinite Good, who is God, in him alone must it find rest and enjoyment'.

Bonaventura's reply to an objection to this assertion reads as follows:

To the objection that the human soul only comprehends (*capit*) finitely, it must be said that, as the soul is itself finite, it does indeed comprehend the Infinite Good finitely. But because that Good *is* infinite, the soul will be entirely swallowed up by him (*ab ipso totaliter absorbebitur*) so that its ability to comprehend (*capacitas*) is bounded on all sides. The soul will not merely rejoice but, as Anselm said, it will 'enter into the joy of the Lord' [Matthew 25:21]. For if it comprehended so much without being overcome or swallowed up, the desire could arise to comprehend something further . . .

Bonaventura then draws the conclusion that the human soul, despite its finite capacity, requires to love that Good who is infinite.

In unimpeachably orthodox writings it was so usual to talk of the soul being swallowed up into God, that it cannot be the verb *absorbere* which worried or puzzled Erasmus' literate friends and which attracted Lee's accusations of sympathies for Beghards and Turlupins. Erasmus never suggested that it was; he is much more specific: Lee and others accused him of believing 'that the soul is swallowed up by the Deity, *just as a tiny drop of water, when put into a barrel of wine, is swallowed up by the wine. . .*' This they saw as part of an heretical conception of the final restoration of all things. Such terms lead one not to Origen's Greece but to late mediaeval Germany.

The words in italics show this to be so. They can be found in writings by Meister Eckhart and Tauler. Had this analogy of the soul's being swallowed up into God like a drop of water in a wine-barrel become the hallmark of heretical mystical movements in German lands? It seems so, certainly. Erasmus is able to reject it with vigour, since he never wrote any such thing.

In the fourteenth century Meister Eckhart's doctrine had been the subject of prolonged scrutiny. Finally, just after his death, pope John XXII condemned several of his propositions with the bull *In agro Dominico*, promulgated at Avignon on 27 March 1329. (The authenticity of this bull has been questioned, but that is of no consequence to the points made here. Cf. *Dictionnaire de Théologie Catholique*, s.v. *Beghards*.) The tenth of the condemned propositions concerns the total transformation of the soul into the Godhead:

We are totally absorbed into God [Eckhart said] and are changed into him in a similar way as the bread is changed into the body of Christ in the Sacrament. I am so changed into him that he makes me one being with himself—*not* a similar being. By the living God this is true: there is no distinction here.[1]

Now Meister Eckhart did explain such an absorption into God in terms of a drop of water in a wine-barrel. He does so in his *Talks of Instruction*, when urging the desirability of frequent communion. By the act of communicating, the pious are said to be transformed into God and made one with him; this union with God is closer than the union of body and soul:

This union is much closer than that of a drop of water poured into a barrel of wine. There is water and there is wine; but they are so transformed into one, that all creatures would be unable to tell the difference.

(Disiu einunge ist vil naeher, dan der einen tropfen wazzers glizze in ein vaz wînes: dâ waere wazzer und wîn, und daz wirt alsô in ein gewandelt, daz alle creatûren niht enkûnden der undescheit vinden.)[2]

---

[1] See, in general, J. M. Clark, *Meister Eckhart: An Introduction to a study of his Works with an Anthology of his Sermons.* For the bull *In agro Dominico* see *ibid.*, p. 253f.; consult especially G. Théry, 'Ed. critique des pièces relatives au procès d'Eckhart . . .' in *Archives d'Histoire doctrinale et littéraire du moyen âge*, I, 1926, 129–268; III, 1928, 325–443; IV, 1929, 233–392.

[2] Meister Eckhart, *Die deutschen und lateinischen Werke* ed. J. Quint; vol 5, *Traktate*, p. 269 and p. 354.

Eckhart's editor in his notes adds other uses of the same analogy in Tauler. There is no need to reproduce them here.

J. M. Clark and J. V. Skinner point out a parallel analogy in St Bernard's treatise *De Diligendo Deo*, in chapter 10.[1] This parallel is indeed instructive, for it shows the gulf separating what, despite his hyperbole, the saint meant and what Erasmus was wrongly accused of preaching. St Bernard's language is no less bold than Eckhart's, but despite it all, the soul's continued individuality is assured and the analogy is with 'much wine', not a barrelful of it:

Oh love, holy and chaste! Oh passion, sweet and delightful! Oh direction of the will (*intentio voluntatis*) pure and cleansed—all the more cleansed and pure in that nothing of self is left mixed in with it; all the more sweet and delightful in that what it feels is totally divine. To be affected thus is to be made into God (*sic affici, deificari est*), just as a small drop of water poured into much wine seems totally to abandon itself, as it takes on the savour of the wine and its colour; just as a red-hot, glowing iron becomes like the fire, putting off its own and former shape . . .

All human affections will melt away from man as he merges into the divine will:

Otherwise, how will God be 'All in all' if anything of our own is left behind in man? The substance will indeed remain, but in another form, another glory, another power. When will this be? Who will possess it?—'When I shall come and appear before the face of God' [Psalm 41/42, 3] (*PL* 182, 991AB).

Is there a problem of orthodoxy here? Well, St Bernard is a saint, so probably not. Anyway, for him man was not destined to be so swallowed up as to loose his identity. The verb *deificari* means 'to be made into God', but with an element of pious hyperbole: for Eckhart it is to be taken literally—or so his judges opined. Bernard does not imagine the soul being absorbed into the Oneness of God to the point of extinction. But one can understand the ravages such doctrines wrought on untutored or unbalanced minds. Folly is like Bernard where many doctrines are concerned, but she is far less bold in her choice of terms to render the idea of union with God. She remains anchored in Scripture or in Catholic tradition. Nothing that Erasmus wrote in the *Moria* justifies accusations of sympathies with Beghards, Turlupins or any allied heretics. But Erasmus could certainly have been more discreet.

[1] *Meister Eckhart, Selected Treatises and Sermons*, London 1958; edition used, Fontana Library, 1963, p. 89.

And in one way Erasmus *is* closer to Eckhart: both make the eucharist the prime vehicle of union with God.

Meister Eckhart was a subtle and learned scholar. His judges may not have understood his paradoxes and hyperboles. But the mystical enthusiasts who followed Tauler and Suso in the fourteenth and fifteenth centuries were often simple clergy, unlettered monks and nuns, as well as pious laymen. Inevitably they did fall into heresy. In the supposititious Eckhartian tractate *Schwester Katrei*, that simple, misguided and silly nun tells her confessor that she has 'become God'. Modern scholarship can hold that Eckhart taught no such thing. But, however unfairly, contemporaries of Erasmus did apparently attribute both the tractate and such doctrines to Eckhart. The excesses and the heretical simplicities of Tauler's and Suso's loosely associated 'Friends of God' and their successors were things which any prudent man would distance himself from. That is what Erasmus was doing when he denied ever suggesting that the soul was absorbed into God like a tiny drop of water was absorbed into a barrel of wine.

Such an analogy had been used by Eckhart, by Tauler and doubtless by their followers. Expressed in homely German to men and women who knew what it was to have barrels of wine in their cellar, it was destined to be successful. But to the theologically naïf it was as dangerous as it was memorable. And eventually it did lead to errors which do superficially sound like Folly's doctrines. During the interrogation of the heretical Beghard Hartmann, he asserted that man may become one with God, so that—

Unus est cum Deo et Deus cum eo unus absque omni distinctione.[1]

He is one with God, and God is one with him, without any distinction.

To hostile eyes which pass inexcusably swiftly over the page, this could seem to correspond to Folly's teaching that, through the Communion, man becomes one with God and with his fellow men—so rising to the new life that he seeks to become *unum cum illo, unum item inter sese* ('one with him, one, too, with each other'). But that, as we saw, means something very different (p. 125).

The charge of teaching that 'everything will be as it was before the creation of the world' Erasmus never apparently felt called upon to answer, except by denying ever having had anything to do with it. It doubtless arose from his allusion to *summo illo bono omnia in sese rapiente* ('the Supreme Good catching away all things into himself'). I think Erasmus saw this as a way of alluding to John 12:32: where Christ

---

[1] Döllinger, *Beiträge zur Sektengeschichte des Mittelalters*, II, p. 384; cited *Dictionnaire de Théologie Catholique*, s.v. *Beghards, Béguines héterodoxes*, col. 533.

asserts that he will 'draw all things unto himself'. The Vulgate reads *omnia trahem*, 'I will draw *all things*'. The *Novum Instrumentum* follows the Greek: *omnes trahem*, 'I will draw *all people*'. But Erasmus came to prefer the meaning given by the Vulgate; in this he was influenced by Augustine (see *Annotations*, LB 6. 391E). So in the *Paraphrases* we hear of Christ ruling in heaven, *unde esset omnia revocaturus ad se*, 'from whence he will call all things back to himself' (*LB* 7, paraphrase of Luke 23:24). If that is what Folly meant, then such a doctrine is quite orthodox.

Lee's accusations of Beghardism and Turlupinism could be answered. But answered they had to be. Erasmus was a Low-German living in German-speaking lands. He was being accused of holding views held by those heirs to Eckhart and his followers who are sometimes given a rather spurious semblance of unity under the name of the 'Friends of God'. Any Low-German can be expected to have had at least some knowledge of such movements and of their doctrines: and a man who knows a heresy can be suspected, however wrongly, of having sympathy for it. (So thought Egmontanus, Béda and the Sorbonne: EE X, 34n.16).

(iv) *The spirit in its own kingdom*

There is a tantalisingly quiet dropping of a phrase from Folly's peroration in late 1516. Erasmus felt it wise to drop it because it too could give a handle to those who were on the look out for heterodoxy in the *Moria*.

Erasmus never specifically and textually wrote of the resurrection of the dead in terms of a spiritual or aetheric body, distinct and different from the earthly one put off at death. It is always a question of man's earthly body being rendered spiritual as, in the fullness of time, it doffs its earthy limitations, donning immortality and incorruptibility. (Origen can be quoted in the same highly orthodox sense; cf. *Contra Celsum*, PG 11, 1465, 32.) But was Erasmus always as clear as he ought to have been about the soul's pre-existence—or non-existence—before it joins with a body to give men and women their individual lives on earth? (The pre-existence of the soul has no place in Catholic Christianity after the early centuries of its formative period.) And did he take sufficient care to distinguish his concept of the eventual clothing of the soul in its own, resurrected, spiritualised body from the neo-Platonic belief in an afterlife lived in an aetheric spiritual body? These questions arise from the discreet omission of an important phrase from all (authorised) editions of the *Moria* from 1516 onwards.

The first version of the *Moria* supplied two reasons why the spirit could more easily swallow up the body in the life to come. They are presented in a strikingly parallel construction.

partim quod jam velut in suo regno est, partim quod jam olim in vita corpus ad hujusmodi transformationem repurgarit atque extenuarit.

partly because it is in its own kingdom, as it were: partly because, formerly in this life, it will have purged and fined down the body for such a transformation.

The first of these clauses could give readers grounds for thinking that Erasmus held the heretical doctrines of the pre-existence of souls and of an afterlife lived in a neo-Platonic aetheric body. The spirit is aetherial; the term *aether* meant that uppermost region, that heaven, where God reigned in state. The neo-Platonic *aetheric body* is indeed in its own kingdom when it leaves behind the dross of the world and returns to the *aether* from which it came. If Lee, Dorpius, or anyone else suspected that he meant that the aetheric *spirit* was *in its own kingdom* in the sense that Christian man will live immortal in the aetherial regions, clad in a purified aetheric body, then he was very wise indeed to strike it out without a word. At the very least Folly's expression in the original version suggests the doctrine of the pre-existence of the soul. In his later writings Erasmus avoids alluding to the *spirit* in this context and is at pains to condemn Platonic associations. It was wiser to talk of 'the soul' and to use more traditional terms.

As for the phrase given above in italics, it just had to come out.[1]

The soul can then be thought of as a queen—but as a queen who has no kingdom save that of her Beloved Lord.

When Erasmus struck out the reference to the spirit in its kingdom, he also added marginal notes inviting the reader to think of the ecstasy of the soul in terms of Origen's commentaries on the *Song of Songs* (see below, p. 185). In the *Song of Songs* (1:4) we read that 'the King hath brought me into his bedchamber'. Origen applies this to the soul: being the bride she is 'brought into the bedchamber of the King and

---

[1] *Partim quod jam velut in suo regno est* was definitively stricken out of the 1516 Froben edition (sig. y4r°), remaining absent from the Froben editions of 1519 (G4r°), 1521 (Z6r°) and 1522 (Z6r°), as well as from the Soter edition of 1523 (p. 346), the Badius edition of 1524 (N8v°), the Cervicornus-Hitorpius edition of 1526 (X4v°), the Sebastian Gryphius edition, probably of 1529 (G5r°), and the Froben edition of 1532 (X4r°). (Editions in which Erasmus presumably had no hand retain the phrase.) Since neither the Lug. Bat. *Opera* nor Kan give a critical text, the phrase is not only missing from available editions and translations, but no hint of its absence is given. Yet one expects a second *partim* in Latin after the first. As it stands after the excision, the sentence is noticeably lopsided. Even if we did not know that a phrase had been left out, we would have been justified in suspecting it.

made a queen. She it is of whom it is said [Psalm 44:10], The queen standeth by thy right hand' (*PG* 13BC). Great wealth is stored up for her. Glorious riches await the soul. St Paul wrote of them when he exclaimed: these are the things which 'eye hath not seen, nor hath ear heard; nor have there entered into the mind of man what God prepared for them that love him' (*PG* 13. 98D). The allusion to I Corinthians 3:6 leads on to St Paul's teachings after his rapture; St Paul is the privileged man, 'who said that he had been caught up into the third heaven and from thence into paradise, and heard ineffable words which man may not utter' (*PG* 13. 99C).

The importance of these two allusions is very great. Both appear in Erasmus' writings, the first in the *Moria*, the second in the *Paraphrases*. Neither of them is quoted directly from the Vulgate: in both cases they are idiosyncratically cited as Origen gives them in Rufinus' version. Origen's *Homilies on the Song of Songs* are a rich source of material for understanding Erasmus, and not only in the *Moria*. It is sad that Erasmus felt obliged to drop the allusion to the spirit reigning in her kingdom. It expressed an idea which, to judge from the Listrius annotations to the *Moria*, meant something very real to him.

(v) *The soul, an exile seeking her homeland*

Erasmus dropped the word kingdom. He did not abandon the basic idea which it conveyed. In other works he uses the word *patria* (homeland, fatherland) for the heaven towards which the soul—not the spirit—strives to return, while sojourning here on earth. (The verb he associates with this idea remains *peregrinari*, to be an exile.)

That the soul should wish to return to its fatherland is a commonplace of philosophical writing since Boethius, who refers to the soul's return to its *patria* in the *Consolation of Philosophy* (III, prose 12; Loeb, p. 300, lines 28/9). According to Boethius, the soul, on reaching heaven may say: 'This, I remember, is my native land (*patria*); here was I born; here will I stay' (IV, metre 1, lines 25/26: Loeb, p. 316). But that is 'philosophy' not Christian doctrine; it is not consonant with the Catholic Boethius' theological writings.

Curiously enough, the word *patria*, which, one might have thought, could be taken to mean that the soul was—heretically—returning to its native land is the term affected by Christian writers. Erasmus could have found plenty of orthodox authorities who used it as he did, including Augustine and Bonaventura. I suspect that he was partly influenced by the way in which exegetes glossed Boethius, bringing him close to a virtually baptised Plato in the process. The commentary on the *Consolation of Philosophy* once ascribed to Aquinas explains Boethius' phrase 'to see its *patria* again' in terms of the soul's 'knowing blessedness' (*cognoscere beatitudinem*). In another and fuller gloss, the fourteenth-century Carthusian scholar Dionysius of Lewes explains that the soul will find its *patria*—'that is, the mansion of blessedness' which we call the Empyrean; 'Plato is thought to have written nothing about this, unless that is what he means in the *Phaedo*. [. . .] I am amazed that such a man should be able to expound these things.'[1]

Such writers, like Erasmus, make the soul's journey to its *patria* not a return to a Platonico-Christian heaven from which it had been expelled, but rather a journey from Paradise Lost to the New Jerusalem. Erasmus warned in his *Commentary on Psalm 38* against interpreting the scriptural word *peregrinatio* in purely Platonic terms. The exiled stranger, the *advena* who is man, is not to be understood, we are told, as a pilgrim returning to the heaven from which, as in Platonic doctrine, he was expelled.

Where then *did* this stranger emigrate from? From Paradise. Where did he migrate to? To this vale of tears. Whither does he hasten? To our true fatherland, Jerusalem; there he will see clearly what here he perceives in vain shadow (*in imagine*).[2]

The teachings of Folly here are part of the permanent preoccupations and beliefs of Erasmus as expressed in his later writings.

Erasmus' sense of nuance and style are a help in our understanding this. The soul, we were told, was striving not only towards a taste of heavenly goods; it was striving towards an enjoyment of them—not only, that is, *ad coelestium bonorum gustum* but *ad coelestium bonorum fruitionem*. The word *fruitio* can be searched for in vain in classical Latin writers. It is a late Christian Latin word for a specifically Christian doctrine: it means that 'enjoyment' of God, or that justifiable pleasure in good actions, which the Christian may experience.[3]

For Folly this taste and enjoyment of blessedness is achieved by the soul's being enraptured into God, 'absorbed' into him so that—as is stressed twice in one single phrase—man will be 'outside himself'—(*extra se* and *extra sese*). This ineffable bliss is vouchsafed by the *Summum Bonum* who is God, ravishing all things into himself (*omnia in sese rapiente*). But despite the words *extra se* and *extra sese*, ecstasy as

---

[1] See Boethius, ed. Pseudo-Aquinas, Venice, 1523, and ed. Dionysius Carthusianus, Cologne, 1540, *ad loc*.

[2] *LB* 5. 464F; commenting on Psalm 38:7 (Vulgate): *Verum tamen in imagine pertransit homo*, = Psalm 39:6 (Prayer Book): 'For a man walketh in a vain shadow.' *In imagine* corresponds to LXX *en eikoni*, in an image.

[3] Cf. *Thesaurus Linguae Latinae*, s.v. *fruitio*; also—less useful on this word—*Lexicon Latinitas Medii Aevi*, Brepols, Turnholti, 1975.

Erasmus conceived it is not a Philonic snatching of man's mind away. The mind of man, his *mens*, is caught up into God through divine erotic insanity when it leaves, as it were, this corruptible body, a body purged and purified, *as far as may be* in this world. Such a soul is granted a momentary glimpse of bliss: at the highest it is granted the beatific vision. Erasmus avoids the actual term. Folly chastely calls it *quiddam ineffabile*. At no point of his theology is Erasmus ever closer to Augustine. In *De Doctrina Christiana* (1. 3. 3–6) Augustine makes a sharp distinction between 'to use' and 'to enjoy' (between *uti* and *frui*). Only those things which are to be 'enjoyed' make us blessed (*beati*). 'To enjoy' means to cleave with love to an object for its own sake. We men are but sojourners (*peregrini*), desirous of returning to our homeland (*in patriam redire*). All things on earth and sea are to be used with this end only in view. In this 'life of mortality we are journeying absent from the Lord' (*peregrinantes a Domino*—II Corinthians 5:6):

If we desire to return to our homeland where we can be blessed, we must use this world, not enjoy it, so that 'the invisible things' of God 'may be perceived by our understanding through the things which are made' [Romans 1:20]—that is to say, so that we may lay hold of things eternal and spiritual by means of those things which are corporeal and temporal (*ut de corporalibus temporalibusque rebus aeterna et spiritalia capiamus*).

And after a few pages, Augustine goes on to praise Christian folly (*CCSL* 32. 1. 3. 3–6:11 and 12). As a reminder of the continuity of such themes, we may note that St Bernard says much the same things in much the same terms, in his sermon *De Peregrino* (*PL* 183. 183f.).

The man who uses the world in the way that Augustine and Erasmus wish him to will enjoy in his soul a vision of bliss. And such beatitude is the lot of all the pious dead as well, as, ecstatically happy, they await the gift of personal, individual, perfect immortality.

4. *The Resurrection: meanwhile, a foretaste of the future in this life*

Jam haec foelicitas quamquam tum demum perfecta contingit, cum animi, receptis pristinis corporibus, immortalitate donabuntur, tamen quoniam piorum vita nihil aliud est quam illius vitae meditatio, ac velut umbra quaedam, fit ut praemii quoque illius aliquando gustum aut odorem aliquem sentiant. Id tametsi minutissima quaedam stillula est ad fontem illum aeternae foelicitatis, tamen longe superat universas corporis voluptates, etiam si omnes ómnium mortalium deliciae in unum conferantur, usque adeo praestant spiritalia corporalibus, invisibilia visibilibus. Hoc nimirum est quod pollicetur Propheta: *Oculus non vidit, nec in cor hominis ascendit, quae praeparavit deus diligentibus se* (Scheurer H3r⁰–v⁰; Kan 188).

This happiness will only be attained in perfection when the souls receive back their original bodies and are endowed with immortality; yet, since the life of the pious is nothing other than a practising of that life, or as a shadow of it, they also sometimes have a taste or odour of that reward. It is only the smallest of drops in comparison with that fountain of everlasting joy, but it nevertheless surpasses all bodily pleasures—even if all the delights of all mortal men were gathered together into one single man. That is the extent to which the spiritual surpasses the corporeal; the invisible, the visible. This is most certainly what the prophet promises: 'Eye hath not seen, neither hath there entered into the heart of men, what God hath prepared for them that love him' [Isaiah, as cited by St Paul, I Corinthians 2:9; Vulgate reading].

Here Folly is at her most specifically Christian both in word and doctrine. The language and the thought both conform to the long tradition of ecstatic theology in the Church. However great the blessedness of the ecstatic soul, caught away to God in death and rapture, such a state is but a provisional one. The hope of the Christian lies not in an immortal soul—and certainly not in the permanent absorbing of his soul or spirit into the Godhead—however much beatitude the soul may enjoy in such a state, pending the resurrection: it lies in immortality. Immortality is the state of mankind after the resurrection. Without the body there is no such thing as human immortality. The soul is not naturally immortal: as St Paul stresses to Timothy, it is God 'the only Potentate, the King of kings, the Lord of lords, who only hath immortality' (I Timothy 6:16). In his *Paraphrases* Erasmus underlines the point: 'It is God who only hath immortality *ex sese*'—as a property of his own being. And in his *Annotations* he insists, on Ambrose's authority, that St Paul (despite a certain ambiguity in the Greek) is writing not of Christ but of God the Father, to whom, in a sense peculiar to him, immortality belongs. There is no question of course of stripping the two other Persons of the Trinity of such an attribute; but in Holy Writ 'all is referred to the Father as author: immortality, life and light are from him' (*LB* 6. 946D).

Folly passes straight on from the rapture of death to the granting of immortality in one's original body. No Platonist or neo-Platonist would give a moment's support to such a doctrine. For such philosophers it would be the height of perversity to thrust the soul back into its body—however purified—once it had secured a happy and blessed release from the contagion it represents. Where such basic doctrines are concerned Erasmus remains firmly inside Catholic orthodoxy. As he restates this doctrine in his *Commentary on the 3rd Psalm*, the full import of it comes strongly across:

We who die in the faith of Jesus Christ die in the firm hope of a better life and so fall asleep rather than die. Meanwhile the body, which is to live again at the trumpet-blast of the angel, rests rather than lying dead in the grave; it is already freed from all the harm of pain and toil with which it was afflicted, and in its own time will be brought back to life. And indeed the souls enjoy calm repose (*placide quiete fruuntur*) until they each receive back the tent-companion (*contubernium*) of their body.

Meanwhile, as baptised Christians who strive to avoid evil for Christ's sake, 'we are buried with him who happily passed a sabbath in the tomb, rising again with him into the New Life'. While in this mortal body we must fear the attacks of the Enemy, until 'death is finally swallowed up (*absorpta*), so that we may say: "Death where is thy victory"' (*LB* 5. 239A–F).

Erasmus often emphasises, following St Paul, that the resurrected body will be a spiritual one not an animal one (cf. for example *LB* 5. 246A–D). But there is no beating about the bush: as Folly affirms, immortality is granted *receptis pristinis corporibus*—when the souls receive back their original bodies. This doctrine of the soul's awaiting the resurrection of the body is spelled out with care in the *Sermon on the 4th Psalm*: there is no perfect repose for them who remain in the tabernacle of the body here on earth; they will find repose only in that safest of mansions which God has prepared for them. There, removed from evils of life, they enjoy the repose of the blessed (*quietam beatam agunt*). To the eyes of fools they appear dead, but they are in peace, their hope is full of immortality. The happiness of such blessed souls is not yet complete (*absoluta*): they desire to clothe themselves in the body they have put off. This causes them no anguish, for they have perfect trust in God.

Erasmus states this again in his *Annotations*, commenting on I Corinthians 15:49: 'We bore the image of the Old Adam by sinning and dying: we shall bear the image of the Second Adam and in some way imitate his immortality. The beginning, and a kind of practising (*meditatio*) of that, is here [on earth]' (*LB* 6. 740. 42).

There is no need to insist further on the two terms *illius vitae meditatio* ('a practising of that life') and *velut umbra quaedam* ('or as a shadow of it'). It suffices that we realise yet again that this practising of the life to come consists in experiencing that ecstatic rapture which is a taste and an odour of the eternal reward—*praemii illius gustum aut odorem*.

The words *gustus* and *odor* take us to the very heart of ecstatic theology. They occur with great frequency in Origen's *Commentaries on the Song of Songs*, from which they entered into the widest currency (cf. *PG* 3. 95A, 151C, etc.). The idea of tasting the sweetness of the God is often associated with Psalm 33:9 (AV 34:8): 'O taste and see that the Lord is good.' How this is used in the context of ecstasy may be seen from Bonaventura's sermon for the third Sunday in Lent (*Opera*, IX, Quaracchi 1901, 229, col. 2.). Ecstatic amazement comes from contemplating the glory of God's works:

What advantage is there in the word over the thing itself? What is the worth of abstaining from wordly preoccupations, without 'tasting how sweet the Lord is'? What is the use of vowing the perfect life without doing it? As the poet says, 'Anyone can be rich in promises', and as the popular proverb puts it, 'To promise and not to give is to comfort a fool.' Such people seem to take God for a fool.

The way to taste God is through that 'alienation of the mind' which is rapture (*raptus*) or ecstatic madness (*alienatio ecstatica*). Such alone is a love which loves *vehementer*.

Folly maintains that such an experience is 'a taste of that reward' which is eternal life in Christ—a *praemii illius gustum*. So too does Bonaventura: if anyone should taste (*gustaverit*) with the 'tongue of his heart' the sweetness of the heavenly rewards—the *dulcedo caelestium praemiorum*—then anything else whatsoever will have a bitter taste (*Soliloquium* 2. 2: *Opera*, VIII, Quaracchi, 1898, 47).

As for the sweet odour of God, a principal authority for the mystics is Ecclesiasticus 24 (Vulgate, 20ff.; AV, RV etc., 15ff.): 'As cinnamon and aspalathus, I have given a scent of perfumes; and as choice myrrh, I spread abroad a pleasant odour . . .' In the hierarchy of mysticism, smelling the pleasant odour of God comes first: tasting God's sweetness comes next. As Bonaventura exclaims in the *Soliloquium* (partly following St Anselm whom he cites in error as St Bernard): 'O Lord, if thine odour is so pleasant, how sweet is the sweetness of thy taste!' That is why the soul dares to say that the odour of God is not enough: it wants to enjoy his taste. And that is enjoyed in that 'sober drunkenness', that *sobria ebrietas*, by which ecstasy has been known from the earliest Christian fathers (*Opera* VIII, 51 etc.). Folly, like Bonaventura, is using the standard language of Christian ecstasy.

This applies also to the emotive hyperbole with which this taste is praised: it is 'but a drop' in comparison with the 'fountain of everlasting joy': it nevertheless surpasses all bodily pleasures—which, of course, for Erasmus, means all non-spiritual, all visible ones. Mystics are in agreement over this. Bonaventura cites Bernard to show that the soul which burns *vehementer* with divine love enjoys a taste of what is good. This *gustus boni* may be tiny—*licet exiguus*—but it is the sweetest of all the delights with which God restores the afflicted soul. He then goes on to cite Hugo of Saint-Victor to prove that this is what makes the pious begin *totaliter a se ipsis alienari*—'to be madly driven entirely from themselves' as the soul, by the elevation of the mind (*mentis elevatio*), is drawn away from earthly things. In some miraculous way the soul is raised above itself and above all created things in a divine intoxication. The soul tastes of that fountain of life which makes it drunk with sober drunkenness.

This passage of St Bonaventura, with its frequent citings of Scripture, of Bernard, Anselm, Augustine, Chysostom and others, is a most useful one for placing Folly's praise of ecstasy within a broad and long tradition of similar theological concern. Anyone who, with Erasmus in mind, follows up the references in the excellent footnotes in the Quaracchi edition will throw much light on to Erasmus' thought—and save himself a lot of time.

Folly is preaching the philosophy of Christ, not just in a general way but quite specifically. The words she utters here correspond closely to what Christ is made to say in the *Paraphrases*. Her hyperbole was designed to show not simply that spiritual goods are superior to those of the body, but that they are pre-eminently and infinitely so.

That is the extent to which the spiritual surpasses the corporeal (*usque adeo praestant spiritalia corporalibus*), the invisible, the visible. This is most certainly what the Prophet promises: 'Eye hath not seen' etc.

The same words come from Christ's lips in the paraphrase on that great spiritual commonplace which is John 3:5–8. The rebirth of Christians is not only superior (*praestantior*) to the bodily birth, but infinitely so—of the same degree of magnitude as the spirit's superiority to the flesh or of God's to the body. Fleshly people only acknowledge fleshly things, perceptible to the senses. 'Yet the things which cannot be seen exist pre-eminently' (*praestantissime sunt*); they have the greatest power, whereas the flesh is weak and powerless. This rebirth is achieved by God. 'By hidden inspirations—*arcanis flatibus*—the minds of men are caught up by the spirit of God and transformed', even though the eye cannot distinguish this (*LB* 7. 520C–E).

The last word on this subject can be left with Erasmus' Paul. Erasmus returns to the themes of Folly's eulogy in an important paraphrase of Romans 8: 18: 'For I reckon that the sufferings of this present time are not worthy to be compared with the glory that shall be revealed to usward.' The context requires him not to compare the joys of the future reward with earthly joys but with earthly sorrows: apart from that the meaning is the same: Christ achieved good by bearing evil; he entered into his kingdom through obedience; through shame he came to glory; by death he achieved immortality. We must do the same, in due time dying with him, so that we may live with him for ever.

That is the rule joined to our inheritance which, being an immortal and so great a one, transcends the entire capacity and thought of the human mind; if you were to gather together all the afflictions of this life in one single man, they would be light when weighed against his reward: the future glory which is prepared for men and which they, as it were, purchase with their troubles.

In this life we have an earnest of heavenly reward which awaits us.

A certain, secret taste is meanwhile given us inwardly through the Spirit. But we shall have it wholly when, after the resurrection of the body and the casting off of the harmfulness of mortality, we reign immortal with the immortal Christ (*LB* 7. 802F).

The phrase we meet here, 'if all the afflictions of this life *you were to gather together in one man* (*in unum hominem conferas*)' strongly recalls Folly's assertion about the primacy of the taste and odour of heavenly bliss, 'even if all the joys of all mortal men *in unum conferantur*'. It is this which makes me conclude that Folly's assertion should not be rendered as, 'brought together into one', but as, 'into one single man'. The sense would then be: even if one single man had experienced in himself all the earthly joys which all mankind had ever tasted, he would have known nothing at all compared with the taste and odour of the Beatific Vision vouchsafed to the soul in ecstatic rapture.

This is what you would expect. The 'fountain of eternal bliss', the *fons aeternae foelicitatis*, is what was purchased by the death of Christ; it is what Erasmus later calls the *fons omnis laetitiae nostrae*, 'the fountain of all our joy' (*LB* 5. 313C—on the 22nd/23rd psalm).

An interesting change that Erasmus made here was to replace the Vulgate translation of Isaiah 64: 4, as cited by St Paul in I Corinthians 2: 9, so as to bring it in conformity with the meaning implied by Greek usage. He incidentally inserted a clause omitted in the first versions: Folly first cited 'the Prophet' as saying: 'Eye hath not seen, nor *hath* there entered (*ascendit*) into the heart of man what God hath prepared for them that love him.'

This is finally put right in 1523: the phrase 'nor hath ear heard' is inserted and *ascendit* is changed to the plural *ascenderunt*. Once more one can see the influence of Origen at work here. Some seven years before Erasmus changed *ascendit* to *ascenderunt* he inserted the note advising the reader to read Origen on the *Song of Songs*. As Rufinus rendered that work, St Paul says, as Folly does in 1523, *ascenderunt* not *ascendit (PG* 13. 98D). He could have worked out the right translation for himself, but Origen must have prompted him.

He pointed out in his Annotations that Valla had already reminded readers that a Greek singular verb governed by a neuter plural must, by normal rules of grammar, be translated as the Latin plural (*LB* 6. 667 11). The conservatives attacked him for that too! (For the reply to Edward Lee on this issue, see *LB* 9. 217DE.) (Already in the earlier editions Erasmus had altered the last words of this sentence as they appear in the Vulgate from *iis qui diligunt se* to *diligentibus se*. In both cases the meaning is the same: 'to them that love him'; the reading adopted in the *Moria* is the one later adopted in the *Novum Instrumentum* also.)

In the *Paraphrases* Erasmus points out that it was the *stulta crux Christi*, the foolish Cross of Christ, which opened up such truths to those who 'philosophise by faith, not by reason'. And with a glancing blow at Ficino and his school, he includes among the princes of this age who would not see this, not only Caiaphas, Pilate, the Pharisees and the Devils, but the Magi and the Philosophi (*LB* 7. 865AB). This does not, I think, refer to the Magi who visited the infant Christ. Erasmus is condemning by implication those who seek to complicate the simplicity of Christ's religion with magical and philosophical arguments. The cap fits many a Florentine Platonist.

The general preoccupations of Erasmus, leading on as they do to II Corinthians 4: 18, recall what Origen wrote in *On the First Things (Peri archōn)*. Like Erasmus after him he spells out that the resurrected body will not be a new or different one—whatever Greek philosophers may say; it will be the same one, transformed into something better. According to Origen it is life in this spiritualised, immortal body which is alluded to in Isaiah's cry: 'Eye hath not seen nor hath ear heard, nor have there entered into the heart of man what God hath prepared for those who love him' (*PG* 11. 337C–339C).

The economy of man's salvation is now complete.

In this world, the pious man strives to make his entire life conform to the spirit, spiritualising his animal body and his *anima*, practising death by ecstatic rapture. This rapture is a foretaste of that insanity of death, when the soul definitively departs from its earthly tabernacle. Caught up into God, the soul, ecstatic in the profoundest of senses, tastes beatitude and awaits in confidence the return of its tabernacle, now transformed into an eternal dwelling at the Resurrection. That tabernacle will then have ceased to be mortal, corruptible, animal, polluting. It will be a dwelling-place fit for the soul to dwell in in the heavens.

5. *Divine insanity: the 'good part'—of Folly, of Mary, of Christ's philosophy*

Atque *haec est* Moriae *pars, quae non aufertur* commutatione vitae, sed perficitur (Scheurer H3v°; Kan 188).

And this is Moria's part, which is not taken away [Luke 10:42] by the exchange of life [cf. Matthew 16:26; Mark 8:37] but 'made perfect' [cf. Matthew 5:48].

How grimly humourless some of Erasmus' enemies were! Most of today's readers know that *Haec est Moriae pars, quae non aufertur* is a happy and pious pun. The allusion is to Luke 10, when Christ rebuked Martha and praised Mary. Martha was cumbered about with much serving, whereas Mary simply sat at Jesus' feet and heard his word. Martha asked Jesus to tell Mary to help with the meal. He replied:

Martha, Martha, thou art careful and troubled about many things: but one thing is needful: and Mary hath chosen that good part which shall not be taken away from her—*Maria optimam partem elegit quae non auferetur ab ea.*

Folly's pun means that the 'good part' that Mary chose was the path of Christian Folly. It is well known that Erasmus later replaced *Moriae* by *Mariae*, dropping the pun and making it a straight allusion to Luke 10: 42. This was in fact done in time for the 1516 Froben edition and repeated in all the editions of Froben and others which drop the phrase *partim quod jam velut in suo regno est. Moriae* is retained in others which Erasmus had no hand in.

If 'Mary's part' and 'Moria's part' are different ways of alluding to the same religious attitude, we would expect Erasmus to read Christian folly into St Luke's attractive account of the clash between the contemplative Mary and the busy, Women's Institute figure of Martha. This expectation is borne out by Erasmus' later writings. Again he had changed a word, but not his mind. Mary is described in the *Paraphrases* not simply as a woman who listened to Jesus' teaching, but as one who was 'caught up' (*rapiebatur*) so that, having forgotten other things, she would not be 'torn away'. Martha was loved by Jesus and approved by him, but Mary had chosen the stronger part; 'having forgotten the things of the body', she concentrated 'entirely on the things of the soul'. It is of basic importance to Erasmus' conception of insane rapture that the subject of them, like Mary here, forgets where she is and forgets worldly things.

In the *Paraphrases* Christ goes on to say that, while it is in some ways right to be occupied with such things as Martha was, in the last resort they only concern this mortal body of ours, the needs of which will cease when immortality is bestowed:

> But he who casts away such cares and is entirely caught up towards heavenly things takes a short cut (*compendium facit*); he concentrates on one thing only, but that one thing is more excellent than all the rest. Such happiness as he has will not be taken away; it will be increased when what is imperfect shall be abolished and what is perfect shall be revealed . . . (*LB* 7. 379AF).

In the *Sermon on the 4th Psalm* also Erasmus uses the contrast of Martha and Mary as a means of teaching the primacy of divine things 'which really are', *quae vere sunt*. Mary, seated at Jesus' feet, is the mind, the *mens*, which has found repose from all carnal affections. Others may sit at the feet of Aristotle, Averroes or of the legal glossators Bartholus or Baldus: the truly wise sit at the feet of Jesus (*LB* 5. 275F). The words of the Vulgate, *non auferetur ab ea* ('shall not be taken from her') link the account of Martha and Mary with the parable of the talents, which is revealed by Christ as meaning that 'unto him that hath shall be given: but from him that hath not, shall be taken (*auferetur ab illo*) even that which he hath'. Erasmus explains in his *Paraphrases* (Luke 8: 18; *LB* 7. 362D–F) that the goods which are not taken away consist in the acceptance of the mystical sense of the Christian religion, which is cherished in the soul like a treasure.

These are the things that Folly implied when she adapted to her smiling use the 'good part' which the Marian Moria chose. The strongest proof of the continuity of these ideas in Erasmus' teaching of the philosophy of Christ is what we read in *On Preparation for Death*. We are treated to the same themes as in Folly's praise of ecstasy, based on the same scriptural texts. Some have already been quoted from this passage to make other points: all them could have been, for all are relevant. We have St Paul's injunction to use this world as though we used it not, since the form of the world is but a passing show and we are only travellers in it. 'The things which are seen are temporary: the things which are unseen are eternal.' And then, as though despairing of ever making people see his point in the *Moria*, he says of such a Christian way of life, not that it is Moria's part, nor even that it is Mary's part: it is *magna Christianae Philosophiae pars* (the great part of Christian philosophy):

> And this is the great 'part' of Christian Philosophy, which prepares us for death, so that we learn, by contemplating the things which are eternal and heavenly, to despise the things which are temporary and earthly. Plato judged the whole of philosophy to be a practising of death.

And we are told what we now know already: such a 'practising of death' is a 'preparation for and, as it were, an exercise in dying'. Plato is a guide, but he does not go the whole way:

There is eternal truth in some human disciplines, but it never provided anyone with true blessedness. Here [in Christian Philosophy] he who made the promise is eternal; he through whom he made it is eternal; the things which are promised are eternal; they bring eternal happiness to those who embrace them by faith and eternal unhappiness to those who neglect them. Such a practising of death is practising the true life. It makes clear what the Philosopher promised: that the soul, its burden lightened, may emigrate from its bodily home; that, indeed, with joyful spiritual rapture (*alacritate spiritus*) and throwing itself about with joy (*gestiens*) as though leaving a dark and troublesome prison, it leaps into blessed freedom and into that lovable light that knows no darkness.

The allusions to Scripture that Erasmus then assembles are to themes we have met many times in this study: Wisdom 9:15: 'For a corruptible body weigheth down the soul, and the earthly frame lieth heavy on a mind thinking many things'; David's prayer in Psalm 141/2:7, duly Hebraicised and Platonised: 'Lead my soul from prison, so that it may confess thy name, O Lord'; St Paul's anguished cry in Romans 7:24: 'O wretched man that I am! Who will deliver me out of the body of this death?'; and two more of his sayings: Philippians 1:21: 'For me, to live is Christ, and to die is gain'; and—in some ways the most conclusive of all—Philippians 1:23: 'I desire to be loosed, and to be with Christ.'

Throughout the whole of our lives we must carry out this practising of death (*LB* 5. 1295D–1296B). That is what Folly also maintains.

But, while all men and women must strive to practise death in this way, only a chosen few achieve that special 'separation' of body and soul by which the pious, here and now, on this side of the grave, become, as it were, totally outside themselves.

6. *The gifts of the enraptured: the appearance of madness*

Hoc igitur quibus sentire licuit (contingit autem perpaucis) ii patiuntur quiddam dementiae simillimum, loquuntur quaedam non satis coherentia, nec humano more, sed dant sine mente sonum, deinde subinde totam oris speciem vertunt. Nunc alacres, nunc dejecti nunc lachrymant, nunc rident, nunc suspirant, in summa vere toti extra se sunt (Scheurer H3v°; Kan 189).

Those who are allowed to experience such things—and it comes to very few—suffer something very like being out of their minds: they say things which are not sufficiently connected together and not in the manner of men;

they utter mindless sounds, and thereupon change the entire 'fashion of their countenance' (Luke 9:29). They are now transported with joy, now dejected; now weeping, now laughing, now sighing: to sum up, they are, in truth totally outside themselves.

(i) Privileged babbling

Folly is about to reach her concluding words. Everything she says now deserves to be carefully weighed, for this is the end towards which her eulogy tended.

We are left in no doubt that the ecstasy she has been praising is a rare privilege. Two hyperboles are used to show this. Those whose souls are caught up out of their bodies, delighting in the odour and taste of God, not only seem mad to a casual observer; what they experience is *quoddam dementiae simillimum*: it is as like dementedness as it is possible to get.

This divinely prompted state so akin to *dementia* is something vouchsafed to man by God—something which only happens *quibus sentire licuit*, 'to those to whom it is permitted'. And those are few, very very few, in number.

The phrase 'it comes to very few', *contingit autem perpaucis*, arrestingly recalls what St Bonaventura wrote on this subject in his commentary on Peter Lombard's *Sentences*—*contingat paucissimis*, which means the same thing. This coincidence of expression reinforces the coincidence of meaning. Bonaventura is a good guide to Erasmus' meaning—he is also a useful shield from ignorant criticism, as Erasmus showed in his *Annotations* (II Corinthians 5, St Paul's ecstatic insanity, cited on p. 152). Folly and Bonaventura are describing that highest form of ecstasy which is rapture. In the words of Bonaventura:

Those who, on account of the excessive sweetness [of the taste of God] are raised into ecstasy, are sometimes raised up further, as far as rapture, although this comes to very few.

qui prae nimia dulcedine modo elevantur in ecstasim, modo subelevantur usque ad raptum, licet hoc contingat paucissimis.[1]

From late 1516 onwards, the 'Listrius' note to the passage of the *Moria* which concerns us now draws attention to both the ecstasy and the rapture:

Rapture and ecstasy are called insanity; we do not take this straightforwardly nor as referring to ordinary insanity, but only in a certain manner (*quodammodo*).

---

[1] *Opera*, III Quaracchi, 774 ab, on *3 Sentences, d. 35 a.1, quaest. 1.*

That is why *quandam* is added, lest the peevish or those who hurl abuse should seize the opportunity of making false interpretations (*calumniandi*).

The reader is begged not to remain at the level of the words but to weigh the matter (*rem ipsam expendere*). 'If anyone does that, could anything more holy and pious be said on such matters?'

Indeed, when Erasmus writes of rapture he is writing of one of the greatest of mystical privileges.

Folly proceeds to describe very briefly those outward signs of rapture which make the favoured man appear like a madman; this leads on to the two most famous of scriptural ecstasies. Enraptured men do not speak coherently or connectedly (*loquuntur quaedam non satis coherentia*); what they say does not sufficiently follow from the context. Elsewhere Erasmus makes such a phenomenon typical of all ecstasy (see p. 231). And it is no accident but something directly owed to the Holy Ghost himself, that there are things in the Scriptures that, at a literal level, appear 'absurd or quite incoherent' (*absurda minimeque cohaerentia*) (*LB* 5. 870Af.). So, too, men, under the influence of the Spirit 'do not speak in a human fashion', but *dant sine mente sonum* ('utter mindless sounds'); such a phenomenon is discussed, unsympathetically, by Erasmus in his annotations on I Corinthians 14:7 and 14 (*LB* 6. 729C–730D). As for the contention that enraptured mad-seeming men 'change the entire fashion of their countenance', that is basic to the theory of both madness and rapture. When even Christ was praying during the Transfiguration (Luke 9:29) 'the fashion of his countenance was altered' (*species vultus ejus altera*): and when David (in a psalm quite fundamental for the understanding of Erasmus' doctrine of ecstatic folly) 'feigned madness before Ahimelech', he did so by 'changing his countenance' (*mutavit vultum suum*).

(ii) *Laughing and weeping fools*

Such men are indeed outside themselves, to all outward appearances merely mad. Under the weight of such ecstatic amazement men vary between intense joy and deep depression: they are, as Folly puts it, *nunc alacres, nunc dejecti*—here again we have ecstasy linked with Cicero's term *alacritas*, a transport characterised by joy.

It might seem that two such straightforward notions as *alacres* (joyful) and *dejecti* (depressed) need no comment. But they do. At one level we may note that these twin phenomena are often attributed to divine fools and seen as a sign of their ecstasy. As the Bollandist fathers wrote of St Symeon Salos ('The Fool')—who was a 'fool for Christ's sake'—'No one more wisely showed the world to be foolish; no one more learnedly laughed as he wept, or wept as he laughed, at the folly of the world.'[1]

Stulti propter Christum—fools for the sake of Christ—drew their name from I Corinthians 4:10, where these words occur. A long line of Greek Orthodox saints cultivated madness as a form of holiness. I have not included them in this book because I am not certain what influence they may have had on Erasmus. The presence of so many refugees from Byzantium may be supposed to have made such men and their theology more widely known. It is perhaps indicative that Jacopone da Todi, that disturbing thirteenth-century Italian Franciscan poet and ecclesiastical statesman who cultivated divine madness (*santa pazia*), was reburied in 1596 in the church of San Fortunato at Todi; Bishop Angelo Cesi enshrined his remains in a magnificent tomb. He placed on it an inscription stating that as 'a fool for the sake of Christ, he deluded the world in a new manner and seized hold of heaven'—*stultus propter Christum, nova mundum arte delusit et coelum rapuit.*[2]

The influences on Erasmus that can be checked and verified are, by their nature, bookish. But a current of sympathy for divine madness ran right through the middle ages and the Renaissance. When Erasmus writes about the symptoms of such an ecstasy as was 'most close to madness', many had seen with their own eyes strange and mad-seeming behaviour in pious men and women, things which they interpreted as Erasmus did, as signs of exceptional favour from the Godhead.

(iii) *The enraptured soul: Origen on 'The Song of Songs, which is Solomon's'*

It is safer, no doubt, to follow the books, whenever we are guided to them. From 1516 onwards Erasmus provides us with such a guide. It points to a vital work, which readers of the *Moria* really ought to know.

It is a note attributed to Listrius which shows us the way. It is intended to explain why men who know what it is to be caught up in ecstasy are 'at times transported with joy, at times dejected—*nunc alacres, nunc dejecti*:

The reader would understand this better if he were to read Origen's *Commentaries on the Song of Songs*—how the bride is variously affected as the groom now withdraws himself, now shows himself and reveals his power.

[1] Cited by Sarah Murray: *A Study of Andreas, the Fool for the Sake of Christ*, Borna, Leipsig, 1920, p. 8. n. 3.

[2] On Jacopone da Todi consult Raby, *History of Christian-Latin Poetry*, Oxford, 1953, pp. 430f; Evelyn Underhill, *Jacopone da Todi, Poet and Mystic, 1226–1306*, London, 1919. There is a good edition of Jacopone's *Laude* by F. Mancini, Laterza, 1974.

Elizabeth of Schönau, an ecstatic often confused with Elizabeth of Hungary, is cited too: Faber had included her in his 'three spiritual virgins' (1513).

Origen's *Commentaries on the Song of Songs* survive, partially, in Rufinus' translation only. Many of Erasmus' central ideas and favourite scriptural texts are to be found there. It was a good work to allude to: it does indeed throw light on to the spiritual ups and downs of the soul; it is concerned with ecstatic joy, while avoiding the word *ekstasis* and—as always with Origen—playing down the actual departure of the soul from the body even when his terminology encourages such notions. Erasmus also was led to play this down, as far as the *Moria* is concerned, while in some ways emphasising it in his exegetical works, thus bringing them closer together.

Another attraction of the work as a means of explaining the *Moria* is the fact that it started a major theme of Christian writing destined to last into modern times. Origen was the first Christian writer to interpret the *Song of Songs* as an allegory of both the Church's and the soul's love for God; the erotic imagery of that passionate poem was used to give an idea of the intensity of the love. By the end of the middle ages such themes were mystical commonplaces, though few knew Origen at first hand.

Erasmus occasionally uses the theme of bride and Groom, of lover and Beloved. Origen handles that theme with consummate artistry, an artistry which can even survive Rufinus' Latin translation. Without in any way lessening the passionate love of the soul for her beloved King and Bridegroom, Origen conveys the white-hot, mind-abstracting love of the soul in terms which make her divine, erotic love incontrovertibly close to the 'sober drunkenness' of spiritual ecstasy. Erasmus encouraged the reader to interpret the *Moria* in the light of this love.

In Origen's *Commentaries on the Song of Songs*, the soul is rendered amazed (*miratur et stupet*) by the riches of her Lord (*PG* 13 88A). The thought of him fills her full of joyful transport (*alacritas*). The merely animal man laughs at the spiritual meanings of Scripture: the spiritual man finds his deepest truths in them (97A). Christ, for the sake of his bride, emptied himself and took on the form of a slave (98A). When the soul is introduced into her King's bedchamber (*Song of Songs* 1:3), she rejoices and is full of happy exultation (99CD). She enjoyed his breasts (*ubera*) more than wine. (*Song of songs* 1:3, LXX and Vulgate). She will eventually rejoice even more fully 'in the plenitude of spiritual doctrine' (100CD). Like the Queen of Sheba visiting Solomon, [I/III Kings 10, II Chronicles 9] she will understand enigmas and come close to her Lord; like Mary also, who 'chose the best part, which shall not be taken away from her' (107D). The soul awaiting her Lord is like

Mamre who [in Genesis 18:1, 2] sat outside under an oak, at the door of the tabernacle, lifting up his eyes and looking forth. It is important that he should have been sitting outside:

The mind is indeed *outside*, placed outside its body (*extra corpus posita*); far from bodily thoughts, far from carnal desires. Because it is placed outside all these things, God visits it (121D–122C).

Christ resolves spiritual enigmas. We must be content to remain in darkness, until it is infused with light. Only then can the soul come to whatsoever things are true (*ad illa quae vera sunt*). The soul needs this darkness, to shield it from too much light (153C). This last theme is an exception, meaning little to Erasmus.

The soul is brought into the 'house of wine' (*Song of Songs* 2:3), where banquets are prepared. She already glimpses the King's bed-chamber: she yearns to enjoy the wine of delight and happiness (154CD). This is the wine which the saints get drunk on: the 'new wine' of God (156BD). In such a banquet the spiritually drunken souls find true communion with their Lord and with each other, so that we, the faithful, 'are all one in him' (*ut omnes in ipso unum sumus*: 163B).

Then comes the long passage which specifically concerns the Listrius note, as is shown by the verb used for the Groom's 'withdrawal' of himself, *subducere*. Origen's Groom is sometimes present; it is then that he teaches. At times he is said to be absent: it is then that he is desired. We know when he has been withdrawn (*subduci*) and when he is present (*adesse*) by the presence or lack of spiritual insights (168C–169A).

In reading what follows we must remember that, in the most carefully prepared and most fully authorised of all the editions of the *Moria*, this is how we are invited to interpret the ecstasy of the ecstatic Christian lover, dazed and distracted by his *mania erōtikē*.

The most relevant part of this long passage is devoted to explaining *Song of Songs* 2:8:

The voice of my Beloved! Behold, he cometh
Leaping upon the mountains, skipping upon the hills.
My Beloved is like a roe or a young hart:
Behold! he standeth behind our wall;
He looketh in at the windows;
He sheweth himself through the lattice. My beloved spake, and said unto me:
Rise up my nearest one, my fair one, my dove, and come away . . .

This is linked with 1:4

> The king hath brought me into his bedchamber.

Origen comments thus:

Nevertheless the Groom, inasmuch as he is a man, is not to be understood as being always in the house nor always remaining with the bride who is set within the house. He frequently goes out; she, violently moved by love for him, yearns for him when he is absent; but occasionally he comes back to her. That is why, throughout the whole book, the Groom is sometimes yearned for as though absent, sometimes is present, talking to the bride.

The bride herself, since she has looked upon the many and marvellous things in the Groom's bedchamber, seeks to enter into the house of wine as well [*Song of Songs* 2:4]. Having entered there and having discovered that the Groom, inasmuch as he is a man, has not remained in the house, she will be 'driven out' by love for him; she will go forth outdoors herself and wander widely round about outside, without going inside the house; she keeps a look-out, on every side, for when the Groom should come back to her.

Then suddenly she sees him, crossing over the peaks of the neighbouring mountains with huge leaps, coming down to the house in which the bride is shaken by her love for him and is aflame with passion. And when the Groom reaches the wall of the house, he lingers a while behind it, carefully examining something, as is his wont, and considering it in his mind. Then he, too, feeling something of love for his bride, uses his height, which reaches up to the windows of the house. Part of these windows is more like a lattice. He leans a little through the windows—he is much taller than they are, reaching beyond the higher part, which, as we said, is divided by lattice-work.

Then he looks in and addresses the bride, saying to her: 'Arise and come, my nearest one, my fair one, my love' . . .

. . . Sometimes she is visited by him; sometimes she is left alone, so that she may desire him more.

This, with its emphasis on love for God conceived in terms of eros and on the way in which the soul in its agitation wanders about 'outside', has unmistakable ecstatic potentialities.

And the terms used are very passionate; the soul is twice described, for example, in this very passage as being *sollicita* by her love for the Groom; moreover, because of this, she *aestuat*. *Sollicitare* basically means 'to move violently, to shake, to agitate'; so, too, *aestuare* means not only 'to burn' or 'to be hot', but implies a raging passion, akin to a stormy sea. Similarly the soul is not merely *agitata* but *exagitata*—driven outside by her violent affections. This sense of being 'driven outside' is the proper meaning of the verb; it is reinforced by the words which follow it, *exierit foras*, 'she will go forth out of doors'. All these words are appropriate for a soul driven to distraction by her yearning 'to go out'—'outside' her body, or herself—so as to join her loving God in rapturous union.

Origen applies this passionate text to the soul within the Church, whose 'walls' are the solidity of sound doctrine.

By these walls the Groom is said to stand. Compared with them he is so great, so lofty, that he surpasses the entire building. He looks in at the bride, that is, at the soul. He does not yet show himself to her openly and entirely, but, looking in as through a lattice, encourages her, calling upon her not to remain seated lazily within but to come out to him outdoors (*exire ad se foras*), so as to see him—not through windows or lattices, nor yet 'through a glass, darkly, but face to face', issuing forth outside.

The emphasis on being 'outside' is linked with I Corinthians 13:12, which is cited in the last sentence above. Origen continues:

But since she cannot gaze upon him yet—since he is not standing before the wall but behind it—he leans in through the windows, which are certainly open to let in the light to illuminate the house. The Word of God [the *Sermo Dei*], leaning down and looking through the window, calls upon the soul to arise and to come unto him ... And so the Word of God [now called, indifferently, the *Verbum Dei*], looking in through the windows and casting his gaze upon his bride, the soul, encourages her to rise up and to come unto him—that is, to leave behind corporeal and visible things and to hasten towards things invisible and spiritual (*invisibilia et spiritalia*), 'because the things which are seen are temporal, and the things which are not seen are eternal' [II Corinthians 4:18]. ...

The fact that the Groom is said to look through the lattice of the windows certainly means that, while the soul is placed within the house of the body, it cannot grasp the naked, open wisdom of God; nevertheless, through the patterns, signs and portraits of things which are visible, she contemplates the things which are invisible and incorporeal. And there is the Groom, looking in at her through the lattice.

The terminology and thought here are strikingly Platonic, marrying Christian texts to the theory of those celestial 'ideas', of which earthly things are but the shadows.

Christ stands behind the wall of the Old Testament, allowing himself, when the time is ripe, to be glimpsed through the lattice of the Law and the Prophets. The Church must not remain seated, satisfied with the mere letter of Scripture; God urges her to 'go out, to come outside to him'. Unless she does go outside, unless she does advance from the letter to the spirit, she cannot be wed to her Groom nor find fellowship with Christ.

He calls her, therefore, from the carnal to the spiritual; from the visible to the invisible; and from the Law to the Gospels.

The 'fragrant odour' of Christ draws her forth. But the lattice is beset by devils; only our Lord and Saviour can draw his beloved safely through the lattice, which he must break and tear apart.

For Christ, when he ascended into heaven, led captivity captive [Ephesians 4: 18], not only leading forth our souls but raising their bodies—the Gospel testifies that the bodies of several of the saints were raised up, appeared to many and entered into Jerusalem, the Holy City of the living God [Matthew 27:52–3] *PG* 13. 167C–184B.

It is in the light of such exegesis of the *Song of Songs* that Erasmus invites his reader to interpret the violently changing passions of the loving souls of the pious. Their transports of joy, their fits of depression, are analogous to the trembling emotion of a loving bride, shut up in the kind of house a maiden might inhabit in ancient Byzantium. There are, indeed, so many of Erasmus' major themes to be found in the Commentaries of Origen on the *Song of Songs, which is Solomon's* that he has the right to be taken seriously when the note eventually appended to this passage is a solid finger-post pointing towards them. He had already said as much in the *Enchiridion* (*LB* 5. 8CF).

This citing of them in the Listrius footnote was not the sign of a passing interest only. In the *Commentary on the 38th Psalm*, for example, the theme of the bride and her loving Groom who comes down to her, leaping across the hill tops is powerfully evoked—and evoked in a way that Origen himself might have admired. It is applied to Christ's love for his Church; to the primacy of the spiritual as seen in the New Testament even above the great peaks of the Old Testament—'Job, Melchisedec, Abraham, Isaac, Jacob, Moses and the rest of the Prophets.' Christ leaps over them, the sole of his foot touching them as he leaps over them like Remus hopping over the puny walls Romulus was building for Rome (*LB* 5. 420CF).

Folly concludes her description of the emotional upheaval of the pious with the words: *in summa vere toti extra se sunt*: 'to sum up, they are, in truth, totally outside themselves'. The sign-post leading us to Origen invites us to think of this in terms of the passionately loving soul, 'driven out' by love for Christ, 'issuing forth' from her house and 'wandering widely about'. Once more, the later explanation lessens the ecstatic implications without effacing them. In Origen's commentary the soul is at her happiest when she is shut up at home, catching signs of the Groom as he comes leaping down the hillsides to gaze in at her through the grill of her lattice-windows. In the *Moria*, on the contrary, terms such as *extra se* imply at times that it is precisely when the soul is outside, not inside, that she meets her God in rapturous union.

This was an aspect of ecstatic rapture that Erasmus felt called upon to play down from late 1516. But in this part of the *Moria* neither of these senses of *extra se* seems to be the dominant one. What makes these pious men 'totally outside themselves' is the extreme irrationality of their behaviour. Why! Anyone would think they were demented, to judge from their incoherent speech:

> Those who are allowed to experience such things—and it comes to very few—suffer something very like being out of their minds (*patiuntur quiddam dementiae simillimum*).

To be, or to seem to be, outside oneself; to be in the eyes of carnal men mad; so to behave that you do indeed—and not only to carnal men—appear to be quite mad: such are the symptoms of that high rapture which St Paul himself called madness and which Erasmus saw as the highest form of ecstatic Christian folly.

The words *dementiae simillimum* imply that the ecstatic really does seem to be out of his mind; there is no question of amiable eccentricity. There is no suggestion that the majority of men would have any way of telling the difference between such an ecstasy and a raving madness calling for chains and restraint.

7. *The raptures of Paul and of Peter: learned banter and Montanist heresy*

Mox ubi ad sese redierint negant se scire, ubi fuerint, *utrum in corpore an extra corpus, vigilantes an dormientes*, quid audierint quid viderint, *quid dixerint*, quid foecerint non meminerunt, nisi tanquam *per nebulam ac somnum*; tantum hoc sciunt se foelicissimos fuisse, dum ita desiperent. Itaque plorant sese resipuisse, nihilque omnium malint, quam hoc insanię genus perpetuo insanire. Atque hęc est futurę fęlicitatus tenuis quaedam degustaciuncula.

Verum ego jamdudum oblita mei *huper ta eskammena pēdō*. Quamquam si quid petulancius aut loquacius a me dictum videbitur, cogitate & stulticiam, & mulierem dixisse. Sed interim tamen memineritis illius Graecanici proverbii, *pollaki toi kai mōros anēr katakairion eipen*, nisi forte putatis hoc ad mulieres nihil attinere. Video vos epilogum expectare, sed nimium desipitis, siquidem arbitramini me quid dixerim etiam dum meminisse, cum tantam verborum farraginem effuderim. Vetus illud *misō mnamona sumpotēn*: novum hoc, *misō mnamona akroatēn*. Quare valete, plaudite, vivite, bibite, Moriae celeberrimi Mystae.

Finis Moriae In gratiam Mori (Scheurer H3v°; Kan 189–90).

As soon as they have come back to themselves, they say that they know not where they have been, 'whether in the body, whether out of the body' [II Corinthians 12:2], whether 'awake or sleeping'; they do not remember what they heard, what they saw 'what they said' nor what they did, except through a cloud or a sleep [Luke 9:33 etc.]. But this they do know: that they were most happy when they were out of their senses like this. And so they weep over having ever come back to their senses again, and would like nothing better than to be for ever insane with this kind of insanity. And this is a thin little taste of future happiness.

In truth I [Folly], having long since forgotten myself, have 'jumped too far over the pit'. However, if anything said by me seems too wanton or too garrulous, do reflect that both Folly and a woman have actually stopped talking! And meanwhile, do remember that Greek proverb, 'A fool often says a word which is opportune' [*Adages* 1.6.1]—unless of course you think that it does not apply to women . . .

You are expecting an epilogue, I can see—but you are very much out of your senses if you think I can still remember what I said when I poured out such a mash of words. There is an old proverb: 'I hate a drinking companion with a memory' [*Adages* 1.7.1]; here is a new one: 'I hate a pupil with a memory'. So fare ye well; clap, be alive, imbibe, ye most festive priests of Folly.

The end of the *Moria*, written for More.[1]

(i) *Folly's concept of ecstasy: the themes intertwine*

Folly has only three more sentences to say before her short, pithy epilogue brings her declamation to a close. We are faced with the kind of exegetical delight which often confronts those who attempt to explain witty or comic authors of any profundity: the juxtaposing and intertwining of different levels of thought, of different uses of language. The last sentence, just before Folly confesses that she has 'forgotten herself', takes us into the mystical joys of the life everlasting. Then we are immediately plunged into playfully erudite and refined banter. If would be tempting to think that one can consider these things apart, first explaining the 'serious' end of Folly's eulogy of ecstasy, then teasing out the humour from the humanist banter. But it cannot be done. The one depends on the other. And Erasmus' difficulties arose at least as much from the witty end as from any other part of his book.

The 'serious' part at first seems to pose few problems: read quickly it seems simply to resume what has been said already: the Christian

---

[1] For the translation of the phrase *Moriae celeberrimi Mystae* as 'most festive priests of Folly', cf. Pierre Mesnard, 'Erasme et la conception dialectique de la folie' in Enrico Castelli (editor): *L'Umanesimo e "La Follia"* (volume two in the series *Fenomenologia dell'arte e della religione*) Edizioni Abete, Rome, s.d., p. 55.

ecstatic, soul-departed in a mad and happy rapture, eventually comes back to himself, returning to sad sanity from happy insanity.

And what an insanity it is! Oh to be insane like that for ever! But no ecstasy lasts for ever—not even the ecstasy of death. All enraptured souls return to their bodies in the end. As far as this world is concerned, that is a sad and bitter truth.

One thing we are never allowed to forget: this ecstasy is a madness. The man who knows what ecstasy is, having experienced it, 'would like nothing better than to be forever insane with this kind of insanity'. Like many other forms of madness, this ecstatic insanity is character-ised both by the madman's not knowing what he was doing when he was beside himself and by his not remembering it afterwards, except as through a cloud or in a dream.

Writing this, Erasmus was giving hostages to Fortune, thrusting weapons into the hands of his enemies. Unwittingly, imprudently or how you will, Erasmus was adopting theological attitudes and using a theological terminology which even men of good intent might well suspect of being seriously heretical. Yet all that Folly is apparently doing is moving her theme of madness into the area of belief associated with the ecstasies which befell St Paul on one occasion and St Peter, St James and St John on another.

Given Erasmus' knack of arousing resentment and hostility among widely different sorts of men, one could foresee what would happen: some misunderstood the subtle complexities of his thought and his humour. Others, not unskilled in such matters, smelled heresy in his ambiguities; and, up to a point, they may have been right.

Cardinal Prince Pio da Carpi was in some ways the easiest opponent to answer. Like a comic colonel on the stage he thundered on about Julian the Apostate and Porphyry, so repetitively overstating his case that he weakened it. Erasmus replied with bitter dignity that he was sure that Cardinal Pio must have felt his own self to be displeasing when he wrote such things—things 'neither true nor pious'. The play on Pio's name—*Pius* of course in Latin—was wounding and effective.[1] Edward Lee was a more serious matter: his accusations had concerned named heresies which had long been ravaging German lands—lands with which Erasmus, as a German, was associated. Who made the most serious of the accusations I do not know, but Erasmus' own writings suggest that it was made as soon as the *Moria* appeared, lasted for many years and was specifically renewed about May 1515—that is, about the time that Dorpius' criticisms needed to be answered.

---

[1]See Pio da Carpi, *Thirty-six Books against Places in the Lucubrations of Erasmus*, Paris, 1531; and Erasmus' *Reply to Albert Pio*, LB 9. 1109Eff.

The charge was that of Montanism. A great deal depends upon what is implied when Folly asserts that ecstatics 'do not remember . . . what they said' (*quid dixerint . . . non meminerunt*). This theme is taken up, with apparently innocent jesting, in Folly's non-epilogue: 'I have long since forgotten myself . . . you are out of your senses, if you think I can still remember what I said . . .'

The basis of the jest lies in the close parallel between Folly and Socrates (*Phaedrus* 263D). Socrates too, once inspiration had left him, 'forgot' how he had defined love at the beginning of his eulogy of it. As he said, 'I was in such an ecstasy that I have forgotten'. But his ecstasy was a clear case of spiritual possession (*egō gar toi dia to enthousiastikon ou panu memnēmai*). To link such an 'enthusiasm' with Peter and Paul was simply asking for trouble. Yet that is what Erasmus did, just before Folly's final joke.

Jests such as these can be made to reek of Montanism. Before we deal with that it is best to see what Erasmus implies by his appeals to the Scriptural ecstasies of Paul or of Peter.

(ii) *The rapture of Paul: a rapture in the body?*

Folly alludes to St Paul's rapture to the third heaven and to Paradise when she asserts that, once they have come back to themselves, ecstatics say that they do not know whether their ecstasy had been experienced in the body or out of the body.

We know of St Paul's rapture through his own account in II Corinthians 12. He talks of it in an arrestingly impersonal way, as something which befell a man he knew. He would have told nobody about it; only his duty to the Church at Corinth made him reveal it. This is an aspect of Christian ecstasy which more effusive ecstatics have tended to overlay. Some of the greatest saints talk so discreetly and indirectly about their ecstasies that it is possible to doubt whether they are describing their own experiences or not. St Paul was obliged foolishly to boast in the interests of the faithful:

I must needs glory, though it is not expedient; but I will come to visions and revelations of the Lord. I knew a man in Christ, fourteen years ago (whether in the body I know not, or whether out of the body, I know not: God knoweth), such a one caught up even to the third heaven. And I know such a man (whether in the body or apart from the body, I know not: God knoweth), how he was caught up into Paradise, and heard unspeakable words which it is not lawful for man to utter . . . I am become foolish. Ye compelled me (II Corinthians 12:1–4, 11).

There is a large amount of writing on this rapture: Paul's credentials as an apostle largely depend on it. Much of it can be ignored by students of Erasmus, provided that the basic importance of Paul's rapture is not lost from view. At the centre of Paul's religious conviction is an ecstatic experience. He had glimpsed eternity; he had been vouchsafed the beatific vision; he had seen God face to face: theologians describe it in various ways, but Folly is speaking of such an ecstasy as that.

St Paul does not, as Folly's context might suggest, show any confusion about his rapture. He states where he was caught away to; he remembers the experience in detail. His only doubt concerned the manner of it: was he transported bodily to heaven or not? God knows; he does not.

St Paul hesitates because rapture can mean both the catching up of the soul and also the very material whisking away of a person from one place to another. Philip is the standard example of physical rapture. It happened to him on the Gaza road, immediately after he had baptised the Ethiopian eunuch:

And when they were come up out of the water, the Spirit of the Lord caught away Philip, and the eunuch saw him no more: and he went on his way rejoicing. But Philip was found at Azotus (Acts 8: 39–40).

In the paraphrases Erasmus gives due importance to this rapture, explaining that Philip was 'set down in the nearest town, Azotus', by an angel of the Lord.

St Paul's rapture could have been an analogous one, different in degree but not in kind. His rapture probably took place on the road to Damascus (Acts 9:1–9). Now the distance from the Damascus road to Paradise is greater than that from the Gaza road to Azotus; but distance means nothing to God. In the eyes of later theologians the additional miraculous element would lie—if Paul had been physically taken up to heaven—not in the huge distance involved but in an earthly body's being able to sustain exposure to the spiritual purity of those higher regions. In practice most theologians were probably convinced that St Paul was caught up in the spirit; such an interpretation dominates among platonising Christians. St Paul's rapture became for many the best-known of all cases of rapture *extra corpus*—a rapture in which the soul or spirit is caught up outside the body, either in appearance or reality. On the other hand since St Paul himself hesitated, a physical rapture in the body is not ruled out. The Greek fathers seem overwhelmingly to have taken St Paul's ecstasy to have been a rapture in the spirit not in the body. Through Latin fathers such as Ambrose and Augustine similar interpretations reached the whole western Church and flourished there—whether in Bernard, Aquinas or Bonaventura and their many followers, or in religious manuals such as Raynerius of Pisa's *Pantheologia*.[1] A valuable insight into scholastic attitudes towards St Paul's ecstasy is provided by Peter Lombard (*Collectanea in Epistolas Divi Pauli, PL* 192. 79–84). Some Renaissance speculations appear particularly bold: Ficino, who knew better than Paul himself, said that the apostle was caught up neither in the spirit nor the body: he was caught up in his spiritual body. (Erasmus writes as though such speculations need not even be noticed—once he has cut out that bothersome phrase about the spirit in its Kingdom.) In 1531 Charles de Bouëlles devoted a dense little treatise to St Paul's rapture (*De Raptu Pauli*). A most useful compendium of orthodox views is to be found in the *Institutions* of J. Viguerius (1565); *De Raptu sive extasi*, p. 96 v° ff.

Both the originality and the debt to tradition of Erasmus' theology of ecstasy stand out more vividly if the *Moria* is read in the context of acknowledged mystical writers. A striking feature of the *Moria* is Folly's avoidance of grades or ladders of ecstasy. A useful standard of contrast is supplied, say, by Richard of St-Victor. Richard saw the 'first grade of violent love' as betokened by the arousing of the thirst of the soul. In the second grade, the soul is athirst towards God (*ad Deum*). The third grade sees the soul athirst in God; the fourth and last finds the soul athirst 'in accordance with God' (*secundum Deum*).

It would at first seem that Erasmus has placed Folly's eulogised ecstasy in this third grade; it is in this third grade that the mind is drunk and begins to taste the sweetness of God:

The soul thirsts towards God when it desires to go entirely over to God in ecstasy (*mentis excessus*) so that, having quite forgotten its own affairs, it can truly say, 'whether in the body, whether out of the body, I know not: God knoweth'.

But Folly also includes elements which Richard places in the fourth grade, when the soul 'goes out' (*exit*) for God's sake, sinking below self on behalf of one's neighbour (Richard of St-Victor, *De IV Gradibus Violentae Charitatis, PL* 196. 1215f.).

Richard is cited as an example not as a source; all Christian mystics afford a place of honour to Paul's rapture. But some are more preoccupied than others with the implications of it. If St Paul's spirit (or his soul) was actually, physically and in fact, ravished out of its body into the third heaven, what happened to the body meanwhile? Was it left as though dead? Was it left really dead? Did the soul really and truly leave the body as it does in death? And if so, what does this imply?

---

[1] I have used a later edition of this useful mediaeval work: *Pantheologia*, Venice, 1585, *De Raptu*, pp. 804 ff.

(iii) *Augustine supplies some of the answers. A rapture like Paul's—'awake or asleep'?*

A major work of Augustine for mystical writers is *De Genesi ad litteram*. The twelfth book is devoted to visions and revelations as well as to such matters as Paradise and the third heaven. Folly makes what is probably a somewhat garbled allusion to it when she adds after the reference to St Paul's hesitations the words 'whether waking or sleeping' (*vigilantes an dormientes*). These words also appear in I Thessalonians 5: 10, in a context having little immediate bearing on the *Moria*: we are with Christ 'whether we wake or sleep'; but it is the context of *De Genesi ad litteram* which makes them relevant to the *Moria*.

Augustine was concerned to understand what Paul implied by his inability to say whether he was caught up in or out of his body. He writes as follows in the chapter where 'this problem is unknotted':

The apostle took great care to distinguish what he knew from what he did not. There remains to say that he himself did not know whether, when he was caught up into the third heaven, he was still in the body as the soul is in the body when the body is said to be alive—*if a man be waking or sleeping or even alienated from his bodily senses in ecstasy*—or whether on the other hand it had entirely left his body, which lay dead until the soul came back to those dead limbs once the revelation was over. In that case he was not in a waking sleep, nor did he come back to his senses again having been alienated in ecstasy, but, being dead, he was brought back to life again. What he saw when he was caught up to the third heaven—what he confirms that he knew—he saw in fact, not figuratively (*imaginaliter*). His mind was alienated from his body; but it is not certain whether his body was left quite dead or whether his soul (*anima*) remained there as it does when the body is alive. He was caught up to see and to hear those things of his vision which cannot be uttered. That, no doubt, is why he said: 'Whether in the body, whether outside the body, I know not' (*PL* 34. 458; *De Genesi* 12. 5. 14).[1]

It was Augustine not Paul who associated the idea of 'whether waking or sleeping' with the apostle's hesitations. But once used by such an authority in such a context it became attached to many accounts of St Paul's rapture. This fact explains, I think, Folly's phrase, 'whether awake or asleep'. Augustine's words were quoted through the centuries. Erasmus would have known them at second hand as well.

Augustine's hypothesis that Paul may have left a corpse behind him during his rapture does not find a great deal of support. St Bernard for example, does write of rapture as a death but one where the soul is not

[1] In the original the words in italics are: *sive vigilantis, sive dormientis, sive in extasi, a sensibus corporis alienata* . . .

caught away from life on earth but from its snares. Such a death does not destroy life, it transforms it (*De Diligendo Dei* 10. 27 etc.). Folly is nearer this tradition. However much the ecstatic soul is presented as being 'outside the body'; however much the pious ecstatic is caught up 'outside himself', this is never thought of as actually dying. It was by misunderstanding points such as these that Pio could ramble on about Porphry, while others can believe that Erasmus was an actual follower of Plotinus. Folly repeatedly uses such words as *velut* ('as if') or *perinde quasi* ('as though'); she does not see ecstasy as a real freeing of the soul from the body but as a way of making it *paulo liberior*, 'a little more free'. Despite the frequent hyperbole, Folly sees ecstasy not as a death but as a practising of death in Christian madness.

Nevertheless, Erasmus apparently attaches Folly's eulogy of ecstasy to St Augustine's treatise by echoing a phrase he helped to make famous. He later, however, saw fit to pull the ecstasy praised in the *Moria* farther away from *De Genesi ad litteram*. For reasons of his own he subsequently wished to play down a concept of ecstasy in which a man may be said to be alienated from his bodily senses.

It is not certain that Folly is echoing *De Genesi ad litteram*, though it is, I think, probable. St Paul never describes his rapture in terms which imply that he did not know whether he were asleep or awake. That is a later accretion.

One of St Augustine's hypotheses implies acceptance of the Pauline tripartite division of man, seeing him composed of a body, which is kept alive by the *anima* even when the mind—the *nous*, *mens*, or *spiritus*—is actually and in reality caught up outside that body. One might have expected Erasmus to have had considerable sympathy for such a theology of ecstasy; in practice I cannot recall any of his works where it is unambiguously implicit let alone explicit. Erasmus' concept of ecstasy has no room for a litter of dead bodies temporarily abandoned by their souls; it is one reconcilable with Augustine's hypothesis but by no means necessarily the same as it.

(iv) *The rapture of Paul: a double rapture*

The allusion to St Paul's rapture is so obvious a one that it is important to try and find out how Erasmus interpreted the apostle's experience. That may well throw further light on to the *Moria*. In the *Paraphrases* Erasmus adds further details. They emphasise that Paul's rapture was one of exceptional splendour:

I know a man [says St Paul, as paraphrased] who, fourteen years ago was caught up—in the body or outside the body I know not; God knows. But he was caught up into the third heaven and from there was further caught up into Paradise. In both he heard words so ineffable that they may not rightly be uttered by mortal men.

Not every theologian thought of St Paul as being doubly enraptured. To be caught up to the third heaven is privilege enough. Yet, for some, Paul was caught up immeasurably higher. Was this double rapture already accepted by Erasmus when he wrote the *Moria*? Probably, as it derives from both Origen and Ambrose. The passage from Origen on the *Song of Songs* was translated above (p. 171). Ambrose expounds the same doctrine (*PL* 17. 348–9): St Paul was caught up beyond all the stars of the firmament, to where the blessed spirits dwell.

Renaissance scholars continued to attach the greatest importance to St Paul's rapture. For Guillaume Budé it was the decisive sign of his superiority even to Socrates. Socrates brought philosophy down from heaven to earth, so as to improve the morals of men; to Paul was revealed in his rapture the greatest of truths: that Christ, both God and man, was born to raise the study of wisdom from earth to heaven (*De Transitu Hellenismi ad Christianismum*, in Opera I. 166D). Great though the ecstasy may be which Erasmus praises, it may not be quite so exceptional as that, at least after all the implications of what he was saying had sunk in. Folly, in the *Moria*, does associate her 'insane' ecstatic love for God, her *mania erōtikē*, with such an exceptional privilege. Erasmus is a little more circumspect later.

If Erasmus did draw back a little from a particular concept of ecstasy it may not be simply because Paul's rapture was too great a favour to be generally applied to even an élite of pious ecstatics. It may also be a result of his increasing doubts about Pseudo-Dionysius. The easiest way to defend this particular concept of ecstasy would have been to quote from *De Divinis Nominibus*. His doubts about Dionysius brought him troublesome allies. He had to remind his critics that Luther followed him in this, not he Luther. Later Calvin joined the band: he believed, using words which recall what Folly said, that St Paul's rapture was of a kind vouchsafed to very few (*paucissimis datum*); he goes on to trounce 'that trifler Dionysius' who dared to adulterate Holy Writ with his *Celestial Hierarchies* (*Corpus Reformatorum* 78. Calvin 50, 137f. cf. ibid., 76, Calvin 48, 423: on II Corinthians 12 and Acts 17:34).

Had Erasmus been able to swallow his doubts about Pseudo-Dionysius he would have conciliated many orthodox Catholics, not all of them die-hard Sorbonagres.

(v) *Folly's rapture and the 'rapture of the three disciples'*

Folly's allusion to II Corinthians 12 and St Paul's rapture jumps out from the page. Few can have been put off by Kan's failure to point it out. The allusion to the ecstasy of Peter, James and John is another matter. That does not leap to our attention; yet it was destined to be much more important: very much more. It is so central to Erasmus' doctrine of ecstasy—and ecstasy is so central to his religion—that ideally every subsequent allusion to it should be noted and analysed. Representative examples are studied in the following pages.

According to Folly those who come back to themselves after an ecstasy do not recall 'what they said' (*quid dixerint*). When defending the *Moria* Erasmus treats those words as an allusion to the ecstasy of St Peter and his two apostolic companions at the Transfiguration. In fact the whole of the end of the *Moria* is seen as an allusion to the events portrayed in Matthew 17:1–8; Mark 9:2–8; Luke 9:33–end. This 'ecstasy of the three disciples' makes an important contribution to the *Moria* in its own right; it also provides Erasmus with a broad bridge over which he could make an orderly strategic withdrawal.

At the Transfiguration the 'fashion of Christ's countenance was altered and his raiment was white and glistering'. Moses and Elijah appeared with him and spoke of his coming death. Peter, James and John, who witnessed this vision, were struck with fear and driven into an ecstasy of amazement. Peter began to utter curious nonsense—some said pernicious nonsense—as Moses and Elijah were about to withdraw:

And it came to pass, as they were parting from him, Peter said unto Jesus: 'Master, it is good for us to be here; and let us make three tabernacles, one for thee, and one for Moses, and one for Elijah'—not knowing what he said (*nesciens quid diceret*) (Luke 9: 28–33).

By Erasmus' time this amazement of Peter and his two companions had long been seen as the standard example of that ecstatic stupor for which Rufinus' *Origen* and Erasmus both use the verb *obstupesco*. It is an ecstasy in which the pious man is thunderstruck, dazed, beside himself with terror, joy or amazement. All three synoptic Gospels stress that the three disciples were sore afraid. Luke follows Mark in saying that Peter 'wist not what he said' (*nesciebat quid diceret*).

These elements make up the special quality of the ecstasy of the three disciples. Important additional elements, all Scriptural, are the fact that the apostles awoke from a sleep (Luke 9:32) and that the events were enrapt in a cloud (Matthew 17:5; Mark 9:6; Luke 9:34).

The ecstasy of amazement should not be thought of in modern terms as a case of shock. It is a gift of grace. When Erasmus felt called on to defend the *Moria* it was this Petrine ecstasy which he threw into relief. He specifically justifies the very end of the *Moria*—the part we are considering now—in terms of the 'ecstasy of the three disciples'. He does so clearly and unmistakably, but time has obscured his meaning. Moreover, the words to which he appealed—*quid dixerint* ('what they said')—seem so colourless in themselves that their source has not been generally recognised and so their import has not been grasped.

The first attempt to bring the ecstasy praised by Folly in line with that of the three disciples is to be found in the letter to Dorpius (May 1515). After defending his use of Platonico-Socratic *furor* to show how the pious are 'swallowed up into God', Erasmus adds:

'But,' you say, 'you are not opposed to the matter: it is the actual words which are offensive to pious ears.' But why are those pious ears not offended when they hear Paul talking of 'the foolishness of God' and 'the folly of the Cross'? Why do they not bring a charge against St Thomas who wrote thus about St Peter's ecstasy: 'When he was piously silly—*pie desipit*—he began his speech about the three tabernacles'? That holy and happy rapture he called *desipientia* ('foolishness'). And yet those words are sung in churches (*EE* 2. 337. 495f.).

This appeal to Thomas Aquinas is important, aimed at claiming the support of that great scholastic whom many of his critics venerated as all but infallible. Aquinas does indeed make the Transfiguration into a major event in the unveiling of Christian truth. The experience of the three apostles was on a par with St Paul's rapture, though apparently different in kind. Both Paul and the three disciples were vouchsafed *visions*—not in the sense that they saw something imaginary, but in the sense that they had a glimpse of divine realities. What St Peter saw momentarily at the Transfiguration was an unveiling of the glory of Christ in majesty (*Summa Theologica* 3^a. 45 *in toto*). Moreover, in his commentary on Matthew's account of the Transfiguration, Aquinas asserts that 'Peter spoke foolishly (*insipienter*) and so was unworthy of a reply' (*Super Ev. St. Matthaei Lectura*, ed. Raphael,. 1951, p. 219, 1433).

Erasmus appears to be alluding to words of Aquinas figuring in a hymn or collect. I cannot trace them to him. Conservative theologians could hardly object to a doctrine backed by him and encapsulated in a liturgical collect. If Aquinas wrote them, his support would be welcome.

The letter to Dorpius was followed three years later by another apologetic one. In this letter, addressed to Martin Lypsius on 7 May 1518, Erasmus was forced to be even more specific. He now had to answer attacks by Edward Lee.

These indirect replies to Lee are long and weighty. At times a marked defensiveness is noticeable. He attempts to play down the importance of his theme of ecstatic Christian folly and of the *Moria* in general. It would be unwise to take these words out of their context, as though they represented Erasmus's mature and untramelled judgment on the *Moria*. They are better seen as part of the defence of a worried man:

Finally the false accusation that Lee makes about the ecstasy of the three disciples I judge to be unworthy of a refutation. Lee pictures to himself an ecstasy in which a man is entirely torn away from all bodily sensations. But men are also deranged (*delirant*) by fear and by joy, so that they know not what they say, or have gone outside themselves in some other respect (*alioqui exciderunt*). It is said of Peter that 'he knew not what he said'. That is enough for me in a playful work; and we were treating folly, not theology (*EE* 3. 843. 94).

In other words Erasmus is claiming that the *Moria* is concerned with the kind of ecstasy associated with that of the three disciples at the Transfiguration. It is clearly—perhaps even, by implication, exclusively—concerned with the ecstasy of amazement. This can only with some difficulty be applied to the whole of Folly's praise of ecstasy; but it could be reasonably applied to the last part of it which concerns us now.

The final words translated above should be noted. Erasmus suddenly claims the right to be less precise in a playful work—*in opere ludicro*—than he would be in a theological one. That is a fair way from the assertion that the *Moria* is the *Enchiridion* with a smile. It is also not really true. The theology of the *Moria* is very precise indeed. So is its language. The only slackness lay in two or three misquotations of Scripture, which are no more pardonable in a comic work than in a work of manifest scholarship and which were put right in later editions. But the most dangerous part of the *Moria* does seem to have been the final words of the non-epilogue. Jests on theological subjects can be taken very literally by theological sobersides.

(vi) *Peter 'knew not what he said': the risk of Montanism*

Were Lee's accusations too close for comfort? Theological enemies are often adept at finding wilful heresy in casual ambiguities. Erasmus' comportment, from almost as soon as the *Moria* was published, shows that the bone of contention lay in the crucial words: 'what they said, what they did. . . they do not remember' (*quid dixerint, quid fecerint . . . non meminerunt*). Rival theologies can be made to depend upon them. One of the theologies is heretical . . . Montanism.

Either Erasmus had partly fallen into the Montanist heresy or else some of his contemporaries believed they had grounds for thinking that he had. The Montanist heresy is not an inappropriate one for a student of the early Church to fall into: it was a very early heresy, redolent of classical assumptions.

The Montanists, who flourished during the life of Tertullian, had first been noticed about the year 172. Following Montanus they claimed to have special prophets and prophetesses who uttered revelations during insane ecstatic trances. They tended to believe that all true prophecy was like their own and, specifically, that the Old Testament prophets were inspired just as theirs were.

What made the risk of Montanism particularly dangerous for Erasmus was its conceiving of ecstasy as a kind of mindless madness, an *amentia*. The great Tertullian's treatise *De Ecstasi* has not survived his opponents' destructive urges, but we do know that, both as a Catholic and as a Montanist, Tertullian thought of ecstasy as a form of *amentia* (PL 2. 726; notes to ch. XLV). He says so specifically in his work *Against Marcion* (PL 2. 491A: ' . . . *in estasi, id est, amentia*). So too in his treatise *On the Soul* he adopts the terminology of the Septuagint, having an *ekstasis* fall upon Adam during the extraction of his rib and the creation of woman. In itself, that was normal enough; but he describes this ecstasy too as an *amentia*, adding that such mindless madness is 'that spiritual force in which prophecy consists' (PL 2. 684B).

Erasmus could safely call Christianity a form of madness: the paradox was not entirely new. He could follow a major Catholic tradition in thinking of ecstasy as a *mentis excessus*, a rapturing of the mind out of the body. The danger to orthodoxy came when he ran these two currents together. To talk of ecstasy in terms of insanity and *amentia*, and then to have your returned ecstatic 'not remembering what he said', was positively to invite dangerous associations with that Phrygian heresy which Montanus taught, which seduced Tertullian and which Renaissance erudition risked bringing back to life.

The Catholics maintained that the Montanist prophets were possessed by devils. As usual, they set about destroying their opponents' case and writings, while making attempts to refute their doctrines. The Montanists' conception of ecstasy was Philonic, a Christianised form of pagan spiritual possession. The ecstatic prophet was thought to have been taken over by the Holy Ghost or a good spirit. In this respect their trances were analogous to those of the Sibyls. A feature of such a spiritual possession, admitted by the Montanists and attacked by the Catholics, is that the prophet does not know what he says or does during his ecstatic trances. This point was seized upon by the Catholics from the outset. Since Erasmus makes his ecstatics 'insane', and since they too do not remember what they said or did, an accusation of Montanism could be levelled against him, even by men of goodwill.

For centuries one of the main authorities for condemning the Montanist heresy (which was also known as the Phrygian heresy) was the 28th (or 48th) section of the *Treatise against Heretics* by Epiphanius, a learned, fourth-century Cypriot bishop. This section is known as *Contra Phrygastas*.

Epiphanius' treatise is quite a disturbing one to set down beside the *Moria*—if, that is, you want Erasmus to be always orthodox on all subjects. Epiphanius makes a frontal attack on the Montanist conception of *ekstasis* as a kind of *mania*. He devotes considerable attention to the Montanist claim that the true ecstatic prophet 'does not know what he says or does' (*agnoei gar ha phthengetai te kai prattei*: *PG* 41. 864B). By coincidence no doubt, those compromising words are virtually translated into Latin by Folly (*quid dixerint, quid foecerint non meminerunt*). Epiphanius rejects the claim that Montanist prophets are like those of the Old Testament: the Montanists are possessed by evil spirits; as for the Old Testament prophets, they know what they said while they said it—and they remembered it afterwards.

Most of the writings of the Montanists were suppressed, but it can be seen that they attached great importance to the ecstasy of the three disciples: a considerable part of *Contra Phrygastas* is taken up with showing that this ecstasy at the Transfiguration was *not* a case of Montanist prophesying.

What then is the meaning of the statement found in Mark and Luke (though not in Matthew) that Peter spoke oddly, because he did not know what he was saying?

Epiphanius' answer is essentially to define *ekstasis* another way. He points out that *ekstasis* can mean a state of dazed amazement. Under the influence of such a *stupor* a man may well be somewhat confused. There may be a dream-like, cloudy quality about the ecstatic's behaviour but there is no total unawareness—nothing there would justify the assertion that the true ecstatics knew not what they said or what they did.

In the history of ecstasy it is important to distinguish between a general state of dazed confusion on the one hand and a total unawareness of what one had said. or done on the other. The first is not remotely Montanist; the second may well be so. Where matters of this importance are concerned it is vital to look at one's texts very closely. Folly does not assert that ecstatics, once they have come back to themselves, 'do not remember what they heard, what they saw, what they said nor what they did'. To stop there would be to read Erasmus like a Lee, a Béda or a Pio da Carpi. What she says is, that they do not remember what they were saying *nisi tanquam per nebulam ac somnum* ('except through a cloud or a sleep'). These are echoes of the accounts of the Transfiguration. Later, such aspects are emphasised in the various paraphrases, doubtless with one eye on what had been written long before in the *Moria*. So in the paraphrase of St Matthew's account of the Transfiguration we are told that Jesus wanted to reveal to chosen disciples the form of his countenance as it would be when he would come to judge the world. He did this *velut per somnium*, 'as though through a dream'. That is why the three apostles were as though 'suddenly snatched from their sleep'(*experrectis a somno*). They were dazed with fear and astonished (*expavefactis igitur et attonitis discipulis*). This account in the paraphrase of St Matthew (*LB* 7. 94f.) is paralleled by that of St Mark (*LB* 7. 224Df.). That of St Luke makes similar points (*LB* 7. 371f.).

One might have thought that that was enough to put everyone's mind at rest. Erasmus' conduct shows that it was not. And the main trouble was probably caused by a joke which badly misfired.

(vii) *Folly's Montanist epilogue*

If Erasmus had stopped before Folly's last canter, he would have saved himself a great deal of bother. The ecstasy of the three disciples could be pressed into service to explain the faulty memory attributed to ecstatics. Even if one felt a certain doubt about its total appropriateness, as I do, the doubts could be stifled. But then Folly is allowed to give, as it were, the game away.

The end of the *Moria*, when Folly comes back to herself, is one of those complex jests beloved of Renaissances authors and readers. The title of the *Praise of Folly—Stultitiae Laus—*is ambiguous. It means both the praising of folly and the encomium declaimed by Folly. A similar complexity is jestingly put before the reader in Folly's last sentences.

Suddenly and unexpectedly we are shown that Folly herself has been speaking in ecstasy! It is all of course a joke; Erasmus' tongue is firmly in his cheek. But it is a dangerous joke, since it only apparently makes sense if ecstatics, on their return, *do* forget what they said:

In truth I have long since forgotten myself (*oblita mei*) . . .   You are expecting an epilogue, I can see—but you are very much out of your senses (*nimium desipitis*), if you think I remember what I said . . .

The last words are *quid dixerim meminisse*. They directly appeal to what has just been cited seriously above to describe the confused state of the returned ecstatics: *quid dixerint . . . non meminerunt* ('they do not remember what they said'). How can Erasmus get out of that? There is no amazement; no *stupor* is possible here. Folly's joke really does seem to imply a concept of ecstasy too close for comfort to Montanist assumptions.

Erasmus' model for the Folly of the non-epilogue was Socrates (*Phaedrus* 263D). But to attempt to hide behind the amnesia of that sage enthusiast would have been to play into the hands of his critics.

Would it not have been enough for Erasmus to say it was all a joke and to leave it at that, cutting out a word or two from this section and putting a word or two back in their place? He did just that. But he did much more as well. The basic theme of the end of the *Moria* was one he could only make a limited compromise over. It was too important to him to allow of a fundamental re-writing. But before looking at how Erasmus explained away the Montanism of Folly's own ecstasy, it is useful to look at what he wrote immediately after the *Moria* was published.

(viii) *Taking up an anti-Montanist attitude (I): St Basil*

Erasmus realised the dangers of confusing his doctrines in the *Moria* with the Phrygian heresy of Montanus almost as soon as the work appeared in print. That can be inferred by the first literary work he then undertook—a translation of the Preface to St Basil's *Commentary on Isaiah*. This he completed in 1511. The original manuscript was in Grocyn's library. Erasmus had doubts about ascribing the work to Basil the Great, but he realised that it was far from negligible, whichever Basil wrote it. So he translated it into Latin, submitted it to John Fisher, bishop of Rochester, and hoped for patronage. Fisher, always friendly, was not over-impressed; he even wondered whether Erasmus had simply tidied up an earlier Latin version.[1]

The choice of text is very important. Erasmus' version is recommended reading for all students of the *Moria*. This page or two of Basil on Isaiah is a vital clue to Erasmus' intellectual preoccupations in the months following the appearance of Folly's eulogy. (In 1518 Erasmus' version of the Preface of Basil was published by Froben together with the *Enchiridion*.)

Even a quick reading of Erasmus' *Basil* shows a striking overlapping of vocabulary and concern with the end of the *Moria*. It is impossible to look at the last pages of the *Moria* and the few pages of this version of Basil without noticing the fact.

For St Basil, a good prophet sloughs off the skin of the Old Adam and receives divine inspirations (*divini afflatus*); he then conforms his life to what the Spirit means him to. Pious men can receive revelations

[1] Cf. J. Rouschausse, *Erasmus and Fisher. Their Correspondence*, Paris, 1968, notes on pp. 87–8.

of spiritual realities (*res verae*) in visions or by hearing voices and so on. But what Basil will not allow is that Isaiah, say, or Ezechiel uttered words which they could not understand. That would be to make them possessed, in a Philonic or Montanist rapture.

But there are those who say that they prophesied when they were caught up outside themselves (*extra se raptos*), their mind being swallowed up by the Spirit (*a spiritu absorpta*).

Since, in form of words at least, that is precisely what Folly said, one reads on attentively, for this is an opinion which St Basil is condemning. He goes on to add:

It is truly abhorrent to the manifestation of the divine presence that someone who is seized by the Godhead should be mindless (*amentem*); that, when he begins to be full of the divine decrees, he should then be out of his own mind (*propria . . . mente excidat*), and that he who is of use to others with his utterances should be of no use to himself. To sum up: how can it be fitting that anyone should be made very like a madman (*simillimus insano*) by the Spirit of Wisdom, so that the Spirit of Understanding should exclude coherency (*cohaerentia*)?

Of all the works Erasmus could have translated, why did he choose this one? The impact of these words is considerable. They read like a recantation. In fact they are not: they are in the nature of a *distinguo* and of a strategic withdrawal. Basil asks: Can the Light cause blindness and bring darkness into the soul? No. That is the property of diabolical possession:

It appears not to be lacking in verisimilitude that an evil, diabolical power, lying in wait for human nature, should confound the mind. Anyone saying that the presence of the Holy Ghost produces such an effect speaks impiously. Moreover, if saints be wise men, how can they not conform and correspond to what they themselves prophesied: 'The wise man understands what proceeds from his own mouth; he carries understanding on his lips' [LXX/Vulgate, Proverbs 16:23].

How St Basil reconciles this assertion with the ecstatic language strewn throughout the Septuagint and by no means absent from the New Testament is then explained. The terms which Erasmus uses to render this passage call forth some technical reflexions:

If—because Isaac was caught up outside himself (*extra se raptus*) at the entrance of his son, and because David spoke in his mind-departed state (*in excessu suo*)—they therefore imagine the saints to have been caught up outside themselves (*extra se rapi*), then let them understand that it is astonishment and amazement which are called rapture (*raptus*).

In other words, the more colourful ecstatic terminology is merely figurative and hyperbolical. What is meant by these terms is what one reads in the Bible: 'Heaven was amazed: the earth was terrified.' (This is a loose allusion to LXX Jeremiah 2:12.)

This translation of Erasmus' can be read in *LB* 8. 486F–487A. It is profitable to compare it with Basil's original text, which may be found in *PG* 30. 125C–128A. In fact the full force of what Erasmus is doing only comes across if you do confront his translation with the original Greek. In this paragraph Basil sharply condemns those who 'falsely allege' (*katapseudontai*) that the saints prophesy in ecstasy. Erasmus translates this by the more neutral verb *fingo*, which can mean to imagine, to conceive or to represent, and does not necessarily bear the sense of falseness so obvious in the original. It can be used to apply to a work of 'fiction'.

Even more important is the fact that Erasmus chooses translations which echo phrases frequently used in the *Moria*. Where Erasmus says that Isaac was *extra se raptus* ('caught up outside himself'), Basil says merely, *exestē Isaak*. The allusion is to LXX Genesis 27:33, which in the Vulgate is rendered by *expavit Isaac* ('Isaac was terrified'); the Vulgate moreover, emphasises the element of fear: *expavit Isaac stupore vehementi* ('Isaac was terrified with a "vehement" amazement'). The natural translation of *exestē Isaak*, especially in context, is that 'Isaac was amazed'. Why then does Erasmus say that Isaac was 'caught up outside himself', if not to bring his Basil closer to the language of Folly?

Erasmus follows Basil in retaining the ecstatic meaning of LXX Psalm 115: 2: *Egō de eipa en tē ekstasei mou* (I said in my 'ecstasy'). David is alleged to have spoken in *excessu suo* as in the Vulgate. The word *excessus* inevitably suggests that mind-departing ecstasy which is *mentis excessus*. It would have been more natural to have rendered this too by a verb suggesting amazement.

The next phrase supplies even clearer evidence. Basil wrote: 'Because of this, they falsely allege *paraphora* against the saints' (*PG* 30. 126C). *Paraphora* means 'a going outside', frequently with respect to the mind, distracted or deranged. Erasmus rendered this sentence as: 'They therefore imagine the saints to have been caught up outside themselves' (*extra se rapi*). Then Basil's statement that *ekstasis* in the Bible really means *ekplēxis* (fear or consternation) is expanded; the one word *ekplēxis* is turned into Latin by means of both *admiratio* (astonishment) and *stupor* (amazement). The *ekstasis* which this represents for Basil is then rendered by Erasmus as *raptus*, so making it into a rapture. Finally, Basil's allusion to LXX Jeremiah 2: 12: 'Heaven *exeste* . . .' is translated as 'Heaven *obstupuit* . . . ,' by, that is, that verb *obstupesco* which, in the *Moria* too, is used for the ecstasy of amazement.

Erasmus was already by this time a man with a fastidious feeling for words. He was sharply aware of shades of meaning. Neither chance nor ignorance can explain why he consistently confused his categories in this way. Moreover, what Erasmus did here he did again, more than once, later; he deliberately confounds the two main kinds of ecstasy, while insisting that he means the ecstasy of amazement. When challenged about the ecstasy which Folly is constantly praising in the very terms which St Basil condemns if taken other than figuratively, Erasmus follows Basil and refers the reader to the ecstasy of amazement —the *stupor* which struck the three apostles at the Transfiguration. Folly talks of *mania, furor, amentia*, 'vehemence'; of men being 'caught up outside themselves', of incoherence, and of ecstasy being 'very like madness'; the whole of her peroration revolves about a man being '*as it were*, outside himself' in a mad, selfless ecstasy, uttering words and doing things which he does not understand or even remember. These are, textually, the very ideas and expressions which Basil condemns, unless, that is, they are used figuratively for the ecstasy of amazement. Taken literally they may oblige one to think of diabolical possession and are certainly capable of a Montanist interpretation.

Basil's *Preface to Isaiah* is a standard anti-Montanist work. His arguments and authorities were taken over and used by Jerome in his own *Preface to Isaiah*, itself a standard antidote to Montanism. A quick translation of Basil's preface was an effective way of protecting oneself from accusations of potential seriousness.

Erasmus partly succeeded in detaching himself from smears of Montanism. Indeed he became an authority to quote against it. This can be seen from an interesting paragraph entitled *De Ecstasi* in P. J. Olivarius' book *On Prophecy and the Prophet Spirit*. It reads as follows:

It is not really relevant to our subject to say much about *ecstasis*, but since many thought that the holy prophets foretold in ecstasy, and a few thought the same of John in Revelations, we will say a little about it. *Ekstasis* means in Latin *mentis stupor* (an amazement of the mind) or *alienatio* (a loss of reason). Hence *ekstatikos*: astonished (*attonitus*) or mad (*mente captus*). For *ekstasis* is not the raising up of the spirit (*elevatio spiritus*). When anyone is raised up in that most noble part of the soul which is called the spirit, he is not mad (*non mente captus*). Therefore whoever it was who wrote *On the Spirit and the Soul*—for Erasmus does not think that that book was by Augustine—was certainly not versed in Greek literature. In Revelations, John often says he was 'in the spirit'. That egregious expositor explains that he was 'in ecstasy'. Montanus, the author of the new prophesying, thought that prophets, when they foretold the future, were in ecstasy, and insane so that they could not understand what they were foretelling.

St Jerome bitterly attacks Montanus in that learned preface which he prefixed to the *Commentaries on Isaiah* . . .[1]

Erasmus had chosen his first piece of work after the *Moria* with striking ingenuity. But one cannot help feeling sometimes that he had had a close shave.

From the moment Erasmus presented Basil in his contrived Latin version to Fisher he always puts the emphasis on the ecstasy of amazement. At first sight this is rather odd. The earliest church fathers were hostile to certain kinds of ecstasy because of Montanist heresies. Not so the later ones. So great an authority as St Augustine allows one to take Old Testament *ekstasis* to mean either the ecstasy of amazement or that *mentis excessus* in which the soul is raptured outside oneself. Such doctrines were widely held in the most orthodox of circles. Erasmus could certainly have done the same in a more usual, less whimsical, less paradoxical, less madcap context. But he chose to associate ecstasy with insanity, and insanity with incoherent speech and with an unawareness on the part of the ecstatic of 'what he said'. That left him with no option but to throw into relief that *extasis stuporis* which does allow there to be some degree of incoherence on the part of the enraptured. Otherwise it is hard to see how he could rightly have escaped the accusation of Montanism. Taken literally, the end of the *Moria* is indeed heretical. Orthodoxy is saved only if many of its terms are taken figuratively and if, as Erasmus strenuously claims, the ecstasy he is talking about is such as befell the three disciples during the Transfiguration of their Lord.

(ix) *Taking up an anti-Montanist attitude (II): marginal notes to the 1516* Moria *on Folly's Montanist epilogue*

Erasmus saw that he had to find some way of stopping the reader from interpreting the final jest about Folly's own ecstasy in too literal a sense. If he failed to do so, then the *Moria* ended with an at best ambiguous attitude towards Montanism. Erasmus defused these potentially dangerous statements with two notes.

The first is placed against *oblita mei* ('I have forgotten myself'):

[1] Petrus Johannes Olivarius Valentinus; *De Prophetia & Spiritu prophetico*, dedicated to Stephen [Gardiner] bishop of Winchester, Basle, 1543; *BL*, at *3166.b.10*.

oblita mei: because it is not appropriate that Folly should talk about such mysterious matters. She does the same at the end of the disputation as she did at the beginning, feeling that the matter might at first appear too hard.

This thrusts aside any suggestion that she had 'forgotten herself' in the sense that she 'knew not what she was saying'. She had simply forgotten her rôle as a Fool.

The note placed against *video vos epilogum* is even more ingenious:

You are expecting an epilogue I can see—but you are very much out of your senses if you think I can still remember what I said (*quid dixerim meminisse*) . . .

The 'Listrius' note reads:

She aptly pretends forgetfulness in an epilogue which consists in repeating what has been said; that cannot be done except from memory.

(*Video vos epilogum*: Apte praetexit oblivionem in Epilogo, qui constat repetitione eorum quae dicta sunt, quod nisi a memore fieri nequit) (*BL* 1476, bb. 10; sig. zr°).

So Folly did not actually speak as one who 'knew not what she was saying'; she did not actually forget what she uttered in ecstasy. It was all a pretence: an ingenious literary device to avoid a tedious recapitulatory summing-up in the epilogue . . .

The purging of the text of the *Moria*, the additional marginal notes and the letter to Dorpius are all part of the same movement of self-defence and public explanation. I know of no manuscript or printed source which contains an open accusation of Montanism against the *Moria*. Yet all these actions, like the oddities in his translation of Basil's preface to Isaiah, are designed to avoid it.

Erasmus fights his battle for Folly's concept of ecstasy on two fronts. He tones down the implications of what Folly says, yet he introduces the very same notions discreetly elsewhere. It was in fact important to Erasmus that an enraptured ecstatic should 'forget himself', at least to a degree. So even St Paul is shown as being forgetful. This transpires from the *Annotations*, when Erasmus is commenting on St Paul's exclamation (Galatians 2:20): 'I live, yet not I, but Christ liveth in me—a life however which now I live in the flesh, I live through faith in the Son of God. . .' Erasmus notes that Paul breaks off what he was saying *'velut oblitus sui'*, 'as though he had forgotten himself' (*LB* 4. 811C). The importance of this remark lies partly in the fact that this text was *the* ecstatic text *par excellence*.

(x) *Peter 'knew not what he said': further Epiphanian solutions*

In some ways Erasmus' ingenuity made matters very much worse. The effect of explaining away Folly's Montanist jesting is to throw us back to the serious use of the expression 'they do not remember what they said'; this had been applied a few lines earlier to pious ecstatics who have come back to themselves. In that moving and emotive climax there can be no question of literary pretence to avoid being tedious in an epilogue. One wonders how Epiphanius' anti-Montanist assertion that Biblical ecstasy means ecstatic amazement can be brought to bear on that troublesome passage.

To enter constructively into Erasmus' thought it is helpful to look at what he later wrote about the ecstasy of the three disciples at the Transfiguration, since it is in such terms that he defended himself. Nothing that Erasmus ever subsequently says about the Transfiguration is likely to be irrelevant to an understanding of the *Moria*.

If we were studying a game of chess or a set of cynical political manœuvres we could coldly note that to hide behind Gospel accounts of Peter's confused utterances during the Transfiguration would be a good tactic to adopt in order to establish anti-Montanist credentials. But we are not doing that. Erasmus' adult life was devoted to furthering the Catholic faith as he conceived it. The intellectual and spiritual tensions aroused in him by the need to reconcile what he wrote in the *Moria* and what he translated in his *Basil on Isaiah* must have been very great indeed. Erasmus' writings show that he needed to defend the kind of madness which Folly elaborated upon, not out of the prickly vanity of an author but from the deepest roots of his convictions.

St Mark's and St Luke's account of the Transfiguration are even more important to Erasmus than St Matthew's. If they do use essentially the same words about St Peter's incoherence during the Transfiguration as Folly does—and if they use them in the same sense as he does—then Erasmus' defence is unshakeable. But the *ifs* are important. By *nesciebat quid diceret* Mark does not mean that Peter did not know, once his ecstasy was over, what he said during it; he means that Peter knew not what he was saying—or what he should say—as he spoke while witnessing such a vision. The traditional English translation is 'Peter wist not what he said'. But that is ambiguous in a way that neither the Greek nor the Vulgate is; both mean, 'Peter wist not *what he was saying*'. Similarly in Luke's account, Peter uttered his confused speech *nesciens quid diceret*. Again, he spoke 'not knowing *what he was saying*'. This is not a quibble. A major theological distinction is involved. Erasmus had two alternatives: he could deny he ever meant that the pious ecstatic utters words which are incoherent when he says them and which, as a separate issue, he largely forgets when the ecstasy is over; or else he could so interpret what he wrote as to safeguard orthodoxy. Any other alternative might lead to an assumption of heresy. What he certainly does is to confuse his traces. The tenses of *quid dixerint . . . non meminerunt* in the *Moria*, as well as the context, mean that ecstatics 'do not remember' (*non meminerunt*) 'What they were saying in the past' (*quid dixerint*)—*memini* is a defective verb, past in form, present in meaning. So it can be interpreted in the light of what was said of St Peter. Folly spoke, not knowing 'what she was saying' while she was speaking. So far, so good. St Peter did the same.

Even then it was not enough simply to cite the example of the three disciples at the Transfiguration: the right theological conclusions have to be drawn from that event. Erasmus had to choose from among several interpretations or else, selecting his materials, work out a full interpretation of his own.

He concentrates upon the assertion that Peter 'knew not what he said' because it is that phrase above all which traditionally justified the ecstatic interpretation placed upon his confused utterance. This was the case as early as Origen who, in his *Commentary on Matthew*—the only Gospel commentary of his partially to survive—believed that Peter was possessed by a devil, since the words he uttered were an attempt to persuade Jesus to remain safely on the mountain, instead of coming down again to die for us men and for our salvation. Origen cites both Mark and Luke in his Commentary (Latin version):

Mark adds that Peter 'did not know what he should answer' (*nec enim sciebat quid responderet*). Luke writes that Peter spoke, 'not knowing what he was saying' (*nesciens quid loquebatur*). But if Peter uttered these words 'not knowing what he said', we must consider whether he perhaps spoke in ecstasy (*per excessum mentis*) moved by a hostile spirit—for we cannot believe it was the Holy Spirit (*PG* 13. 1074Af.).

The Holy Ghost had not yet appeared among men who believed in Christ—that occurred at Pentecost. Despite the offence he knows he may give, Origen insists that no good spirit could cause to be uttered the bad advice given by St Peter on the mountain.

Here was Origen, normally an ally, giving ammunition to Erasmus' enemies.

This passage of Origen was well-known: it was cited in the *Catena Aurea* of Aquinas. It could offer no comfort to Erasmus: if this were true, then Folly had been unwittingly championing diabolical possession. That is indeed one of the risks Erasmus ran.

Tertullian is equally clear that the key idea is Peter's 'not knowing what he said'. He uses this fact to defend Montanist prophesyings:

In what way did he not know what he said? Is it more appropriate that he should be mistaken or that he should have spoken through that ecstasy of grace, that mindlessness which we defend on behalf of the new prophesying? (*PL* 2. 413C).

. . . an ratione quam defendimus in causa novae prophetiae gratiae ecstasin, id est amentiam convenire?

This is as worrying as Origen's contention: here is an important Erasmian idea, linking *ekstasis* with *amentia*, but defended by the greatest theologian whom Montanism perverted from orthodoxy. The only solution for Erasmus was to link the ecstasy of the *Moria* ever more firmly with that ecstasy of fear or amazement, that *ekstasis phobou*, which Epiphanius saw as the orthodox rival to that mind-departing ecstasy, that *ekstasis phrenōn*, which could open the way to thoughts of diabolical possession. But he had to do it in ways which avoided the pitfalls of such un-Catholic interpretations as those represented by Origen or Tertullian, both authors whom he knew well.

One way Erasmus faced this problem was by widening it, reminding scholars that Socrates made a distinction between prophets and seers. Essentially the Montanists thought of their prophets as *vates*, as seers, ecstatically possessed. But Christians also traditionally allowed an important place to seers: all Montanist prophets were seers, but not all seers were Montanists.

Allusions to Plato or Socrates—contrary to what Erasmus' other writings might lead one to expect—are very, very rare in the *Annotations on the New Testament*. I can recall only two which are relevant to Folly: one (already studied) was the additional note on Theophylact's linking of Socratic *furor* and Pauline erotic madness. The other is analogous, telling the reader how an evangelical prophet differs from a Classical pagan one. The annotation concerns I Corinthians 14:1–5, which reads:

Desire earnestly spiritual gifts, but rather that ye may prophesy. For he that speaks in tongues speaketh not unto men but unto God; for no man understandeth, but in the Spirit he speaketh mysteries. But he that prophesieth speaketh unto men edification, comfort, consolation . . .

In the *Annotations* (*LB* 6. 728CD) Erasmus warns that no gift of the Spirit is to be despised, but some are higher than others. The prime gift is prophecy. But it is important to realise what prophecy means:

In this passage Paul does not mean by *prophetia* the ability to predict the future; he means the interpretation of the Holy Scriptures. In like manner Plato distinguished seers (*vates*) from prophets (*prophetae*). Seers, seized by the Godhead, do not themselves understand what they say (*nec ipsi quod loquuntur intelligunt*). Their speech is wisely interpreted by others.

Erasmus adds that the imperative verb, 'Desire earnestly', is *diōkete* not *zēlōte*. Both mean 'desire', but *diōkein*, the verb used by St Paul here, means 'to desire *vehementius*'.

The full import of this note is not easy to define. It is a note where silences are eloquent. Erasmus is presumably reminding his readers that, while prophets in the New Testament sense have nothing to do with foretelling the future—their privilege is to declare the real spiritual sense of Scripture—nevertheless prophets akin to classical seers do have a share in the divine *charismata*, none of which is to be despised. Such *vates* do not understand what they say. In this respect at least they are not unlike St Peter at the Transfiguration.

Such an idea would not have been new to Renaissance ears. Both the mosaic floor of Sienna Cathedral and the widely sung hymn *Dies irae* proclaim that Christ's return in majesty to judge the world in the Day of Wrath is testified to by David and the Sibyl:

> Dies irae, dies illa
> Solvet saeclum in favilla
> Teste David et Sibulla.

Oh Day of wrath! That day will loosen the bonds of the world in ashes, as David and the Sibyl bear witness.

St Augustine had included both the Cumaean Sibyl and Virgil among the seers prophesying the advent of Christ (*City of God*, x. 27).

Without taking up a position, Erasmus leaves his options open. His theology of ecstasy seems to owe something here to Augustine. Bartholomew of Medina sums up this Catholic doctrine conveniently in his commentary on part of Aquinas' *Summa Theologica*: St Jerome denied the Montanist assertion that prophets speak in ecstasy 'in such a way that they know not what they said—teaching others while they themselves were unaware of what they said'. (He does this, incidentally, in his *Preface to Isaiah*, which uses the same texts and arguments as St Basil.)

Augustine (*lib. 9 in Genes. qu. 80*) said that, since ecstasy is accustomed to be found in the revelation of great things, nobody should doubt that prophets sometimes do experience ecstasy.

St Jerome is not held to mean that an ecstatic prophet always understands everything he says: he is taken as condemning those who maintain that they utterly fail to understand what they say in their ecstasy (*ut omnino nescirent quid loquerentur*). Such is an excellent way of approaching what Erasmus seems to mean. Folly does not say that pious men remember nothing of their ecstasies; she says they only remember them as through a sleep or a dream—like the apostles at the Transfiguration in fact.[1]

Erasmus is also prepared to defend the proper place of ecstatic utterance, meaningless to men, meaningful to God. Unlike many of his contemporaries he did occasionally get near to realising that the gift of tongues may mean the ecstatic gibberish of *glossolalia*. But Erasmus is very clear on this: men may well utter incoherent speech under the power of the Spirit, but they are not prophets unless they can later explain what their strange utterances meant: 'some of them do not adequately understand them themselves' (*LB* 7, paraphrase on I Corinthians 14:2–5). Nothing at all in the *Moria* suggests a sympathy for ecstasies like that, but their reality is not denied.

What Erasmus does venerate and cherish is something much fuller and more rounded. It is a form of the ecstasy of amazement such as befell the apostles at the Transfiguration, but consistently enriched with elements more normally associated with the ecstatic drunkenness of Greek and then Latin tradition and with that 'vehement' *mentis excessus* which has all the symptoms of the mind's apparently succeeding in making itself a little freer from its body. This can be seen from the ways in which Erasmus wrote of the Transfiguration, even years after the *Moria* was first conceived. On each and every occasion he wrote as if he had the *Moria* directly in mind. That is what one would expect: he had publicly explained the end of the *Moria* as being an echo of the ecstasy of the three disciples. That could never be forgotten.

Erasmus found help in many authorities for his marrying together of the two main orthodox concepts of ecstasy. Theophylact was particularly helpful. So were the Greek fathers in general as were Ambrose, Jerome, Bernard, Bonaventura. Theophylact in his glosses on St Mark's account of the Transfiguration explains Peter's nescience in terms of a temporary mental derangement: the three disciples, terrified by the Light, 'were not in their right minds (*ou gar ēn ontōs en tōi idiōi noi: PG* 123. 581B). This accords with what Erasmus says later.

Eleven years after the publication of the *Moria* Erasmus still talked of the ecstasy of the three disciples in the same terms as in the *Moria*. This can be seen from his *Paraphrase of St Matthew* (1522): the apostles witnessed the Transfiguration 'as though just awakened from a sleep'. They were 'astonished'; 'terrified'.

---

[1] See Bartholomew of Medina: *Expositio in 1ᵃ 2ᵃᵉ Angelici Doctoris . . .*, Salamanca, 1588, p. 303 col. ii.—p. 304 col. i.

So Peter, not sufficiently in control of himself (*nondum satis sui compos*) but entirely enraptured (*totus raptus*) by the joy and majesty of the sight, said what he did say. So too, when the vision departed, the disciples, having received back their souls (*receptis animis*) lifted up their eyes and saw no one there (*LB* 7, paraphrase on Matthew 17:4–8).

Such terms are worth pondering over: the ecstasy of amazement is being consciously drawn closer to that mind-departing ecstasy so evident in the *Moria*. Erasmus similarly emphasised the elements of rapture in the *Paraphrase of St Mark* published the following year, 1523: Peter was 'enraptured'; he was 'not sufficiently in control of himself'; the vision had made him act 'as though he were drunk'. The cloud came upon the disciples, lest they be 'swallowed up' by the splendour; they had experienced a taste, a *gustus*, of the divine. But most telling of all is the detail of the explanations of Peter's strange utterances:

For, as though caught up outside himself, he knew not what he said. So great a fear had amazed the souls of mortals, not yet able to receive the majesty of God (*LB* 7. 224D).

Etenim, velut extra se raptus, nesciebat quid loqueretur. Tantus pavor obstupefecerat animos mortalium, nondum capaces divinae majestatis.

In the *Paraphrase of St Luke* Peter is shown to have uttered his strange speech in a state of ecstatic drunkenness: 'Peter spoke these things, not knowing what he said, as though drunk on the sweetness of the vision' (*LB* 7. 371).

The fact that these disciples—like Folly's ecstatics—only saw through a cloud and so were not fully aware of it all—is brought to the fore with quiet emphasis.

This desire to bring together the two major forms of ecstasy within the context of the ecstasy of amazement is too consistently present for it to be other than conscious and purposeful. Many further examples could be cited. One more, which is perhaps particularly helpful, is the account of St Peter's other major vision—the one related in Acts 10 and 11, in which he saw a table-cloth descending from heaven, laden with foods which included ones considered ritually unclean by the Jewish community in the Church. Erasmus constantly expounds this in terms appropriate to a mind-departing rapture.

The account in Acts tells how Peter came to see this vision. He was up on the roof, praying; and then, at the sixth hour, being hungry, he fell into a trance—*epepesen ep'auton ekstasis*. Erasmus translates this with vigour in his *Novum Instrumentum*. The Vulgate reads, *cecidit super eum mentis excessus*: 'a mind-departing-ecstasy fell on him.' Erasmus makes it more vivid. This ecstasy *irruit super eum*: 'rushed down upon him.' (Acts 10:10.) The effect of using this vivid verb is to increase the element of sudden rapture. The verb was carefully chosen. By using *irruo* Erasmus quietly associated Peter's sudden ecstasy with that other ecstasy which *irruit super Abram*—which 'rushed down upon Abram' in Genesis 15:12. And, indeed, the Septuagint uses the same words for Abraham's ecstasy in Genesis 15:12 as St Luke does for Peter's in Acts 10:10: *ekstasis epepese tōi Abram*. Whatever it was that happened to St Peter had already befallen Abraham in former days. If the Vulgate was right to use *irruo* for Genesis 15:22, then Erasmus could do so for Luke 10:10. Both were manifestations of the same thing.

When Peter told the Church in Jerusalem what he had seen in this vision (Acts 11:5), he related how he had seen it *en ekstasei*—in an ecstatic trance, no doubt. The Vulgate renders this as 'I saw a vision in a rapture' (*Vidi in excessu mentis visionem*) using the term *mentis excessus* with which we are by now so familiar. Erasmus stresses the actual rapture. In his *Novum Instrumentum* we find this phrase rendered as *Et vidi, raptus extra me, visionem*. So Peter's vision was seen while 'he was caught up outside himself . . .'

It is this aspect which is twice thrown into relief in the *Paraphrase of Acts* (1524). Acts 10:10 is further expanded to show that Peter, while hungrily praying, was 'caught up in the Spirit' (*raptus est Spiritu*). So, too, when Peter tells the Church of his experience (Acts 11:5) he is paraphrased as saying:

I ordered food to be prepared. Meanwhile I was caught up (*raptus sum*) and in ecstasy (*in ecstasi*) I saw a vision . . .

And when that vision was over Peter—where nothing in the original obliges him to do so—is made to use the expression *reversus ad me*. He had, in other words, 'come back to himself', exactly like the pious ecstatics praised by Folly. He was, in fact, a Christian madman, 'insane' as Folly had conceived of insanity some thirteen years earlier.

(xi) *The happiness of the Christian madman*

The few lines of Folly's peroration that we are studying contain a ringing allusion to the happiness of those enraptured Christian fools. Such ecstatic madmen, when they have come back to themselves (*ubi ad sese redirent*) may forget many things; but this they do know: that they were most happy when they were most out of their senses. With such an insanity, they could wish to be insane for ever and ever.

Erasmus is applying to Christian madness, which brings the Christian fool into contact with the eternal realities, the lesson he drew in the

Adages from a Greek proverb which he found in Plutarch and latinised as *Insania non omnibus eadem* ('Madness is not the same for everybody'). Horace's Stoic convert Damasippus is cited to prove the truth of the saying. (The third satire of Horace's third book, in which Damasippus appears, is given over to mocking the various insanities of mankind. It was certainly one of Erasmus' models.) Erasmus talks of madmen he has met, including one who thought he was the greatest sinner there had ever been, one who thought he was Christ, one who thought he was God. The pride of place is given to a poor fool cited by Athenaeus who fondly believed he owned all the ships he saw coming in and out of harbour, together with all their merchandise. Unfortunately, his brother cured him . . .

After he had come back to himself (*ad se reversus*) he used to say that he had never lived happier [than when he was mad] (*Adages* 3. 10. 97; *LB* 2. 949D–950A).

The Christian madman differs in one way only from such an idiot. He weeps because he wishes he could be mad like that, not for all his life but for all eternity. Ordinary madmen are, in the last resort, not unlike More's wife who could be happily fooled with trinkets. Christians are satisfied with nothing less than eternity. And the blessedness of such eternity the Christian fool will, if he is enraptured, ecstatically glimpse: 'and this is one, thin little taste of future happiness.'

It is a commonplace of ecstatic theory that rapture is a gratuitous glimpse of eternal blessedness. To the enraptured soul is vouchsafed a momentary sight of eternal reality; it is granted the beatific vision of that Supreme Good who is God and whom redeemed man will eternally enjoy hereafter. No one on whom has been bestowed such a sign of divine favour can ever be the same again.

St Paul had such a favour bestowed on him: that was agreed by all who wrote on him; so too did the three disciples at the Transfiguration. Both these ecstasies play a central rôle in the Christian religion. Both play a central rôle at the climax of the *Moria* and in Erasmus' theology generally. Few things which Erasmus subsequently wrote are more indicative of the spiritual depths lying just below the surface of Folly's happy closing pages than the various paraphrases of the Gospel accounts of the Transfiguration. This major event in the life of the Church is the yardstick against which Erasmus invites us to measure the heights and the depths of Christian folly.

Erasmus believed that Christ chose Peter, James and John for the privilege of witnessing his Transfiguration because they were capable both of believing what they saw and then keeping appropriately quiet about it until the time came to publish it abroad. That is why Christ took them—only them—to the mountain. The scriptures simply tell us that the mountain on which that great drama was played out was high: 'Jesus took them to a high mountain' (*in montem excelsum*).

In this study we have so often met *vehemens* used as a pious etymological pun that I apologise for having to emphasise it yet again. But return to it we must: the context makes it particularly important. Erasmus' various paraphrases of the three accounts of the Transfiguration in the New Testament show that it was not merely a joke when Folly brings *vehemens* close to the sense of 'bearing the mind away'. In the paraphrase of St Matthew's account, the mountain of the Transfiguration is not said to be simply high (*excelsum*); it is said to be *vehementer excelsum*, 'mind-enrapturingly high' (*LB* 7. 94F.). This is not a passing flight of fancy. Erasmus returns to the same phrase one year later, in his paraphrase of St Mark: there too Christ took the three chosen disciples away to a *montem vehementer excelsum* (*LB* 7. 224A). So, yet again, the mountain is said to be 'mind-enrapturingly high'.

The use of the adverb *vehementer* links the episode as paraphrased with Erasmus' Latin translation in the *Novum Instrumentum;* whereas the Vulgate states that the disciples 'greatly feared (*timuerunt valde*), the *Novum Instrumentum* says that they were 'vehemently' frightened (*et territi sunt vehementer*). This is Erasmus' version of Matthew 17:6; *vehementer* renders the word *sphodra*, which does indeed combine the notion 'exceedingly' with an element of violence[1]

(xii) *A privilege to be secretly cherished*

The Transfiguration led to vehement ecstasy because Christ vouch-safed to his three chosen disciples a glimpse of himself in glorious majesty. The full force of this revelation can only be appreciated if we recall that Erasmus held a kenotic theology of the Incarnation. During his life on earth, Jesus of Nazareth appeared to be a man among men, differing mainly from the others in seeming at times mad enough to be restrained in fetters. Then suddenly, without warning, perched on the top of a mind-enrapturing mountain, Peter, James and John saw Jesus as the Christ in majesty. No wonder they were driven into an ecstasy of amazement such as Folly eulogised.

It is helpful to look yet again at the paraphrase of St Mark's account of the Transfiguration: the people did not realise that Christ must appear twice, first lowly and abject, secondly in majesty, 'when he will take unto himself his whole body, the Church, purged of all evils'.

[1] Those who rely on the Lug. Bat. *Opera Omnia* may like to note that the Greek and Latin have been seriously misplaced at this point. The Greek of Matthew 17:6. is on 83A; the Latin on 92A.

Christ knew that some probably doubted this, so he strengthened their resolve saying:

Consider what I told you to be certain: the Son of Man whom you now see lowly and will soon see cast down below all men, will appear in Fatherly Majesty, with all the angels and his chosen followers. That time is not far off. There are those among you who, before they die, shall see the kingdom of God come with power.

This is an allusion to Matthew 24:30 and Luke 21:27, where Jesus tells of the Second Coming, when, in the midst of trials, tribulations and calamities, men 'shall see the Son of Man coming on the clouds of heaven with power and great glory'. (What is implied is that the Church still awaits that day; but she is sure it will come, since unimpeachable witnesses have glimpsed it already in visions.)

Even the disciples did not understand what Christ meant: the meaning was indeed 'not simple'.

However, lest his disciples should begin to doubt that what he had promised concerning the majesty of his Second Coming would indeed occur one day, he wished to offer them, before their death, a taste of that future majesty, insofar as mortal nature can grasp it. And so, after six days, Jesus attached to himself three out of the chosen twelve, as being exceptional. To these he would entrust this vision, which they would keep silent about until the time came to declare it.

These were the three disciples, Peter, James and John; these three alone Jesus took away to that mountain vehemently high. Those whom Jesus deems worthy of such a vision must be 'free from care'—free, that is, from that *sollicitudo* about worldly matters which was emphasised in the *Moria*.

What happened to those three disciples we now know. They were caught away in an ecstasy of amazement, full of joy and fear. The chief of them babbled nonsense, knowing not what he said, as though he were drunk. Such an ecstasy is virtually indistinguishable from a bout of temporary insanity; but the man who has been vouchsafed such a vision treasures it as his greatest joy, for it was a foretaste of eternal happiness. Such a man knows better than to boast of his rapture. He will only do so if the interests of the Church require it. And even then he may well do so obliquely.

In the paraphrase Mark—or is it now Erasmus?—adds this comment:

Even today Christ deems some chosen ones—who have been carried up to the mountain of pure contemplation—worthy to be offered a taste of eternal happiness by means of private inspirations. People dwelling on the plains do not understand this; and if anyone were to tell them, they have no faith (*LB* 7. 224AB).

Dignatur enim et hodie quibusdam selectis, subvectis in montem purae contemplationis, aliquem aeternae felicitatis gustum praebere secretis afflatibus. Hoc nec intelligit populus in campestribus versans, et si quis narret, non habet fidem.

CHAPTER SIX

The Inspired Exegesis of a Christian Prophet

Folly arbitrarily finished her declamation, lest it went on into infinity. This book too must draw to a close for much the same reasons. A useful way to achieve this desirable end is to look at one of Erasmus' psalm commentaries, the Commentary on psalm 33(34).

A case could be made out for looking at others as well, especially at the Commentary on the 38th (39th) psalm, which is one of the most striking examples of Erasmus' writing as a prophet. The commentary is also deeply personal in tone, written by an Erasmus who is tired of the world and who yearns to die. But extensive reference has already been made to it in this book, since, as late as 1535, it still revolves around the same subjects which characterise the *Moria*—the importance of those invisible things which 'really are'; the higher insights which made the Biblical Jeduthun into a wise man like the bold philosopher who left Plato's shadowy cave; the reality of Christian folly. It also alludes to precisely that passage on the *Song of Songs* of Origen which the Listrius footnote of late 1516 cited to explain the joys and fears of the Christian soul (*LB* 5. 420CD).

Nevertheless, the Commentary on psalm 33 is even more helpful for understanding the long-term importance of Folly's version of the mad philosophy of Christ within the corpus of Erasmus' mature theology.

Benedicam Domino is one of the psalms which bears a title. Erasmus read into the title profound mystical meanings of direct relevance to his doctrine of prophetic Christian madness. In the Vulgate this title appears as *Psalmus David quum David mutavit vultum suum coram Abimelech* (A psalm of David, when David changed his countenance before Ahimelech).

The force of these words lies in the fact that 'to change countenance' means to feign madness; that is in fact the alternative reading of the title in the Revised Version; it is also the translation adopted in the Revised Standard Version: 'A psalm of David, when he feigned madness before Ahimelech, so that he drove him out, and he went away.' (In English we say Ahimelech not Abimelech.)

The allusion in the title is to an episode related in I Samuel (I Kings), 21: David was fleeing for his life from Saul, the royal father of his beloved Jonathan. He came 'to Nob, to Ahimelech the priest'. His feigning of madness took place not at Nob but before Achish, the King of Gath, whose courtiers terrified David (who was trying to avoid Saul's justified fear of his pretensions to the royal power) by recalling how the Israelites had sung that 'Saul hath slain his thousands, and David his ten thousands'. Nevertheless the feigning of madness is said to have taken place 'before Ahimelech'. (Ingenious explanations are traditionally given for this.)

David in his terror sought refuge in an appearance of raging lunacy:

And he changed his behaviour before them, and *feigned himself mad* in their hands, and scrabbled at the doors of the gate and let his spittle fall down upon his beard.

Then said Achish unto his servants, Lo, ye see the man is mad: Wherefore then have ye brought him to me? Have I need of madmen, that ye have brought this fellow to be mad in my presence? Shall this fellow come into my house?

David therefore departed thence, and escaped to the cave of Adullam; and when his brethren and all his father's house heard it, they went thither to him. And everyone that was in distress, and everyone that was in debt, and everyone that was discontented, gathered themselves unto him. . . . (AV I Samuel 21:10–22, 2; LXX etc., I Kings 21:10–22, 2).

Erasmus takes this as having an inner meaning of prophetic relevance to Christ.

He relates the literal meaning first (*LB* 5. 369–70), saying that David 'changed his countenance, simulating madness, then collapsing in the hands of the leaders . . . (*mutavit os suum, furorem simulans, subinde collabens inter manus ducentium . . .*) (*LB* 5. 370D).

This is doubly interesting. First we have *furor* used for the madness, a choice of word which brings the madness potentially into the context of Socratic *mania*. Next we have the actual phrase *furorem simulans* which has no counterpart in the Septuagint nor in the Vulgate. Allusions to David's 'feigning madness' are found in the Authorised Version and all modern translations; they derive directly or indirectly from Hebrew sources. The Septuagint simply says that David '*prosepoiēsato* on that day', apparently with the sense that he 'feigned himself a false character'; the Vulgate, very differently, says that David 'fell down (*conlabebatur*) in their hands', presumably in a swoon or a fit. Erasmus keeps this phrase, but interpolates before it the allusion to 'feigning madness' accepted by modern scholarship (cf. the *New English Bible*: David 'acted like a lunatic in front of them all'; AV and RSV: David 'feigned himself mad in their hands'). This meaning is central to Erasmus' exegesis. Here is one of the cases where he did apparently owe something important to a tradition of scholarship which had not entirely divorced itself from the Hebrew. His main sources of inspiration, challenge and knowledge where this psalm is concerned are Augustine's commentaries on it (*PL* 36, 300–322) and St Jerome's *Appendix Breviarum in Psalmos* (*PL* 26, 919). It is instructive to compare Erasmus' commentary with these texts and with midrashic commentaries (e.g. W. G. Braude's translation of the *Midrash on Psalms*, Yale U.P., 1959, p. 410).

Erasmus regards this strange episode in the life of David as a Silenus, as one of those apparently ugly matters which can be opened up to reveal hidden mysteries. The surface meaning seems to have little relevance for Christians, but 'if the Lord will deign to be with us while we extract the kernel, while we grind out this fine flour, while we open up this Silenus, your souls will delight in spiritual delights; they will feed on wholesome food and be amazed into contemplation of divine wisdom' (*LB* 5. 371A).

The full force of this claim is by now apparent. By divine providence, David's life was a prefiguration of the life of Christ. The hidden correspondences between the history of David and the history of Christ can be revealed by prophetic exegesis. The truth revealed is so staggering that it may lead to an ecstasy of amazement. (This last phrase translated contains the ecstatic verb *obstupesco*.)

The true value of the account of David's feigned madness lies in its hidden correspondences with Christ's life on earth. Otherwise, Erasmus asks, what point would there be in this story? Many similar things may be read in prophane literature: Ulysses and Brutus, for example, also feigned madness; so too have many criminals. But no Christian should believe that the account of David's simulated madness is important only for its historical content, since all that took place in Biblical history was part of a special divine dispensation. Behind David must be seen Christ.

If we open the Silenus we shall see that other and much more sublime David hiding within that mortal David, and in Saul we shall see another and much more pernicious Tyrant. If we open the eyes of faith we shall see in that fugitive, hungry man, 'changing his countenance' and exposed to so many perils, him who is truly called King of heaven and earth, the Lord Jesus Christ.

Similarly, behind Saul we shall see the prototype of Satan. The gate by which we must enter to understand this mystery is a low one. We must bow our heads. Once inside we find the majesty of God.

Christ 'changed his countenance' for our sakes even in Holy Writ; for his sake let us change our palates and our eyes, so that, as this psalm says, we shall 'taste and see how sweet the Lord is' [Psalm 33/4:1–3; 9].

In other words, Christians may have a taste of the divine majesty of Christ by contemplating the truth providentially hidden within the Silenus of the Old Testament accounts of David's feigned madness, truth which Erasmus is about to reveal for his readers to taste. Such a 'taste' is analogous to the experience of the three disciples at the Transfiguration, who also were amazed by a glimpse of Christ in majesty, which for them, too, was a foretaste of heavenly bliss.

But the wisdom of this world puffeth up. We must beware of it.

If there be any one among you who appears to himself to be wise, let him follow Paul's advice and become a fool with Christ, the Prince of this world, so that he may be truly wise. Those who are swollen up by Aristotelian, Averroistic or Platonic philosophy, are accustomed to despise the mystical allegories of Scripture; some even laugh at them and reckon them to be dreams.

Such men attack the practice of Christ and the apostles, for Christ took the brazen serpent held aloft in the desert [Numbers 12] to refer to himself [John 3]. Similarly Christ [in Matthew 12] showed that the story of Jonah and the Whale, spiritually understood, referred to his own resurrection. 'You see what great divinity that Silenus enclosed!'. It is impious not to believe the historical truth of the manna which was given to the Jews in the desert: it is equally impious not to believe it to contain a deeper meaning. Christ showed it to be an allegory of himself. So, too, when the resurrected Christ was walking with two of his disciples, the Gospel tells us how, 'beginning with Moses and all the prophets he opened the Scriptures for them' [Luke 24:27]. What does this mean, 'he opened (*aperuit*) the Scriptures'?

He showed them the allegory hiding in the historical events. What does it mean, 'beginning with Moses?' It means he began with the figures (the *figurae*) of the Pentateuch. The difference between a figure and a prophecy is that a figure is a dumb man or a speaking deed (*figura est mutus sive factum loquens*) while prophecy is a speaking voice (*Prophetia est vox loquens*). Both may be a form of the seer's art (*vaticinium*).

Erasmus is writing in the light of assumptions about language, semeiotics, divination and hidden truth widely held by scholars during the Renaissance. Language was not considered to be unique; it was a series of verbal signs, corresponding to other symbolic forms of communication and often less certain than concrete signs, gestures and actions. The true adept at interpreting prophecies had to be as skilled at understanding non-verbal signs as he was at interpreting those treacherous, ambiguous, aural or written signs which are words. (The fullest exploitation of such themes by a Renaissance writer of genius is that of Rabelais, for whom it is a major element in his religious philosophy as well as in his comedy. The belief, however, was of the very widest currency.)

The explanation of what Erasmus means by a *factum loquens* was destined to become one of the great themes of the Renaissance. (Rabelais uses exactly the same example in the *Fourth Book of Pantagruel:* so does Francis Bacon in *The Advancement of Learning*.) Sextus Tarquinius sent a message to his father Tarquin the Proud to find out what he should do during a period of unrest. Tarquin the Proud said nothing; but he took the messenger into his garden and swished off the heads of the tallest poppies. The messenger understood nothing of this: he simply related what had happened. But Sextus Tarquinius understood all right what was meant by this secret mystery, this *arcanum*: his father was advising him to cut off the heads of his most outstanding subjects. Erasmus relates this gruesome story, not in order to approve of such butchery, but to show how actions and gestures can convey definite meaning. He believes that the Old Testament is full of such meaningful signs and symbols, placed there by the providence of God.

This, indeed, is what the apostle wrote to the Hebrews [1: 1]: 'In sundry and divers ways God spake in time past unto the fathers by the prophets' [Cf. the Annotation on this verse, *LB* 6. 983C].

God spoke by his action of founding the world; whatever is beautiful in the world speaks in its own way of the power, wisdom and goodness of the Creator. That is what is meant by the psalmist: 'The heavens declare the glory of God; and the firmament showeth his handy work' [Psalm 19:1]; and 'There is no speech nor language where their voice is not heard' [19:3; Vulg. 18:4].

God has spoken to us by the precepts of the law of Moses; he has spoken through figures; he has spoken by the prophets; and he has spoken through mystical historical events (*per historias mysticas*). All these things have their own tongues, talking to us of spiritual wisdom. But we must not be deaf to them, as though we were Stoics,

Epicureans, Jews or atheists like Anaxagoras. John the Baptist showed us that Christ is manifested in such figures, when he said, 'Behold the Lamb of God, which taketh away the sins of the world'[John 1:29]. Moses struck water from the rock; but Paul showed the spiritual meaning of this when he wrote [I Corinthians 10:4]: 'They drank of the spiritual rock which followed them: and that rock was Christ.' Who would have dared to interpret it that way, without so sure an authority? Paul, writing to the Corinthians [I, 10:11] stated that 'all those things happened to them figuratively (*in figura*); they were written for us, upon whom the end of the world hath come.'

Erasmus gives further examples from Peter and from Acts. It is not enough to read the Scriptures as we would read Herodotus or Livy; for in the Scriptures the Holy Ghost has hidden Christ. After all Paul said [II Corinthians 3:6]: 'The letter killeth: but the spirit giveth life.' The letter has its place; but what good does it do to read of the brazen serpent raised up in the wilderness, if you are not led from it to Christ? 'Life is where Christ is.' This counsel will be useful to you not only here, but whenever you hear anything read out from the Holy Bible, or whenever you read it yourself.

This assertion is a most useful antidote against the opinion that Erasmus was above all an erudite philologist, quietly restoring the text of the New Testament in a spirit of scholarly calm and detachment. None of Erasmus' Biblical exegesis corresponds to such an anachronistic notion, least of all his explanation of the Old Testament. The exegesis of this psalm which Erasmus is about to embark on consists in a spiritual unveiling of its *arcana*, of its hidden religious mysteries. Erasmus is conscious of following the footsteps of Christ and the apostles, for Christ and St Paul did just that. They acted as prophets. As Erasmus put in his *System of True Theology* (1518), 'Paul called the interpretation of hidden Scripture (*enarrationem arcanae Scripturae*) not *philosophy* but *prophecy*. Prophecy is a gift of the everlasting Spirit' (*LB* 5. 76C). The force of this contention lies in his belief that this gift of the Spirit was still vouchsafed to chosen vessels in his own time. Paul had such a gift: so does the inspired exegete today. As he wrote in *Ecclesiastes or How to Preach*—one of his very last works, dating from 1535:

The Spirit of Christ is at work even today in the prophets; for I call prophets those who open up the mysteries of hidden scripture (*qui explanant arcanae scripturae mysteria*). Paul places this kind of prophecy amongst the chief gifts of the Spirit [I Corinthians 12:10, etc.]. Diligence on our part is also required—not that the Spirit should work less in us, but work more secretly (*LB* 5. 798F).

Erasmus believed himself to have such a prophetic gift. *The Commentary on Psalm 33* stresses from the outset that he is concerned to explain the hidden mysteries—*the arcana*—of this psalm (*LB* 5. 369BE). The importance that he attaches to his gift of prophecy is shown by his long and passionate defence of the reality of the hidden sense to be found in Scripture.

What Erasmus found in the psalm *Benedicam Domino* was a feigned madman, David; he forefigured the madness of Christ and his followers.

Erasmus believed that several kings of Gath were called Ahimelech, just as several kings of Egypt were called Pharaoh (*LB* 5. 379BC). This particular Ahimelech was surnamed Achish. Erasmus gives the 'early doctors' of the Church, the *prisci doctores*, as his authority for saying this. So David 'changed his countenance' before both Ahimelech the priest and before Ahimelech Achish, the King of Gath. Before the priest he hid his fear and pretended to have important business on behalf of his king; before Achish he concealed his sanity (*sana mens*) making a show of madness (*insania*). So too did Christ 'change his countenance' when he appeared as a gardener to Mary Magdalene and when he appeared as a mere traveller to the disciples on the road to Emmaus.

The Hebrew names providentially contain the mystical meaning of *Benedicam Domino* and I Samuel 21. *Ahimelech* is explained as 'My Father the King'; as for *Achish,* it means 'How is this?' To the eyes of faith these names are peculiarly appropriate to the Children of Israel in that they claimed God as their Father, yet all too frequently they confronted his miraculous revelations with an unbelieving *Quomodo est?* ('How is this?'). When Christ offered them the truth to make them free, they replied, 'We are Abraham's seed, and were never in bondage to any man' (John 8:32–3). They were lying: they did not follow Abraham; they were slaves of the letter, of vice, of the Devil. In the same way, when Christ revealed his miracles they had no faith saying, *Quomodo est,* 'How is this?' (e.g. Matthew 22:45). This name applied to Nicodemus (John 3:4–9) and even to the Blessed Virgin who replied to the Angel Gabriel at the Annunciation, *Quomodo fiet istud,* 'How can this thing be?' (Luke 1:34).

The examples of *Quomodo* listed by Erasmus are quite ingenious (*LB* 5. 379D–380C). For his Hebrew etymologies he is following a tradition going back to St Jerome as well as to St Augustine, who is, indeed, a major source (*PL* 36. 300ff). Erasmus is accepting here a doctrine of the real meaning of names, which Renaissance philologists justified by their understanding of Plato's dialogue, the *Cratylus*.

Inspired prophetic exegesis then leads on to the question, How can men hope to see the glorious face of Christ, which is so similar to the Father's, when they could not even gaze on the face of Moses, whose countenance 'shone by reason of his speaking with God, so that he had to put on a veil'? [Exodus 35:29–33; II Corinthians 3:13]. Any allusion to the glorious face of Christ in majesty serves to remind us that that is precisely what the apostles ecstatically glimpsed at the Transfiguration.

Moses wove a veil: so too Christ veiled his divine nature with a mortal body. What would be a greater 'changing of countenance' than the Word becoming flesh, crying as a babe at his mother's bosom? Here Erasmus is remembering his Origen and the kenotic theology which Folly took over from him and St Bernard.

He continues, still in an Origenistic vein: 'Your piety should not be offended if we lisp unutterable things with the words of men. David pretended to be a madman.' There is no pretence in Christ: he did not doff his divine nature; he veiled it for a time and took our nature upon him. 'He did not pretend to do so.' His only pretence was to be a sinner on behalf of us all. Yet Christ did 'change his countenance'. This was perceived by Isaiah with prophetic not corporeal eyes: 'He hath no form nor comeliness; we have seen him, and there was no beauty. We have seen him despised and the least of men, a man of sorrows and acquainted with weakness. His face, as it were, was hidden from us . . . ' And Erasmus recalls all of this famous passage of Isaiah 53, in that Latin of St Jerome which seems so cramped beside the glories of the Authorised Version. Similarly, Christ 'changed his countenance' when, in that mystical psalm (21: 7; 22: 6) he exclaimed: 'I am a worm, and no man, a reproach to men and the reject of the people.' This man of sorrows was Jesus, that kenotic lunatic who saved mankind by his madness:

You can see, dearly Beloved, what majesty of mysteries lies hidden within the Silenus of this history [of David's feigning madness]. What David did was not all that important, but what was represented to us by this history was a sight full of wonder for the very angels.

Good, then. We leave David and come to Christ, we leave the letter that kills and find the life-giving Spirit. Let us take care to love what we understand; let us strive to imitate the sight which is set before us.

Some strive to apply all the detail of this history to Christ; that is pious, but not necessary. There is much detail interwoven into the history which is not relevant to the allegory.

What is not, I think, to be neglected, is how appropriate it is to Christ that David should have simulated dementedness or epilepsy (*morbis comitialis*) so that he might slip away. Pious ears are shocked if anyone attributes raging madness (*furor*) or mindlessness (*amentia*) to Christ; and yet the title of this psalm virtually does, saying, 'he changed his countenance'. They can barely stand the word *pretended*; in no wise can they stand the word *lie*. It is not surprising if these words horrify Christian ears when applied to Christ, for Jews cannot bear to hear them attributed to David; they absolve David with the excuse that the spirit of the Lord rushed upon him, seeing that, formerly, those whom the spirit of prophecy seized upon manifested some appearance of mindlessness. Thus Saul was seized by the Spirit and prophesied; and elsewhere he danced naked among the prophets.

This is an allusion to two episodes in I Samuel. In the first (10:10ff.) 'the spirit of God came upon Saul and he prophesied among the prophets'. Again (19:23f.) the spirit of God came upon Saul 'and he went on and prophesied until he came to Naioth in Ramah. And he stripped off his clothes also and prophesied before Samuel, and lay down naked all that day and all that night'. (I cannot recall that Saul ever danced while prophesying; perhaps Erasmus is confounding him with David who danced before the Lord, clad in a linen ephod: II Samuel 6:14ff.; cf. I Chronicles 15:29.)

Erasmus goes straight on to tell of the odd conduct of a nameless prophet in I (III) Kings 20:35f., 'who said to his fellow by the word of the Lord, Smite me, I pray thee. And the man refused to smite him', and so was eaten by a lion. Another man did smite him. Erasmus relates this event and comments on it:

And in III Kings 20, a prophet threatened with death a man who would not wound him when ordered to do so; after he was wounded by another, he sprinkled his face and eyes with dust so as not to be recognised by the king. That is not far from madness, were it not to be excused by the working of the Spirit (*per spiritus energiam*).

As in the *Moria*, we are left in no doubt that prophetic *furor* is closely akin to apparent lunacy.

The Gentiles attribute to prophets a raging madness which we prefer to call ecstasy (*furorem tribuunt vatibus, quam malumus ecstasin dicere*). Whenever the divine power works upon a mortal organ, to sober men it seems like a form of dementedness (*LB* 5. 381E).

Having shown how David was obeying his true King, who was God, and so was blameless when he deceived men who deserved to be deceived, Erasmus continues with his prophetic exegesis:

Let us apply our mystical ears to these mystical matters; then there is no stumbling-block. Let us not draw away from the footsteps of the apostles. The blessed Paul wrote thus to the Corinthians (I, 1:21): 'For after that in the wisdom of God the world by wisdom knew not God, it pleased God by the foolishness of preaching to save them that believe.' If God had remained in his wisdom, no mortal wisdom, however sublime, could ever have attained a knowledge of God. So God came down from his incomprehensible wisdom and in some way lowered himself to our folly, so that he might gradually bear aloft our sluggishness, away from our first gross attempts at true wisdom. Parents lisp in this way to their babes; so too do very learned men adjust themselves to the capacities of ignorant children: if they did not do so, their disciples would remain fruitless. The apostle continues: 'We preach Christ crucified, unto the Jews a stumbling-block, and unto the Greeks foolishness' (I Corinthians 1:23). You see, Christ yielded up none of his perfect wisdom, but displayed to men a certain kind of folly, beneath which is hidden wonderful wisdom—provided that faith imparts teachableness to the mind.

Here we have the same sort of expression as in the 1522 *Moria*—*quandam stulticiae speciem*, 'a certain kind of folly'. The self-emptying of Christ is now partly a kind of teaching-aid rather than the pouring away of deity as humanity is assumed. But Christ's *kenōsis* included apparent madness and is still conceived as a self-emptying of the Godhead.

Erasmus continues by alluding further to I Corinthians 1, now citing verses 24 and 25:

The apostle adds: 'But unto them which are called, both Jews and Greeks, Christ [is] the power of God and the wisdom of God. Because the foolishness of God is wiser than men: and the weakness of God is stronger than men'. And so David did not 'change his countenance' before just anybody, but only before Ahimelech—that is before Jews who had ears and heard not, who had eyes and saw not, who had a heart, but one waxed gross so that they could understand nothing except what could be perceived by the outward senses.

These harsh words applied to Ahimelech and, by extension, to unbelieving Jews who remain in their faith, is an allusion to Christ's condemnations in Matthew 13:13–15 and to two other important developments of the theme, in St John's Gospel and in the Acts of the Apostles. In all these cases the New Testament authors are appealing textually to Isaiah's condemnation of his unbelieving countrymen (*Isaiah* 6:9–10 and context).

St Matthew reports Christ as saying:

Therefore speak I to them in parables: because they seeing see not, and hearing they hear not; neither do they understand . . . For this people's heart is waxed gross . . .

The same theme is taken up by St John (12:38–40) and by St Luke in Acts 28:26–7.

The importance of this appeal by Erasmus to Isaiah's condemnation of the gross-hearted people of Israel is considerable. In the context of the New Testament it justifies Christ's preaching of the Gospel in a hidden, enigmatic way—in parables that is. (Scriptural parables are *not* ways of revealing religious truths to simple understandings; they are ways of hiding it from everybody except from those to whom God chooses to unfold their meaning.) And Erasmus is himself unfolding a parable, sure that many will not believe him.

This concept of the parable can be used to lend authority to a most rigorous form of predestination. Erasmus is careful to see that it does not do so. In Acts this text is specifically taken to justify the spreading of the Gospel to chosen Gentiles—with a strong implied condemnation of the Jewish majority. The Jews agreed to meet Paul by appointment; he expounded his matter, 'testifying the Kingdom of God, and persuading them concerning Jesus, both from the law of Moses and the prophets'. Some believed; others did not. Paul then quoted Isaiah's bitter condemnation of his people:

Well spake the Holy Ghost by Isaiah the prophet unto your fathers, saying:
   Go thou unto this people and say,
   By hearing ye shall hear, and shall in no wise understand;
   And seeing ye shall see, and shall in no wise perceive;
   For the heart of this people is waxed gross,
   And their ears are dull of hearing,
   And their eyes have they closed;
   Lest they should see with their eyes and hear with their ears,
   And understand with their heart,
   And should be converted, and I should heal them.
   Be it known therefore unto you, that the salvation of God is sent unto the
      Gentiles, and they will listen.

Erasmus is in the position of Christ and of St Paul. He is expounding hidden truths on the basis of the Old Testament. And he knows that many will scoff. But he will not allow this to be taken in a Lutheran sense as a deliberate hardening of the hearts of the Jews on the part of God. In his *Annotations* (*LB* 6. 71F, § 12) he cites the famous text '*I will harden Pharaoh's heart*' (on which Luther partly based his rigorous doctrine of absolute predestination to salvation and reprobation), and then insists that neither that text nor Christ's words warrant such a harsh interpretation of the divine will. The paraphrase of the relevant part of St Matthew's Gospel has textual similarities with the part of his psalm commentary we are now studying. It is a useful clue to what is implied by Erasmus' quoting of it here. Unlike some modern translations which suggest that the Gentiles will listen *also*, the original Greek and the Vulgate both seem to mean that the Christian message will pass from the Jews, who reject it, to the Gentiles, who will not. That is the sense which Erasmus develops in his paraphrase of Acts 28:26f.: the Jews have rejected the Gospel message which was offered to them: the Gentiles, however, will abandon their idols and believe (*LB* 7. 770BC). It is not presented as a divine plot: the incredulity of the Jews is a human, not a divinely induced state. But Erasmus will not turn this into a condemnation of Jews alone. Unbelieving Gentiles come in for their share of condemnation.

It is this Scriptural context which partly explains the apparently anti-Jewish savour of what is to follow, a savour by no means typical of all of Erasmus' judgments on the Jews and certainly distinct from his attitude to Jewish converts. It would be wrong, too, to emphasise it even here: it is part of a scathing condemnation of Gentile, Jewish and Christian unbelief. What Erasmus most feared was the 'judaïcising' of Christianity—the abandoning of its spiritual truths in favour of legalism and mere ceremonial. A possible rebirth of paganism seemed to him to be a real, but a lesser danger. In Erasmus a condemnation of Jewish incredulity, which makes Christ's sacrifice on the Cross a stumbling-block, is normally balanced by a condemnation of the arrogant philosophy of the Gentiles, for which it was mere foolishness. So it is here. As he wrote in 1526 to Simon Pistorius, in a letter partly intended for the ears of Duke George of Saxony: 'You are afraid of paganism: I am afraid of Judaism, which I see taking over everything' (*EE* 6, p. 402, line 91). That is not an example of proto-Fascism, but a severe judgment of a party within the Church. Not unreasonably he betook himself to a major commonplace of the New Testament: the condemnation of the unbelief with which both Jesus and St Paul had been faced and which Isaiah was believed to have foreseen. This is a way of showing that the battle against incredulity which Christ and his apostles had engaged has never been won: the good fight has still to be fought—and with extra zeal in face of the incredulity and gross hearts of his contemporaries.

To return to the Commentary on Psalm 33/4, Erasmus goes on to say of Christ:

When we hear that his relations prepared chains to bind him saying [Mark 3: 21] 'He is raging mad—*in furorem versus est*'; when the Pharisees say, 'Thou art a Samaritan, and hast a devil' [John 8:48], adding that he had Beelzebub and cast out devils in his name, do we not seem to hear Ahimelech saying: 'You see the man is mad; wherefore then have ye brought him to me? Have we need of madmen, that ye have brought this fellow to be mad in my presence? Send him away, lest he come into my house' [I Samuel 21:14–15]. The Jews do not have Christ in their synagogue or temple today, because they thrust him out. And when he taught in Nazareth in the synagogue, the Ahimelechites 'thrust him out of the city and led him unto the brow of the hill that they might cast him down headlong' [Luke 4:29]. And finally, outside Jerusalem, he was crucified and buried. Ahimelech was disturbed by the semblance of an epileptic (*specie epileptici*): more gravely were the Jews disturbed by the new doctrine of Christ. That is why Paul says: 'Unto the Jews a stumbling-block' [I Corinthians 1:23]. The Lord did not preach to the Gentiles, but his doctrine, in Paul, seemed foolishness to the Gentiles. When Paul preached in Athens those *morosophoi*—those 'foolish-wise' Epicureans and Stoics, that is, who professed the foolish wisdom of this world—said: 'What does this *spermologus*, this babbler, mean?' He seemed to be announcing new devils. It seemed foolish to them to promise the resurrection of the dead, and even more foolish that God wished to save the whole world through a man condemned and crucified (*LB* 5. 382).

Such was their human wisdom, leading to a trust in human virtue or even to atheism. Erasmus' condemnations do not apply only to Jews and Gentiles. Christ's own followers fall into the same trap.

And again when the Lord revealed the mystery of the eating and drinking of his body and blood, did he not seem to be insane even to his own disciples? They said, 'This is a hard saying. Who can hear it?' [John 6:60]. And indeed for those who only understood according to the flesh, nothing is more demented than this saying. Yet, 'following the spirit', these same 'words are spirit and life' [John 6:64].

Again when Christ said [John 8:58], 'Before Abraham was, I am', they took up stones as though confronted by a man raging mad and demented (*velut in furiosum ac dementem*). And indeed, to those who were ignorant of the mystery, his speech was neither consistent nor coherent (*nec consistit nec cohaeret*).

Here, then, as in the *Moria*, are divine folly (*stultitia*), divine madness (*furor*) and divine lunacy (*dementia*) manifesting themselves in incoherent speech. Indeed, here it is applied to Christ himself, as seen in some of the holiest parts of the Gospel writings. The implications are then developed; Erasmus finds it somewhat forced to apply the words of the title of the psalm, *He drove him out, and he went away*, to Christ's transferring the Gospel to the Gentiles. Many do so; he does not mention St Augustine by name; he is one of those whose interpretation he is rejecting. But it was David who was driven away, not Ahimelech. It is more pleasant and less forced—*mollius*—to take these words another way: David when he was driven away was a 'figure' of Christ, who was sent away as a weakling and a fool (*stultus*), until he cried from the Cross, 'It is finished.'

It was right for Christ to hide his countenance this way; for as Paul wrote (I Corinthians 2:8), 'If they had known it, they would not have crucified the Lord of Glory'. Satan, too, had to be deceived:

If Satan had not been taken in by the appearance of human weakness, he would not have incited the Jews, whom he had held captive for centuries, to sacrifice the victim who set them free.

Here, then, is God's madness seen in the *kenōsis* of a self-emptying Christ who had to hide his deity—hiding it from his own people in their own interests and, on a cosmic scale, hiding it from the great enemy of the human race in the interests of all mankind. And, as usual, Erasmus applies this lesson to judaïcisers and neo-Gentiles among the Christians:

So, as it had been written, the Son of Man was thrust out, and went away. Would there were not people like Ahimelech and Achish amongst the Christians; for them, holy writ is a stumbling-block and the doctrine of Christ—so different from the wisdom of this world—seems to be full of dementedness (*LB* 5. 383).

That is what they think when they hear the beatitudes and commandments such as the injunction to love those who hate you, to bless those who curse you, and to leave all for Christ.

To strive towards such things is the profession of all Christians; not to follow them always is of the nature of human weakness. But to mock at them is pagan impiety or Judaic incredulity. From such an evil, dearly Beloved, we who profess Christ must be as far removed as possible (*LB* 5. 383C).

Too many who profess Christianity are pagan in their lives and passions, being neither entirely pagan nor entirely Christian.

We, dearly Beloved, are sheep; and if we are not, let us strive to be so . . . A sheep needs neither halter, reins nor goad: he knows the voice of his shepherd and follows it, So may we be simply obedient to the doctrine of Christ, nothing doubting concerning his promises. He does not deceive; he does not abandon his little lambs who depend on him.

Following the example of David, let us 'change our countenance before Ahimelech'; let us seem fools to the world, so that we may be wise before God; let us seem out of our minds (*amentes*), so that we may be sober to God.

This is yet another strong appeal to St Paul's madness for God (II Corinthians 5:13): 'For if we are beside ourself, it is for God, if we are sober, it is for you.' The man who makes himself seem mad in men's eyes is seen by God to be truly sober:

Let us be imitators of the blessed Paul, as he was of Christ. He made himself 'all things to all men, so that he might gain them all'. [I Corinthians 9:22—but, in fact, Paul only hoped to gain 'some']. And just as David seemed to Ahimelech, so Paul seemed to Festus, from whom he heard (Acts 26:24): 'Much learning, O Paul, doth make thee mad'. Asserting his authority among the Corinthians, Paul put on the mask of a fool saying (II Corinthians 12:11) 'I am become a fool . . . ye have compelled me.' And in the same epistle (5:13) he said, 'For whether we are beside ourselves, it is to God; or whether we be sober, it is for you' (*LB* 5. 383D–384A).

Erasmus cites this last text as it appears in the Vulgate not in his *Novum Instrumentum*. But that is a minor matter. For him the sense is the same: Paul was 'mad to God'.

These words were published nineteen years after the *Moria*, years full of anguish and strife when Luther and others rose up against him on one side and when a myriad of enemies confronted him within his own Church. Yet the message does not differ. The way of Christ is a way which does not seem amiably eccentric to men of this world; it seems mad with the madness of the raging lunatic whose words do not always make coherent sense. Such a man may force himself to be 'sober' for the benefit of his fellow men, but he has his bouts of spiritually drunken madness when he is 'beside himself for God'.

That is why the ecstatic madness of the Christian fool is always to be praised.

And it is why, despite the odd remark occasionally cited to suggest the contrary, Erasmus was so deeply devoted to the Old Testament, in which he saw a divinely contrived foreshadowing of what was made manifest in the New. To meditate upon the mystery of these correspondences was one of the ways in which a spiritual man might achieve an ecstatic glimpse of the majesty of God and of his providence. For him, as constantly for the fathers and the many who followed them, the Old Testament is composed of shadows, of *umbrae*. These shadows are given substance by the realities of the New Testament. To be satisfied with the shadows is to remain carnal madmen, insanely content with flickerings within Plato's cave. Better far to read the pagan poets allegorically than the Old Testament 'carnally', for the sake of its shadows alone. To allegorise the poets is at least to find in them the partial truths of inspired philosophers. But to read the Book of Chronicles or the Psalms unspiritually is no more relevant to the

Christian life than reading Livy. The reason for this is not that Erasmus somehow equated the Bible with pagan literature. Quite the
reverse. It is because the Old Testament is unique and its relation to the
New Testament is a source of wondrous amazement. (*LB* 2. 733CD;
LB 5. 9Af.; 29A-F; 117F; 172B; 172F; 418; 551CF; 1019C etc.)

Erasmus exemplifies an unbroken tradition of Christian mystical
exegesis. Its implications are staggering and recognised as such. The
Old Testament was written under the promptings of the Holy Ghost.
At any point we may hear Christ talking through it. But that is not the
beginning and end of its power. Erasmus did not merely believe—nor
did the Church—that the life of Old Testament characters had been so
narrated as to prefigure Christ and his Church: he believed that, under
providential grace, those lives had been, in very fact, lived in such a
way that they correspond to Christ and his Church. (*LB* 5. 271A to at
least 378F.) They correspond as shadows correspond to the realities
which project them.

The task of the prophetic exegete is to unveil this mystical correspondence.

One starts with the literal truth of Old Testament shadows. The
mystic import of them may well be unravelled with the 'real,' that is,
the etymological meaning of the Hebrew names. All the flowering of
Erasmus' theme of *Iduthun* as a foreshadowing of Christ, leaping from
hill-top to hill-top like the soul's Beloved in the *Song of Songs*, derives
from a seed sown by Jerome, for whom *Iduthun* means *Transiliens
eos*, 'Leaping across them' (*PL* 23. *De Hebrais Nominibus*, 827, s. v. 71
Psalterio).

Erasmus, every bit as much as Jerome, say, or, centuries later,
Rabanus Maurus, believes one must pass from the shadows to the
truth (*PL* 33. 258, col. ii; *PL* 109. 457C). When Erasmus read in psalm
22/3 the words, 'He restoreth my soul,' he saw in them the crucified
and triumphant Christ (*LB* 5. 314Df.). That was the sense of the 'table'
which was 'spread'. Erasmus narrates this in the person of Christ
himself:

You, Father, wipe away the sadness of the Cross; you have changed the grief
of death into the joy of resurrection. My head, covered with filth and spit,
swollen up with blows from men's fists, crowned with thorns and having no
beauty nor comeliness, you anointed with the oil of happiness; the cup which
you handed me to drink, I drank. It was not inefficacious, but resplendent,
bathed in light and powerful. It made many drunk, to the point of despising
riches, family, stripes, stakes, racks and life itself. It did not contain the water
of the letter which the Jews drank before my death, but the 'must', the new
wine, of the Spirit. Babylon has its cup too; so do the philosophers: but your
cup alone offers this drunkenness. This loving-kindness was not for me alone,

Father; you wished it to remain for ever with my bride, the Church, for whom I drank it (*LB* 5. 315A–D.).

Such a way of seeing the correspondences between the two Testaments was, already in the *Enchiridion*, a gateway to ecstasy. The books of the Old Testament are to be meditated upon:

Think them to be, as they are, pure oracles, deriving from the sanctuary of the divine mind. If you approach them humbly, with piety and veneration, you will feel yourself ineffably breathed upon by the Godhead, seized, caught up, transfigured; you will see the wealth of that richest Solomon, the hidden treasure of eternal Wisdom (*LB* 5. 8D).

To see the force of such mysteries is to drink from those twelve mystic fountains of the forty mansions of the children of Israel (*LB* 5. 7B; Numbers 33:9). To unveil them is to make the souls of your readers to be amazed in rapture (*obstupescere*, *LB* 5. 371). Exegetes by the score, in an unbroken line from the fathers, had made the same claims. Many have been studied by Henri de Lubac (*Exégèse Médiévale*, Paris, 1959 I, 2, 633f.). To take an example almost by chance, an expositor such as Garnier of Rochefort (*PL* 205. 730B) shows, like Erasmus, the soul astonished (*attonita*), as the mystery of the correspondences make it amazed (*obstupescit*). Centuries before, Origen had done the same, seeing allusions to such rapture in I Thessalonians 4:16: 'And we shall be caught up with them.'

Erasmus is at one with Augustine: to perceive the way in which the two Testaments are in hidden conformity is to be granted a glimpse of the divine Majesty; it results in 'a peaceful amazement, as in the stupefaction of ecstasy' (*pacifica admiratione . . . quasi ecstasis sopore . . .*; *PL* 36. 824, 19, col. ii.).

Erasmus was a scholarly philologist; but he claimed to be far more: a prophet in the wake of Christ, Paul, Origen, the fathers and their successors. He, like they, opened up the *arcana Scripturae*, the spiritual meaning of the New Testament and the secret yet revealed truths veiled in what was, for him, the *Silenus* of the Old Testament. Such an exegete is a prophet whose world is marked by amazement, astonishment, spiritual drunkenness, ecstasy, rapture. He does not mind seeming to be mad: David, Christ and Christ's disciples are mad in that sense too.

That is why the gift of prophecy is so intimately connected with ecstatic folly as well as with scholarship. The prophetic exegete does not deal with dry-as-dust texts in order to conjure up some cardboard historical Jesus. For Erasmus such a prophet enables those who hear him to glimpse the face of Christ in Majesty, as the three disciples did on that mountain vehemently high. And such a prophetic exegete is vital for that harmony in the dwellings of the Church that is so amiable; he is the agent through whom men themselves may be metamorphosed, rather as Christ was on that mountain:

When the gift of prophecy is given to a man who purely treats and dispenses the word of God, people listen to it with religious attention and reverence, not as the words of a man but as the words of God himself. Meanwhile he who teaches is so affected that you can feel the spirit of Christ speaking through the human mouth. Sometimes the spirit of Christ can be seen to be present in the hearers. Some sigh; some burst into tears; the faces of some grow happy. In short you would say that they had all been transfigured.[1]

---

[1] *LB* 5. 477D: *On the Amiable Concord of the Church*: a prophetic exegesis of psalm 83/4, 'How amiable are thy dwellings'.

APPENDIX A

The 1514 Interpolations into Folly's Peroration

(i) *The fascination exerted by the 1514 interpolations*

The expanded *Moria* of 1514 led to the complete eclipse of the original version. The interpolations are so successfully satirical and aggressive that writers on Erasmus still tend to take their examples from them.

To study them in even a little detail will be the subject of another book. They can best be understood in the light of the *Novum Instrumentum* and its *Annotations*. Other theological works of Erasmus are relevant too. That is a remarkable fact. The *Moria* was central to Erasmus' thought: it was never peripheral, not even when he was approaching death. The 1514 additions form no exception. On the whole the 1514 interpolations add less than one might expect to the subject of this book—Erasmus had said all he wanted to say about ecstatic folly in the *Moria* of 1511. He felt no call to expand it in 1514. From 1516 onwards he did see the need for caution, explanation and discreet emendation. It is in other works that he chose to write about ecstatic folly. But Erasmus' concern, for example, to mock those who believe they are honouring Jesus by drawing him with a halo, with two fingers raised in blessing, is doubtless connected with his kenotic conception of the incarnate Christ as a self-emptying suffering fool, living as a harassed man amongst men (Kan 12—'chapter 53'). Similarly his concern to interpret Hebrews 11: 1 as a call for faith in things invisible is directly concerned with his belief in the reality of those unseen things which 'really are' (Kan 118; cf. *Etudes Rabelaisiennes* II, 1959, *L'Evangélisme de Rabelais*, ch. 1).

Some of the funniest and most hard-hitting satire of scholastic ignorance and over-subtlety in the 1514 *Moria* can be directly parralleled by remarks in the *Annotations*. Among other things this may be connected with the Occamists' denial of the possiblity of enjoying the beatific vision this side of the grave (*LB* 5. 435C).

The violence of the antimonastic satire in 1514 partly resulted from the attempt of the prior of the convent at Steyn—the convent to which he still owed canonical obedience—to lure Erasmus back to the monastic life. Erasmus replied that the call of biblical scholarship was more important than monastic feasting and coarseness (*EE* 1, no. 296, to Servatius Roger).

The onslaught against war-mongering popes is Erasmus' reaction to the death of that bellicose pope Julius II (13 February 1513). It would have been more noble, no doubt, if this attack had been published during Julius' life, but it was not. Leo X, who succeeded to the papal throne (11 April 1513) was a different man altogether: suave, learned, urbane, he appreciated and protected Erasmus. When he read the *Moria* he commented that he was 'delighted to see Erasmus' in it. (In a 1514 addition Folly refers again to Erasmus by name.) Leo X was man-of-the-world enough to appreciate jokes at the expense of his war-mongering predecessor (*EE* 3. 749).

All these additions change the balance of the *Moria*. But they do not affect the ecstatic ending. Only changes from 1516 onwards do that—with the exception of an ingenious elimination of a serious, elementary, embarrassing error; that was put right in 1514.

(ii) *Bearing fools gladly; and covering up a gaffe*

Even in the case of copious interpolations made just before the peroration, few are important for the understanding of ecstatic folly. Some of the scriptural texts are still cited 'carelessly', as Kan points out (*Réforme et Humanisme*, ed. J. Boisset, 1975, pp. 154–5). This 'carelessness' may mean that he was using intermediate sources yet to be identified.

But the longest interpolation of all is very interesting. It extends from the third line of Kan 165 to the last line of Kan 173. All of this was represented in 1511 by a handful words: *et libenter fertis insipientes ad se refert* ('and Paul applies to himself, Ye bear fools gladly'). *Quid quod palam stultitiam precepit* ('That openly taught folly'). Those words did not go out by chance. They were compounding a gaffe.

This massive interpolation is partly a diversionary skirmish.

In 1511 Erasmus had made Paul say, 'Who is foolish? I am more' (*insipiens quis est? Plus ego*). In 1514 Paul says—correctly this time—'I speak as a fool, I am more' (*ut insipiens dico, plus ego*). A theological gulf separates the gaffe from the true quotation. The first version has Paul delighting in being more foolish than the other apostles; what he actually wrote was an apology for having to indulge in the foolishness of boasting: 'Are they apostles?—I speak as a fool—I am more so.'

How could a scholar justify making such a serious error, one which lessens the support which Paul was alleged to afford to Folly's concept of Christian folly? Erasmus' defence was to attack. His main shafts are directed at Nicolas of Lyra (d. 1430) and at scholastic boobies generally. Nicolas of Lyra was that 'ass at the lyre' which a Greek proverb used as a symbol of crass ineptitude (*Adages* 1. 1. 35). Erasmus spreads a trail of confusion; in the course of doing so he hides all trace of his schoolboy error.

Folly is made suddenly to shift her vantage-point. Unless one realises that there is an interpolation involved, it is easy to get confused. Folly—who has now just cited Paul correctly—pretends to believe that only pedantic Greek scholars get her wrong. The Beta if not the Alpa of *Graeculi* is Erasmus. The word *Graeculi* is a pun on *graculi* (jackdaws). Like the jackdaws in Aesop's fable they dress up in borrowed finery. They also peck eyes out.

What these *Graeculi* maintain—and what Folly is made ironically to seem to condemn—is the true sense of St Paul, as duly corrected and as Erasmus interpreted him in all seriousness. That can be shown by comparing the 1514 *Moria* and the *Annotations on the New Testament*. The resemblances are close and textual.

Paul was afraid he might seem 'rather arrogant' (*arrogantius*). He 'anticipated objections with a pretended excuse of folly' (*praemuniit stultitiae praetextu*: Kan 165). What he actually wrote was, *ut minus sapiens dico* . . . ('As less wise I say . . .', II Corinthians 11:23). By now all memory of the original error has disappeared.

Folly in her temporary paradoxical role of scholastic thick-head leaves the Greekifiers to squabble over such things: she will follow those good theologians who are dull and gross, *pingues et crassus*! The chief of these dullards, Nicolas of Lyra, thought that Paul meant by the words, *As less wise I say*:

If I seem to you to be foolish by putting myself on a par with false apostles, I shall seem to you to be more foolish by placing myself above them (Kan 167).

(The wretched Nicolas did write this nonsense.) Then Folly makes an 'ecstatic' jest: poor Nicolas subsequently drifted off in another direction, *velut oblitus sui*—'as though he had forgotten himself'.

Erasmus says the same thing less paradoxically in the *Annotations*: St Paul was afraid of seeming 'rather arrogant', so he 'anticipated objections with a pretended excuse of folly'. (The words used are exactly those just quoted from the *Moria*.) He goes on to dismiss these Greekless scholastics who try to treat Scripture with 'glosses botched together from here and there'. His concern is with the good, original Christian fathers (*LB* 6. 790f.).

To gloss a fresh Latin version of the *New Testament* is an awesome task for a Renaissance humanist evangelical. But Erasmus does not have one mask for the *Moria*, another for the *Annotations*. The same bitterness can be found in both. There is even room in some of the *Annotations* for satirical laughter.

The *Paraphrases* are, on the whole, more eirenic. But even there Erasmus rarely loses a chance to defend the doctrines of the *Moria*. There II Corinthains 11:23 is expanded so that Paul says:

In those things which truly make for the glory of an apostle, I excel even them. They are Ministers of Christ, granted; but to speak foolishly yet truly—I am more (*LB* 7. 936F).

The *Annotations* are full of matter directly relevant to the *Moria*, full of echoes of Folly's actual words. They also throw much indirect light on Erasmus' difficulties. Erasmus was attacked for calling his brother Christians fools! Christ had forbidden it: 'Whoever shall say, O fool! shall be in danger of hell fire' (Matthew 5:22). The trouble was, that Christ in Matthew 5:22, did use the word *Mōros* here for fool. (The Latin reads *fatue*—fatuus, 'idiot', in the vocative.) Erasmus replied by saying that Matthew wrote in Hebrew not Greek; we do not know what word Christ condemned. (A dangerous ploy in an age seeking Christ's *ipsissima verba* in the Scriptures.) Erasmus had quoted St Jerome as saying that the word *raca*—which Christ condemned as well—though with lesser threats—meant the same as *fatuus*. That, said Erasmus' enemies, was to make Christ unjust, condemning similar offences with different punishments. (The sense of *raca* remains obscure.) Erasmus contends that Christ's condemnations only apply to an angry use of the words, *Thou fool!* Anyway, when Paul says that God chose the *mōra*, the foolish things, of the world he meant humble and unworldly people. Paul himself accepted the epithet *stultus*: 'not that he was really a fool, but because it is a fool's business to boast about oneself.' You can call a man a fool if you seek to correct him (*LB* 6. 57D).

If the *Moria* proves anything, it is that if you start calling your brother a fool even in good, clean, constructive, Christian fun, then you are in for trouble.

(iii) *Stretching skins (I)*

'Chapter 64' is entirely made up of the continuation of this 1514 addition.

Folly again shifts her ground. Theologians believe they can act like God. That is the implication of Folly's next words:

But why should I anxiously defend myself with the example of one man [St Paul], when it is the public right of theologians to stretch out the heavens—holy Scripture that is—like a skin? (Kan 167)

This is a jesting allusion to Psalm 103:2 (Vulgate), where God is described as 'stretching forth the heavens as a skin'. Bad theologians do that when they do violence to the sense of Scripture.

Erasmus makes two interlocking points in this 'chapter': it is right to do violence to pagan authors in order to spread Christian doctrine; it is wrong to stretch and twist the words of Scripture.

St Paul twisted a pagan text when he preached at Athens (Acts 17: 22–3). He claimed that he had seen an altar inscribed 'To the Unknown God'. In fact (according to St Jerome), the altar was inscribed 'To the Gods of Asia, Europe and Africa, and to Unknown and Foreign Gods'. That is a permissible way to treat pagan writings; it gives you a handle for preaching the Gospel.[1]

The same points are made in the *Annotations* (*LB* 5. 501E), where Paul is praised for his cunning (*vafritia*). His affability, moreover, should be imitated by those who seek to convert pagans and ill-educated princes. They should be prepared to 'dissemble many things'. So, too good men may live in court for religious purposes, 'gradually creeping into their princes' affection, even though they have unwillingly to connive at some things'.

The *Moria* was dedicated to such a man; he did not follow Erasmus' advice to its logical conclusion.

Erasmus shocked his public by accusing Paul of cunning. He goes over the case again in his *Apology against Faber Stapulensis* (*LB* 9. 51A). Then Béda objected. Erasmus again defended Paul's cunning, his *vafritia*, by citing Horace who praised the satirist Persius as a *vafer*, a

---

[1] A phrase near the beginning of 'Chapter 64' long defeated me. The meaning is clear—very clear if one compares it with what Erasmus wrote in his *Apology against Faber Stapulensis*, where the same subject is treated in much the same terms (*LB* 9. 51A). But the actual words are difficult to construe.

Eramus wrote:

. . . cum apud divum Paulum pugnent divinae scripturae verba; quae suo loco non pugnant, si qua fides *pentaglōttō* Hieronymo . . .

Normally in Erasmus *pugnare* means, when applied to words or phrases, 'to clash with their context'. As he points out in his defence against certain Spanish monks, *pugnare* is often applied to *quod dissentit*, 'what differs from, or disagress with' (*LB* 9. 1085BC). Yet that is not what the words seem to mean here. It is not a question of 'words which disagree with holy Scripture, words which, in their context do not disagree [with it]'; I once thought that Erasmus was using *pugnare* with the dative to mean 'to fight for', on the analogy of *militare*. He would then have been referring to words which 'fight for the Gospel' (cf. J. Boisset, editor: *Réforme et Humanisme*, Montpellier, 1977, pp. 155–8). In fact Erasmus is alluding to the practice of preaching the gospel on the basis of words wrenched from their context; Jerome did, citing Paul at Athens. Erasmus is unhappy about this, except in particular circumstances, including jests. All this is clear from his annotation on I Corinthians 7:1.

man who cunningly corrected vices with friendly laughter (*LB* 9. 716Af.).

The defence of *vafritia* is in part a defence of the jesting artfulness of the *Moria*. But in the end Erasmus withdrew. When some ministers of Strasbourg claimed that St Paul had done what Erasmus and Jerome said he had, he condemned them for it:

'Paul,' they say, 'twisted the title of the altar at Athens into a means of preaching the Gospel.'

Erasmus retorted that it was more likely that Paul did indeed see an inscription reading 'To the Unknown God'. Even if we accept what Jerome said, there was no deceit (*fucus*) on Paul's part (*LB* 10. 1590f.). But *fucus*, deceit, is far removed from the artfulness which *vafritia* can suggest, when thought of in terms of the satirical Horace.

(iv) *Stretching skins (II)*

Whatever Paul did he did for the sake of Christ's Gospel. But what are we to make of the ignorant preacher who applied to the flayed Bartholomew the words of Habbakuk 3:9: 'The skins of the land of Midian did tremble?' That was 'stretching skins' with a vengeance...

Late in his life (in the *Ecclesiastes or How to Preach* of 1535), Erasmus alluded to this silly preacher twice more. He admits he only knew of him on sound second-hand authority (*LB* 5. 1041E). He apparently regarded his account of this preacher in the *Moria* as a good joke used for pious ends. He contrasts such a proper use of humour with monastic scurrility. His explanation is relevant to his humorous use of St Paul's *Plus ego*, 'I am more' (see above, p. 133). And he again refers to St Paul's sermon 'On the Unknown God' (*LB*. 863A–C and context). St Paul in Athens remains the model of the ingeniously cunning preacher; the idiot with his 'skins of the land of Midian' remains the example of what not to do.

The main body of 'chapter 64' is taken up with the attack on Julius II, together with an attempt to take the sting out of a literal interpretation of Christ's words to the apostles in Luke 22:35–6:

But he that hath a purse, let him take it, and likewise his scrip: and he that hath no sword, let him sell his garment and buy one.

Here is Christ, telling men to buy a sword! How desperately and repeatedly did Erasmus expand and emend his long Annotation on these verses to make them refer to a sword of the spirit and to conform to Erasmus' pacifism! In the end he failed to convince even himself that they bear that meaning and no other. Once more the *Annotations* echo the *Moria* in detail. Erasmus' belief, passionately held in 1514, was that these words were an enigmatic way of preaching his own brand of spiritual Christianity. To take them otherwise was to resemble that stupid preacher with his 'skins of Midian'.

Worse: it was to be like that English clerical buffoon who thought that St Paul lent his authority to the killing of heretics because he told us to *devitare* them (Titus 3:10). *Devitare* means to avoid them. The English cleric thought the verb was made up of the privative *de* plus *vita* life; for him Paul meant, 'take their life away' (Kan 172). In the *Annotations*, John Colet is made to vouch for the truth of this story (*LB* 6. 973D).

In this major addition to the 1511 *Moria* Erasmus was correcting a gaffe, justifying his brand of humour, defending his particular kind of classical–Christian syncretism, and preaching what he believed to be the full, peaceful, tolerant doctrine of Christ, a doctrine which seems foolish to the world.

This particular interpolation ends with three Pauline quotations new to the *Moria*.

And again Paul says: 'As a fool receive me'; and 'I speak not after the Lord, but, as it were, in foolishness'. And again elsewhere, he says, 'We are fools for Christ's sake.'

Et rursum, *Velut insipientem accipite me*. Et, *Non loquor secundum Deum, sed quasi in insipientia* [II Corinthians 11: 16 and 17]. Rursum alibi [I Corinthians 4:10]. *Nos stulti propter Christum.*

You hear what a great proclaiming of folly from so great an authority! And he openly enjoins folly as something of the first necessity and exceedingly full of salvation.

By the time he came to write the *Paraphrases on the Epistles to the Corinthians* in 1519, Erasmus interpreted the first two quotations differently: Paul was admittedly boasting in a way more foolishly human than is in accord with the pure spirit of Christ (*LB* 7. 936BD). Not so in the case of his claim to be a 'fool for Christ's sake'. In the paraphrase Paul speaks at this point with a truly Erasmian sarcasm:

We are despised as fools for the sake of Christ, because we preach him crucified and lowly: you, as wise men, lift up your hearts by faith in Christ! We are weaklings, casting ourselves down for the glory of Christ: you are strong and swollen up. We are despised and obscure: you are prominent and famous. (*LB* 7. 871S).

Paul's 'foolishness' consists in toiling and suffering, even though others get the reward, and in preaching the kenotic doctrine of Christ.

(v) *Folly as an excuse before God*

The last of the major additions comes just before Folly breaks off, lest she go on to infinity. It partly consists of a list of Old Testament *loci* taken, it seems, from a Concordance. More important is Christ's cry from the Cross: 'Father forgive them; they know not what they do' (Luke 23:34; Kan 180).

Erasmus devotes a long explanation to this in the *Paraphrase of St Luke*, dedicated to Henry VIII in 1523. It is a plea for peace; Christ, at the very moment of his triumph, when he was about to go to the heavens whence he would call all things back to himself, presented himself as the exemplar of tolerance. His Cross was placed so as to be seen from Asia, Europe and Africa. His victory is ours—but Christ wants his disciples to have nothing carnal. All must be 'according to the Spirit' (*LB* 7. 462A–463A).

In the *Moria*, St Paul is then cited as saying that he obtained mercy because he did the evil he had done before his conversion 'ignorantly' (I Timothy 1:13). This ignorance, says Folly, was a form of folly: 'What does *I did it ignorantly* mean, but that Paul acted through folly not evil intent? And what does *I therefore obtained mercy* mean, if not that he obtained it by pleading folly?'

There is seriousness behind all this. Some theologians such as Theophylact did urge ignorance as an excuse before God (cf. Theophylact on II Corinthians 11:19). But to call this ignorance *stultitia* seems an isolated idea. It is not followed up in the *Annotations* or the *Paraphrases*.

The harvest might seem small, but it is not. The additions of 1514 link the *Moria* inextricably with the major exegetical works of Erasmus, as well as with the last works he wrote, including the *Ecclesiastes or, How to Preach*.

Closer still, where ecstatic folly is concerned, are those later commentaries on the psalms, where Erasmus poured forth what he believed to be inspired prophetic insights into hidden mysteries. There we find expounded not the cunning *vafritia* of 1514 but the pious ecstasy of 1511.

These commentaries provided a wide field for Erasmus' emotions and for his imagination. His works on the New Testament were held on a tightish rein by the Greek texts he had to explain and by his patristic and philological scholarship. Not so his works on the psalms. What these psalms might have meant in the original Hebrew concerns him hardly at all. He sees them as a series of hidden truths, waiting to be revealed by divine inspiration working through a chosen vessel: an exegete inspired by the Spirit. When Erasmus expounds the psalms he breaks away from the cramping restraints of philological scholarship, finding himself free to range over the limitless fields of allegory and enigmatic mysteries.

What he finds in these psalms is not so much David or Jeduthun but Christ the madman, Christ the self-emptying God, Christ the preacher and the example of the divine and ecstatic dementedness of truly spiritual philosophy.

APPENDIX B

The end of the *Praise of Folly*
(1511 Scheurer edition)

(beginning on line 15 of G5r°)[1]

Atqui fortassis apud Christianos, horum levis est auctoritas. Proinde sacrarum quoque literarum testimoniis (si videtur) laudes nostras fulciamus sive (ut docti solent) fundemus. Principio veniam a theologis praefate ut nobis fas esse velint. Deinde quoniam arduam rem aggredimur, & fortassis improbum fuerit denuo Musas ex Elicone ad tantum itineris revocare, praesertim cum res sit alienior, fortasse magis conveniet optare, ut interim dum Theologum ago, perque has spinas ingredior, Scoti anima paulisper ex sua Sorbona in meum pectus demigret, quovis histrice atque ericio spinosior, moxque remigret quo lubebit, vel *es korakas*. Utinam & vultum alium liceat sumere, & ornatus adsit theologicus. Verum illud interim vereor, ne quis me furti ream agat, quasi clanculum magistrorum nostrorum scrinia compilaverim, quae tantum rei theologicae teneam. Sed non adeo mirum videri debet, si tam diutina (quae mihi ar G5v° ctissima est) cum theologis consuetudine, nonnihil arripui, cum ficulnus etiam ille deus Priapus, nonnullas graecas voces legente domino, subnotarit tenueritque. Et Gallus Lucianicus longo hominum convictu, sermonem humanum expedite calluerit. Sed jam ad rem bonis

---

[1]The text has been reproduced as it stands except (1) for the expansion of all abbreviations apart from the ampersand; (2) for an occasional change of punctuation in the interests of clarity; (3) for the usual distinguishing between u and v, i and j; (4) for manifest errors.

The following errors have been corrected:

comunem for *communem* and *meditatonem* for *meditationem* (H1r°)

cognatonem for *cognationem* (H1r° and H2r°)

praedicant for *praedicat* and *postrema* for *postremas* (H1v°)

fruitonem for *fruitionem* (H2v°)

est for *esse* (first line); *animantium* for *amantium*; *transformatonem* for *transformationem* (H3r°)

communatone for *commutatione* (H3v°)

All italics are my own; there is no typographical distinction of quotations in the original versions. Greek words have been transliterated.

avibus. Scripsit Ecclesiastes capite primo: *Stultorum infinitus est numerus*. Idem cum exclamat: *Vanitas vanitatum & omnia vanitas*, quid aliud sensisse creditis, nisi quemadmodum diximus, vitam humanam nihil aliud quam stulticiae ludicrum esse? Ciceronianę laudi album addens calculum. Rursum sapiens ille qui dixit: *Stultus mutatur ut Luna, sapiens permanet ut sol*, quid aliud innuit nisi mortale genus omne stultum esse? *soli deo* sapientis nomen competere. Siquidem Lunam, humanam naturam interpretantur, Solem omnis luminis fontem esse deum. Huic astipulatur quod ipse Christus in evangelio negat, quemquam appellandum bonum, nisi deum unum. Porro si stultus est quisquis sapiens non est, & quisquis bonus idem sapiens auctoribus Stoicis, nimirum mortales omnis stulticia complectatur necessum est. Iterum Salomon capite. xv. *Stulticia* (inquit) *gaudium stulto* videlicet manifesto confitens, sine stulticia nihil in vita suave esse. Eodem pertinet illud quoque: *Qui apponit scientiam, apponit dolorem, & in multo sensu multa indignatio*. Proinde nec puduit tantum regem hujus cognominis, cum ait capite xxx: *Stultissimus sum virorum*. Neque Paulus ille magnus gentium doctor, stulti cognomen illibenter agnoscit: *Insipiens quis est*, inquiens, *plus ego*, perinde quasi turpe sit vinci stulticia. Et *libenter fertis insipientes*, ad se refert. Quid quod palam stulticiam praecipit: *Qui videntur esse sapiens inter vos, stultus fiat, ut sit sapiens*. Iillud G6r° haud scio an mirum videatur, cum deo quoque nonnihil stulticiae tribuit: *Quod stultum est*, inquit *dei, sapientius est hominibus*. Porro Origenes interpres obsistit, quo minus hanc stulticiam ad hominum opinionem possis referre, quod genus est illud, *gentibus quidem stulticiam*. Neque vero temere est, quod deo stulti tam impense placuerunt: opinor propterea, quod quemadmodum summi principes nimium cordatos suspectos habent & invisos, ut Julius Brutum & Cassium, cum ebrium Antonium nihil metueret, utque Nero Senecam, Dionysius Platonem, contra crassioribus ac simplicioribus ingeniis delectantur, itidem Christus *sophous* istos suaeque nitentes prudentiae, semper detestatur ac damnat. Testatur id Paulus haud quaquam obscure cum ait: *Quae stulta sunt mundi elegit deus*, cumque ait, *deo visum esse ut per stulticiam servaret mundum, quandoquidem per sapientiam restitui non poterat*. Quin ipse idem satis indicat clamans per os prophetae: *Perdam sapientiam sapientium, & prudentiam prudentium reprobabo*. Rursum cum patri agit gratias, quod *salutis mysterium celasset sapientes, parvulis* autem hoc est stultis *aperuisset*. Huc pertinet quod passim in evangelio Pharizeos & scribas, ac legum doctores incessit, vulgus indoctum sedulo tuetur: quodque parvulis, mulieribus ac piscatoribus potissimum delectatus esse videatur. Quin & ex animantium brutorum genere, ea potissimum placent Christo, quę a vulpina prudentia quam longissime absunt, eoque asino maluit insidere, cum ille (si libuisset) vel leonis tergum impune potuisset premere. Ac spiritus ille sacer *in columbae specie* delapsus est. Pręterea cervorum, hinulorum, agnorum, crebra passim in divinis literis mentio. Adde quod suos ad immortalem vitam destinatos, G6v° oves appellat, quo quidem animante non est aliud insipientius, vel Aristotelico proverbio teste *probateion ēthos*, quod quidem admonet ab ejus pecudis stoliditate, sumptum in *stupidos & bardos* convicii loco dici solere. Atqui hujus gregis Christus sese *pastorem* profitetur, quinetiam ipse agni nomine delectatus est, indicante eum Johanne: *Ecce agnus dei*; cujus rei multa fit & in Apocalypsi mentio. Hec quid aliud clamitant, nisi mortalis omnis [1514, more clearly, *mortaleis omneis*] stultos esse, etiam pios? Ipsum quoque Christum, quo nostrae stulticae subveniret, cum esset sapientia patris, tamen quodam modo stultum esse factum, cum hominis assumpta natura, *habitu inventus est ut homo,* quemadmodum & *peccatum factus est*, ut peccatis mederetur. Neque alia ratione mederi voluit quam per stulticiam crucis, per Apostolos idiotas ac pingues: quibus sędulo stulticiam praecipit, a sapientia deterrens, cum eos ad *puerorum, liliorum, sinapis & passerculorum* exemplum provocat, rerum stupidarum ac sensu carentium, soloque naturę ductu, nulla arte, *nulla sollicitudine* vitam agentium. Praeterea cum vetat *esse sollicitos,* qua essent apud praesides oratione usuri, cumque interdicit ne *scrutentur tempora vel momenta temporum*, videlicet ne quid fiderent suae prudentiae, sed totis animis ex sese penderent. Eodem pertinet quod deus ille orbis architectus interminatur, ne quid *de arbore scientiae* degustarent, perinde quasi scientia foelicitatis sit venenum. Quamquam Paulus aperte *scientiam* veluti *inflantem,* & perniciosam improbat, quem divus Bernardus opinor secutus, *montem* eum in quo *Lucifer sedem* statuerat, *scientiae montem* interpretatur. Ac ne quae sunt infinita persequar, utque summatim dicam, videtur omino Christiana religio quandam habere cum stulticia cognationem, minimeque H1r° cum sapientia convenire, cujus rei si desyderatis argumenta, primum illud animadvertite, pueros, senes, mulieres ac fatuos, sacris ac religiosis rebus praeter caeteros gaudere, eoque semper altaribus esse proximos, solo nimirum naturae impulsu. Pręterea videtis primos illos religionis authores mire simplicitatem amplexos, acerrimos literarum hostes fuisse. Postremo nulli Moriones magis desipere videntur, quam ii quos Christianae pietatis ardor semel totos arripuit, adeo sua profundunt, injurias negligunt, falli sese patiuntur, inter amicos & inimicos nullum discrimen, voluptatem horrent, inedia, vigilia, lachrymis, laboribus, contumeliis saginantur, vitam fastidiunt, mortem unice optant. Breviter ad omnem sensum communem prorsus obstupuisse videntur, perinde quasi alibi vivat animus, non in suo corpore, quod quidem quid aliud est quam insanire? Quo minus mirum videri debet, si Apostoli *musto temulenti* sunt visi, si Paulus *judici Festo* visus est *insanire*. Sed postea quam semel *tēn leontēn* induimus, age doceamus & illud, foelicitatem christianorum, quam tot laboribus expetunt, nihil aliud esse, quam insaniae stulticiaeque genus quoddam. Absit invidia verbis, rem ipsam potius expendite. Jam primum illud propemodum Christianis convenit cum Platonicis: Animum immersum illigatumque esse corporeis vinculis, hujusque crassitudine praepediri, quo minus ea quae vere sunt contemplari fruique possit. Proinde Philosophiam definit esse *mortis meditationem*, quod ea mentem a rebus visibilibus ac corporeis abducat, quod idem utique mors facit. Itaque quamdiu animus corporis organis probe utitur, tamdiu sanus appellatur, verum ubi, ruptis jam vinculis, conatur in libertatem asserere Hıv° sese, quasique fugam ex eo carcere meditatur, tum insaniam vocat. Id si forte contingit morbo vitioque organorum, prorsum omnium consensu insania est. Et tamen hoc quoque genus hominum videmus futura praedicere, scire linguas ac literas, quas antea nunquam didicerant, & omnino divinum quiddam prae se ferre. Neque dubium est id inde accidere, quod mens a contagio corporis paulo liberior, incipit nativam sui vim exercere. Idem arbitror esse in causa, cur laborantibus vicina morte, simile quiddam soleat accidere, ut tanquam afflati prodigiosa quędam loquantur. Rursum si id eveniat studio pietatis, fortasse non est idem insaniae genus, sed tamen adeo confine, ut magna pars hominum meram insaniam esse judicet, pręsertim cum pauculi homunciones ab universo mortalium coetu tota vita dissentiant. Itaque solet iis usu venire, quod juxta Platonicum figmentum opinor accidere iis, qui in specu vincti, rerum umbras mirantur, & fugitivo illi qui, reversus in antrum, veras res vidisse se praedicat, illos longe falli, qui praeter miseras umbras nihil aliud esse credant. Etenim sapiens hic commiseratur ac deplorat illorum insaniam, qui tanto errore teneantur, illi vicissim illum, veluti delirantem, rident atque ejiciunt. Itidem vulgus hominum ea quae maxime corporea sunt, maxime miratur, eaque prope sola putant esse. Contra pii quo quicquam propius accedit ad corpus, hoc magis negligunt, totique ad *invisibilium rerum contemplationem* rapiuntur. Nam isti primas partes tribuunt divitiis, proximas corporis commodis, postremas animo reliquunt, quem tamen plerique nec esse credunt, quia non cernatur oculis. Ediverso illi primum in ipsum deum, rerum omnium simplicissimum, toti nituntur, secundum hunc, & ta H2r° men in hoc, quod ad illum quam proxime accedit, nempe animum, corporis curam negligunt, pecunias ceu putamina prorsus aspernantur ac fugitant. Aut si quid hujusmodi rerum tractare coguntur, gravatim ac fastidienter id faciunt, *habent tanquam non habentes, possident tanquam non possidentes*. Sunt & in singulis rebus gradus multum inter istos diversi, principio sensus tametsi omnes cum corpore cognationem habent, tamen quidam sunt ex his crassiores, ut tactus, auditus, visus, olfactus, gustus. Quidam magis a corpore semoti, veluti memoria, intellectus, voluntas. Igitur ubi se intenderit animus, ibi valet. Pii quoniam omnis animi vis ad ea contendit quae sunt a crassioribus sensibus alienissima, in his velut obbrutescunt atque obstupescunt. Contra vulgus in his plurimum valet, in illis quam minimum. Inde est quod audimus nonnullis divinis viris accidisse, ut oleum vini loco biberint. Rursum in affectibus animi, quidam plus habent cum pingui corpore commercii, veluti libido, cibi somnique appetentia, iracundia, superbia, invidia; cum his irreconciliabile bellum piis: contra vulgus sine his vitam esse non putat. Deinde sunt quidam affectus medii, quasique naturales, ut amor patris, charitas in liberos, in parentes, in amicos, his vulgus nonnihil tribuit. At illi hos quoque student ex animo revellere, nisi quatenus ad summam illam animi partem assurgant, ut jam parentem ament non tanquam parentem (quid enim ille genuit nisi corpus? quamquam hoc ipsum deo parenti debetur) sed tanquam virum bonum, & in quo luceat imago summae illius mentis, quam unam summum bonum vocant, & extra quam nihil nec amandum, nec expetendum esse praedicant. Hac eadem re H2v° gula reliqua item omnia vitae officia metiuntur, ut ubique id quod visibile est, si non est omnino contemnendum, tamen longe minoris faciant quam *ea quae videri* nequeunt. Ajunt autem & in sacramentis, atque ipsis pietatis officiis, corpus & spiritum inveniri. Velut in jejunio non magni ducunt, si quis tantum a carnibus coenaque abstineat, id quod vulgus absolutum esse jejunium existimat, nisi simul & affectibus aliquid adimat, ut minus permittat irae quam soleat, minus superbiae, utque ceu minus jam onustus mole corporea spiritus, ad coelestium bonorum gustum fruitionemque enitatur. Similiter & in synaxi, tametsi non est aspernandum quod cerimoniis geritur, tamen id per se aut parum est conducibile, aut etiam perniciosum, nisi id quod est spiritale accesserit, nempe hoc quod signis illis visibilibus repraesentatur; repraesentatur autem mors Christi, quam domitis, extinctis, quasique sepultis corporis affectibus, exprimere mortales oportet, ut *in novitatem vitae* resurgant, utque *unum cum illo, unum* item *inter sese* fieri queant. Hec igitur agit, hec meditatur ille pius; contra vulgus sacrificium nihil aliud esse credit, quam adesse altaribus, idque proxime, audire vocum strepitum, aliasque id genus cerimoniolas spectare. Nec in his tantum quae dumtaxat exempli gratia proposuimus, sed simpliciter in omni vita refugit ab his quae corpori cognata sunt, ad aeterna, ad invisibilia, ad spiritalia rapitur. Proinde cum summa sit inter hos & illos omnibus de rebus dissensio, fit ut utrique alteris insanire videantur, quamquam id vocabuli rectius in pios competit quam in vulgus, mea quidem sententia. Quodquidem magis perspicuum fiet, si (quemadmodum pollicita sum) paucis demonstraro, summum illud premi H3r° um, nihil aliud esse quam insaniam quandam. Primum igitur existimate Platonem tale quiddam jam tum somniasse, cum amantium furorem omnium foelicissimum esse scriberet. Etenim qui vehementer amat, jam non in se vivit, sed in eo quod amat: quoque longius a seipso digreditur, & in illud demigrat, hoc magis ac magis gaudet; atque cum animus a corpore peregrinari meditatur, neque probe suis utitur organis: istud haud dubie furorem recte dixeris, alioqui quid sibi vult, quod vulgo etiam dicunt: *Non est apud se & ad te redi & sibi redditus est*? Porro quo amor est absolutior, hoc furor est major ac foelicior. Ergo quaenam futura est illa coelitum vita, ad quam piae mentes tanto studio suspirant? Nempe spiritus absorbebit corpus, utpote victor ac fortior. Idque hoc faciet facilius, partim quod jam velut in suo regno est, partim quod jam olim in vita corpus ad hujusmodi transformationem repurgarit atque extenuarit. Deinde spiritus a mente illa summa mire absorbebitur, quippe infinitis partibus potentiore, ita ut jam totus homo extra se futurus sit, nec alia ratione foelix futurus, nisi quod extra sese positus, patietur quiddam ineffabile a summo illo bono, omnia in sese rapiente. Jam haec foelicitas quamquam tum demum perfecta contingit, cum animi, receptis pristinis corporibus, immortalitate donabuntur, tamen quoniam piorum vita nihil aliud est quam illius vitae meditatio, ac velut umbra quaedam, fit ut praemii quoque illius aliquando gustum aut odorem aliquem sentiant. Id tametsi minutissima quaedam stillula est ad fontem illum aeternae foelicitatis, tamen longe superat universas corporis voluptates, etiam si omnes omnium mortalium deliciae in unum conferantur, usque adeo praestant spiritalia corporalibus, invisibilia visibilibus. Hoc nimirum est quod pollicetur H3v° Propheta: *Oculus non vidit, nec in cor hominis ascendit, quae praeparavit deus diligentibus se*. Atque *haec est* Moriae *pars, quae non aufertur* commutatione vitae, sed perficitur. Hoc igitur quibus sentire licuit (contingit autem perpaucis) ii patiuntur quiddam dementiae simillimum, loquuntur quaedam non satis coherentia, nec humano more, sed dant sine mente sonum, deinde subinde totam oris speciem vertunt. Nunc alacres, nunc dejecti, nunc lachrymant, nunc rident, nunc suspirant, in summa vere toti extra se sunt. Mox ubi ad sese redierint negant se scire, ubi fuerint, *utrum in corpore an extra corpus, vigilantes an dormientes*, quid audierint, quid viderint, *quid dixerint*, quid foecerint non meminerunt, nisi tanquam per nebulam ac somnum; tantum hoc sciunt se foelicissimos fuisse, dum ita desiperent. Itaque plorant sese resipuisse, nihilque omnium malint, quam hoc insanię genus perpetuo insanire. Atque hęc est futurę fęlicitatis tenuis quaedam degustaciuncula. Verum ego jamdudum oblita mei *huper ta eskammena pēdō*. Quamquam

si quid petulancius aut loquacius a me dictum videbitur, cogitate &
stulticiam, & mulierem dixisse. Sed interim tamen memineritis
illius Graecanici proverbii, *pollaki toi kai mōros anēr katakairion eipen*,
nisi forte putatis hoc ad mulieres nihil attinere. Video vos epilogum
expectare, sed nimium desipitis, siquidem arbitramini me quid dixerim etiam dum meminisse, cum tantam verborum farraginem
effuderim. Vetus illud *misō mnamona sumpotēn*: novum hoc, *misō
mnamona akroatēn*. Quare valete, plaudite, vivite, bibite, Moriae
celeberrimi Mystae.

Finis Moriae In gratiam Mori.

Index

1. Scriptural passages

(Page numbers are in bold type)

2. *Works of Erasmus*

3. General

(See also Contents, pp vii–x)

Abraham, Abram, 50, 51, 190; Jews not true followers of, 229; 'Before Abraham was, I am', 235

Achish, King of Nob, 'surnamed Ahimelech', 224f.; meaning of name, 229f.

Achrida, 145

Adam, 49, 153; and Eve, 153; the Old Adam, 175, 206

Aesop, 243

aetheric body, 170

Agricola, Rudolph, 157n.

Agrippa, Henry Cornelius, 7

Ahimelech, 184, 223ff.; Chapter 6 *passim*; meaning of name, 229; Ahimelechites cast out Christ, 235

Alcibiades, see *Silenus*

Aldus, 2, 24

Alexandria, 19, 49, 55; see also *Philo*

Allen, P.S., H.M., xv, 2, 3, 4

Ambrose, St, xviii, xx, 10, 55, 60–1, 126, 143, 174, 195, 216; on 42 mansions of children of Israel, 60, 65; Chapter 6, *ad fin.*; and *Commentary on Corinthians*, 144f.; on Paul's rapture, 195–9

Ammonius, Andrew, xvf.

Anaxagoras, the atheist, 228

Anselm, St, 165; confused with St Bernard, 176

Antwerp, 4, 6, 12, 82

Aphthonius, 7, 8

Apollo, 140

Aquinas, Thomas, St, xix, 9, 37, 57, 142, 195, 201, 215; respect for Ps.-Dionysius, 20; commentary on Ps.-Dionysius, 57; on the mass, 120; on ecstasy and *erōs*, 134, 142ff., 152; neo-Platonic tendencies, 134; see also *Medina, Bartholomew of*

Aristotle, 20, 33, 53, 86, 87, 108, 110, 181, 226; wrote dubiously about soul, 108, 136, 139ff.; scepticism, 134; *Catena aurea*, 213; *De Anima*, 107; *Metaphysics*, 81

astral body, 159ff., 169ff.

Athanasius, St, xxii, 50, 151, see also *Theophylact*

Athenaeus, 219

Athens, xiii, 19, 20, 49, 94, 235, 245

Augustine, St, xx, 1, 10, 18f., 25, 35, 37, 44, 49, 53–5, 58, 61, 64, 116, 126, 143, 146, 169, 195f., 239; and Origen's doctrine of the

mass, 121; double resurrection of man, 121 etc.; on the New Life, 122; on state of souls at Second Coming, 137; credited with saying of Bonaventura, 152; on pre-existence of souls, 155f.; and *patria* of soul, 171ff.; on *extasis admirationis* and *mentis excessus*, 210; on ecstatic prophets, 215; on etymology, 229f.; *Adversus Faustum*, 44f., 144f.; *De Doctrina Christiana* 18, 35, 76f., 110, 154, 172; *De Genesi ad litteram*, 49, 197f., 215; on psalm 30, 58f.; on psalm 33, 225f.; Pseudo-Augustine's *De Spiritu et anima*, 229f.

Averroës, 53, 181; Averroists, 134–5, 226

Avignon, 166

Azotus, 92, 195

Babylon, 46

Bacon, Sir Francis, 227

Badius, Conrad, 6, 170n.

Baldus de Ubaldis, 181

Barozzi, Pietro, bishop of Padua, 135

Bartholus of Sassoferrato, 181

Basil the Great (and Pseudo-Basil), xx, 54–5; *On the Holy Spirit*, 117, 209–12; *Commentary on Isaiah*, preface translated by Erasmus, 206; anti-Montanism of, 206ff.; and St Jerome, 209ff.; insists that ecstatic terms be taken figuratively, 209

Basle, 3, 6, 106, 118, 120, 145, 221n.; City Museum, 4; Dominican Library, 146; University Library, 145, 150; see also *Theophylact*

Béda, Noël, 9, 106ff., 117, 245

Beëlzebub, 234

Bellay, Guillaume du, 2; the family of, 9

Beghards, 164ff.; interrogation of Hartmann, 168

Benedict, St, praised, 112; English Benedictines' ugly yelling, 119

Beraldus, Nicolaus, 147

Bernard of Clairvaux, St, xviii, 38, 44ff., 55, 58, 111, 195, 216, 230; an ecstatic, 111ff.; held up as example, 112; ecstasy as deification, 167; confused with Anselm, 176; ecstasy and *erōs*, 134ff.; 'spiritus est ubi animat', 152f.; *De Ascensione Domini*, 46ff.; *De Excessu qui contemplatio dicitur*, 46; *De Diligendo Deo*, 167, 198; *In Cantico Sermone*, 46; *De Peregrino*, 46, 154, 173; *Soliloquium*, 152